Windows® 2000 DNS

New Riders

Other Books by New Riders Publishing

Windows NT Power Toolkit
Stu Sjouwerman and Ed Tittel, 0-7357-0922-X

Planning for Windows 2000
Eric Cone, Jon Boggs, and Sergio Perez, 0-7357-0048-6

Windows NT DNS
Michael Masterson, Herman Kneif, Scott Vinick, and Eric Roul, 1-56205-943-2

Windows NT Network Management: Reducing Total Cost of Ownership
Anil Desai, 1-56205-946-7

Windows NT Performance Monitoring, Benchmarking and Tuning
Mark Edmead and Paul Hinsburg, 1-56205-942-4

Windows NT Registry: A Settings Reference
Sandra Osborne, 1-56205-941-6

Windows NT TCP/IP
Karanjit Siyan, 1-56205-887-8

Windows NT Terminal Server & Citrix MetaFrame
Ted Harwood, 1-56205-944-0

Cisco Router Configuration & Troubleshooting
Mark Tripod, 0-7357-0024-9

Exchange System Administration
Janice Rice Howd, 0-7357-0081-8

Implementing Exchange Server
Doug Hauger, Marywynne Leon, and William C. Wade III, 1-56205-931-9

Network Intrusion Detection: An Analyst's Handbook
Stephen Northcutt, 0-7357-0868-1

Understanding Data Communications, Sixth Ed.
Gilbert Held, 0-7357-0036-2

SQL Server System Administration
Sean Baird, Chris Miller, et al., 1-56205-955-6

Domino System Administration
Rob Kirkland, 1-56205-948-3

Understanding Directory Services
Beth & Doug Sheresh, 0-7357-0910-6

Understanding the Network: A Practical Guide to Internetworking
Michael Martin, 0-7357-0977-7

Internet Information Services Administration
Kelli Adam, 0-7357-0022-2

Inside Windows 2000 Server
William Boswell, 1-56205-929-7

Windows 2000 Active Directory
Edgar Brovick, Doug Hauger, William C. Wade III, 0-7357-0870-3

SMS 2 Administration
Michael Lubanski and Darshan Doshi, 0-7357-0082-6

Windows® 2000 DNS

Roger Abell
Herman Knief
Andrew Daniels
Jeffrey Graham

New Riders
201 West 103rd Street
Indianapolis, Indiana 46290

Windows® 2000 DNS

FIRST EDITION: April, 2000

International Standard Book Number: 0-7357-0973-4

Library of Congress Catalog Card Number: 99-068975

04 03 02 01 00 7 6 5 4 3 2 1

Interpretation of the printing code: The rightmost double-digit number is the year of the book's printing; the right-most single-digit number is the number of the book's printing. For example, the printing code 00-1 shows that the first printing of the book occurred in 2000.

Composed in Bembo and MCPdigital by New Riders Publishing

Printed in the United States of America

Trademarks

Warning and Disclaimer

Publisher
David Dwyer

Associate Publisher
Brad Koch

Executive Editor
Al Valvano

Managing Editor
Gina Brown

Product Marketing Manager
Stephanie Layton

Acquisitions Editor
Leah Williams

Development Editor
Allison Johnson

Project Editor
Kristy Knoop

Copy Editors
Keith Cline
Christy Parrish

Indexer
Larry Sweazy

Manufacturing Coordinator
Chris Moos

Book Designer
Louisa Klucznik

Cover Designer
Aren Howell

Composition
Scan Communications Group, Inc.

Contents

About the Authors

Roger Abell has been involved in computing long enough that the first computer he was allowed to power up and down filled a room required punched cards and had a control program called a monitor, from which early operating systems evolved. Today Roger, an MCSE, MCP+I, MCDBA, and MCT, is employed at Arizona State University as a Technology Support Analyst Coordinator and has been evaluating Windows 2000 since 1996. His career spans administration of IBM mainframes, UNIX multiuser hosts, including a massively parallel system with 4,096 processors, and Windows NT domains; it also spans software engineering, systems design, and application development and programming. Through these years, Roger has had the pleasure of teaching programming languages and concepts at the university and community college levels to a couple thousand students. Although also cultivating a small and select set of clients, when possible he enjoys getting away into the American Southwest outback for hot spring campsites, amateur geology and mineralogy, nature studies, and enjoyment.

Herman Knief is currently working as the IT and Network Lead for AuctionWatch.com, Inc. where he is responsible for the corporate infrastructure of the company and the network architecture. AuctionWatch.com is the leading auction portal site and has experienced tremendous growth since their inception in 1999. Herman has also held senior level positions as the Director of Technical Services with Taos, "The SysAdmin Company," and as a Network Architect for GTE at the Pentagon. Herman is also the co-author on *Windows NT DNS*, published by Macmillan, and has written articles on such varying topics as "Virtual Private Networks" and "Security in Mixed Environments" for *Security Advisor* magazine.

Andrew Daniels works as Manager of Operations for NetLedger Inc., an anytime-anywhere accounting firm delivering tools for small businesses. As Manager of Operations at NetLedger, Andrew is responsible for the several thousand pieces of hardware, operating systems, and his department is responsible for supporting the application and network. Andrew has been working with computer systems for more than 10 years and has been involved in several large e-commerce implementations and on-going maintenance of sites including Levi Strauss (Levi's, Dockers, Slates), Walgreens Pharmacy, Logitech, and Eckerd Pharmacy. Andrew continues to focus on enterprise-level systems, network, security installations, and administration. Andrew currently lives in Silicon Valley, California and enjoys camping, site seeing, traveling, and reading in his spare time. Andrew can be reached through email at `bitshark@hotmail.com`.

Jeffrey A. Graham is a Senior Systems Administrator working at AuctionWatch.com as the Operations Lead. Jeffrey is certified as both a Windows NT and a UNIX administrator. Jeffrey's responsibilities include overseeing a team of systems administrators operating the AuctionWatch site, specification of platforms and systems designs, implementation of designs, and basic jack-of-all-trades. Jeffrey specializes in large-scale systems and enterprise services. Jeffrey has effectively designed, rolled into production, and managed DNS, Sendmail™, LDAP, security tools, and other enterprise services in small-, large-, and enterprise-sized networks.

About the Reviewer

Neil Ruston works for Perot Systems at a large Swiss bank in the London, U.K. office. He has been working in the IT industry for 10 years, initially designing and deploying NetWare 2/3/4 networks. He has CNE 4. More recently, he has been designing NT-based networks, and has an MCSE. He was involved in the Microsoft *Joint Development Program* (JDP) project and designed and deployed an Active Directory and DNS topology as part of the JDP program. He has used Windows 2000 since Beta 2.

To those with the ability to forge new information technologies and especially those with the insight, the skill, and the courage to place these into production as they emerge.

—Roger Abell

To Edie, my loving and patient wife, and Kekoa and Kainoa, the greatest sons a dad could ask for.

—Herman Knief

To my close friends who have fed, entertained, taught, and forced me to maintain sanity by going home when I worked more than I should. You all know who you are.

—Andrew Daniels

To the women in my life: Tammy Webb, for being there and for all the help she was during the writing of this book (and from all of us, thanks for all the food); Nancy Graham, for bringing me into this world; and finally, Jola Janczewski, for giving me my initial break into this field. Thanks to all of you for being there for me.

—Jeffrey A. Graham

Acknowledgments

Roger Abell

I would like to thank my parents, Marjorie and Dan Lennon, and my entire family for understanding my long absences during the writing of this book. Neil Ruston provided a valued technical review for which I would like to thank him. And I would especially like to thank the many people at New Riders for their confidence in this project and their great support and expertise in bringing this together.

Herman Knief

I want to thank all the people at New Riders for their patience and understanding as we worked through iteration after iteration of this material (primarily due to Microsoft's ever-changing code). Many thanks to my co-authors and to the editors, for making this a reality, even though there were times I thought this would never end. And finally, thanks to the reviewers for their contributions and countless cycles as the iterations of material flowed to and fro.

Jeffrey A. Graham

Writing this book has very much opened my eyes to how difficult it actually is to produce something that will be useful to the reader. I hope that this book has been some help in ironing out problems for a number of fellow systems administrators in the field. All of us also realize how much weight it is possible to gain when you eat while writing. (Hi Tammy!)

Tell Us What You Think

As the reader of this book, you are the most important critic and commentator. We value your opinion and want to know what we're doing right, what we could do better, what areas you'd like to see us publish in, and any other words of wisdom you're willing to pass our way.

As the Executive Editor for the Networking team at New Riders Publishing, I welcome your comments. You can fax, email, or write me directly to let me know what you did or didn't like about this book—as well as what we can do to make our books stronger.

Please note that I cannot help you with technical problems related to the topic of this book, and that due to the high volume of mail I receive, I might not be able to reply to every message.

When you write, please be sure to include this book's title and authors as well as your name and phone or fax number. I will carefully review your comments and share them with the author and editors who worked on the book.

Fax: 317-581-4663

Email: nrfeedback@newriders.com

Mail: Al Valvano
Executive Editor
New Riders Publishing
201 West 103rd Street
Indianapolis, IN 46290 USA

Introduction

The *domain name system* (DNS) has for years served as a glue binding the world's networks together into a cohesive communications grid. DNS has not stood still, however, continuing to change to meet new needs and challenges arising from the explosive growth of the Internet and from its many new and emerging uses.

At its most basic, DNS is a vast index that allows communications to connect points anywhere in the worldwide network through the use of friendly names. In this, it is much like a phone book, except it is a distributed system, as if the A section of the phone book were in Phoenix, the B section in London, the C in Tokyo, and so forth.

Since the middle of the 1990s, DNS has been enhanced in a number of ways. Methods for distributing the data more efficiently have been added. Methods for automating entry and update of the data have been defined. The increased use of networked systems, especially for sensitive purposes, has led to new ways to secure both access to the DNS data and also to control what is in the data. The many new uses of the Internet have led to the definition of a new resource data record, so the DNS services can now be used to locate new types of network resources.

This book is about DNS, how it is designed, and how to correctly run it to interoperate with the DNS servers run by thousands of others worldwide. The practical issues behind planning DNS services, and the tools available to assist in running DNS, are treated at length.

This book is also about the Windows 2000 use of DNS, and about the DNS server provided with Windows 2000. This newest version of Windows places DNS at the very center of its core architecture. Windows 2000 relies on and exercises DNS in ways, and to an extent, that quite possibly has never before been seen in a commercial operating system. The new version of DNS provided in Windows 2000 is much different and improved from the version provided in Windows NT, supporting most of the recent changes to DNS. The Active Directory then adds further considerations related to the use of DNS, as do the interoperation capabilities of the networking services in Windows 2000. The included material is intended to assist in finding a map through all these alternatives and to provide an ongoing reference for maintaining the health of the deployment services.

Who This Book Is For

Individuals newly placed into the situation where they now need to run DNS will find a complete introduction to the domain name system. Client use of DNS, the varieties of DNS servers, the interserver operations, and information handled by DNS the are explained and completely documented.

Individuals experienced in running DNS, either in UNIX or Windows NT, will find the information needed to extend their experience into DNS on the Windows 2000 platform. How current (with the many newer changes to DNS) the Windows 2000 DNS server is, which changes are too new, and how this all compares to the most recent BIND levels is laid out to assist in interoperability planning.

Individuals evaluating and designing the use of DNS to support Windows 2000 and its Active Directory will find information current to the initial release. What alternatives exist and their implications are detailed, and indications are made of where new developments are anticipated. Unlike most information now available on this, here the conclusions have been left to the reader with the focus instead on making sure the reader is fully informed.

Individuals administering Windows domain deployments and supporting Windows clients will find the "whole picture" addressed. Windows uses more than just DNS for name services, and the interoperation of these can be at times confusing. This book addresses these administrative needs by covering DNS, but also WINS and DHCP services and their interfacing with DNS.

How This Book Is Organized

This book develops on these topics in three phases. The first chapters of the book set the framework by covering DNS, staying close to industry-standard DNS as found in all servers. The middle chapters cover the issues the administrator faces in designing and securing DNS services, in planning for interoperation, and in understanding the needs and features unique to Windows 2000 compared to other DNS servers (as exampled by BIND). These middle chapters finish up by looking at the Windows 2000 DNS Server in detail, its installation and configuration, and by looking at the tools, utilities, practices, and frequent tasks involved in running DNS in general and in Windows 2000 specifically. The closing chapters focus on client issues and the additional services in Windows 2000 that can be coupled to DNS. These chapters cover configuration of Windows clients and understanding how those configurations impact the use of NetBIOS and DNS by Windows systems, and also cover the installation and use of DHCP and WINS services.

I

Understanding the Domain Name System

1

Introducing the Domain Name System

THIS CHAPTER REVIEWS THE FOLLOWING:

- **Name Registration, Resolution, and Distribution.** The domain name system (DNS), above all, is a directory of registered computer names and Internet Protocol (IP) addresses that can be instantly located. This section provides an overview of how the name service that's a critical part of the DNS registers, resolves, and distributes computer names. DNS servers can be used to locate services in a domain that they are authoritative for as well. You can send a query looking for a service in a domain rather than a system and still get back an IP number if this functionality is implemented. Note: Windows 2000 requires the use of Service (SRV) (mentioned later) records.
- **Host Name Characteristics.** The rules for DNS host naming are important to consider when you choose just one name or when you're planning to name thousands of computers. This section describes the rules you need to know and has suggestions for making good name choices.
- **Fully Qualified Domain Names.** Computers on the Internet are all members of a domain. This section describes domain names and fully qualified domain (host) names and how they're formed.

This book is about the *domain name system* (DNS), both for the newcomer and the seasoned DNS administrator. This book is also about the new Windows 2000 DNS

Server, and about the use of DNS in Windows. No prior knowledge of DNS should be needed, but those with this background will quite possibly discover a number of new things. This is not said out of a belief in the quality of the information here or a belief that there are holes in the reader's background.

The Windows 2000 system uses DNS like no prior Microsoft product—in fact, like no prior product. Although this book begins by examining and explaining DNS as it is, the worldwide standard, it ends in a fairly complete review of the Windows 2000 specifics. In between, this book discusses the use of BIND for Windows 2000, Windows 2000 DNS for non-Windows environments, new DNS features and concerns, and accustomed DNS practices within new interfaces.

Windows 2000 places DNS in a very central and heavily used role supporting the Active Directory domain environment. Ask 100 professionals seasoned in deploying Windows 2000 what 10 things are the most essential to "do right," and very close to 100 of the 1000 "must-know" items mentioned will be DNS. From the Active Directory design stages right on through to the most taken-for-granted daily user actions, Windows 2000 systems' vital signs are keyed to DNS, one way or another.

This tour starts with DNS itself, seeing what it is, its definitions, how it works, how it is used in any system—whether the time-honored BIND version or the Windows 2000 one. By the end, you will have seen the features of this new release and a number of issues and alternatives for their use within the Windows environment.

This chapter introduces the DNS without making any assumptions about your prior knowledge except that you know a bit about how computers work and how they interact with the Internet. Those who need an introduction or refresher on DNS and DNS servers can benefit from reading it. Here you can learn conceptually, and in some small degree of detail, what the DNS is and how DNS is servers make it work for millions of computer users in homes and businesses around the world.

Name Registration, Resolution, and Distribution

Transmission Control Protocol/Internet Protocol (TCP/IP) communication happens between computers using their IP addresses. For this reason, an IP address is required for every computer on the Internet to give it a unique identity.

The DNS is the de facto method for registering computer names and IP addresses. The Internet community developed DNS to enable computer hosts anywhere to locate others by friendly names rather than their more cryptic IP addresses. DNS is an evolving service that is continually upgraded via suggestions in the *Internet Engineering Task Force* (IETF) drafts and *Request for Comments* (RFCs). You learn later in this book where to find these drafts and RFCs.

Don't confuse a DNS server with DNS itself. DNS servers are merely tools of the domain name system (or its robots, so to speak) doing the routine work needed to make the domain name system function. This chapter covers the domain name system and DNS servers. It's important to keep the difference in mind.

DNS servers give clients (individual users, application servers, and even other DNS servers) a way to store and retrieve the host names and IP addresses of other hosts. A *host* is another name for a computer or network entity, and a *host name* is the name a computer goes by in the domain name system. One important concept is the concept of a namespace. The namespace is the whole space on the Internet that is composed of the unique and human-friendly names for these hosts.

Every host name and its IP address are stored in one or more DNS servers, enabling everyone in the world with Internet access to retrieve a host's IP address just by name. For this to work, DNS servers must communicate reliably with each other to bind every branch of the Internet domain name tree together into one comprehensive system. This domain name tree is the skeleton of the namespace, which DNS servers can climb and traverse as they work. Chapter 2, "How DNS Works," fully examines how DNS works and discusses exactly what the namespace is.

Perhaps the two most fundamental name service concepts you can learn are registration and resolution. They are important requirements for understanding DNS names and DNS servers. But first, let's take a quick look at what we register and resolve: host names and IP addresses.

Host Names and IP Addresses

DNS data files match names with numbers. Telephone directory services resemble the DNS in the sense that they, too, are systems in which names are stored and matched with numbers to identify destinations.

Even though there are other parts to DNS records and some complicated aspects to the DNS itself, the most fundamental use of DNS, and its highest value to most users, is its capability to match host names with the numeric IP addresses to which they belong and to give out that information on demand.

Host Name Registration

Host's names and IP addresses have to be registered. Registration involves just recording a name and IP address in a directory or listing. Registration methods can be manual or automatic, static or dynamic. DNS servers, in the past, received original host registrations via manual input, which means that hosts in a DNS server's list must be put there, or registered, by someone entering them at a keyboard. The recent trend is to have hosts registered dynamically, with updates being triggered by a *Dynamic Host Configuration Protocol* (DHCP) lease or being done directly by the hosts themselves with dynamic DNS updates.

DNS registrations are manual and static unless you are using dynamic DNS like that available in Windows 2000. Usually someone must manually update a host's record when any of its information changes. Figure 1.1 depicts individual hosts that have been registered with a DNS server. Fortunately, the most critical information in a DNS server is just a name and an IP address. (Chapter 4, "Domain Information Details," introduces some important exceptions.)

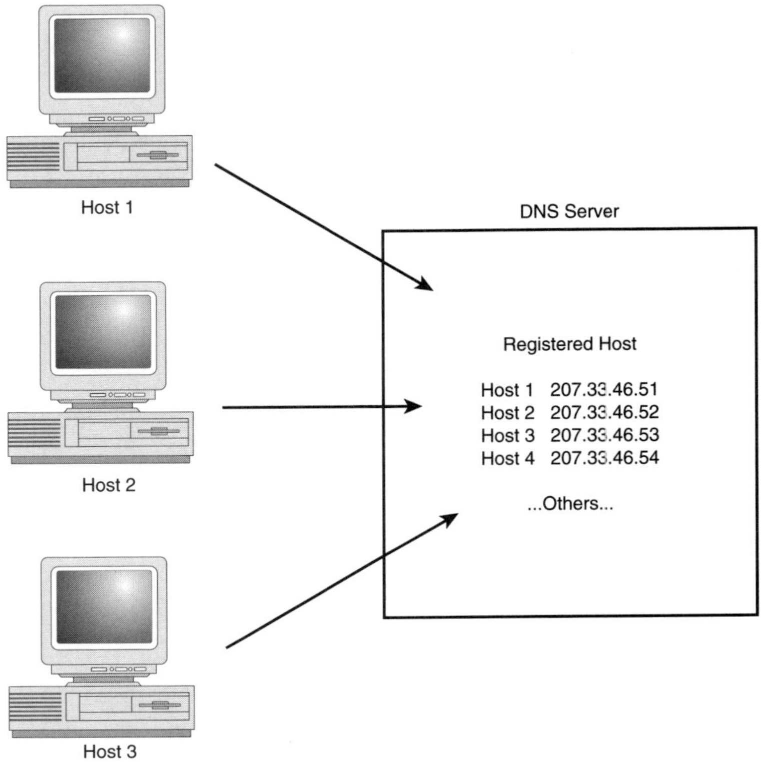

Figure 1.1 Individual hosts are registered with a DNS Server.

Figure 1.1 doesn't show how host names are registered because there isn't just one way. Manual registrations are most common, and there are a few ways to register names automatically. One way to register automatically is for a DNS Server to refer to a Windows Internet Naming Service(WINS) server. The interactions of DNS and WINS are mentioned throughout this book, and Chapter 16, "WINS: Legacy Name Services and Resolution," describes the intricacies of this registration method.

Another method of registering automatically occurs when a DHCP server registers names with DNS servers capable of handling *dynamic DNS* (DDNS). DHCP servers automatically issue IP name and address information to clients when they start up. This is the easiest way to use almost any DNS server because it is the most fully tested and supported. This method works quite well in almost all cases. After the registration has been completed (especially if you have notification enabled), all DNS servers receive that registration information.

Most computers are manually registered with one DNS server, which is usually in the same building, campus, or at least in the same organization. Mid- and large-size organizations almost always have their own DNS servers. It's often faster and easier to edit your own host list than it is to call someone else, such as an *Internet service provider* (ISP), to record every change for you. With Windows 2000 or UNIX, if you have an internal environment, you will most likely need to run DNS yourself internally.

Hosts must be registered in one DNS server: the primary server. Secondary servers automatically get all their data from a primary DNS server. Administrators like the backup this gives them, and it lets them place servers with identical databases in several locations. A headquarters office, for example, might have a primary DNS server; remote locations could each have a local secondary server for speedy lookups and to protect against network failures that would make the primary server unavailable. This allows all the servers to find hosts whose names have been registered, and to do it close to the clients wanting to use those names. If DNS goes down in your network, whether Windows 2000 or other, it is catastrophic for your hosts' availability. You will definitely want to put in multiple DNS servers. You obtain some load balancing as well if you have some machines resolve off of the secondaries.

Host Address Resource Records

The main purpose of name registrations, regardless of how they're performed, is to record the name of a host and its IP address in a place that's accessible to other machines that need the information. An entry is called a *resource record* (RR). RRs come in many varieties, which Chapter 4 describes in more detail.

Figure 1.2 shows the host records of several machines as they appear in the DNS management console of Windows 2000.

If you used a UNIX DNS Server with text-based configuration files, the entries would look something like the hosts recorded in the following records. (IN means Internet, and A means address.) If you use Windows 2000 DNS, you can also store this information in identical files, but you do not have to do so. The first column (with host1) refers to the host name, the second column refers to the type of record (in this case Internet,) the third column is the type of resource record (A for Address), and the fourth column is the IP address:

```
host1    IN    A    207.33.46.51
host2    IN    A    207.33.46.52
```

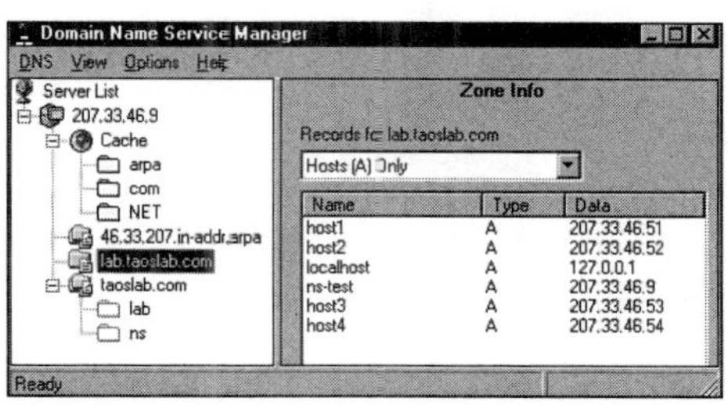

Figure 1.2 Viewing host Address (A) records.

host3	IN	A	207.33.46.53
host4	IN	A	207.33.46.54

Host Name Resolution

Once registered, a host's name can be resolved. *Resolution* is the client's process for looking up the registered name or service to learn its IP address. After the client gets a target host's IP number, it can communicate with it directly on a local network, or it can reach out through one or more routers to a remote network.

It may seem obvious that there's usually a single DNS server for many registered hosts. It's worth noting, however, how this fact makes it a quick matter to resolve the names of other hosts also registered in the same server. Organizations with thousands of hosts need only a few DNS servers.

Figure 1.3 illustrates how a DNS client resolves the names of other hosts listed in the DNS Server where it, too, is registered.

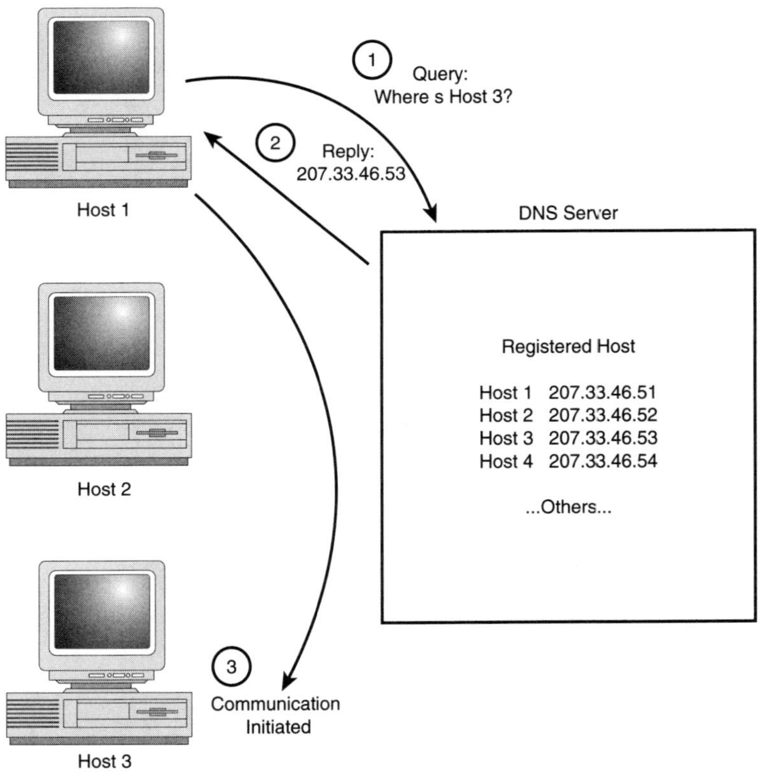

Figure 1.3 A DNS client queries a DNS Server to resolve a host name.

Resolvers

The explanations of name queries in this chapter may seem to imply that DNS servers do all the name-resolving work. Let's clarify this. The main actor is actually an invisible resolver program that runs on all DNS-enabled computers that use TCP/IP. Resolvers convert compatible path statements involving networked host domain names into queries. Resolvers can even cache previously located hosts, speeding up connection times.

Resolvers are everywhere, local and remote, on clients and DNS servers alike. DNS servers use a resolver to query other DNS servers when called upon to do so, which can be often. When a DNS client acts like a client, its resolver is used. When a DNS server acts like a client, its resolver is used. When a DNS server acts like a server, it's responding to a client's resolver, and the client may be another DNS server.

RFCs

International standards-setting authorities and voluntary regulating bodies work together to preside over the Internet. These regulating bodies use RFCs and working committees to openly evaluate new ideas for standards, receiving them from bright individuals and commercial interests. Some RFCs become standards. To view RFCs, visit the Domain Name Services Resource Directory at www.dns.net/dnsrd/.

Agencies with standards-setting influence over DNS, Internet protocols, and the Internet itself include the following organizations:

- Internet Architecture Board (IAB)
- Internet Assigned Numbers Authority (IANA), www.iana.org
- Internet Engineering Steering Group (IESG), www.ietf.org/iesg.html
- Internet Engineering Task Force (IETF), www.ietf.org
- Internet Society (ISOC), www.isoc.org
- Internet Network Information Center (InterNIC), www.internic.net

RFC 1034, " Domain Names: Concepts and Facilities," indicates that resolvers require access to at least one name server to obtain their information directly, or to pursue the query using referrals to other name servers. RFC 1034 (pages 5 and 6) says, "From the resolver's point of view, the domain system is composed of an unknown number of name servers. Each name server has one or more pieces of the whole domain tree's data."

Resolvers usually have one of the following results to pass back after queries (from RFC 1034, page 29):

- **One or more RRs giving the requested data.** In this case, the resolver returns the answer in the appropriate format.
- **A name error (NE).** This happens when the referenced name does not exist. For example, a user may have mistyped a host name.
- **A data not found error.** This happens when the referenced name exists, but data of the appropriate type does not.

Resolvers are located on the same machine as the program that requests the resolver's services, but it may need to consult name servers on other hosts. RFC 1034 (page 28) says, "Because a resolver may need to consult several name servers, or may have the requested information in a local cache, the amount of time that a resolver will take to complete can vary quite a bit, from milliseconds to several seconds."

Reverse Lookups

So far, all this discussion has illustrated is how DNS maps names to IP addresses. But it can also map IP addresses to names. Because the data files in DNS servers are automatically ordered or indexed to quickly find names, reverse lookups on IP addresses require a special IP-first database order as well. Reverse lookups are also sometimes called *inverse queries*.

The database DNS servers use to perform reverse lookups is called an *in-addr.arpa zone*, or Internet address zone in the arpa domain. If you look at Figure 1.2 carefully, you'll see the 46.33.207.in-addr.arpa zone at the bottom belongs to the name server. This in-addr zone contains a database of IP addresses mapped to names that the server can use if you need to look up a name by using the IP address. Chapter 4, where address Pointer (PTR) records are covered, discusses how this reverse mapping is built.

Reverse lookups are not nearly as useful as forward lookups, but they do happen. Most reverse lookups are performed to find the name of a local host when the user, such as a system administrator, already knows its IP address. The practical use of reverse lookups is to discover the *fully qualified domain name* (FQDN) of a known IP. *File Transfer Protocol* (FTP) servers sometimes use reverse lookups to verify that connecting hosts are actually who they say they are. Otherwise, such tools as `nslookup` are required to use the reverse lookup feature (see Chapter 12, "Troubleshooting Tools and Utilities"). This technique is just one more way to verify that the connecting machine is not spoofed or otherwise faked. This helps to lessen (but does not eliminate) attacks.

DNS Server Search Order

You can decide where DNS clients look first, second, and so on to resolve names. Figure 1.4 shows the search order used by a Windows 95 client. The first DNS server listed, 192.168.1.24, is where the client itself is registered as a member of the example.net domain. If the client fails to get an answer from the first server in the list, it continues asking with the second and third servers. Windows 2000 client settings allow many more servers to be listed here. Chapter 14, "Windows Client Configuration and Resolution," covers configuring the different client versions in some detail.

The DNS server where your clients need to be registered is a primary server for their own domain, and most administrators set their clients' search server to the IP address of the same server. But there's no reason why the search servers must be the same as the primary—or server of registration. In fact, it is common to provide secondaries specifically for client use. When dynamic DNS registration is used, if the client does try to register with a secondary, the secondary forwards it to the primary for the

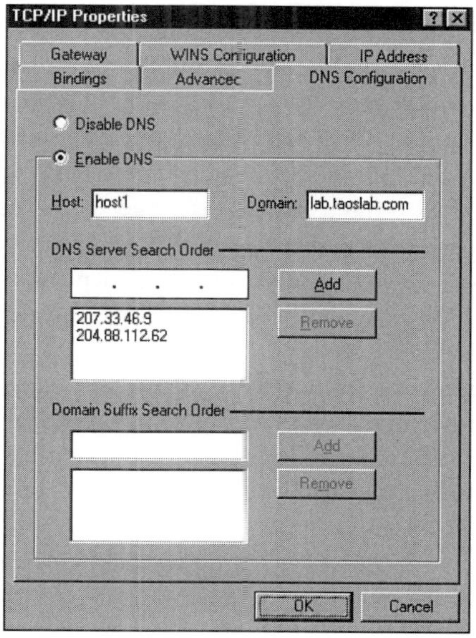

Figure 1.4 DNS Server search order is optional.

client, so there is no real harm. There are many strategies for the types of servers used for different needs, as discussed later.

The search order is entirely up to you. The DNS servers that your machine queries for resolutions and the DNS servers where it's registered do not have to be the same. Second and third search servers can also be any you like, such as one in another domain, an ISP's name server, or any other that'll respond quickly to queries. Searching through the list halts as soon as a server responds with an answer.

Host Name Distribution

No single DNS server holds the names of all the world's hosts. That would be impossible. The distance it would create between you and such a master DNS server, if one existed, could be great and the database size enormous. Imagine the computing power and bandwidth that it would take to make a single central DNS server work for the whole Internet. In addition to this, if the master DNS server failed the entire Internet would fail throughout the world! Instead, host names are distributed among many DNS servers.

Name distribution solves one problem, but it creates another problem for clients. How can a client know which DNS server to query? The domain name system solves this by using a top-down tree structure for host names, where each host is a leaf on some branch and each branch has a domain name. It's important to realize that every host you'll have is associated with a domain.

How many DNS servers are needed then? Although the real number is unknown and varies for practical reasons, the theoretical minimum is one DNS server for each branch in the domain name tree.

When a client needs another host's IP address, it usually queries its own DNS server first—that is, if it's the first in search order. If that server doesn't have a record for the host being sought, as is often the case, the query gets passed up the hierarchy of DNS servers, so to speak, to a higher server. Eventually, one with the capability to answer the query is found. To fully understand this codependence of DNS domains and servers, it might help to imagine the domain name tree itself as a hierarchy of names, as Figure 1.5 illustrates.

Every DNS server, unless it's isolated for a special reason, fits somewhere into the overall Internet domain hierarchy with other servers. No DNS server is an island unto itself. Each one assumes responsibility for domain name-service duties, even if only for the names that belong to a small organization or some part of a large one.

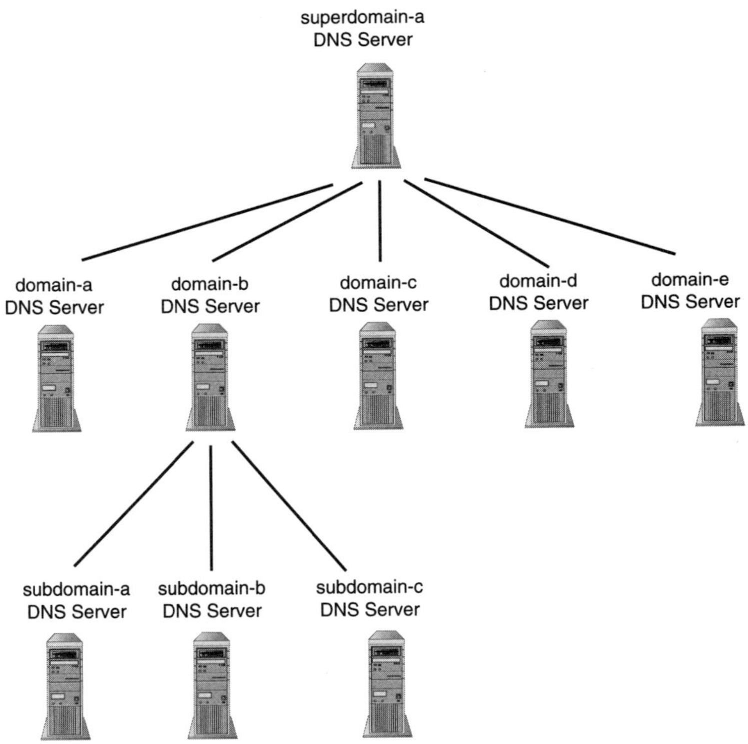

Figure 1.5 All DNS servers have a place in the name tree.

Private DNS Servers

It's possible to operate DNS servers in private networks that are not connected to the Internet. You can even physically connect servers to the Internet, but not let them participate in the public namespace. Unless private servers are isolated, they can cause serious conflicts. IP numbers get allocated (see Chapter 6, "Working with Service Providers"), and domain names must be registered (see Appendix D, "Registering Addresses on the Internet").

To establish a private network, you must isolate it from the public network and you should use IP numbers reserved for private use only. If you use IP numbers that are routable and not assigned to you and you later decide to connect to the Internet, you have a number of issues to overcome. RFC 1597, "Address Allocation for Private Internets," examines these issues. Like the public network, private networks also need root name servers. Appendix B, "RFCs Related to DNS," explains RFCs and tells you how to get them. Public root servers are described in RFC 2010, "Operational Criteria for Root Name Servers," and 1034, "Domain Names: Concepts and Facilities," describes root server design. A root server is a server that is either actually or artificially at the top of the DNS namespace.

Host Name Characteristics

Following the most restrictive advice of Internet RFCs, domain host names (such as those given to UNIX computers) can be up to 24 characters long. Note that Windows computers can have two names, a Windows networking (NetBIOS) name and a DNS name. Figure 1.4 shows the Windows 95 DNS tab of the TCP/IP properties, where you can enter host and domain names, but the Windows computer name doesn't go there. It goes in the Identity panel and can't be any longer than 15 characters. Windows computer names are short and simple, like the following:

hostone

hosttwo

hostthree

They could be long and complex, like the following, but then they'd be illegal in the Identity panel where the NetBIOS namespace surfaces:

host1-o12s-3t4n5a6m7e8-1

host2-o23s-4t5n6a7m8e9-2

host6-o37s-8t9n0a1m2e3-3

The wisest way to solve this dilemma is to choose a name that satisfies the criteria of both the domain namespace and the NetBIOS namespace. This means that names have to be short—15 or fewer characters—and have only characters legal in both spaces. If you assign a name greater than 15 characters, Windows 2000 truncates it for NetBIOS use.

For servers and other frequently used hosts, you should choose names that people can remember. Simple, functional names are best. Before you implement DNS, you can come up with an intuitive naming convention for user workstations, such as tcarter-pc for Trent Carter's PC, hknief-ws for Herman Knief's workstation, and so on. Servers should also follow a naming convention. You can first select a natural realm from which to select their names. This easily creates easy-to-remember associations between all like hosts, such as titanic, enterprise, and mayflower named after ships, and paris, munich, and seattle named after cities. Users at a new site, once set up, were delighted that I had named all their new printers after volcanoes. This is fine for a small organization, but when you grow larger and you still want to make this work, you have to develop subdomains (and very likely when even larger, you need to employ standard naming conventions that become cryptic to the users).

Incidentally, InterNIC, or NIC as it's sometimes called, is the agency that manages domain name registrations. Appendix D explains how to register a new domain with NIC.

IP Host Names

The Internet community provides some rules for naming hosts. If you don't follow them carefully, you can create problems for users or applications that try to access your computers. RFC 952 is an authoritative standard defining valid host names, and it describes what makes names valid, or legal. RFC 1035, "Domain Implementation and Specification," is also authoritative. The following are some practical naming guidelines excerpted from RFC 952:

- A name is a text string of up to 24 characters drawn from the alphabet (A–Z), digits (0–9), minus sign (–), and period (.). Periods are allowed only when they serve to delimit components of domain style names; this means that you cannot use a period in the actual host name. Note that the 24-character limit is part of RFC 952 and not a limitation from Windows. Unless you override the defaults, DNS is not case sensitive.
- No blank or space characters are permitted as part of a name.
- No distinction is made between upper- and lower-case letters.
- The first character must be a letter of the alphabet.
- The last character must not be a minus sign or period.
- Single character names or nicknames are not allowed.

Some names don't follow the standard. Take 3com.com, for example, which obviously violates the rule that the first character not be a digit. Although there are some contradictions between RFC documents and some practical relaxation of the standards, it's a good idea to follow them as closely as you can. Domain names follow much the same rules.

RFC 1035: Host Name Recommendations

RFC 1035, "Domain Implementation and Specification," provides an especially helpful grammar for domain names, if you're familiar with formal computer language forms. The following excerpt is from pages 6 and 7 of that document:

2.3. Conventions

The domain system has several conventions dealing with low-level, but fundamental, issues. While the implementor is free to violate these conventions within his own system, he must observe these conventions in all behavior observed from other hosts.

2.3.1. Preferred name syntax

The DNS specifications attempt to be as general as possible in the rules for constructing domain names. The idea is that the name of any existing object can be expressed as a domain name with minimal changes.

However, when assigning a domain name for an object, the prudent user will select a name which satisfies both the rules of the domain system and any existing rules for the object, whether these rules are published or implied by existing programs.

For example, when naming a mail domain, the user should satisfy both the rules of this memo and those in RFC-822. When creating a new host name, the old rules for HOSTS.TXT should be followed. This avoids problems when old software is converted to use domain names.

The following syntax will result in fewer problems with many applications that use domain names (such as mail, Telnet).

<domain> ::= <subdomain> | ? ?

<subdomain> ::= <label> | <subdomain> ?.? <label>

<label> ::= <letter> [[<ldh-str>] <let-dig>]

<ldh-str> ::= <let-dig-hyp> | <let-dig-hyp> <ldh-str>

<let-dig-hyp> ::= <let-dig> | ?-?

<let-dig> ::= <letter> | <digit>

<letter> ::= any one of the 52 alphabetic characters A through Z in upper case and a through z in lower case

<digit> ::= any one of the ten digits 0 through 9

Note that while upper- and lowercase letters are allowed in domain names, no significance is attached to the case. That is, two names with the same spelling but different case, are to be treated as if identical.

You can find more information about the rules for creating valid host names in RFCs 1123 and 1912. Good sources for all Internet RFC documents are www.isi.edu/rfc-editor/ and www.merseyworld.com/techwatch/standards/.

Windows (NetBIOS) Computer Names

Windows computer names must be 15 or fewer characters long to satisfy the NetBIOS length requirement. Don't depend on case to make names unique: Host-One, HOST-ONE, and host-one are equivalent on UNIX and Windows computers alike. Windows computer names can have characters that aren't allowed in DNS. Problems arise if names with invalid characters are registered in DNS, either manually or through the automatic WINS feature, which is described in Chapter 16. Windows computers should use valid DNS characters only so that problems can't arise. The following sample names are valid in WINS, but not in most DNS servers:

1isAnumber (beginning with a digit not allowed with DNS)

under_score (underscore character not allowed with DNS)

space ghost (space character not allowed with DNS)

This is good advice: Use only DNS-legal names for Windows computers. During a migration/upgrade you may need to maintain two separate naming schemes, but you should really try to avoid this.

Fully Qualified Domain Names

Host names aren't truly complete unless they include the domain to which the host belongs. Of course, if you're using a computer in the same domain as the host you seek, your resolver probably appends the domain name for you after making the helpful assumption that you're in the same domain. If the computer you seek is in another domain and DNS fails to find it, however, it may be that you're using an unqualified domain name—one that doesn't include domain membership information. Most operating systems provide a means for you to customize the behavior of this guess-and-append process.

A FQDN is the host name plus the full path, listing all domain memberships in a series. Domain names are joined together in series to indicate exactly where the host logically resides. Another way to put it is to say that FQDNs are fully expressed host names because they leave nothing unsaid. FQDNs contain directions leading to the very top of the domain tree where all domains and hosts are rooted. The FQDN of a Web server at acmecompany might be www.acmecompany.com, for example, or if the host www resides in the sales department's subdomain, its FQDN might instead be www.sales.acmecompany.com. When names are given like acmecompany rather than acmecompany. they are sometimes referred to a relative, and properly speaking only the form ending with a period (.) is a FQDN. This distinction can be quite important in understanding and controlling the resolution process. The trailing period actually indicates the very root of the domain tree.

FQDNs are practical. Electronic mail, for example, uses fully qualified domain names in the recipient's email address. Take janicejones@acmecompany.com, for instance, in which the recipient's name, janicejones, is followed by the @ symbol. Following @ is the mail server's FQDN or alias, which in this case is the name of an organizational domain where the mail server resides, followed by its top-level domain: .com. The .com domain means that acmecompany is a commercial organization.

Selecting a Domain Name

Selecting a domain name can be an involved task. With the popularity of the Internet reaching an ever increasing high in recent years, some have found great profit in domain name speculation. That is to say that individuals have registered many domain names for themselves, in the hope that another less fortunate individual will start a company and legitimately try to register the same domain name. If the domain name in question is already registered, the second individual must choose another, or can try to persuade the first party to part with the domain name . . . usually with a lucrative outcome. When preparing to register a domain name, take time to think of several good names, preferably that have meaning for their intended use. Try to stay in the confines that were set up for the *top-level domains* (TLDs). The .com for commercial use, .net for network-related activities or service providers, and .org for non-profit or social organizations are relatively unrestricted anymore. By properly using the TLDs, entities have many opportunities to have similar names, but they can still distinguish themselves based on their intent or purpose. The .edu, for educational, and the .gov and .mil, for government and military are restricted in terms of who may register. Additional TLDs such as .law, .inc, .mail, .games, .learn, and so on provide an even greater number of choices—provided that speculators don't consume all of them. The use of acronyms is a great way to come up with domain names. Keep in mind, however, that the shorter the domain name, the more likely that someone has already registered the name.

In many ways, registering a domain is like trying to get personalized license plates for your automobile. One must be flexible and a little creative to come up with something unique. When ready to attempt the registration of a domain name, the InterNIC has many tools available to help with the discovery of unique names and the registration process. For information on the InterNIC, see www.internic.net. There are a number of new TLDs as well, if you are interested in them. There are far too many to list here, but this information is freely available on the Internet.

Summary

This chapter introduced fundamental DNS concepts and some rules for naming. The remainder of this book covers information you need for setting up and administering a DNS server.

> **IP Addresses**
>
> Every computer on the Internet has an IP address. An IP address is four numbers in a row, each ranging from 0–255 and separated by dots, such as 123.21.99.1, or 10.1.1.3. Individual IP addresses can be assigned automatically or manually. For most purposes, DNS doesn't care about the way they're assigned. A new standard, called IPv6, may be implemented; you will find more information about this later in the book.

2

How DNS Works

THIS CHAPTER WILL DESCRIBE HOW DNS servers work, how they work together, and how they respond to name queries by reviewing:

- **A Hierarchy of Hosts and Domains**—This section shows how the domain namespace is like a tree (a hierarchy of computer names that are all related to organizations). It explains how subdomains divide the namespace up into manageable units and how delegations tell one DNS server how to query other servers, if needed.
- **Domains and Zones**—The relationship between a domain and a DNS server can vary; it's not always one server per domain. DNS servers use zone files that determine precisely what domains and hosts they manage. Zones give DNS administrators enough flexibility to make one DNS server handle one or more domains, parts of one or more domains, or combinations thereof. Zone data, which is at the heart of DNS administration, is introduced in this section. Note: Some servers do not use zone files to store information on the zone, secondary servers might just have a running copy in memory, and Windows servers can have the zone information stored in Active Directory.
- **Resolving Client Requests**—What happens if a client sends a name query? This section illustrates the client-query resolution process in detail, using an

example query. It also explains the recursive and iterative query modes that DNS servers can use. The example shows how a query can walk up the DNS name tree to the root server and back down another branch to satisfy a client's request.

- **Overview of Tools**—This section covers the basic tools that you can use to help you with DNS issues, including information gathering, troubleshooting, and other tools. It gives you a small initial tool chest for working with, and understanding, DNS.

DNS is a practical repository and clearinghouse for network host and domain names, treating every host name as a symbolic address—because names are convenient and easier to remember than numbers.

DNS client features are most apparent in the application-networking layer where uniform resource locator (URL) names, for example, open quickly in browsers to reveal Web pages from anywhere. The lower, transport, layer communicates information over the network. DNS clients and servers use the connectionless User Datagram Protocol (UDP) protocol on port 53 for queries and responses and the Transmission Control Protocol (TCP) protocol on port 53 for server-to-server connections. The reason that DNS clients and servers use connectionless UDP is simple. The traffic being propagated over UDP does not require an established response; if the communicator does not receive the necessary information, the resolver resends until it receives a response (as described in the "Resolving Client Requests" section found later in this chapter). As for server-to-server communication, only a connection-based protocol, such as TCP, can be used, because these servers must relay important resource record (RR) and serial information, which is only replicated every so often. Without this information, servers are out of synch with each other and are unable to provide a reliable service.

A Hierarchy of Hosts and Domains

When the Internet (originally called the ARPAnet) was small, a single, consolidated `hosts.txt` file was distributed around the network for performing host lookups. As the Internet grew, the old model of host file distribution became inadequate. The DNS architecture was developed to replace the old, file-based method of performing host lookups. DNS established a distributed data model that resembles a file system tree, as shown in Figure 2.1. Architecturally, the DNS is a distributed, hierarchical, client/server database-management system.

The tree-like model is distributed, because each registered domain provides its own database listings to contribute to the overall architecture, as shown in Figure 2.2.

At the peak of the hierarchy is the root of the domain tree (usually represented by a "`.`" dot) that consists of root-level name servers. These root-level name servers have initial pointers heading down to the first-level domains, or top-level domains (TLDs), such as `.com`, `.org`, `.mil`, and `.edu`. Additionally, there are more than 200 geographic TLDs and the list is growing. TLDs were initially managed by Internet Authorized

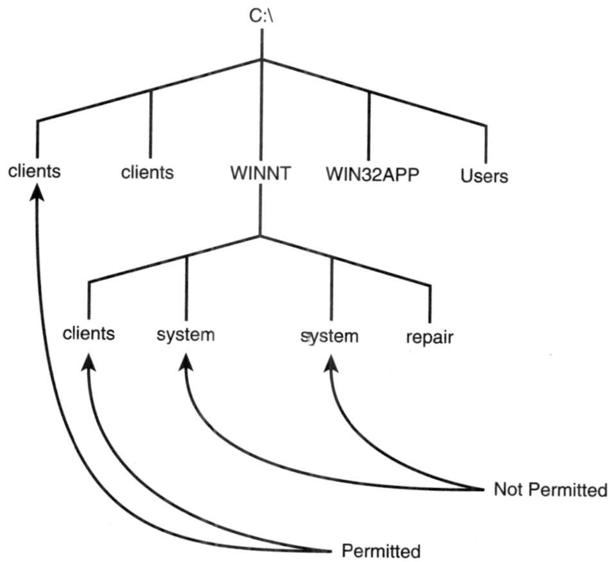

Figure 2.1 A DNS tree, like a file system tree, requires unique names at each level.

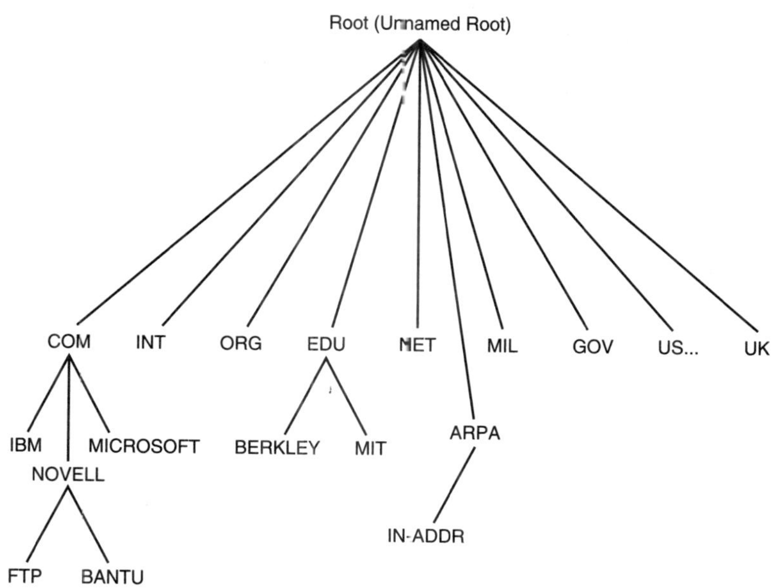

Figure 2.2 The DNS name tree hierarchy starts with the root domain.

Numbers Authority (IANA); however, several TLDs have been delegated to organizations for management, such as Internet Network Information Center (InterNIC). InterNIC manages among others `.com`, `.org`, `.net`, and `.edu`. This is an evolving space because of the abundance of registrations during the 1980s and 1990s, and it is subject to change. We've attempted to list a broad spectrum of these TLDs in Appendix C, "Top-Level Internet Domains."

Hosts within the domain name hierarchy can exist at any level below the root. Because the name tree is a hierarchy and not flat, host names have to be unique only within each small branch of the domain. For example, `www` could be the host name of several Web servers within a single company, as long as each machine resides in a separate branch of the domain hierarchy. For example, `www.xyz.com`, `www.corp.xyz.com`, and `www.eng.xyz.com` are all valid host names that correctly resolve to unique hosts, although each host has the same name. This basic principle also provides for uniformity in naming conventions across domains for File Transfer Protocol (FTP) sites, Web sites, name servers, and so on.

Root-level DNS servers are much like those used by corporations and educational institutions all around the world, but these servers reside at the most privileged place on the Internet—that is, above even the first-level domains, such as `.com` and `.org`. Table 2.1 shows the all-important first levels in the domain name hierarchy.

An easy way to remember DNS levels is to recall that the root domain has only a dot (.). TLDs have one name, and second-level domains (SLDs) have two names.

A key difference between root-level name servers and an organization's name servers is that root servers contain pointers back down to all the registered SLDs, such as `example.net` or `college.edu`.

SLDs are organizational or geographic, categorized by the last part of the domain name, or suffix. For example, `microsoft.com` is owned by Microsoft Corporation. Most domain suffixes give a clue as to what kind of organization owns them.

Table 2.1 **Domain Name Hierarchy**

Domain Name	**Position in Hierarchy**
.	The root is the only domain with no name, represented by a terminating dot that's customarily implied.
`.net`	A TLD, or first-level domain name.
`example.net`	A SLD, second-level domain name.
`test.example.net`	A subdomain name, an organizational domain within another.

> **Note**
> First-level domains are actually at the second level if compared with the root, but they're called TLDs. The root domain is not often thought of as a domain, although it is one in every technical sense. The root domain's relatively few root-level members exist solely to support the name tree and its functions.

However, an organization's type is not always that easy to determine by looking at its suffix. Take the `.net` and `.org` domains for example. These are not as clearly defined as the commercial, or `.com`, domain. Although originally intended for Internet service providers (ISPs) and other networking organizations, the `.net` domain has been granted to a number of research projects, such as `handle.net` and `giga.net`.

The `.org` domain was intended for use by nonprofit and federally funded research organizations; however, it has also been used by such government organizations as the High Performance Computing Center (`hpc.org`) and the Integration Technology Office (`ito.org`).

Subdomains

A domain underneath any other is a subdomain so that even TLDs are actually subdomains of the root. However, the variety of subdomains underneath SLDs is huge. Because this is where most subdomains reside, "subdomain" most often refers to one located anywhere beneath a SLD.

Organizations establish subdomains for their own internal reasons. `East.isi.edu` is a subdomain of `isi.edu`, for use by the east coast division of Information Sciences Institute (ISI). Companies sometimes create subdomains to match the internal structure of their corporation. Figure 2.3, in the section "Domains and Zones," illustrates this by showing one subdomain each for Engineering, Marketing, Sales, and HR. Domain subdivisions like this can help to improve the performance of mail servers, name servers, and other services by distributing the workload over several machines within the company's internal network. The division of your subdomain structure is entirely up to you. Your goal should be minimizing overall traffic on the network and providing for whatever requests occur. It is not uncommon for Windows 2000 to use a structure that is similar to domain controller placement, and for similar reasons. You might want to define domains within logical local area network (LAN) boundaries to minimize wide area network (WAN) traffic; you should consider at least putting in a caching name server on each local LAN area.

Domains Versus Subdomains

A logical purist might call all domains underneath the root subdomains just because they're subordinate. However, this use of the term is too broad, and it doesn't adequately distinguish the upper levels. Commonly, administrators call any domain under the second level a subdomain—that is, those having three or more names separated by dots. This distinguishes the TLDs, which are more permanent, from those at the third, fourth, and lower levels.

In practical terms, root-, top-, and second-level domains refer to the firmly established domains high in the name tree, and subdomain refers to domains beneath the second level.

Delegation

This brings up the purpose of delegation—the formal method for distributing the workload among several servers within a domain, such as between the parent domain and its children, or subdomains. The primary server (or servers) is referred to as the Start of Authority, or, in DNS as the SOA, for a domain. The primary server has an indisputable right to answer all queries for its domain or to delegate some of that authority to other servers.

Every TLD is actually a small part of the root domain, and the TLDs are divided even further into the SLD. Delegation is the method root-level servers employ to share responsibility with all other name servers. The result is distributed authority for all the Internet's published host names. By providing this distribution, a key concept of DNS is achieved. No single server can cause failure. The root servers are multiple, as are most, if not all, the TLDs, and your domain should be as well.

If one DNS server cannot answer a query, it can automatically point the client to another server that has been delegated by the involved domain. Subdomains are often handled by delegated servers. Delegations determine what servers are authoritative for the name being queried, and so they determine what servers are queried next if needed. If the authoritative server for your domain doesn't have the answer to a query, then it either doesn't exist in your domain or it exists somewhere else in another domain, in which case a pointer is needed indicating where to send the query (which might be the next level up in the tree). Delegations advertise authoritative name servers for domains; however, in reality, most queries need only be sent to one server by a client. If a client (resolver) receives an authoritative answer back indicating that the host or domain does not exist, it immediately stops looking. The resolver does not follow any more delegations, and it doesn't matter how many of the name servers in its search list it might have formerly contacted.

Delegations tend to point downward from root-level servers, which are at the DNS pinnacle, to top-level DNS servers. Subdomain DNS servers are registered with parent domain servers through Name Server (NS) records. Organizations register their SLDs and DNS servers with InterNIC for delegation from the TLD servers. As discussed earlier, you can have multiple delegations underneath your SLD.

Delegations tend to point both laterally and downward. Lateral delegations identify other name servers at the same level, sharing authority for a single domain level, and downward delegations identify subdomains (see Appendix C). Any public DNS server you have can be delegated by a top-level DNS server as one of its many subdomains.

You delegate a name server by using the NS record. (Chapter 4, "Domain Information Details," describes NS records and shows you how to use them.) NS records specify a list of authoritative servers for the domain. For example, to set up subdomains for an organization, you should make a delegation from the parent domain to the subdomains. If you don't, the subdomains are not resolvable by any outside hosts.

From a DNS client-resolver's perspective, it's as if all registered host addresses are local to their own DNS server. However, that's just the appearance. Delegation tells the local DNS server how to find hosts outside itself, which makes it possible for clients to resolve addresses outside their own domain.

Domains and Zones

Understanding the difference between zones and domains can take a bit of mental effort. The DNS domain name tree provides a branch, for domain names, and leaves, for host names. On the tree, subdomains and the hosts are members of all the domains above them on the tree.

Zones logically overlay parts of the DNS tree structure to determine the names that each DNS server supports. Your DNS server's zone determines the branches that it covers in the name tree, its area, or for which domains (plural!) it has authority.

Figure 2.3 shows one server having a zone of authority that includes both the `mkt` and the `sales` domains. A DNS server can also have a single domain in a single zone. The `eng` domain in Figure 2.3 is an example of one zone having one domain, although it does have two subdomains. Because Windows 2000 zones are used to holding a contiguous branch, which would require the `mkt` and the `sales` domains to both be in separate zones, general zoning rules differ a little.

Interoperabilibty between DNS servers and DNS clients requires zones and delegations because zones determine where names are stored (that is, which DNS server has them) and what path clients and servers should take to communicate with other DNS servers.

A zone can contain records for a single domain, a portion of a domain, one or more subdomains, or combinations of parent and child domains. Having records for multiple domains is especially true for the special class of reverse-address zones that are used for resolving IP addresses to names. Reverse-address zones are described in Chapter 4, in the "Pointer (PTR) Records and Reverse Lookups" section.

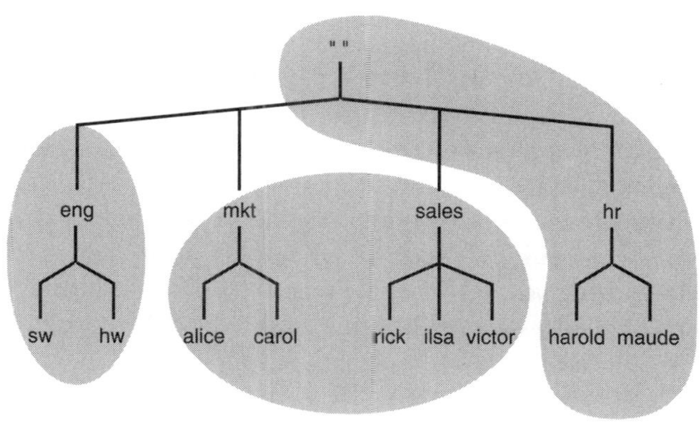

Figure 2.3 Zones determine the domain names that a DNS server manages.

Zones provide the DNS server with its cut, so to speak, of the names that it's supposed to manage, and delegations tell the DNS server where to look if there's a query outside its own zone. Neither zones nor delegations determine which DNS server has the authority to be the original source for a domain's records and which servers are backups. Designating a SOA server as a primary, or SOA, gives it this authority; and designating a server as secondary, or NS, makes it a primary server's backup.

Primary DNS Servers

As discussed earlier, the primary DNS server (the SOA) is authoritative for names in its domain, and it's the one from which all information about the names in that domain is derived. When a primary server starts up, it receives its zone data from the local data in files (or the Active Directory) on the host where it's running. A DNS server can be the primary server for more than one domain at a time, and it can be primary for one domain and secondary for another domain at the same time. Chapter 3, "Name Server Types," explains DNS server types in more detail. However, it's important to realize now that domains and zones are not primary. Only DNS servers can be primary, as the term identifies a DNS server as the authoritative source of a domain's names.

If you want to set up a domain hierarchy for your organization, it's smart to first set up a primary name server for the whole domain. The zone that your server manages should contain all the domain names for that referenced zone. If the server does not contain all of the records for that domain, you must delegate authority to subdomains (*example.net* being divided into: *sales.example.net*, *ops.example.net*, *eng.example.net*, and so on).

By choosing the option to subdomain, you increase your flexibility. In the same token, you potentially increase your workload because each subdomain can have a start of authority; therefore, each time you make a change, you must make in on the designated primary server. Microsoft's usage of the term *zone* is sometimes confusing. As the implementor, you should be careful with verbiage and use.

Secondary DNS Servers

Secondary servers obtain their data from primary servers. When a secondary server starts up, first it contacts the server from which it receives zone data, and then compares its version with the primary's version. If needed, the secondary server performs a zone transfer, pulling the primary server's zone data over to itself. The secondary knows the primary because its name is listed within its files along with SOA and NS RRs. The secondary server is only represented by a NS record, and it does not carry the responsibility of being the SOA because only the primary can have this role. Of course, if the secondary does not yet have the zone data, it needs to use the directives in its startup file to locate its master to obtain the zone data.

Like primary DNS servers, secondary servers are an authoritative place to look up domain names. The difference is that primary servers are the origin, or source, of domain names for other DNS servers needing to import zone files; whereas secondary servers are not the source, or originator, of authoritative data. They exist to provide a backup and to support queries.

Moving Data from Primary to Secondary DNS Servers

With some understanding of domains, zones, and delegation, it's now time to move on to a discussion of the distributed database model that DNS is built on. Zone files are essentially database tables of DNS names, and a primary server has the source zone file(s) for its own domain(s).

Remember that subdomain name servers can take a primary role, effectively splitting a large domain's name list into smaller portions in separate zone files. If a large organization built its name servers using a single domain without subdomains, zone files would also grow large. Large, flat namespaces have another problem: an undivided DNS branch can't support two identical host names. By failing to subdivide domains, large organizations can quickly create for themselves the same problem that the ARPAnet had when it decided to build the DNS architecture. However, that same large organization could divide its namespace into subdomains but still use just one zone file, as Figure 2.3 illustrated. This would overcome only one of these two problems.

Subdividing domains can also improve performance by keeping zone files smaller and easier to manage. A name server should not have to parse an enormous zone file. Although other factors also matter, it's generally true that the smaller a zone file is the quicker the response from a name server. However, subdomains introduce a practical problem. Delegations solve part of the problem by coordinating the relationship between parent and child (subdomain) domains. How does a secondary name server obtain data from an original source—its master name server? The answer is by transferring that server's zone file. This is also called a zone transfer. A zone transfer can be partial or full, depending on the need and the time since the last full transfer was performed. Breaking large zone files into smaller zones also has the advantage of improving zone transfers. That's quite a few reasons to avoid large, flat domain namespaces.

When a primary name server starts up, it merely has to begin responding to name service queries. When a secondary server starts up, it is told to look at a master server (often the primary server) for the authoritative data; it is then given a path and filename in which to store its local copy when the data is received. This is provided by the server's startup information, which is covered in Chapter 4. If a secondary name server is starting up for the first time, or if someone has cleaned out its data directory, the secondary server sends a request to its master server for a copy of the zone file.

A zone transfer operates much like Windows' (NT or 2000) file replication, or its Windows Internet Naming Service (WINS) data replication between name service partners. If a secondary name server has a copy of the primary server's zone file, then it can also begins to provide authoritative answers to name queries. What if a zone file on the primary server is changed or updated? The SOA RR contains fields of information instructing secondary servers how often to check back with the primary for changes. These fields set an expiration, timeout, and refresh frequency. This SOA RR also has a version, or serial, number. For more information about SOA RRs, see Chapter 4.

A secondary server periodically queries the primary server for the zone files it needs refreshed, checking to see if the serial number (an incremented database version indicator) has changed. If so, the secondary server knows that data in the zone has changed, and it initiates the transfer (either a partial or a complete transfer) of the required information. Partial transfers are the incremental transfers defined in RFC 1995, whereby changes only rather than entire zones are transferred.

The secondary server performs a zone transfer only if the serial number has been incremented to a higher number. If, for any reason, the serial number has been decremented, the secondary server assumes that its copy of the zone is more recent, and it continues to use the local copy until the zone expires. If for some reason the serial number needs to roll over to zero, the secondary server's local zone file is erased, and the secondary server then initiates the transfer of a completely fresh zone data file from its master. A secondary can obtain its zone data from the primary or from another secondary, but in either case, it is said to obtain its data from its master.

Both the Windows 2000 DNS Server and BIND version 8 have a notify option to trigger updates. The notify option is specified in RFC 1996. This means that a master server can actually notify secondary servers about changes to speed the propagation of new information. The notify option increases security because a primary server can initiate all zone transfers. Because its administrator furnishes a list of secondary servers to notify, the eligible secondary servers are limited to only those that have been preauthorized. By entirely changing who initiates data transfers from secondary servers to primary servers, a domain's zone file can't be easily stolen. That's an impressive list of reasons to use the notify option as incremental transfer efficiency recommends. However, some BIND 8.1.1 servers are known to dump their core when receiving such transfers from Windows 2000 DNS; so, one should be at 8.1.2 if planning on using BIND secondaries in this way.

Organizations that want DNS queries processed quickly in a global environment can choose to set up secondary servers in different geographical locations, maybe even locating some of their zones in servers owned by cooperating, friendly organizations. Doing this provides better local query performance and adds redundancy that can save the day if Internet connectivity to your site becomes unavailable.

Secondary DNS servers can still provide resolution during a failure, although the destination host might not be reachable. For such services as Sendmail™, this is useful; because if Sendmail™ can resolve the host but cannot create a session for the transfer of a message, it simply queues the message again and tries later. If Sendmail™ cannot resolve the host, it bounces the message and returns an unknown host error.

Windows 2000 steps beyond the standard primary and secondary DNS server distinction by providing for the integration of zone data into Active Directory as a third category of zone. If integrated, there can still be standard secondaries, but there can also be multiple, peer primaries that use Active Directory replication. This is covered in

Chapter 7, "Dynamic DNS and the Active Directory," where a number of DNS issues related to Active Directory technology are discussed.

This chapter has thus far been about the domain namespace and domain name servers. The remainder of this chapter focuses on clients, client queries, and how DNS servers cooperate to satisfy them.

Resolving Client Requests

If a client wants to communicate with a remote system (such as if a user clicks on a link for a Web site), a number of steps must occur before the actual communication with the remote system can begin. The first step is to resolve the remote system's name into an Internet Protocol (IP) address. Clients act as resolvers. To resolve the name of a remote system, the client sends a query to one of its DNS servers. At least one DNS server is designated in the client configuration. You can view a client's DNS server search order in the DNS tab of its the TCP/IP Properties dialog, as shown in Figure 2.4. The opening section of Chapter 14, "Windows Client Configuration and Resolution," gives pointers for locating this in the various Windows clients.

In Figure 2.5, you can see that one or more DNS server IP addresses can be listed, indicating to the client resolver where to ask for the addresses of host names. The client queries the first name server in the list. If the resolver doesn't receive an acknowledgement within a specified time, it'll try the next server on the list until a name server accepts the query.

If a name server accepts a client's query, the client usually just sits back and waits for an answer whereas the name server tries to find an IP address either in its zone files or from other DNS servers to match the host name it received in the query. If the first DNS server accepts the query request but cannot resolve it locally or remotely, it

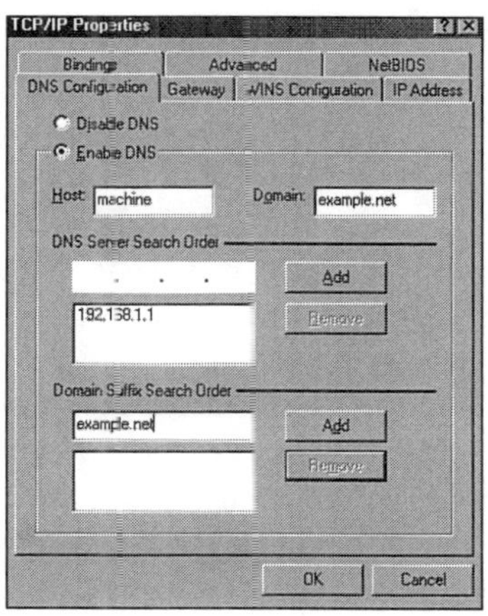

Figure 2.4 A Windows 95/98 client's TCP/IP properties for DNS.

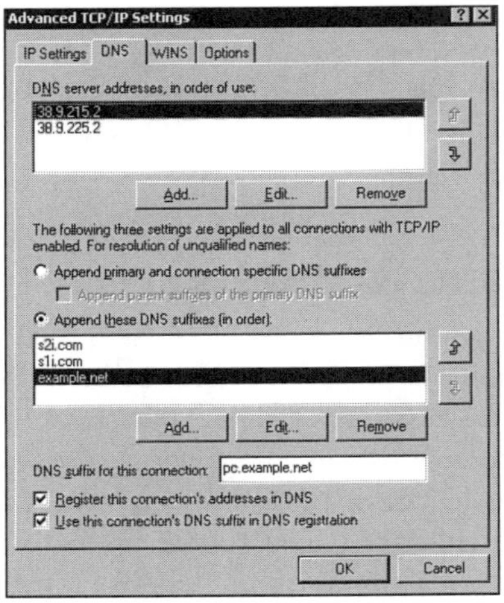

Figure 2.5 A Windows 2000 client's advanced DNS configuration.

returns a name error (NE) response indicating that the domain name is nonexistent. If this occurs, the client does not reissue the query to an alternative DNS server.

If the host name includes the host's domain name, the DNS server uses the additional information to speed its search, possibly even referring the query directly to another DNS server or telling the client the address of another DNS server to query (remember fully-qualified domain names [FQDNs], from Chapter 1, "Introducing the Domain Name System"). If a domain name is not specified, the DNS server might assume that the query is for a host in its own zone file.

Client Request Resolution Walk Through

What follows is a detailed example to help you understand name resolution heuristics. You should walk through the exercise slowly enough to grasp what happens at each step because it illustrates how DNS really works.

You might recall from prior discussions (about FQDNs and the root-level domain) that a trailing period indicates that a host name is fully qualified, meaning that all necessary domain memberships are assumed to be present in its name. If the host name a client is to resolve ends with a trailing period (.), its DNS server does not make further assumptions about domain memberships. Instead, the DNS server begins the query by sending it directly to a root-level server, from which it'll take the shortest possible path down the DNS tree to a server that's authoritative for the sought host's domain. If the name is relative (that is, without any trailing period), the DNS server makes a series of intelligent assumptions in an attempt to reconstruct the host's FQDN.

The behavior of resolvers varies slightly, depending on the source of the code used for the resolver libraries. It should be noted that many standard resolvers perform queries in a couple of steps, based on what the resolver (client) receives from the application it's serving. If the host name `www` is queried, the domain name is appended by default. If the host name `www.isi.edu` is queried, it tries to resolve `www.isi.edu` directly. If the server cannot find `www.isi.edu`, it would then attempt to append the domain name and try the query again.

The difference is that some resolvers distinguish between a FQDN and a host name by looking at the entire string and making a decision based on whether it looks like `www.example.net`, which is a FQDN, or like `www`, which is only a local host name.

For example, let's put our client in the `cnri.reston.va.us` domain and say it's trying to reach the `www.isi.edu` Web site. If the sought host's domain name isn't fully specified (qualified), the server tries to construct the full name. Because this client initially queried it's own DNS server in the `cnri.reston.va.us` domain and did not use a FQDN, the initial search string its DNS server tries looks like this:

```
www.isi.edu.cnri.reston.va.us
```

Notice that the DNS server appended its own domain name, `cnri.reston.va.us`, to the sought host's name. DNS servers assume that a host's name is not fully qualified unless the query includes a trailing period. Only a trailing period confirms that the domain name has been fully specified. Another way to remember this is to realize that `www.isi.edu` is a relative name just as `www` is a relative name that might or might not resolve within the current domain. As long as there's no trailing period, a name's relativity can be assumed by the resolver and it is usually left up to the DNS server to sort out. With an initial search domain of `cnri.reston.va.us`, the name server cannot resolve the host/domain name combination it received. Having failed at properly reconstructing the sought host's FQDN, the next query the DNS server tries must assume that it exists at a higher level. The second query, then, looks like the following:

```
www.isi.edu.example.NET
```

Notice that the `cnri` portion from the first query is now gone. If the name server performing the client's search is not primary for the `reston.va.us` domain and the `cnri` domain as well, it sends the query to another server for resolution. But if the name server is primary, and the request failed to locate the IP address on its second try, the

Note

Resolvers can behave differently from one another depending on how they're designed and configured. The examples furnished in this chapter reveal general truths about how the resolvers work. Factors specific to each resolver can change the methods they use, but they rarely affect the final results.

Some resolvers, for example, assume that a domain name with any imbedded dots (.) is an FQDN, and they pass such names unchanged to a DNS server. This is what Windows 2000 will try first. Others assume that if there is no trailing period, the name must not be an FQDN; therefore, the resolver appends the client's own domain name before passing it to a DNS server. Both assumptions can be wrong. Fortunately, client resolvers and DNS servers combined can successfully parse and resolve most names.

DNS server again reformats the query by dropping another portion of the local domain's name on the assumption that the next higher level can resolve it. This is the DNS server's third attempt.

If the third query also fails, the fourth, in this case, will be a little different. Because there really isn't an `us` domain (`us` is handled by the root), the fourth query actually goes to a root-level server to query for `www.isi.edu`. The name server does not receive an answer for the query from the root-level server for `www.isi.edu`, but instead receives a referral pointing to the authoritative name server for `isi.edu`. The DNS server then sends a query for `www.isi.edu` directly to the `isi.edu` name server.

Because `www.isi.edu` is a valid host in the `isi.edu` domain, the name server for `isi.edu` responds with the IP address for `www.isi.edu`. The local name server then provides the result back to the client, enabling the client to proceed to the next step of downloading the Web page by trying to contact the Web server at the IP address that it just received. The next section clarifies the host-to-address query process in detail.

The preceding has been an example of a recursive query by the name server. Iterative, or non-recursive, name servers can also be set up, and, in fact, the result of an iterative query is like that of a name server querying a root server. The root servers do not perform queries for clients; they merely provide a best guess or a pointer showing where more information can be found.

DNS servers can operate in recursive or iterative modes. In recursive mode, a DNS server becomes the client's agent, communicating with other DNS servers as necessary to retrieve the answer while the client waits. If working a query, a recursive DNS server itself becomes the resolver, or DNS client, to other DNS servers. The Windows 2000 DNS server default mode is to accept recursive queries from clients but to issue iterative queries to other DNS servers except its forwarders.

In iterative mode, a DNS server provides a best guess answer as to which server can answer with authority. Usually this answer is a referral to another DNS server that the resolver, either the original client or another DNS server, can follow. These referrals are sort of like following stepping-stones that lead ever closer to the final destination. This frees an iterative DNS server from further working on the query, because the client resumes working on the query for itself.

Host-to-Address Query Example

The program `nslookup`, which is used in the next example, is described in the "Overview of Tools" section later in this chapter and, in greater detail in Chapter 12, "Troubleshooting Tools and Utilities."

Listing 2.1 is the actual detailed output from `nslookup` for a host-to-address query of `www.isi.edu` by the primary name server for `cnri.reston.va.us`. It shows the kind of communications that occur between clients and servers to resolve a DNS query. Figure 2.6 is a diagram of the query in Listing 2.1.

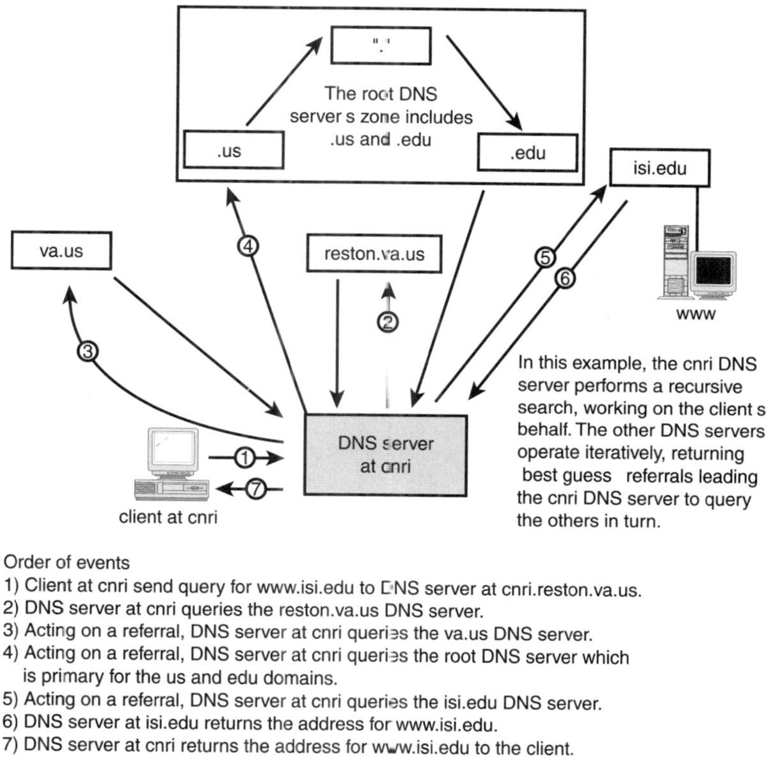

Figure 2.6 A name query follows delegations to traverse the DNS tree.

Listing 2.1 **Recursive Query Example from *nslookup***

```
ns.cnri.reston.va.us:/:1$ nslookup
Default Server: localhost
Address:  127.0.0.1
> ·   set debug

//Initial Query to CNRI Server (#1)

> ·   www.isi.edu
Server:  ns.cnri.reston.va.us
Address:  132.151.1.1

;; res_mkquery(0, www.isi.edu.cnri.reston.va.us, 1, 255)
------
Got answer:
    HEADER:
        opcode = QUERY, id = 4, rcode = NXDOMAIN
```

continues

Listing 2.1 **Continued**

```
        header flags: response, auth. answer, want recursion, recursion avail.
        questions = 1,  answers = 0,  authority records = 1,  additional =  0
    QUESTIONS:
        www.isi.edu.cnri.reston.va.us, type = ANY, class = IN
    AUTHORITY RECORDS:
    ..          > cnri.reston.va.us
        ttl = 3600 (1 hour)
        origin = cnri.reston.va.us
        mail addr = action.cnri.reston.va.us
        serial = 199712220
        refresh = 3600 (1 hour)
        retry   = 300 (5 mins)
        expire  = 3600000 (41 days 16 hours)
        minimum ttl = 3600 (1 hour)

//Referral By CNRI.Reston.Va.US to Reston.Va.US (#2) which Triggers Next åQuery

------
;; res_mkquery(0, www.isi.edu.reston.va.us, 1, 255)
------
Got answer:
    HEADER:
        opcode = QUERY, id = 5, rcode = NXDOMAIN
        header flags: response, auth. answer, want recursion, recursion avail.
        questions = 1,  answers = 0,  authority records = 1,  additional = 0
    QUESTIONS:
        www.isi.edu.reston.va.us, type = ANY, class = IN
    AUTHORITY RECORDS:
    ..          > reston.va.us
        ttl = 21600 (6 hours)
        origin = Gaia.NameTamer.com
        mail addr = hostmaster.NameTamer.com
        serial = 1997091912
        refresh = 21600 (6 hours)
        retry   = 7200 (2 hours)
        expire  = 3600000 (41 days 16 hours)
        minimum ttl = 259200 (3 days)

//Referral By Reston.Va.US to Va.US (#3) which Triggers Next Query
------
;; res_mkquery(0, www.isi.edu.va.us, 1, 255)
------
Got answer:
    HEADER:
        opcode = QUERY, id = 6, rcode = NXDOMAIN
        header flags:  response, auth. answer, want recursion, recursion avail.
        questions = 1,  answers = 0,  authority records = 1,  additional = 0
    QUESTIONS:
        www.isi.edu.va.us, type = ANY, class = IN
```

```
    AUTHORITY RECORDS:
    ->          > va.us
       ttl = 86400 (1 day)
       origin = VENERA.ISI.EDU
       mail addr = us-domain.ISI.EDU
       serial = 971219
       refresh = 43200 (12 hours)
       retry   = 3600 (1 hour)
       expire  = 1209600 (14 days)
       minimum ttl = 86400 (1 day)

//Referral By Va.US through "root" to ISI.EDU (#4,5) which Triggers Next Query
------
;; res_mkquery(0, www.isi.edu, 1, 255)
------
Got answer:
    HEADER:
       opcode = QUERY, id = 7, rcode = NOERROR
       header flags:  response, want recursion, recursion avail.
       questions = 1,  answers = 1,  authority records = 3,  additional = 4
    QUESTIONS:
       www.isi.edu, type = ANY, class = IN
 ANSWERS:
    ->          > www.isi.edu
       internet address = 128.9.176.20
       ttl = 25234 (7 hours 34 secs)
    AUTHORITY RECORDS:
    ->          > ISI.EDU
       nameserver = VENERA.ISI.EDU
       ttl = 130797 (1 day 12 hours 19 mins 57 secs)
    ->          > ISI.EDU
       nameserver = NS.ISI.EDU
       ttl = 130797 (1 day 12 hours 19 mins 57 secs)
    ->          > ISI.EDU
       nameserver = NOC.HPC.ORG
       ttl = 130797 (1 day 12 hours 19 mins 57 secs)
  ADDITIONAL RECORDS:
    ->          > VENERA.ISI.EDU
       internet address = 128.9.0.32
       ttl = 20381 (5 hours 39 mins 41 secs)
    ->          > VENERA.ISI.EDU
       internet address = 128.9.176.32
       ttl = 20381 (5 hours 39 mins 41 secs)
    ->          > NS.ISI.EDU
       internet address = 128.9.128.127
       ttl = 20381 (5 hours 39 mins 41 secs)
    ->          > NOC.HPC.ORG
       internet address = 192.187.8.2
       ttl = 145775 (1 day 16 hours 29 mins 35 secs)
```

continues

Listing 2.1 **Continued**

```
//Answer to Query by ISI.EDU for CNRI.Reston.Va.US (#6) which is Returned åto
Client (#7)
------
Non-authoritative answer:
www.isi.edu
        internet address = 128.9.176.20
        ttl = 25234 (7 hours 34 secs)

Authoritative answers can be found from:
ISI.EDU
        nameserver = VENERA.ISI.EDU
        ttl = 130797 (1 day 12 hours 19 mins 57 secs)
ISI.EDU
        nameserver = NS.ISI.EDU
        ttl = 130797 (1 day 12 hours 19 mins 57 secs)
ISI.EDU
        nameserver = NOC.HPC.ORG
        ttl = 130797 (1 day 12 hours 19 mins 57 secs)
VENERA.ISI.EDU
        internet address = 128.9.0.32
        ttl = 20381 (5 hours 39 mins 41 secs)
VENERA.ISI.EDU
        internet address = 128.9.176.32
        ttl = 20381 (5 hours 39 mins 41 secs)
NS.ISI.EDU
        internet address = 128.9.128.127
        ttl = 20381 (5 hours 39 mins 41 secs)
NOC.HPC.ORG
        internet address = 192.187.8.2
        ttl = 145775 (1 day 16 hours 29 mins 35 secs)
>
```

In Listing 2.1 and Figure 2.6, you can actually see the name server queries climb the DNS tree to the top level and then work its way down another branch. You might also find it interesting that the name server `VENERA.ISI.EDU` shows up in several places. The reference to `VENERA.ISI.EDU` is at the `va.us` level of the query. `VENERA.ISI.EDU` is one of the name servers for the `va.us` domain. You might also notice that the server from the root cache file, `VENERA.ISI.EDU`, was formerly one of the DNS root-level servers. The root server maintained by ISI is currently called `b.root-servers.net`.

Overview of Tools

A number of tools are associated with various facets of DNS. These tools can make the job of understanding what is going on and what might be wrong easier. Understanding the underlying theory of how these tools work enables you to better use them. The tools covered in this section are: Domain Internet Groper (`dig`), ipconfig, netlab, nslookup, ping, traceroute (tracert), netstat, and nbtstat. This is just a brief explanation of this toolkit; you will get more information in Chapter 12. The specific use of each of these tools is described as follows:

- dig—dig is a better nslookup. It tracks more information and is easier to use than nslookup. dig also uses the resolver to perform queries against the distributed DNS database. dig also has a number of options that provide more flexibility on the command line.
- ipconfig—ipconfig shows information about the network settings on the system, it includes things like: IP, DNS server, routing information, netmask, and more. ipconfig also enables you to renew or release all adapters or specific adapters; it also enables you to output the data to a specific file.

  With the introduction of Windows 2000, Microsoft Corporation has added some additional features to ipconfig. Two that help you with the client's resolver cache are:

  - /displaydns—Enables you to display the contents of the resolver cache if any entries exist there.
  - /flushdns—Enables you to purge the cache, which can be very useful if there is corruption or information that has changed that you want to have reloaded.
- netlab—This tool is a freeware program consisting of a number of tools that are easily reached through a graphical tool. This enables easy switching between tools to track down network problems and tools to provide more information on network conditions. netlab puts them all in one place for easy access and enables access to the following network tools: finger, whois, time, quote, ping, trace, DNS, scanner, and info. finger works in user@host or host modes. (In user@host mode it returns information about a specific user at that host, in host mode it returns information on who is logged into the system.) whois returns information from the whois database about a specific domain; you can query different types of whois servers for forward and reverse information. time has two sections to it, daytime (which prints out the date and time in a human readable format for the time at the remote server's location) and clock synchronization which synchronizes your clock to a reference clock. quote connects to a quote-of-the-day server, which is a humorous service offered by some services. ping performs pings as previously described; the ping section has a GUI that enables better control over the ping command. trace is similar to ping but performs tracerts. DNS does basic nslookups. scanner enables the scanning of a network and the control over features, such as port scanning and others. info gives you information on versions of the stack and the system name.
- nslookup—The nslookup tool performs a DNS query to various servers. If nslookup is executed, it queries the default name server unless a different name server is specified. nslookup can be called in two basic modes: interactive and

non-interactive mode. In interactive mode, a number of queries can be performed and a number of options can be set that control how the `nslookup` tool queries the database. `nslookup` uses its own resolver to perform queries.

- `ping`—`ping` is a tool that uses an Internet Control Message Protocol (ICMP). `ping` sends an `ICMP ECHO_REQUEST` to the address that is passed as a parameter. `ping` has a few options that provide for some control over its behavior. `ping` is primarily used to check for a responsive machine on a network.
- `tracert`—`tracert` (also sometimes known as `traceroute`) is a tool that sends UDP packets to a specific address. Usually, groups of three packets are sent out, and each group obtains its time-to-live (TTL) value incremented by one. The TTL parameter is used to determine if a packet of network traffic is to be considered non-deliverable. If a packet is marked non-deliverable, an `ICMP TIME_EXCEEDED` message is sent back to the originating host. This permits the tracking of each step that the network traffic is taking in route to its destination. After the destination address is reached, `tracert` stops sending packet sets.
- `netstat`—`netstat` displays protocol statistics and open TCP/IP network connections. A number of options control what `netstat` displays. Use `netstat /?` to obtain a list of all the options.
- `nbtstat`–`nbtstat` displays statistics using NetBIOS over TCP/IP (NetBT). A number of options are available for `nbtstat` as well. Use `nbtstat /?` to obtain a list of all the options.

Summary

This concludes the introductory explanation of how DNS works. The next few chapters explain DNS server types, their purposes, and how the various server types work together, as well as some detailed information about DNS zone files. Chapter 5, "Dissecting Name Queries," resumes the discussion of client name resolutions with a thorough explanation of iterative and recursive queries.

3

Name Server Types

THIS CHAPTER REVIEWS THE FOLLOWING:

- **Primary Name Servers.** Primary name servers have authority to respond to queries for a zone, and they're the location from which all the zone's address data originates. This section describes the features that make a primary server special. Note that sometimes a primary name server is called a *master* as well. The new term comes from the BIND version 8 configuration file changes. Anywhere primary is referred to in this chapter, the word *master* can be interchanged.

- **Secondary Name Servers.** Secondary name servers are backup servers. They're not where original zone data resides, but they can respond to a domain's queries with authority. Secondaries usually get their zone data from the domain's primary DNS Server. Note that secondaries can be referred to as *slaves* as well.

- **Caching-Only Name Servers.** As the name implies, caching-only name servers cache address data. Caching is a behavior of most servers. Caching-only servers are those designed to do nothing but cache queries. They don't have a zone file populated with lots of hosts, and they don't transfer zones from other DNS Servers. Caching-only name servers answer queries, but not authoritatively. This section describes caching-only servers and explains what makes them valuable.

- **Passing Queries: Forwarders and Slaves.** Forwarders and slaves are DNS servers that have a very special cooperative relationship with other DNS servers for sharing the duty of handling queries. This section explains forwarders and slaves, and explains how they give administrators service design options. Note that the reference to slave here is not the same as a secondary server previously mentioned; it refers to an option rather than a server type.

- **Determining DNS Type.** If you walk up to a DNS server but don't know what role it's playing, this section can show you how to tell the difference between primary, secondary, forwarders, slaves, and caching servers.

A domain name server can perform one role or several roles at once. This chapter provides an overview of the possible roles a server can play. It's important to note, too, that one DNS server can support multiple domains simultaneously while sometimes undertaking a different role for each. Some roles, such as caching only, are necessarily set for the entire server. A DNS server's type, then, is determined when you choose its configuration and the configurations for each domain your server will support.

In addition to explaining potential DNS server roles, this chapter reveals and discusses several architectural options to help illustrate the differences between primary, secondary, forwarder, slave, and caching servers. It's much easier to understand them in the context of practical problems and applications. The only certainty in this regard is that some DNS server will be primary for each domain. The rest is up to you.

Primary Domain Servers

Primary (or master) servers are the engines of DNS, motivating the distribution and lookups of name data throughout the Internet. Primary servers are always the original sources of address data. They have the ultimate authority for the names in their domain, and because they're the primary source of zone files for zone transfers, primary servers alone have the power to determine their domain's information as it is published to any and all other servers needing it. A secondary can also be "master" for a zone transfer to another secondary, but the master files are on the primary. This confusion in language was clarified in RFC 2136, which distinguished a slave, master, and primary master:

- **Slave.** An authoritative server that retrieves the zone transfer and is named in the zone by an NS record.
- **Master.** An authoritative server configured to be the source of transfer data for one or more slave servers.
- **Primary master.** The master server at the root of the zone transfer-dependency graph. The primary master is named in the zone's Start of Authority (SOA) record. By definition, only one primary master server exists per zone.

The publication process begins when an administrator builds a configuration boot file manually, copies one from a UNIX host's BIND DNS implementation, or, more likely, enters all the boot configuration data the server needs through the DNS server's management interface. The Windows 2000 DNS server automatically puts any configuration files in the %windir%\system32\dns folder

Essential information needed to manually configure DNS includes the following:

- The domain's name (must be preapproved by InterNIC if the domain name needs to resolve outside the enterprise)
- The IP address and name of each server for which you want to provide name resolution
- The host name and address of the DNS servers themselves
- The host name and address for each other computer that will be included in the DNS server's zones

See Chapter 11, "Configuring Windows DNS Servers," for step-by-step instructions on installing and configuring the Windows 2000 DNS Server.

Storing Windows DNS Boot Configuration Data

You can store the Windows DNS boot configuration data in multiple ways: via a boot file and via the Registry. By default, the service boots via the Registry. To use a boot configuration file rather than the Registry, you need to set the boot method by selecting the From File option under Load Zone Data on Startup. This selection menu is located in the Advanced tab of the DNS Server properties.

Unlike previous versions of the DNS Server software, the Windows 2000 DNS Server automatically updates the Registry and the boot file when selecting or changing boot methods. (In previous versions, synchronization was a more labor-intensive task, which often turned out to be more painful that fruitful.) The Registry key is HKLM\System\CurrentControlSet\Services\DNS. Chapter 11 discusses the effects of changing storage methods.

With Windows 2000, the choice of using Active Directory–integrated zones is also available, but only for primary zones. Because secondary servers do not modify data, there is no need for the secondary to access the primary data store directly; they just perform zone transfers in the normal fashion. With primary zones, the Active Directory integration means that the zone data is stored in the directory store itself. This provides a more robust means of storing and replicating (transferring) the data. If you are using Active Directory–integrated zones, multiple domain controllers can share being masters for the primary zone information. This integration also enables you to apply access control on anything from the entire store down to a single resource record (RR) as an added way to secure zone data.

Configuration Data and Domains

Microsoft DNS Server can provide configuration files for limited compatibility with the files created on UNIX-style BIND configurations, primarily to make migration to a Microsoft DNS Server easier. The default name for the cache file under Windows 2000 is CACHE.DNS.

Configuration data not only specifies the directory where the server will store such data as zone files and caches, it also contains lists that name the domains the server will support and a directive indicating what type of server the server will be for each domain: primary, secondary, or caching. If the server is using Active Directory, zone data will be stored there. If the server is primary, the boot configuration information includes the source zone file for each domain thus specified. If it is secondary, the IP address of the master server is included so that the server knows where to request updates.

When a primary server is operating, changes you make to the domain are additions or deletions of hosts, subdomains, mail exchangers, name servers, and so on. If you're using a boot configuration file to get the server up and running, you make changes only to the primary server's source files. Name server boot files have a structure that looks like the following. (Comment lines, which begin with a semicolon [;], have been inserted to describe the boot file entries.)

```
; Directory where dns.exe will store backup files:
  directory           c:\winnt\system32\dns

; Directives for name server operations:
; Server Type    Domain          Source
  primary        example.net                 hosts.db  ; Used for forward lookups
                                             (name to IP)
  primary        1.168.192.in-addr.arpa      hosts.rev ; Used for reverse lookups
                                             (IP to name)
  primary        0.0.127.in-addr.arpa        hosts.local  ; Used for internal
                                             communications
  cache                     .                cache   ; Root cache file (names and IPs
                                             of root servers)
```

The preceding example presents a form familiar to UNIX administrators. Windows 2000 DNS ignores the directory directive in this example. Note that files, including the cache file, usually have a .DNS extension in Windows systems unless otherwise specified. Don't worry about all the configuration options at this time. Chapter 11, which covers installation, provides the information you need to understand the options and make decisions. Fortunately, many of the settings are selected for you automatically.

The cache directive references the root domain (.), and the cache file contains the entries with addresses for the primary root-level servers. A root cache file comes with Windows 2000 DNS, but you can always download the most current version from InterNIC at `ftp://rs.internic.net/domain/named.root`. Be sure to rename the file to cache. (Also, don't confuse the root cache file with caching-only servers.) The FTP site is probably the easiest way to get this information. The only time the root cache file needs to be updated is when Internet authorities add a new root-level server (almost never), or when your DNS server is used to support an isolated network for private use. Note that you need these files only if you are going to use the server publicly for Internet lookups. Some companies use an internal and external setup for resolution internally along with Internet addresses; this often occurs on separate machines for internal and external servers.

In the preceding example that shows name server boot file structure, the host.db file contains a text table for the example.net domain. The hosts.rev file contains a text table for the 1.168.192.in-addr.arpa domain, the domain that contains Internet address (`in-addr`) mappings, which is the IP address–to–host name mappings for the 192.168.1.0 network. The directory statement, which is ignored, would tell a UNIX BIND name server that the files are located at the <c:\winnt\system32\dns path.

Secondary Name Servers

A secondary server contains authoritative address data for the domain, but gets it from a primary server via zone transfers. Secondaries are great for data backup, and they relieve the primary server's load by answering queries. BIND version 8 refers to secondaries as slaves.

Secondaries are authoritative because they have local copies of the zone files that are pulled from primaries during zone transfers. The function of the secondary name server are as follows:

- **Distribution of workload over several machines.** Because multiple machines handle queries for a domain, the response time improves when resolving queries. Load distribution comes from the fact that resolvers keep track of what name servers they've used and what the response times were for those servers for each query.
- **Depending on geographic location, routing, and so on, some servers perform better than others.** An intelligent resolver uses that information to choose what name servers it will hit for different requests.
- **Redundancy.** With secondary name servers, a domain call can still be referenced, and queries resolved, even if the primary fails and becomes unavailable. It is especially useful to locate secondaries on physically different networks, even in different parts of the country.

Local Host Resolutions for the Reverse Address Domain and the Cached Root Domain

Directives and the contents of files for the 0.0.127.in-addr.arpa domain and the root cache are usually identical on every machine because every machine has a loopback port with an address of 127.0.0.1. The loopback, often labeled `localhost`, is used for internal communications for network services.

A name server can resolve names by calling itself via the `localhost` address, which speeds the operations of the name server because communications do not actually go out onto the network where there's more latency.

Of course, if you look at this list closely you will see that the multi-master model of Active Directory integrated zones can be used to accomplish all of these, also, even though there might be no secondaries.

The functionality of email is a good example with which to make the redundancy point. Assume that xyz.com has its primary name server in San Jose, California. The administrators decide to put the secondary on a different subnet, but in the same building. If xyz.com loses connectivity to the Internet, it will instantly lose the capability to answer external DNS queries in its domain. If someone tries to send email to xyz.com, for example, the email will bounce, probably with an `unknown host` error.

Now assume that xyz.com decides to put a second secondary name server on the East Coast of the United States, hosted by abc.com. If xyz.com then loses its connectivity, queries will still be answered by the secondary at abc.com. In addition, xyz.com may also have improved overall response when resolving queries to external entities because it has a distributed arrangement enabling queries to come from different parts of the country. An email message sent to xyz.com, for example, would in this instance just be queued again due to delivery problems, rather than bounced.

The following example illustrates what a boot file for a secondary name server might look like:

```
; Directory where dns.exe will look for or store backup files:
  directory     c:\winnt\system32\dns

; Directives for name server operations:
; Server Type   Domain                     Source          Backup
  secondary     example.net                192.168.1.220   hosts.db
  secondary     1.168.192.in-addr.arpa     192.168.1.220   hosts.rev
  primary       0.0.127.in-addr.arpa       hosts.local
  cache         .                          cache
```

Notice in the preceding example that the source of the data for the domains comes from the host 192.168.1.220, and the name server stores a backup copy of the zone file and calls it hosts.db. The secondary name server has the same cache directive as the primary. Note that the name server is a primary for the 0.0.127.in-addr.arpa domain because the loopback address is private to each machine, and therefore each machine is the primary for its own loopback network.

The secondary is not required to store a backup copy of the domain information, although it is recommended. Having a local backup means that the name server starts faster because it doesn't need to contact the primary for the zone info immediately upon starting and, if the data is up-to-date, it doesn't have to transfer more than the check for new zone information. This does not guarantee that the initial set of data is up-to-date, but the name server can at least begin to answer queries based on the data it has.

Caching-Only Name Servers

Caching-only servers can be used to improve the performance of DNS servers on local networks. Where DNS queries frequently hit the same target locations, a caching-only name server can be installed to provide quicker responses to queries without incurring the administrative problems of a primary or secondary name server, or the network overhead of zone transfers. Caching-only servers require little work to set up and operate, as illustrated in the following example:

```
; Directory where named will look for or store backup files:
  directory      c:\winnt\system32\dns

; Directives for name server operations:
; Server Type   Domain                  Source
  primary       0.0.127.in-addr.arpa    hosts.local
  cache         .                       cache
```

The configuration file for a caching-only name server requires only entries for the directory, the loopback domain (0.0.127.in-addr.arpa), and the cache statement itself.

The only requirement for a caching-only server is a valid root cache file that includes the name server itself. Because a caching-only server cannot be authoritative, it should not be delegated for a domain. Caching-only servers can be configured to forward requests and then cache the results for use when responding to future queries.

Caching-only servers are great for organizations that have an ISP providing their primary DNS services and that want to improve performance, and for supporting remote sites with slow links. To set up a caching-only server in Windows, the DNS service first must be installed and started. The cache and loopback is automatically generated as soon as a new server is installed. Then the only required action is to ensure that the service starts up after any Windows server reboots or after other system interruptions. Most installations will not use an Internet Service Provider (ISP) for provision of DNS services used to support a Windows domain environment, but a local cache of external names from one's public name space ISP or from one's internal name servers carries many advantages.

Caching-only servers have several advantages. The main advantage is an increase in performance for many users who would otherwise make one server too busy: The server offloads the query burden to a machine dedicated for the purpose. A disadvantage, however slight, is that caching-only servers may not always have accurate information. You can set its *time-to-live* (TTL) value to control how long a caching-only server keeps cache data before discarding it. One issue with Windows 2000 DNS is that it does implement the NCACHE, or negative response, caching. This usually poses no problem, but can at times lead to some confusion, especially for the DNS administrator making changes and testing.

Passing Queries: Forwarders and Slaves

A DNS server can designate another to be its forwarder, which establishes where future queries are forwarded if it can't answer A slave relationship makes a server dependent on its forwarders to answer queries by restricting its activity—that is, by preventing it from being a client to any other DNS servers. In a nutshell, the fundamental difference between a forwarding server and a slave is as follows:

- **Forwarding server.** Sends queries to a designated machine, its forwarder, waits for short period of time, and then can begin to look for the answer itself.
- **Slave server.** Sends queries to a designated machine, its forwarder, and waits for an answer. Slaves do not try to resolve the queries themselves.

  Note that this use of slave is not referring to a secondary server but an actual functionality called *slave*.

A *forwarder* is a designated machine for handling queries (see Figure 3.1).

Clients, including other DNS servers, wait for a short period of time after sending a query to a forwarder and then can begin to look for the answer themselves if no reply is received, unless they are slaves. Because a lot of traffic can be sent through forwarding DNS servers, they build up a large cache of addresses. This is useful if you want to build up a cache for many users that have well-focused network access patterns.

Figure 3.1 illustrates the following process:

1. A client sends a query to a local DNS server.
2. The local DNS server forwards the request to a forwarder and begins waiting.
3. The forwarder attempts to resolve it locally and if it cannot, it sends the query to a name server on the Internet and begins waiting.
4. If no reply is received, the local DNS server sends the query to a name server on the Internet.

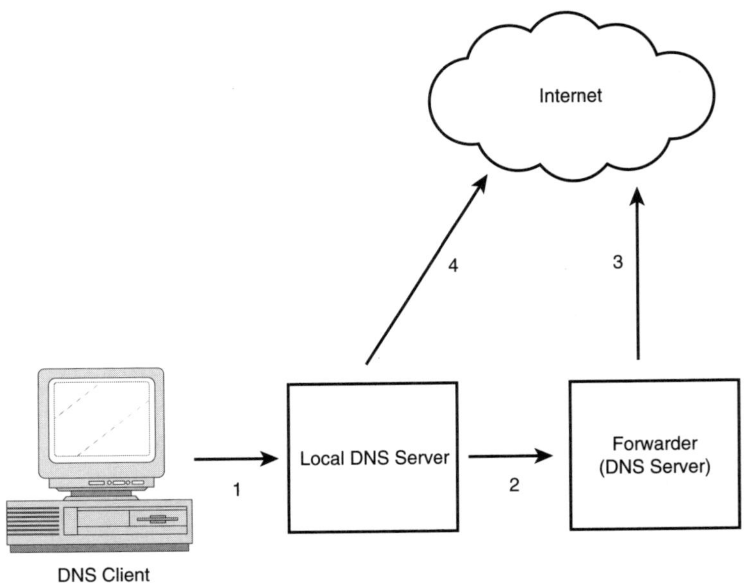

Figure 3.1 A forwarder handles queries on behalf of another DNS server.

Both the forwarder and the local DNS server will eventually get a response, building the cache on both DNS servers.

If a client's name server has a designated forwarder and it receives a query but cannot answer the query from its local zone files or cache, the name server does not then perform a recursive search to find the answer. (Chapter 5, "Dissecting Name Queries," describes recursive queries.) Instead, the name server forwards the query to its designated forwarder. The designated forwarder name server performs the search and provides an answer. If the forwarder does not return an answer, the server then starts a recursive search on its own.

Forwarding has a number of practical uses. One is to forward a query to several DNS servers with the knowledge that they'll all work it, and that this will build a cache of each located host's address; this cache will be useful for subsequent queries by the same or another client. The most frequent application of forwarders, however, is to use dual DNS servers to work through a firewall. Organizations connected to the Internet need to resolve Internet host names, but might not want to expose their entire network to the rest of the Internet for security reasons. In this scenario, an internal DNS server forwards all queries for names outside the organization's domain to an external DNS server for resolution. You can use forwarding so that an internal server gets first crack at the resolution followed by an external server.

Slave servers are those forced to use a forwarder (see Figure 3.2). Slaves send queries to one or more designated forwarder machines and wait for an answer, but

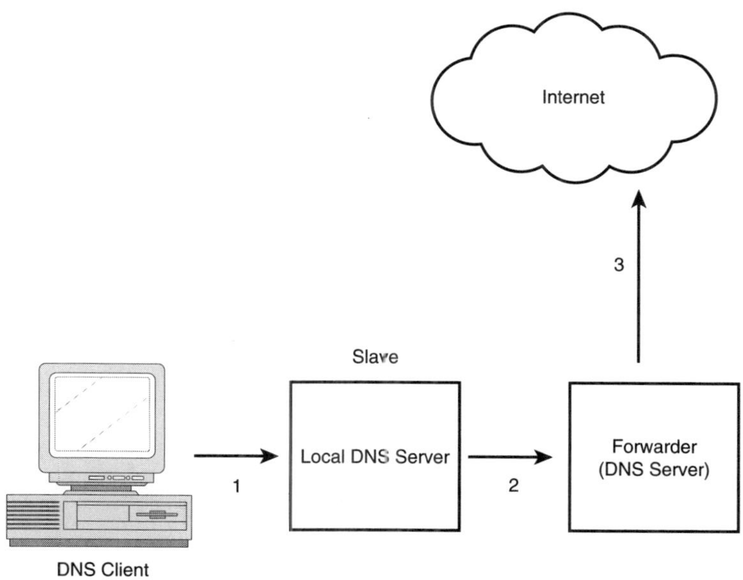

Figure 3.2 A slave must wait for the forwarder's response.

they're not allowed to try to resolve queries for themselves if the forwarders don't answer fast enough. This option is extremely useful as a security measure because it forces all query traffic to go through one path from a slave to a forwarder. It's a great way to penetrate a firewall with authorized, predictable outgoing DNS queries and, as such, can help you implement a good security policy.

Figure 3.2 illustrates the following process:

1. A client sends a query to a local DNS server.
2. The local DNS server forwards the request to a forwarder and begins waiting.
3. The forwarder attempts to resolve it locally and if it cannot it sends the query to a name server on the Internet and begins waiting.
4. If there's no reply, a slave (the local DNS server in this case) will not initiate a query on its own.

Slaves are DNS servers set up to use forwarding, with one additional restriction: Slaves accept responses only for queries from the designated name servers to which they forward queries. This way, going back to the previously mentioned scenario, an internal DNS server provides all name resolution service for internal hosts because looks at internal servers only for resolution. This provides control of whether resolution passes off to Internet servers.

An external name server provides all the external name resolution for the protected hosts and for the organization's publicly known hosts. A DNS server inside the firewall should service the rest of the internal domain to prevent private names and addresses from becoming known. Remember that anything in a DNS server can be discovered quite easily by using simple queries! Windows 2000 with Active Directory integration enables you to control access with *access control lists* (ACLs).

To set up a forwarder, the boot file must have an entry specifying the forwarder by directive, or you must make an entry in the Forwarders panel, which you display by clicking the Forwarders tab in the Server Properties dialog box. To open it, just select Properties on the server. If you check the Do Not Use Recursion check box, you have set up a slave server.

In either case, you must include the Internet Protocol (IP) addresses of the machines that the server will forward to. The following example shows proper boot file entries. Note that the directory is the default location for Windows 2000. I suggest including these, however, because sometimes you will forget where things are and it is nice if something can
tell you where it is:

```
; Directory where named will store backup files:
  directory           c:\winnt\\system32\dns

; Name servers that will serve as forwarders:
  forwarders          192.168.3.72 192.168.1.24
```

```
; Ensures that the name server will not attempt queries
; outside of itself:
  slave
; or, depending on the version:
  option forward-only

; Directives for name server operations:
; Server Type  Domain                    Source
  primary      example.net               hosts.db
  primary      1.168.192.in-addr.arpa    hosts.rev
  primary      0.0.127.in-addr.arpa      hosts.local
  cache        .                         cache
```

Determining DNS Type

The following list summarizes the different DNS server types and may help you to select the kind of server you need to implement:

- **Primary or master.** Authority for one or more zones. A *zone* is the data for one or more domains, and may be data for part of a domain.
- **Secondary or slave.** Also authoritative, but functions as a backup to a primary name server. Gets all zone data from a primary server by transfer.
- **Forwarder.** A DNS server designated by another to handle all its queries.
- **Slave.** A DNS server configured to use a forwarder, but which has no other options. Must use the forwarder for all queries. Note that this is not referring to a secondary.
- **Caching-only.** A server that builds up a cache of addresses by virtue of its own query activities. A caching-only server has no zone data of its own, and only performs queries for clients.

Windows 2000 DNS server can be used to provide any of these; an interesting variation is a slave server except that it is also authoritative for one or more zones. Chapter 11 discusses the set up of these different types in more detail.

You may need administrator privileges to find out what kind of server is running on an existing system; then, you can read the boot file or examine the Registry, or view the DNS server and the zone properties using the DNS management console. The DNS server's function is spelled out in plain English in the boot file of UNIX systems. Statements about the operation of the name server are also listed there, starting with the purpose, or function, of the server in question. For Windows, this file informs you of any zones that are on the server and what is used for the cache file. If your name server is started via the Registry (it can be started via the Registry or a boot configuration file), the boot file contains only a statement mentioning the fact.

Using the DNS server management console, right-click any of the listed zones to open the Zone Properties dialog box. Figure 3.3 shows the General tab that displays information about the zone, indicating whether the server is primary or secondary. If

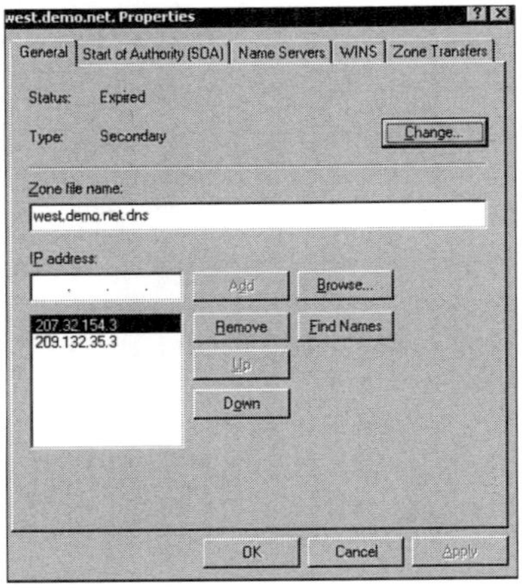

Figure 3.3 Primary servers reference a zone file where data is stored.

no zones (other than the 127.in-addr.arpa) appear, you know that the server is a caching server and possibly a slave. To distinguish these two, examine the cache file, or look at the Root Hints tab of the server properties.

If you don't have administrative privileges for the machine, but you know its IP address, you can query the name server to examine the SOA record of any of its domains. If the source entry in the SOA is for the same machine, it's safe to assume that the machine is primary for the domain.

A secondary server can provide authoritative data for any of the zones it gets by transfer from a primary. Figure 3.3 shows how a secondary is configured. The IP Address area shows how you specify what server(s) are its masters. You can put a secondary server on a local area network (LAN) or LAN segment to provide a dedicated, local query server, reducing wide area network (WAN) traffic and increasing security. Also you may want a caching-forwarding server on a slow link because it reduces bandwidth needs by caching answers for lookups locally.

If the machine in question has no zones, it could be a caching-only server or a secondary that has not yet been delegated for the domain.

Summary

The various DNS server types help you design systems to solve problems and answer name service challenges. Primaries are sources of data, secondaries are backups that help share the query load, caching-only servers can help relieve query and network workloads without adding to your administrative burdens, and forwarders and slaves can increase security and help you to realize the benefits of caching.

Chapter 4, "Domain Information Details," detail how to construct DNS records, what they mean, and how to use resource records to establish relationships between DNS servers.

4

Domain Information Details

THIS CHAPTER REVIEWS THE FOLLOWING:

- **Database Resource Records.** *Resource records* (RRs) make up the contents of zone files and, as such, are at the very heart of DNS. As the name implies, each resource record contains information about a resource that's important for DNS to know about. Among these resources are other DNS Servers and hosts, and now also advertised services. This section identifies major resource record types and explains their use.
- **The Cache File.** The cache file (*root hints*) identifies root-level domain name servers so that any DNS server can easily find the root of the domain name system tree. This section describes the cache file, why it's needed, and how it's used.
- **Delegation.** Registering your primary DNS Server with one of the InterNICs makes it accessible to clients outside your domain needing access to your domain's name list. You publish secondary servers yourself using *Name Server* (NS) records. This section describes the reasons why you would publish other authoritative servers.

If DNS were a creature, it would do some things by instinct, and it would develop other behaviors only after learning. This chapter describes the fundamental things

DNS was designed for, those things DNS does almost instinctively (serving resource information from its zone files), and the various resource record types that you can use to make DNS perform advanced tasks to meet your specific needs (route mail, find service location information, and enhance security infrastructure using key exchange). This chapter does not cover the new dynamic update behaviors DNS has recently learned.

Database RR

Like any relational database, the DNS architecture is made up of tables, each containing a number of records. DNS database tables are called *zone files*. Most of the records have a special meaning because they identify the location of resources, and they may even be associated with records in other tables. Possible resource record types include the *Start Of Authority* (SOA) record, the *Address* (A) record, and the *Pointer* (PTR) record. Detailed coverage of the most common resource record types is provided later in the chapter. Appendix F, "Resource Records and the InterNIC Cache File," provides a complete listing of resource records.

What records you see in a zone file depends on a few things. What zone file is being examined? Forward and reverse lookup zones, for example, have very few record types in common. Another factor determining a zone file's content is what information the DNS administrator wants, or needs, to publish. The rest of this section provides you with a thorough explanation of the most important record types. You should know about them all and how they're used.

When configured to store zone information in files, Windows DNS stores the zone database files in the %windir%\system32\dns directory. Template files are also provided in the .\samples subdirectory to provide examples of the file format.

Windows DNS Server can store configuration and zone information in three places. Configuration information is always stored in the Registry and can also be stored in a BIND-compatible boot file (the sort found on a UNIX machine). Zone information can be stored in zone files or in the Active Directory. The Registry location for the DNS Server boot configuration is HKLM, System, CurrentControlSet, Services, DNS, Zones; the file is named BOOT. Unlike a UNIX NAMED.BOOT file, the Windows DNS Server allows only the primary, secondary, and cache directives in its boot file. Figure 4.1 shows the Advanced tab of the Windows DNS Server properties on a member server.

When the Load zone data on startup setting is changed to From File, a boot file is created from the information in the Registry. When it is changed to From Registry, the prior boot file is moved into the .\backup subdirectory. In either case, the Registry is always maintained with the current information. This change is immediate when the Apply button is used.

What may be misleading here is that zone files are always used for zone storage unless the Active Directory is being used. Despite the description of this option in Figure 4.1, zone data (that is, the actual resource records) is not stored in the Registry. When zone information is stored in the Active Directory, the zone records are converted

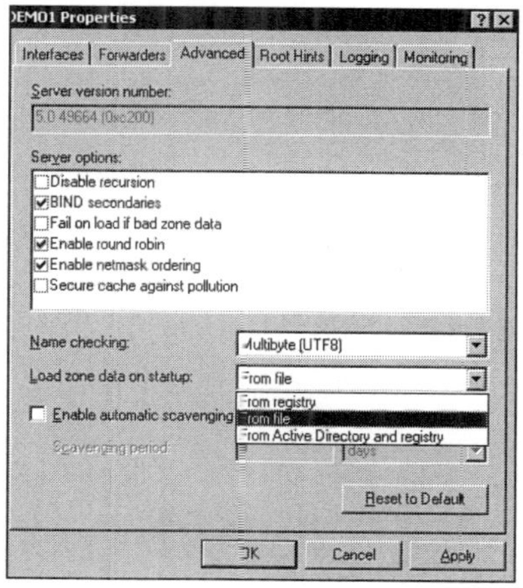

Figure 4.1 The Windows DNS Server Properties dialog box, in which you can set the boot option.

to directory objects visible through Lightweight Directory Access Protocol (LDAP), and there is no longer a zone file on a primary although these are still used on any secondaries. Also, there is then no option to Boot From File.

The zone file formats in Windows DNS are RFC-compliant, and so examples in this chapter apply equally to BIND zone files and Windows DNS zone files. If anything, this chapter includes more information than you'll see in the Windows DNS management interface. Where that's so, just realize that the actual storage is more complex than what you see because the management console is simplifying things by selecting what it presents and by choosing intelligent default values for some configurable options.

RFC 1035, RFC 1183, RFC 1664, RFC 1886, RFC 2052, RFC 2181, RFC 2535, and RFC 2672 (available online from `www.isi.edu`) are the most authoritative documents available describing how to format resource records. Windows DNS formats records automatically when you use the DNS Server management console. If you use the boot file, however, to move files back and forth between Windows DNS and BIND, for example, you need to know precisely how to format records using a text editor, and how to make the boot file acceptable to Windows. One nice feature of the Windows DNS is that it enables you to create a configuration using the DNS Server management console and then to store the configuration to a boot file. This is helpful, of course, if you are moving from Windows DNS to a UNIX/BIND-based solution, not the other way around.

RR Syntax Formats

The following excerpt from RFC 1035 (pages 32–34), written by Paul Mockapetris, explains the syntax of RR formats.

The format of these files is a sequence of entries. Entries are predominantly line oriented, though parentheses can be used to continue a list of items across a line boundary, and text literals can contain CRLF within the text. Any combination of tabs and spaces act as a delimiter between the separate items that make up an entry. The end of any line in the master file can end with a comment. The comment starts with a `;` (semicolon). The following entries are defined:

```
<blank>[<comment>]
    $ORIGIN <domain-name> [<comment>]
    $INCLUDE <file-name> [<domain-name>] [<comment>]
    <domain-name><rr> [<comment>]
    <blank><rr> [<comment>]
```

Blank lines, with or without comments, are allowed anywhere in the file. Two control entries are defined: `$ORIGIN` and `$INCLUDE`. `$ORIGIN` is followed by a domain name, and resets the current origin for relative domain names to the stated name. `$INCLUDE` inserts the named file into the current file, and may optionally specify a domain name that sets the relative domain name origin for the included file. `$INCLUDE` may also have a comment. Note that a `$INCLUDE` entry never changes the relative origin of the parent file, regardless of changes to the relative origin made within the included file.

The last two forms represent RRs. If an entry for an RR begins with a blank, then the RR is assumed to be owned by the last stated owner. If an RR entry begins with a `<domain-name>`, the owner name is reset. `<rr>` contents take one of the following forms:

```
[<TTL>] [<class>] <type> <RDATA>
[<class>] [<TTL>] <type> <RDATA>
```

The RR begins with optional time-to-live (`TTL`) and `class` fields, followed by a `type` and `RDATA` field appropriate to the type and class. `class` and `type` use the standard mnemonics; `TTL` is a decimal integer. Omitted class and TTL values are default to the last explicitly stated values. Because `type` and *class* mnemonics are disjoint, the parse is unique. (Note that this order differs from the order used in examples and the order used in the actual RRs; the given order allows easier parsing and defaulting.)

`<domain-name>`s make up a large share of the data in the master file.

The labels in the domain name are expressed as character strings and separated by dots. Quoting conventions allow arbitrary characters to be stored in domain names. Domain names that end in a dot are called absolute, and are taken as complete. Domain names which do not end in a dot are called relative; the actual domain name is the concatenation of the relative part with an origin specified in a `$ORIGIN`, `$INCLUDE`, or as an argument to the master file loading routine. A relative name is an error when no origin is available.

`<character-string>` is expressed in one or two ways: as a contiguous set of characters without interior spaces, or as a string beginning with a `?` and ending with a `?`. Inside a delimited string any character can occur, except for a `?` itself, which must be quoted using `\` (backslash).

Because these files are text files, several special encodings are necessary to allow arbitrary data to be loaded. In particular:

```
.                   of the root.
@                 A free standing @ is used to denote the current
                    origin.
\X                 where X is any character other than a digit
                    (0-9), is used to quote that character so that
                    its special meaning does not apply.  For example,
                    ?\.? can be used to place a dot character in a
                    label.
\DDD         where each D is a digit is the octet
                    corresponding to the decimal number described by
                    DDD.  The resulting octet is assumed to be text
                    and is not checked for special meaning.
( )                 Parentheses are used to group data that crosses a
                    line boundary.  In effect, line terminations are
                    not recognized within parentheses.
;                   Semicolon is used to start a comment; the
                    remainder of the line is ignored.
```

The syntax representations and examples describing individual RR types later in this chapter are also described in RFC 1035 and RFC 2052. These documents are authoritative references for master file formats. A few observations, however, need to be made:

- RR entries are parsed without case sensitivity, so that hostname = HOSTNAME = HoSTNAme.
- Names in RRs have a length limit of 63 characters per label and 255 characters per FQDN.
- The underscores in *Service* (SRV) RRs are specified in the current revision to RFC 2052 for, perhaps temporary, use in specifying the service and protocol fields. The now current RFC 2052bis draft intended to obsolete RFC 2052 is draft-ietf-dnsind-rfc2052bis-05.txt of November 16, 1999.
- For internationalization, standardized support for enhanced character sets was adopted in RFC 2044, which has since become obsolete by RFC 2279. The UTF-8 standard specified in RFC 2279, which deals with character sets and not DNS specifically, has been built in to the RR support in Windows 2000 DNS.

Underscore Usage

The underscore is commonly used in Windows NT naming schemes, but it's a problem when mapping NetBIOS names to the DNS namespace. Windows administrators need to recognize that the underscore is currently considered illegal in DNS host and domain names. Although some name servers only complain about underscores, others return errors or refuse queries altogether. With Windows 2000, this will typically be less of a problem because the DNS and Windows namespaces need to be tied closely together. However, the fact remains that use of UTF-8 names or of such special characters as the underscore presents a problem to DNS Server interoperation.

SOA Records

The SOA record is a required first entry in all forward and reverse (in-addr.arpa) zone files. SOA records (defined by RFC 1035) provide several key pieces of information that each domain needs. Most importantly, an SOA entry specifies what name server is the source of authoritative information for the domain. Figure 4.2 shows the Properties dialog box for a zone set to the SOA record tab. You can get to the zone properties in the DNS server management console by highlighting the zone's icon in the list in the left pane and then using the context menu (right-click) and selecting Properties.

SOA records are extremely important. They contain the following components. (Some of these values are shown in Figure 4.2.) The following list shows all possible options (but not exactly as they appear in the Windows DNS Server management console). The SOA resource record template looks like the following prototype (refer also to Figure 4.2):

```
<owner> <ttl> IN SOA <zone file source> <mailbox> (<serial> <refresh> <retry>
<expire> <m-ttl>)
```

- `owner.` The SOA owner generally refers to the zone's origin, or what domain the zone file represents. In Windows DNS, owners are the domain names appearing in the server list under server names, and they're automatically entered into the database for you.
- `ttl.` The domain's default TTL is set by the minimum time-to-live value (see the last item in this list, `M-TTL`). This TTL setting, if used, overrides the domain's default TTL value (the `M-TTL`) for the individual record.
- `class.` The class in the SOA defaults to type IN for Internet.

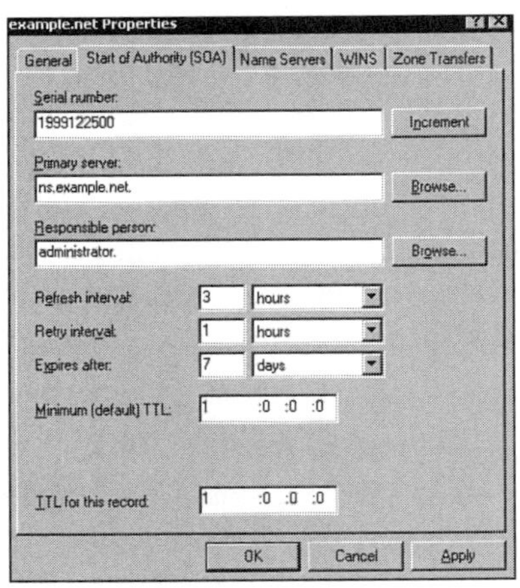

Figure 4.2 Windows DNS Server zone properties showing SOA resource record information.

- `type`. The presence of the letters *SOA* in the type column of a resource record denotes that this is, indeed, a record indicating which DNS server originates authority for the domain.
- `zone file source`. The zone file source is the host name of the primary DNS server for the domain. In Windows DNS, this entry is created automatically when the management interface is used.
- Responsible person mailbox DNS name (`mailbox`). The mailbox is an entry that typically points to the email address of the administrator for the domain. Expressed in a dot format, an example is action.cnri.reston.va.us, which translates to action@cnri.reston.va.us. action would be the mail address probably pointing to the system administrator at CNRI.
- `serial`. The serial number is used for version control. When changes are made to a zone file and the serial number is incremented, the changes are picked up by the slave servers. If it's not incremented, the slave server assumes its data is already correct and does not initiate transfer of refreshed data. A slave requests a serial number from the master and compares it to the one that it currently has. If it finds that the master's number is higher than its own, it initiates a zone transfer. If the master's serial number is equal to the slave's, no zone transfer occurs. If the master's serial number is less than the slave, no zone transfer occurs and the slave logs a message to its error log about the master having a lower number than its own.
- `refresh`. The refresh time tells a slave how often to attempt performing a zone refresh. It's the refresh interval, or cycle. When the refresh time of the slave expires, the serial number is evaluated to determine whether any changes necessitate a fresh transfer. If a change has been made and the serial number incremented, the slaves record the new serial number while reloading the zone. Chapter 5, "Dissecting Name Queries," provides information on incremental and full zone transfers.
- `retry`. The retry interval specifies how soon the secondaries will again try to refresh after a refresh has failed.
- `expire`. Expire time specifies how long the secondary continues to provide authoritative answers when a refresh and retries fail. In the event that a refresh fails because of a primary server's outage, secondaries continue to answer queries until the zone expires. If the primary server comes back online, the secondaries again refresh and everyone is happy. If the zone expires and has not been successfully refreshed, secondaries stop answering queries for that domain.
- `m-ttl`. The *minimum time-to-live* (`M-TTL`) specifies the default value for how long an answer is good (its TTL) when no specific TTL has been provided. When a client queries the DNS server, it takes the TTL information along with the response so that it'll know how long it can use (cache) the answer without having to check back again for changes. If data doesn't often change, the TTL can

be higher. This creates more persistent caches, resulting in fewer queries. Low TTL values cause client caches to expire more quickly, resulting in more frequent queries for exactly the same records. Use of TTL values on resource records is not common, meaning that those resource records have an inherited TTL value that is specified here as the M-TTL on the SOA resource record for the domain.

A typical SOA record might look like this:

```
example.net.     IN     SOA     ns.example.net      root.example.net      (
          19991225000          ;serial
          10800                ;refresh
          3600                 ;retry
          604800               ;expire
          86400      )         ;m-ttl
```

The @ symbol can also indicate current origin (in this case, example.net.), making the following SOA record equivalent to the preceding example:

```
@     IN     SOA     ns.example.net.     root.example.net.     (
          19991225000      ;serial
          10800            ;refresh
          3600             ;retry
          604800           ;expire
          86400      )     ;m-ttl
```

@ equates to the long form: example.net. As mentioned previously, the ttl field is usually ignored because by default, the M-TTL value applies to all records in the zone. Notice that the times are all stated in seconds.

Name Server (NS) Records

Name server records tell DNS what servers are delegated servers for the domain, or for its subdomains. Delegation gives a server authority to answer queries. Delegation is much like a manager delegating work to another person. A name server can delegate the entire responsibility for a subdomain to other servers, or a primary can delegate to secondary servers so that they'll be used for queries even though they are not the origin of address mappings. The section "Delegation" later in this chapter covers delegation in greater detail. Figure 4.3 shows the Properties dialog box for a zone with the NS records tab selected.

NS records are used in both forward and reverse zone files, and they have the following format:

```
<owner> <ttl> IN NS <host.domain-name>
```

The first field of the record is the owner; it indicates the domain for which the name server has been delegated authority. Next is the ttl field, which is usually blank because administrators like to rely on the M-TTL value of the SOA RR instead. Next is the class field, which is almost always Internet (IN). Next is the indication that this is an NS resource record. Finally the name server's host.domain-name consists of a fully

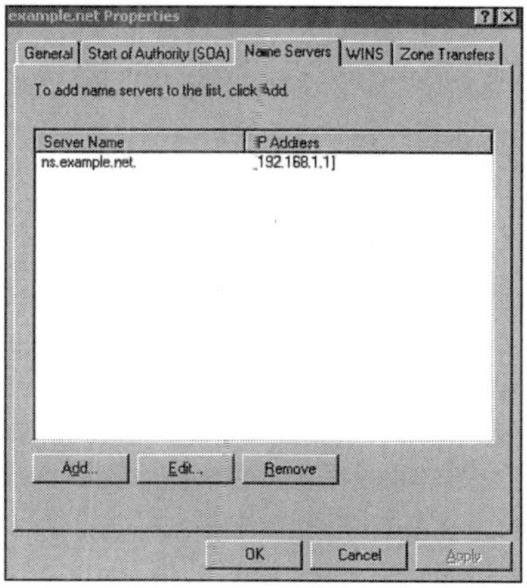

Figure 4.3 Windows DNS Server zone properties showing NS resource record information.

qualified domain name for any server that can provide authoritative answers for the domain. It has a trailing dot to ensure that resolvers understand it's a true fully qualified domain name (FQDN). You can see similarities between NS and SOA records. Both contain owner, ttl, and class fields that are likely to be the same in both records.

There's an NS record for every name server delegated, and "glue" records from parent or root servers to point to the delegated name server. You can specify additional name servers within your domain by using an NS RR, but they are only to be used for internal clients. External organizations will know about the name servers you have registered with the InterNIC and delegated for the zone.

It should probably be pointed out that we have been speaking of delegation in the usual way. Within the Windows 2000 DNS management console, delegation is used somewhat differently. There, one can choose to create NS records either by selecting New Zone or New Delegation. The first creates a new zone, with NS and SOA records, based on assumption of the current server. The second creates a subdomain in the zone at that point, and creates an NS record. Although the Microsoft Windows 2000 documentation is fairly consistent in its use of these terms, one should be aware that delegation often has the rather specific meaning used in this chapter.

An NS record might look like the following:

```
example. net.          IN     NS      VENERA.ISI.EDU.
```

Other, probably more common entries, look like this:

```
                       IN     NS      NS1.ISI.EDU.
                       IN     NS      NS1.USC.EDU.
```

Because the first record in a zone file is the SOA and the owner is declared in the SOA, no owner is specified in the NS records in this example. It is assumed that the owner is the current origin example.net.

Notice that the TTL is not specified in the preceding example NS records, and that the name servers NS1.ISI.EDU. and NS1.USC.EDU. are specified by FQDN with trailing periods. There's no requirement that a delegated name server be in the same domain, which is part of the beauty of the DNS architecture. Here, the name servers actually have different domain name suffixes.

PTR Records and Reverse Lookups

PTR records are keys to reverse address resolution. If you have an IP address of a host and you'd like to know what name the host goes by, a reverse address–, or just an address–, to–host name resolution needs to be available. PTR records make up the bulk of a [reverse network number].in-addr.arpa domain zone file. Figure 4.4 shows the DNS Properties dialog box for PTR records.

The in-addr zone files start off with the SOA and NS records just like any other zone file. The remainder of an in-addr zone file, however, is usually just PTR, and sometimes *Canonical Name* (CNAME) records.

The PTR template looks like this (refer also to Figure 4.4):

```
<owner> <ttl> IN PTR <host.domain-name>
```

If you look at the primary name server for the 1.168.192.in-addr.arpa domain, for example, the entries in its zone file can look like the following:

```
@               IN            SOA      ns.example.net.
hostmaster.example.net.  (20000217000  86400 3600   608400 86400 )
                IN            NS       ns.example. net.
1               IN            PTR      ns.example. net.
10              IN      PTR   machine.example. net.
```

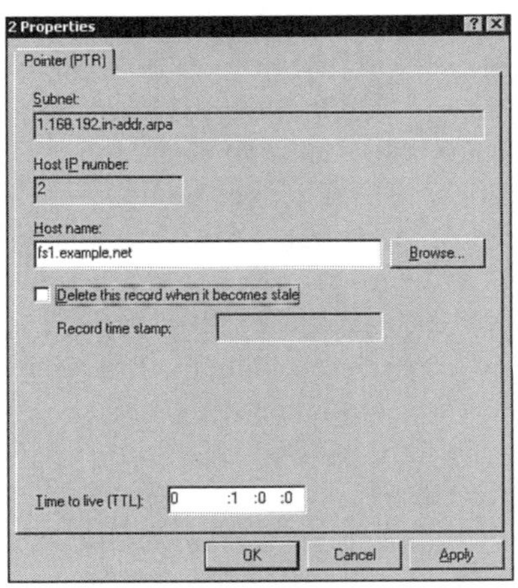

Figure 4.4 Properties of a PTR record in Windows DNS Server.

First of all, notice the trailing period after host names to make sure that no additional information is ever appended to the names. These hosts are fully qualified domain names. If the trailing period is left off, the domain origin is appended to the host names. Because the origin is 1.168.192.in-addr.arpa, it would get pretty ugly fast.

Because this zone file represents a reverse address mapping, the numbers 1.168.192 get appended to the numbers appearing in the PTR records. Hence, the reverse address of ns.example.net is 1.1.168.192. You can turn the numbers around and see that the real IP address is 192.168.1.1.

This example uses the notation of Class C networks. The in-addr zone file might look different for a Class B network. Let's use the 132.10.0.0 network as an example, with a domain name of xyz.com. The boot file entry for such an in-addr zone could be represented as follows:

```
primary     10.132.in-addr.arpa     132.10.inaddr.arrpa.dns
```

The zone file could be set up as follows:

```
@      IN        SOA      ns.xyz.com        root.xyz.com (
20000217001  86400 3600   608400 86400 )
               IN        NS        ns.xyz.com.
1.1            IN        PTR       ns.xyz.com.
1.2            IN        PTR       www.xyz.com.
2.4            IN        PTR       mailhost.xyz.com.
```

Or, the zone file could be set up using the `$ORIGIN` statement to segment the file by domain, as follows:

```
@              IN        SOA       ns.xyz.com        root.xyz.com (
20000217001  86400 3600   608400 86400 )
               IN        NS        ns.xyz.com.
$ORIGIN 1.10.132.in-addr.arpa.
1              IN        PTR       ns.xyz.com.
$ORIGIN 2.10.132.in-addr.arpa.
1      IN        PTR      www.xyz.com.
$ORIGIN 4.10.132.in-addr.arpa.
2      IN        PTR      mailhost.xyz.com.
```

Entering FQDNs with Trailing Periods

In Windows NT 4, Microsoft Knowledge Base article #Q154555 clarified when you should and should not enter FQDNs with trailing periods into the DNS management console. Use FQDNs with trailing periods when specifying servers as DATA in records (NS name server, CNAME canonical name, SOA primary name server, MX mail server, and so on). These fields refer to servers that may or may not be located in the domain, and so, must be fully qualified. They must be fully qualified literally. Otherwise, do not use FQDNs with trailing periods, such as for names located on the server (for hostname A, alias for CNAME, domain for SOA or NS). They'll be qualified by the domain where they're located by the logic of other data records. In the Windows 2000 DNS Server management console, a similar parsing seems to be applied, and whether you can enter periods when they are not needed is at times independent of what is written to the zone file.

This zone file setup can greatly simplify the management of large zone files by dividing zones into logical sections. The `$ORIGIN` statement resets the domain name for all RRs below it so that they reflect the domain name following the `$ORIGIN` statement. The `$INCLUDE` statement introduces even further simplification. `$INCLUDE` enables you to put PTR records for each origin into separate files because it includes those files in the primary zone file at the point where `$INCLUDE` appears. The resulting zone file using this method would look like the following:

```
@              IN       SOA      ns.xyz.com      root.xyz.com (
20000217001  86400 3600 608400 86400 )
               IN       NS       ns.xyz.com.
$ORIGIN 1.10.132.in-addr.arpa.
$INCLUDE sub-net1.db
$ORIGIN 2.10.132.in-addr.arpa.
$INCLUDE sub-net2.db
$ORIGIN 4.10.132.in-addr.arpa.
$INCLUDE sub-net4.db
```

In the preceding example, the three `$INCLUDE` files for the in-addr zones contain PTR records for their respective subnets and hosts.

Sometimes, having in-addr.arpa domains delegated on normal subnet boundaries by full octets does not satisfy one's needs. One ingenious approach to reverse lookups *when classless internet domain routing* (CIDR) is used is based on CNAME records and delegation of in-addr.arpa subdomains. For more information see RFC 2317.

Address (A) Records

A records map host names to IP version 4 addresses. These records are used in forward lookup zone files and in the root cache files. For IP version 6, the corresponding Quad A (AAAA) resource record is used. The format of an A record is similar to an NS record. A record contains an owner, a class, a ttl, the A resource type itself, and finally, the host address. The order of the ttl and class can vary. If you see ttl, for example, before class, it's okay. The Windows 2000 DNS Server will round-robin between multiple A records for the same host, each of which provides a different IP for the host name.

The A record template looks like this (see also Figure 4.5):

```
<owner> <ttl> IN A <address>
```

An A record might look like this:

```
fs1            IN     A    192.168.1.2
```

In an A record, the owner is the host named in the record itself. Because the origin of the SOA is example.net., the entry in the preceding example actually translates into fs1.example.net. This is because fs1 was not recorded with a trailing period. When this occurs, the default behavior of DNS is to append the domain name

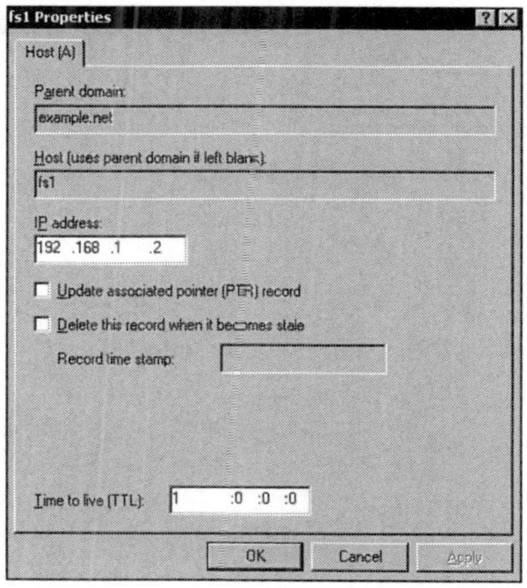

Figure 4.5 Properties of an A record in Windows DNS Server.

of the origin to the resource's name. As a result, queries to fs1.example.net reference this record, and the IP address is returned in reply. Figure 4.5 shows the Properties dialog box for A records in the DNS Server management console.

As in previous examples, the TTL value is derived from the SOA's M-TTL value. `$ORIGIN` and `$INCLUDE` statements may be used with A records. If the primary name server for a domain also serves any subdomains, the `$ORIGIN` statement can be used to reset the origin for those records below it belonging to the subdomains. As with PTR records, `$INCLUDE` statements can simplify zone files by segmenting sets of records into manageable groups and sizes.

Mail Exchange (MX) Records

The `MX` records provide information about where mail can be routed for members of the domain. The MX record format is like the NS record. It contains fields for the owner, the ttl, the class, and the resource itself. In addition, the MX record's preference field enables you to set an order for each target host that can receive mail. Having an MX record point to a machine for mail does not configure that machine to receive mail! Figure 4.6 shows the DNS Server management console dialog box for Properties of MX records.

The MX record template looks like this:

```
<owner> <ttl> IN MX <preference> <exchanger.domain-name>
```

An MX record might resemble the following two examples (also see Figure 4.6):

```
example.net         IN      MX      10      mailhub.example.net.
                    IN      MX      10      mailhub.example.net.
```

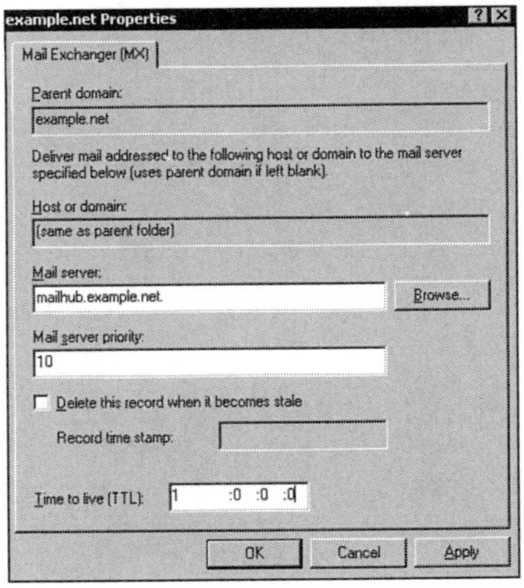

Figure 4.6 Properties of an MX record in Windows DNS Server.

The second line illustrates two things. For one, if the SOA resource record is the last entry in the file to set an origin, NS will automatically become the mail exchanger for mail going to the example.net domain that was specified in that SOA. Be careful: The record order—what immediately precedes an MX entry—has a crucial effect, so if the last entry preceding the MX record is an A type resource rather than an SOA (secondfiddler IN A 192.168.1.32, for example), mailhub would become the mail exchanger for secondfiddler the host rather than example.net the domain! If no owner is specified, DNS always assumes that the owner is the last one specified in preceding records.

You can use the preference field to apply several MX records, each with an exchanger, to a domain. Using the preference field ensures that mail gets delivered and also provides a measure of redundancy. The preference value is a number between 0 and 65535, for which the lower the number the higher the priority.

The following example demonstrates use of the preference field. 10, 20, and 30 indicate preference, in which 10 is preferred over 20, and 20 is preferred over 30.

```
@      IN       SOA      ns.example.net.     root.example.net. (
20000217001       10800     3600     604800      86400)
       IN       MX       10                    mailhub.example.net.
       IN       MX       20                    mailhub2.example.net.
       IN       MX       30                    mailhub3.example.net.
```

In this example, the three MX records are all for the example.net domain. The preference settings indicate that mailhub is the primary mail exchanger.

In the event that mailhub is unavailable or is too busy, mail might be sent to mailhub2. If mailhub and mailhub2 are both unable to respond, mailhub3 is selected.

CNAME Records

The simplest way to describe a CNAME is that it creates an alias. An alias is a name that points to or references another host. You can use CNAME, for example, to run a primary DNS name server and a mailhost on one machine. Figure 4.7 from the DNS Server shows the Properties dialog box for CNAME records.

The CNAME template looks like this:

```
<owner> <ttl> IN CNAME <host.domain-name>
```

Ponder the following scenario: An organization registers ns.xyz.com as the primary DNS server for its domain. The mail program, however, may require that you use a specific computer name, such as mailhost. To solve this problem, you can make the real name of the computer ns.xyz.com, and add a CNAME record to point mailhost traffic to ns.xyz.com. This way, no one but you needs to care that two names or services actually reside at one address. Consider the following scenario: An organization uses ftp.xyz.com as the primary server for its domain's File Transfer Protocol (FTP) traffic. The same organization wants to run a Web server but wants that Web server to appear as www.xyz.com and wants to run it on the same machine as the FTP server. You can add a CNAME record to point WWW traffic to ftp.xyz.com.

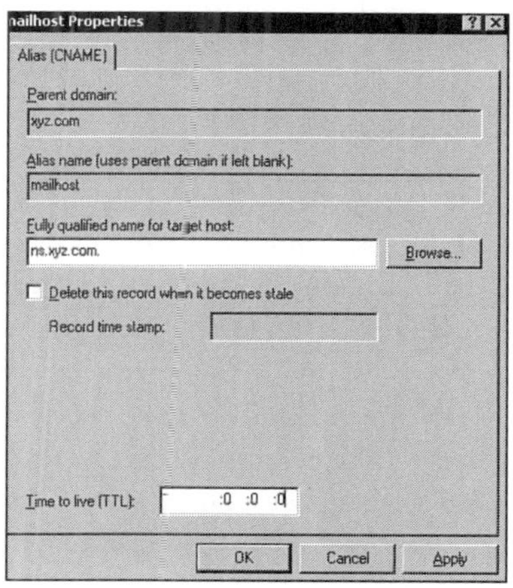

Figure 4.7 Properties of a CNAME record in Windows DNS Server.

Creating Loops with Mail Exchange Programs

You should take precautions not to create loops with mail exchange programs, such as sendmail, because loops make mail undeliverable. Loops just send mail around in circles without making any destination final. This occurs, for example, when a *mail transfer agent* (MTA) sends mail to one machine, which then sends the mail to another, and the last machine sends it back again to the original machine. Some mail programs avoid mail loops by not using MX records for the local host and other machines with equal or lower preferences.

To support this example, entries in the zone file would look like this:

```
@              IN              SOA             ns.xyz.com      root.xyz.com (
20000217001  86400 3600 608400 86400 )
               IN              NS              ns.xyz.com.
ns             IN              A               132.165.23.1
mailhost       IN              CNAME           ns.xyz.com.
ftp            IN              A               132.165.23.2
www    IN              CNAME           ftp.xyz.com.
```

The name mailhost.xyz.com and ns.xyz.com will both resolve properly, resulting with the same IP address, as is so for the WWW aliasing to FTP.

Here's another, simpler example, specifying addresses for FTP and WWW services:

```
Server1            IN     A        10.10.10.10
FTP                       CNAME           Server1
WWW                CNAME           Server1
```

CNAME records can also be used for any other services such as TFTP, FTP, and HTTPS. CNAMEs enable you to represent the hosts that these services reside on with any naming convention you like. CNAMEs can also make it easy to change physical machines while keeping services running. Practical benefits include upgrading servers without disrupting service and improving performance by employing new machines. The CNAME resource record can just be reassigned or pointed to a new host, and the outside world is none the wiser. Note that the SRV records, when used, can also provide this benefit.

SRV Records

The SRV record is technically an experimental resource record. Microsoft chose to build a service foundation that relies on SRV records to locate hosts providing the required services as a way to eliminate the legacy NetBIOS services. Under the old system (NT 4 and older), hosts that provided different services made themselves available through NetBIOS advertisements. Under the new system (Windows 2000), this is accomplished through the use of SRV records. A client must be SRV aware to find the hosts that will provide needed services through these records. In other words, if the client does not know what to ask from DNS, it will not get an answer. Where the client can query for a type of service and, if the query is answered, it receives IP address(es) to contact for the service requested.

An example is a client machine with a user requesting logon. For the user to log on, the client machine must be able to authenticate the user using the correct domain controller. So, the client machine must know where to send the authentication

Pointing to a Host That's Not Real

Neither an MX or an NS record can point to a host that's not real—that is, one named only by a CNAME alias. All hosts specified in NS records must also have an A record in the same zone file for direct resolution. If you forget one of these rules, your name server won't stop operating, but it will generate error messages.

request. The client sends a DNS query for the servers that are the domain controllers for the logon domain. Although the process is actually more involved, with sites coming into play, after the domain controllers have been identified, the authentication process can continue.

SRV records are created by the NETLOGON process to maintain an Active Directory structure if DNS dynamic updates are enabled. Otherwise, a number of SRV records must be manually created. Examples of the types of services that require SRV records are listed here. SRV records can be used to advertise other services beyond these required ones. Figure 4.8 shows the process of creating an SRV record to advertise the HTTP server on the fs1.example.net host.

The format of the SRV records looks like this:

```
<service>.<protocol>  <ttl>  <class>  <priority>  <weight>   <port> <target>
```

Notice the required period between the service and protocol specifications. The <priority> value works much like the MX preference value, to select the preferred provider based on lowest value in this field. Values range from 0 to 65535. The <weight> values come into use when there are multiple records of equal priority for a service. The values should range from 1 to 65535, and queries will be answered in proportion to the weights, effecting a load balancing a little more sophisticated than round-robin. A weight value of 0 should be used when load balancing is not desired. There is a special case value, a single period that may be used in the <target> field to indicate that the service indicated in the record is authoritatively *not* available in the domain.

An example SRV record might look like this:

```
_ldap._tcp     IN   SRV   0 0 389   adserver.example.net.
```

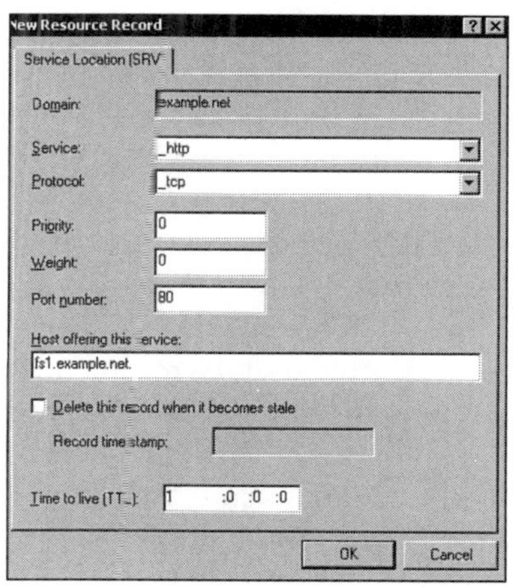

Figure 4.8 Creating an SRV record for _http._tcp.example.net advertisement on fs1.

Some of the SRV advertised service types on which the Active Directory depends are as follows:

```
_ldap._tcp.<domainname> - Allows clients to find ldap servers for a specific domain.
_ldap._tcp.<sitename>._sites.<domainname> - Allows clients to find ldap servers for
a domain that are best for a specific site.
_gc._tcp.<forestname> - Allows clients to find the Global Catalog servers using the
Active Directory root domain.
_gc._tcp.<sitename>._sites.<forestname> - Allows clients to find the best GCs for a
specific site using the Active Directory root domain.
_kerberos._tcp.<domainname> - Allows clients to find Kerberos Key Distribution
Center (KDC) services for the domain.
_kerberos._udp.<domainname> - As above but utilizing UDP rather than TCP.
_kerberos._tcp.<sitename>._sites.<domainname> - Allows clients to find a KDC for a
domain that are best for a specific site.
_kpasswd._tcp.<domainname> - Allows clients to find Kerberos Change Password
services in the domain.
_kpasswd._udp.<domainname> - As above but utilizing UDP rather than TCP.
```

Note also that a number of SRV records with `_mcdcs` as the first qualifier on the `<domainname>` or `<forestname>` are used to structure a queriable tree of the categories of domain controllers and their services that Active Directory clients and services can locate by simple queries as opposed to sequentially chained queries. This is similar to how `_sites` is used to collect together the best service locations for specifically named sites in the Active Directory.

Windows Internet Name Server (WINS) Records

The WINS record type is supported by the Microsoft DNS Server and a select few others, built specifically for Windows 2000/NT. It is not an RFC-compliant RR. The WINS record format is similar to the other records with a couple of minor additions. For an understanding of WINS and its role in acting much like a forwarder to DNS, see Chapter 16, "WINS: Legacy Name Services and Resolution." In a nutshell, when there are clients registered with a WINS server that are not registered in DNS by A records, using a WINS proprietary RR allows DNS to answer queries for those NetBIOS-named clients within the domains in a zone having this WINS record at its root.

The use of WINS and the WINS record in DNS entails a number of issues, which is why a full chapter is devoted to it. Here, note that this record should be omitted from zone transfers to non-Microsoft DNS Servers (with very few exceptions). It is a proprietary extension to the RFCs. So remember, only Windows DNS Servers know what to do with a WINS record. Your ISP, most likely, cannot provide that service for you!

In a clean design, secondaries for the Windows domain would also run Windows DNS, not a UNIX-hosted DNS, so that the WINS records would propagate properly to all servers needing them. This satisfies the design requirement that primary and secondary servers are not only authoritative, but that they can access all the same information. If only some name servers resolve WINS addresses for a domain, clients experience erratic behavior.

The WINS record format in its most basic form looks like the following:

```
<origin> IN WINS <LOCAL> <L lookup-timeout> <C cache-timeout> <WINS-server-IP-addresses>
```

Here, the optional <L lookup-timeout> value is the time DNS waits for a response back from the WINS server, with a Windows 2000 default of 2 seconds. The optional <C cache-timeout> value is the length of time that the WINS response will be cached by DNS, with a Windows 2000 default 15 minutes (given in seconds). Each of these options when used have a required L or C prefix to the value. The optional LOCAL parameter controls propagation in zone transfers. When the option is used, the WINS record will not be transferred. Note that the governing SOA record's M-TTL is not relevant to the WINS record, because in fact the C<cache timeout> parameter determines how long entries are kept by DNS.

An example WINS record looks like this:

```
@  IN WINS LOCAL L 10 C 600 10.52.120.42
```

The easiest way to take advantage of the WINS lookup feature, of course, is to use the Windows DNS management console to add a WINS record to the zone file. To a add WINS record, select the correct zone root node in the DNS management console window, and right-click to select Properties from the context menu. In the Zone Properties dialog box, select the WINS tab. Here you can add the WINS record by adding the IP addresses of WINS servers, as illustrated in Figure 4.9.

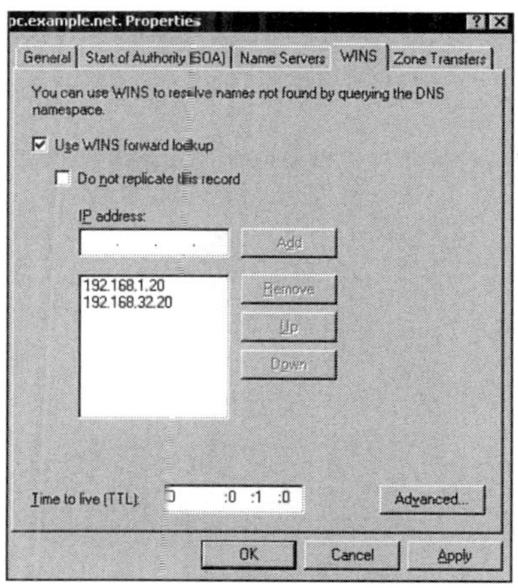

Figure 4.9 Configuring a zone to use WINS forward lookup.

Add only highly reliable WINS servers, and be aware that because DNS must communicate with WINS, if it must try on failure down the listed WINS servers, you have poured some molasses on your DNS Server. As previously mentioned, this record must be at the zone root. This means that any subdomains under the root domain of the zone are WINS enabled. A single NetBIOS name resolved by WINS can thus appear as multiple DNS FQDNs. This is why it is often recommended that a single domain be created and used solely for this purpose, as shown in the figure where a new pc.example.net domain is used. In the Windows DNS Server management console, this new domain has to be created as a new zone.

Windows Internet Name Server-Reverse (WINS-R) Records

The other half of the WINS option is WINS-R record. This resource record is used for in-addr.arpa domains and enables DNS with reverse of NetBIOS names. The format of the WINS-R record is exactly like that of the WINS record; the only difference is the zone file where records get stored, and the final parameter.

The WINS-R record, with the `LOCAL` and `timeout` options having the same meaning as in the WINS record, takes the following form:

```
<owner domain>  IN  WINS-R <LOCAL>  <L lookup-timeout>  <C cache-timeout>
<domain name to append>
```

In the Windows DNS Server management console, the WINS-R record is enabled in the Zone Properties dialog box of an in-addr.arpa domain (see Figure 4.10). Choose the WINS-R tab to use this feature, and specify the domain name that should be appended to the NetBIOS names. There is also an option to specify that the WINS-R records should not propagate in zone transfers when there are DNS secondaries that don't understand the WINS-R record.

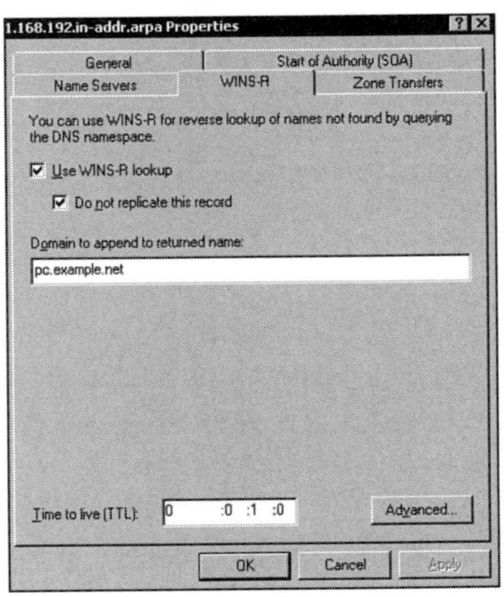

Figure 4.10 Configuring an in-addr.arpa reverse lookup zone to use WINS-R.

The Cache File

The cache file holds the addresses and names of root name servers. The cache file is sometimes called a hint file because it gives the server hints about where to look when it cannot resolve a query directly. The cache file should not be confused with the name server's cache, which is built over time as queries are resolved. Instead, the cache file typically contains the names and IP addresses of the "root"-level servers. Cache file entries for the Internet are static (unless the InterNIC adds a new root server), and they give the server a last-resort outlet in the event it can't locate a host through standard delegations. Microsoft documentation often calls this the root hints file. In Windows 2000/NT, it is provided as the file named CACHE.DNS. Figure 4.11 shows the contents of the DNS Server's cache file. Frankly, it's not very useful as information, but it must be present for DNS to work! A DNS Server assumes that the entries in the cache file are valid and reachable hosts. A severe loop can be created on a DNS Server that cannot reach root servers to resolve queries.

Change your cache file only if your server doesn't connect to the Internet, if you are using a "split-brain" DNS Server design, or when the InterNIC root domain servers change, which is rare. You can download the root cache file directly from the InterNIC via FTP from `ftp://rs.internic.net/domain/named.root`.

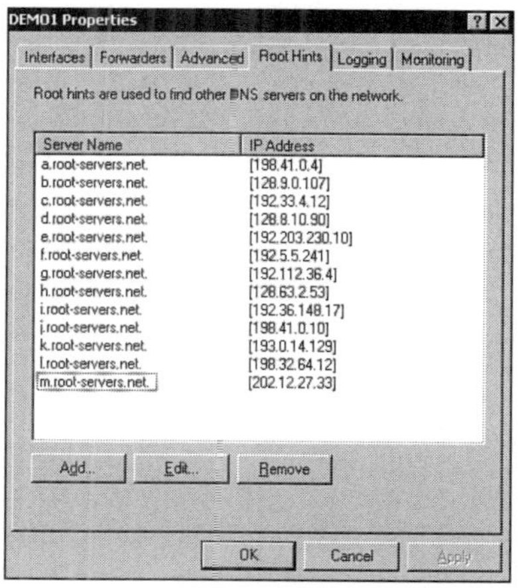

Figure 4.11 The root hints file CACHE.DNS viewed in the DNS server's Properties dialog box.

> **Populating the Cache File**
>
> Make sure that the cache file is populated. If no root-level servers are defined, your DNS server can get stuck in an infinite loop. Because there's no time-out mechanism to save the day if this occurs, you won't be able to resolve any hosts.

Accessing Root-Level Servers with Cache Files

Name servers must answer queries to the best of their ability, even if they don't contain local information enabling them to answer quickly and directly. Recursive queries require a DNS server to obtain an answer from elsewhere. If trying to climb a domain tree does not work, the cache file enables a DNS server to quickly access a root server at the top of the tree where it can find downward referrals in the tree, toward an authoritative DNS server for the specified host's domain.

If DNS is used not connected to the Internet or in a "split-brain" design, the cache file must still refer to a root domain server. If the root domain name server happens to be at the top of the domain tree of a private network, the cache directive in the boot configuration is replaced by a primary directive pointing to a zone file that would contain the name and IP address of the name server itself as the root domain's authority. This is legal and it works fine. The result for a query that such a machine could not itself answer is identical for a nonexistent domain. If the name server can reference a machine that it believes is a root server, the query will still be processed to a happy conclusion. An alternative recommended by Microsoft is to use a cache file edited to contain only "." or only those servers that are to function as root servers in the specific private DNS design.

Delegation

Delegation refers to the act of designating a name server. The first, and required, way to identify an authoritative server for a second-level domain is to register it with the InterNIC. The required way to identify an authoritative server for a subdomain is through delegation from the parent domain. Delegation publishes primary and secondary name servers for your domain/subdomain in the Internet, delegating them as authorities. An NS record is the mechanism you need to delegate a server, with the requirement that the name server be associated with a valid A record. The act of registering a domain with the InterNIC is in reality a request to the InterNIC to delegate authority for your domain to the servers that you specify in the registration template.

If a name server is delegated authority for a domain, clients and other name servers outside the domain can find and use it for their queries. At a very minimum, two name servers, one primary and one secondary, should be identified as delegated authorities for your domain. This doesn't mean that all secondaries must be delegated however. Only the name servers that you want exposed to the world outside the domain need to be delegated.

Secondaries can also be internal to the domain so that only hosts directly configured to use them will ever send queries to these secondaries. If the secondary is delegated, hosts can discover it by NS queries. If a name server is delegated for a domain, but isn't properly configured to operate as a secondary for a domain, hosts that query the domain via that server will receive a "lame delegation" error message.

Once again, it needs be pointed out that the Microsoft DNS Server information sometimes uses the term delegation somewhat differently. In the management console, for example, the task called New Delegation not only creates an NS record but creates a subdomain as well. In this situation, one is actually delegating a new subdomain.

Summary

This chapter has described the information DNS stores, explaining in some detail the most important resource records. This chapter also discussed delegation and assumption of authority, and the cache file (or root hints).

5

Dissecting Name Queries

THIS CHAPTER FIRST REVIEWS THE DETAILS of queries, and then discusses the overall query process, as follows:

- **Iterative and Recursive Queries.** DNS clients can use two types of queries: iterative and recursive. This section describes the difference.
- **Sending the DNS Query.** This section describes what kind of messages fly back and forth between DNS clients and servers.
- **Time-To-Live.** Time-to-live tells clients how long an answer can be trusted, determining how long it can cache the result.
- **The Query Process.** This section sets the discussion of the earlier sections into the context of how the whole process works together to satisfy the DNS client.

Iterative and Recursive Queries

Iterative and recursive queries are the two types of requests that can be sent to a name server. Recursive queries are the most common type sent by clients to their local name servers. When a local name server accepts a recursive query, the local name server itself attempts to find the answer on its client's behalf, and the client waits while the name server does all the work. If the local name server does not already have the answer, it performs a search for the answer, working its way up and down the branches of the domain tree. See Chapter 2, "How DNS Works," for an example of an `nslookup` trace.

For a recursive name query, the DNS server continues to search until it receives an answer. The answer may be the Internet Protocol (IP) address for a host, or it may be that the host does not exist. Either way, the recursive name server reports an answer back to the client.

A name server set up to use a forwarder sends a recursive query to the DNS server designated as its forwarder. The forwarder works the recursive query to find an answer just as it would for any other query. If the client's local server is not a slave, after time it may start working the query on its own, even though it is still expecting to hear an answer from its forwarder. If a local name server is set up to be a slave to a forwarder, things work a little differently. The client can send a recursive query to the local name server; if the name server is a slave, however, it won't work on the query itself, but only forwards it and waits for an answer from the forwarder. It essentially becomes the client's agent, and a slave to the forwarder server. Chapter 3, "Name Server Types," has a thorough description of forwarders and slaves.

Iterative queries differ slightly. The best example of an iterative query is a local name server sending a request to a root-level server. When the local name server for an organization makes a query to a root server, the root server doesn't necessarily take responsibility for answering the query on behalf of the local name server. Another way of saying that is the root server does not accept a recursive query. In fact, the root server can only perform one step to resolve the request, pointing the local name server to another place to query for the answer. This is commonly called a *referral*, and is the resulting answer expected for an iterative query. If a root server is queried for www.isi.edu, for example, it doesn't go to the ISI name server and ask for the address of the host www. Instead, the root server answers back with a hint, telling the local name server to go and query the name server at ISI instead.

The name server answers an iterative query with an "educated guess" based on what it knows. Iterative and recursive queries are discussed in more detail later in this chapter.

Sending the DNS Query

Users start name service queries by trying to access resources on the network. The resource the user is trying to reach might be on another host on the local network or on one halfway around the world. Typically, the user enters the remote host name either by typing it on the command line or going through some application, such as Netscape or Internet Explorer. The user does not, and should not have to, have any knowledge of where the host with that name is located. An entry made in this way then must be converted into an IP address. Again, the user should be shielded from this fact, which is what the following work by the domain name system does.

Depending on the configuration of the user's local machine, the name may be resolved in a number of ways. One way of resolving a host name is to look at a local host's file. The local host's file does not scale very well, which is why DNS was created in the first place. If DNS is the method chosen to resolve the remote host name, the local host references its resolver library to determine whether a default domain has been chosen, a search path has been set up, and what the IP addresses of the name servers are. In Windows NT and 2000, this information is configured on the DNS tab of the Transmission Control Protocol/Internet Protocol (TCP/IP) Properties dialog box, as illustrated in Figure 5.1. (Chapter 14, "Windows Client Configuration and Resolution," discusses the setting of these values on clients.)

After this information has been properly entered, the host can use DNS for host name resolution. After obtaining the IP address of the name server, the local host can send a query to the name server for the remote host's IP address. The format of the IP packet sent to the name server contains five sections, as illustrated in Figure 5.2.

DNS messages (whether queries or answers) contain specific bits of information. The header section, always present, contains information about the packet, including which of these sections are included in the packet, whether this is a query or answer,

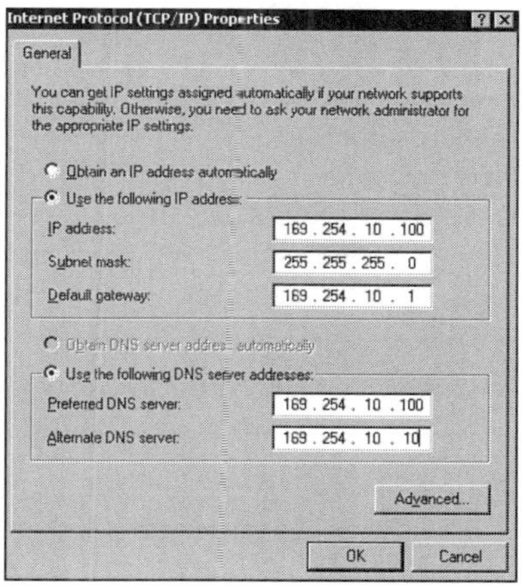

Figure 5.1 The DNS tab of the TCP/IP Properties dialog box.

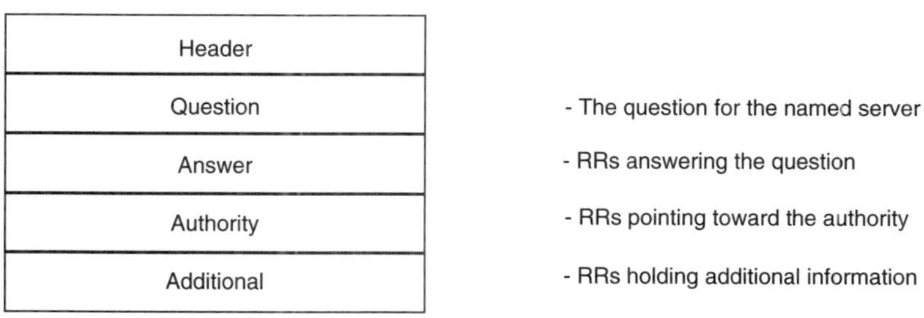

Figure 5.2 Contents of an IP packet sent to the name server.

the type of query (standard, inverse, server status, and so on), whether the packet is an answer, and whether the answer is authoritative. Figure 5.3 illustrates the header format.

The Question section of the packet illustrated in Figure 5.2 contains three pieces of information: the domain name being inquired about, the type of inquiry, and the class of the query. The domain name might actually be a host, but that depends on the type of query being sent. If the user is trying to get to www.isi.edu via a Web browser, the query will be an address query. The packet would contain the host name www.isi.edu in the query section, the type of query would be represented by a code that symbolizes an Address (A) record, and the class would be a code that represents the Internet or IN class. Figure 5.4 illustrates the format of the Question section of the packet.

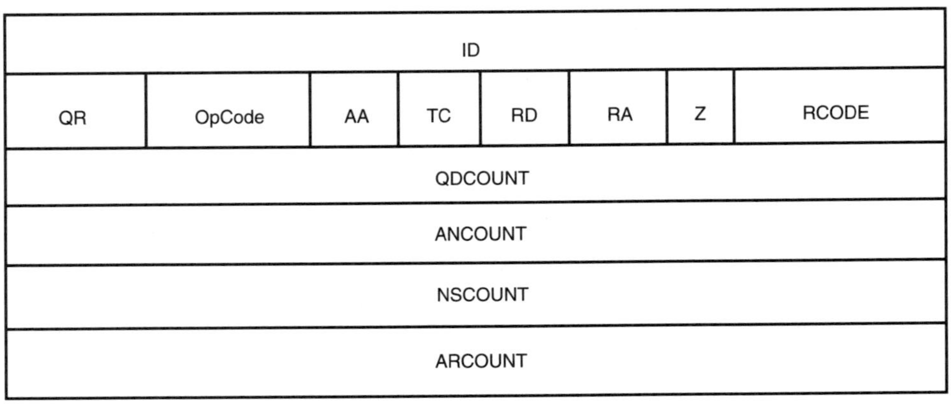

Figure 5.3 Header format of a packet.

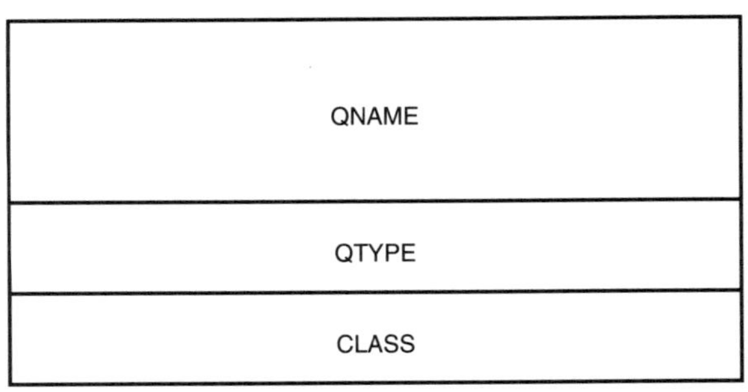

Figure 5.4 The Question field of a DNS message.

RFC 1035

RFC 1035 and updates to it in subsequent RFCs contain more detailed and authoritative information about the contents of DNS messages and how they're encoded.

The Answer, Authority, and Additional Information sections of the packet, as illustrated in Figure 5.2, are all identical in format. The fields included in these sections of the packet include a name, type, class, ttl, length field that specifies how long the resource data field is, and the resource data itself. The name, class, and type fields of the answer should be identical to the question. The ttl field contains the time-to-live for the record data being received, and the Rdata is the actual answer.

In the preceding example, the name field would contain www.isi.edu, and the Rdata section would contain the IP address of the host. Figure 5.5 illustrates the format of the Answer, Authority, and Additional Information fields, all of which are identical.

Now, in the big picture, the client sends the request to its local name server. The name server accepts the query and begins looking for the answer. For the purposes of this exercise, assume that all zone data, authoritative from the server's own delegations as well as nonauthoritative from working earlier queries, is loaded into memory and hence "cached" when the name server starts. If the name server has the information in its cache and the time-to-live (TTL) has not expired, the name server provides the information to the client directly. In this case, the answer returned and the response time greatly diminishes. If the answer returned is not authoritative, the AA flag is not set in the header.

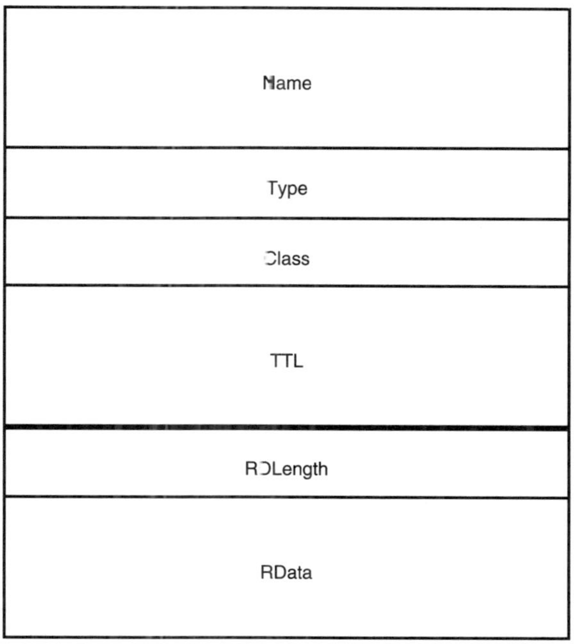

Figure 5.5 The Answer, Authority, and Additional Information fields of a DNS message.

If the answer is not in the name server's cache, the local name server begins querying other name servers, climbing up the domain name tree to the root, and back down another branch to find the answer. In this case, when the local name server does finally get an answer for the client, the AA flag is set, acknowledging that the answer came from an authoritative server. Finally, with the information in hand, the client can proceed to establish a connection to the remote host.

When receiving the response from the name server, the client is normally concerned with the authority status of the answer—that is, if there is a problem reaching the resolved host. A problem occurs if a name server answers nonauthoritatively for a domain for which it is an authority. This usually indicates that someone made a typo or some other error in the zone data.

The following sections, "Cache Hits" and "Cache Misses," illustrate and describe the process of caching results in more detail.

Cache Hits

In a transaction between a client and a name server, if the answer the client is querying for resides in the name server's local cache, the sequence illustrated in Figure 5.6 occurs.

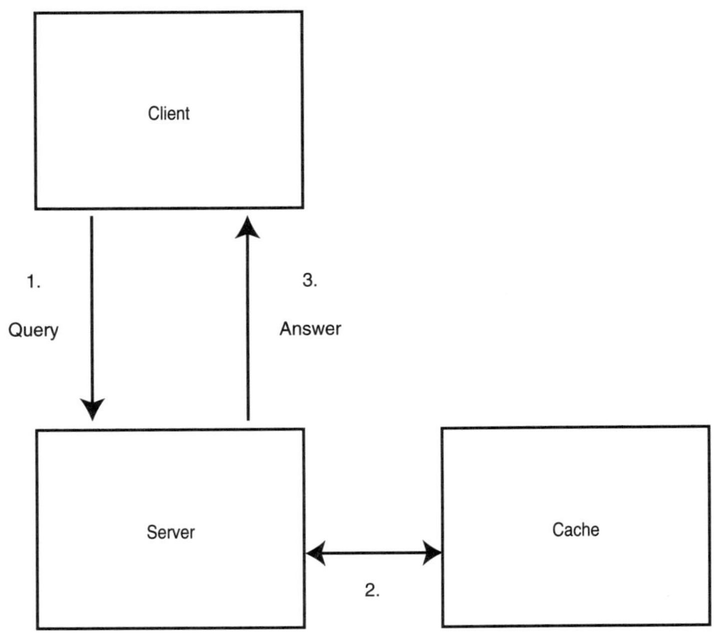

Figure 5.6 Answering a client query from the name server's local cache.

The numbered sequence in Figure 5.6 is as follows:

1. The client sends the query to the name server.
2. The name server checks its local cache.
3. If the name server has the answer in its local cache, the name server returns the answer to the client directly.

Cache Misses

In a transaction between a client and a name server, if the answer the client is querying for does not reside in the name server's local cache, the sequence illustrated in Figure 5.7 occurs.

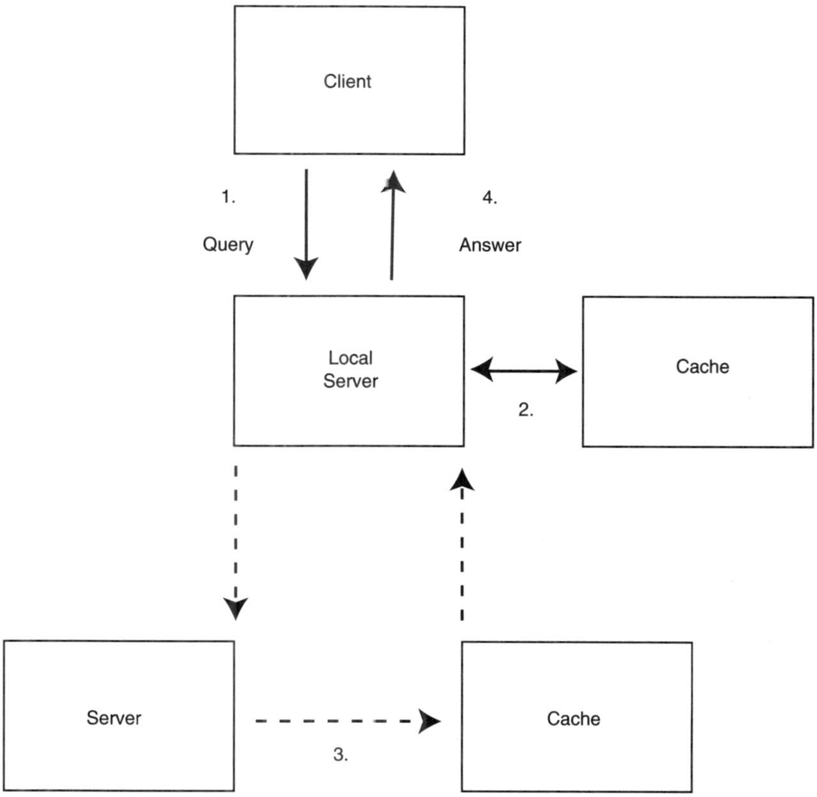

Figure 5.7 Answering a client query from an authoritative server.

The numbered sequence in Figure 5.7 is as follows:

1. The client sends the query to the name server.
2. The name server checks its local cache. If the answer is not in the local cache, the name server must look elsewhere for the information.
3. The name server (depending in its configuration) sends a query to a root-level server, and receives a referral to an authoritative server for the domain in question.
4. After the client's local server has received the answer from an authoritative server, it places the answer in its cache and provides the answer to the client.

TTL

The TTL is a timer that tells a name server for how long an answer is good, after it has contacted an authoritative server. As described in Chapter 4, "Domain Information Details," the TTL can be set on a per-record basis, or it can be set to a default value as specified by the *minimum time-to-live* (M-TTL) in the SOA record for a domain. If the TTL of a single record is set to something other than the default M-TTL, every record following that one will have the same TTL until another record is explicitly set back to the M-TTL. If TTL is set to zero, the client knows that it cannot cache the result.

How the TTL is used is quite simple. When a user's local name server receives a recursive query for information that it does not already have, the local name server must acquire the answer from an authoritative name server for the particular domain through some sequence of steps. After the local name server has received an answer, it caches the answer in the event that some other local host queries for the same information. The TTL specifies how long the local name server keeps the answer it has received and stored in its cache. After the TTL has expired, the local name server flushes the information from the cache and must contact an authoritative name server again if another query is received. If the TTL is set to zero, the answer is not cached, and the data is only valid for the transaction in progress. If the TTL is not zero, the information is cached and used for nonauthoritative answers.

The Query Process

Here the overall processing of query resolution is again looked at, but this time putting it into the overall picture, instead of just focusing on the message context and DNS server actions and responsibilities.

Recursive DNS Queries

Recursive queries force the DNS server to take on the whole burden to retrieve an authoritative answer on behalf of the client. This is illustrated in Figure 5.8, in which the client, pc.acme.com, issues a recursive query to the DNS server, acme.com.

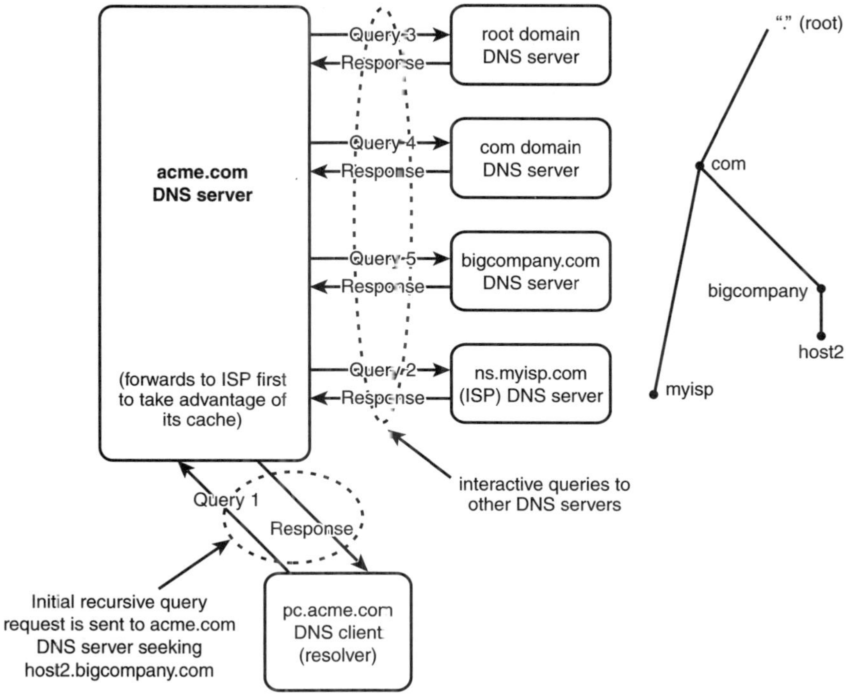

Figure 5.8 Recursive and iterative queries are both required to resolve some client requests.

In Figure 5.8, the DNS server acme.com itself becomes an iterative DNS client/resolver to four other DNS servers after it accepts a recursive query request from pc.acme.com.

When the bigcompany.com DNS server replies with an authoritative answer, acme.com passes it to pc.acme.com, which completely resolves the query. If for some reason a nonauthoritative reply is passed back, the resolution isn't final unless the client is satisfied. After receiving anything but an authoritative reply, a client might use more queries, perhaps to other DNS servers available in its configuration.

If acme.com had refused the recursive query request from pc.acme.com, pc.acme.com would have had to perform all the iterative queries for itself, going to each DNS server in turn, just as acme.com does in Figure 5.8. Client resolvers issue recursive requests almost exclusively, but they are sometimes refused.

The only reply a client accepts from a DNS server in response to a recursive query is success or failure. Until then, the client just waits. If the result isn't an authoritative IP address for the host sought but is instead a "hint" or referral to another DNS server, the client next queries the hint address looking for an authoritative reply.

Recursion means that a DNS server stays with the query on the client's behalf until it's resolved. The DNS server uses its own resolver, switching roles instantly from server to client and back again until it or another server can provide an authoritative reply. Ironically, the DNS server handling a recursive client query usually issues iterative queries to other DNS servers, following their pointers up and down the DNS name tree to reach a server with a match for the queried name, or until an end condition is met such as a timeout or error.

Recursion can happen only if the following conditions are met:

- The client requests recursion.
- The DNS server accepts recursive queries. (Most do, with the exception of root servers.)
- The client's DNS server can't answer out of its own cache or database.

If the client's DNS server can answer out of its own cache or database, it replies immediately, and authoritatively for its own zone data, eradicating the need to perform further queries.

Most resolvers attempt a recursive query first. If the server refuses recursive queries and can't return the address itself out of its own cache or data files, clients usually try again using an iterative query.

Iterative DNS Queries

Iterative queries enable the DNS server to pass back best-guess pointers, also called *hints* or *referrals*. An iterative query may not return a final result, but a recursive query does return a final result. An iterative query may return a partial result, or a suggestion about where to look next. The client (resolver) uses iterative queries to get closer to an answer, iteratively querying other DNS servers until a final answer (resolution), an error, or a timeout occurs. Iteration puts less work on DNS servers but requires more from clients, including the DNS server acting as a client querying upstream DNS servers.

Referring back to Figure 5.8, the second query to ns.myisp.com returns a hint referring acme.com to the root domain DNS server. This repeats until an authoritative answer is received from bigcompany.com's DNS server in response to the fifth query.

If the first DNS server iteratively queried can't return an address, it tells the client which DNS server is the next best to query. The next-best server is usually one somewhere up the name tree closer to the DNS root, or it may be a root server. After a root server has been located, it usually takes very few queries to walk back down the name tree to an authoritative server for the domain sought, which returns the desired address or an error to conclude the original query.

Reverse DNS Queries

Reverse queries are another thing altogether. Recursive and iterative queries are both forward queries, which means that they take a domain name and return an IP number. A reverse query does the opposite; it takes an IP number from the client and returns a fully qualified domain name (FQDN). A special domain was created in the domain namespace for this purpose using reversed IP numbers rather than names. All registered IP numbers are joined to (made members of) the in-addr subdomain of the arpa domain.

Typically, host names can be duplicated because domain name qualifiers separate them sufficiently into domains and subdomains. Because no two hosts in the Internet can have the same registered IP address, they can all be members of one subdomain, but only by number. In this scheme, unique IP numbers replace host names in the domain name hierarchy. In the in-addr.arpa domain, host2.acmecompany.com would have a *Pointer* (PTR) record appearing like the following:

```
2.1.1.10.in-addr.arpa          IN       PTR       host2.acmecompany.com
```

The matching address entry in the acmecompany.com subdomain for this PTR record would look like this:

```
host2.acmecompany.com          IN       A         10.1.1.2
```

In this example, the IP address for host2 is stored in the in-addr.arpa domain and is sorted along with all other registered Internet hosts. To reverse-query host2 (by IP number) requires only that a few numbers be reversed. The FQDN for host2 can then be returned just by querying its reversed IP number in the in-addr.arpa subdomain, where all registered hosts are members known by IP address rather than their domain name.

Seeing Queries at Work

When everything is working, the type of query a client or even a DNS server uses is more important to administrators than users. If you're having performance or resolution problems, you can try changing the default setting. Clients almost always attempt recursive queries. The default for the Windows 2000 DNS Server is also to attempt recursive queries when going to a forwarder, but to any other DNS servers it sends iterative queries. Chapter 11, "Configuring Windows DNS Servers," discusses the specifics for the Windows 2000 DNS Server, including how one can set it to accept only iterative queries.

As stated previously, when everything is working correctly, this entire process should be transparent to the client. The following is a sample of tracing a reverse name lookup started by using the `PING -a [IP address]` command:

```
C:> Ping -a 198.25.40.20
DNS: 0x1:Std Qry for 20.40.25.198. in-addr.arpa of type Dom. name ptr on class
INET addr.
DNS: Query Identifier = 1 (0x1)
DNS: DNS Flags = Query, OpCode-Std Qry, RD Bits Set, RCode-No error
DNS: Question Entry Count = 1 (0x1)
DNS: Answer Entry Count = 0 (0x0)
DNS: Name Server Count = 0 (0x0)
DNS: Additional Records Count = 0 (0x0)

DNS: Question Section: 20.40.25.198.in-addr.arpa of type Dom. name ptr on class
INET addr.
DNS: Question Name: 20.40.25.198.in-addr.arpa
DNS: Question Type = Domain name pointer
DNS: Question Class = Internet address class
```

You can notice that the Question name is the IP address backward, 20.40.25.198.in-addr.arpa of type PTR.

```
DNS: 0x1:Std Qry Resp. for 20.40.25.198.in-addr.arpa of type Dom. name ptr on
class INET addr.
DNS: Query Identifier = 1 (0x1)
DNS: DNS Flags = Response, OpCode-Std Qry, AA RD RA Bits Set, RCode-No error
DNS: Question Entry Count = 1 (0x1)
DNS: Answer Entry Count = 1 (0x1)
DNS: Name Server Count = 0 (0x0)
DNS: Additional Records Count = 0 (0x0)

DNS: Question Section: 20.40.25.198.in-addr.arpa of type Dom. name ptr on class
INET addr.
DNS: Question Name: 20.40.25.198.in-addr.arpa
DNS: Question Type = Domain name pointer
DNS: Question Class = Internet address class

DNS: Answer section: 20.40.25.198.in-addr.arpa of type Dom. name ptr on class INET
addr.
DNS: Resource Name: 20.40.25.198.in-addr.arpa
DNS: Resource Type = Domain name pointer
DNS: Resource Class = Internet address class
DNS: Time To Live = 86400 (0x15180)
DNS: Resource Data Length = 23 (0x17)
DNS: Pointer: frenchy.example.net
```

This sends the IP address to the DNS server and asks for the host name associated with the name. As you can see, all the work happening behind the scenes is beyond the client's view. Remember that if the DNS server doesn't have this name in its tables and cache, the DNS server actually does the work of finding the answer, which in the end as shown here, is all that the client wants and all that it sees. In this case, things were actually quite involved behind the scenes. The name corresponding to the IP address being recursively queried here is a NetBIOS name registered with WINS. In this case, therefore, the DNS server that resolved the query must have been enabled by a WINS-R record (discussed in Chapter 4). That DNS server then did an Adapter Status on the IP address instead of going to WINS or finding the information in its in-addr.arpa delegations. The point is, to the client, everything is much the same no matter how much work and what kind of work the recursive query triggers.

Summary

This chapter described how standard DNS queries work. The query process is also described in other places in the book, Chapters 2 and 3, for example, but not as completely as presented here.

6

Working with Service Providers

THIS CHAPTER REVIEWS THE FOLLOWING:

- **Making Yourself Known on the Internet.** Selecting and registering a domain name.
- **General Considerations for Name Service with Internet Service Providers (ISPs).** A discussion of whether ISPs can provide the required services for your organization.
- **Getting Online and Setting Up Your Servers.** After you have the required pieces, how do you pull them all together?
- **Making Changes to Your Name Server.** Sometimes things change—companies move or change ISPs, for example, and that typically means changing Internet Protocol (IP) addresses.

Making Yourself Known on the Internet

The first thing to consider when an organization wants to connect to the Internet is, how will it be known or found? Good domain names that have meaning are those easily found by targeted audiences. Many organizations choose to abbreviate their name to make up a domain name, or select a phrase that relates to their business. With the Internet boom over the past few years, it has become a real trick to find a domain name that someone else has not already registered. In general, when trying to select a name it is advisable to identify several names that you think you like, before going to the InterNIC whois records. For those unfamiliar with the whois database, the InterNIC provides a mechanism to check the availability of domain names, prior to submitting a registration request. Basically, when querying the whois database, you get one of two responses. The first response is the detail information about the owner of the domain name that has been queried. For those looking to register a new domain, this is not the answer you want to find. The second response would give a No match for "domain.org," which means the domain name you've typed in the query is available. At this point, you should take action quickly to reserve or register the domain name. Recently, some relief has come to the search for a unique name, with the addition of seven new *generic top-level domains* (gTLDs). The new gTLDs are: .cc, .arts, .firm, .nom, .info, .rec, .web, and .shop. These gTLDs provide some breathing and growing room as additions to the existing .gov, .edu, .org, .com, and .net, making available many more names for the choosing.

In the past, you just registered the domain, and it was yours for 90 days, even if you didn't pay for it. If the domain registered was one that you intended to use, you paid the fee and that was that. Currently, you have several options when selecting where to register domain names. You can, of course, register the domain through Network Solutions as many people have done for years, or you may choose to go with one of the alternative registrars. In either case, the process doesn't change too greatly, but the option of reserving (also called parking) a domain name is now available and doesn't require the name server information to be supplied. Basically this gives you the option of holding a domain name until the decision is made to use the domain. The privilege of parking a domain usually costs a bit more than a simple registration, because of the overhead on the part of the registrar, who actually registers the domain and holds the administrative reigns until you decide to activate it. I have been told that some places (in the United Kingdom) will park domains without charging additional fees, but I've not come across them personally. Another change is that most registrars now require payment upfront for registering or parking a domain name. For more information on the registration process, refer to Appendix D, "Registering Addresses on the Internet."

General Considerations for Name Service with ISPs

Internet service providers (ISPs) are the means by which most organizations connect to the Internet. In the past, many organizations, especially those without an MIS staff or those unable to afford an MIS staff, would rely on ISPs to provide basic name server service (for a fee). In situations where the ISP will host the DNS server, an organization may choose to implement a secondary locally. This provides locally available authoritative information and gives the organization the assurance (because the secondary will have a copy of the zone data) that the ISP is publishing the correct information and making changes in a timely manner. The organization may also choose to just implement a caching-only name server to improve performance in answering common name queries by building a local cache. Either of these solutions relieves the organization of some of the administrative problems and overhead, but also leaves the organization at the mercy of the ISP for security and when it comes time to make changes.

Without a tremendous amount of work, an organization could run its own primary name server, and with Windows 2000, this basically becomes a necessity for the Windows services to operate properly. In this scenario, the ISP may provide a secondary name server for a level of redundancy. This offers a couple of nice benefits. For one, the organization is free to make and implement changes at will, instead of when the ISP gets around to it. Also, it allows the outside world to resolve host names for your domain, even when your Internet connections fail. This is especially important for services such as email, which may not be able to deliver the mail if the server is not reachable, but will queue it for some period of time and periodically retry the delivery. If your mail server is not even resolvable, mail will be "bounced" back to the sender with messages about the user and/or domain being "unknown."

In an ideal scenario, the ISP would assign and delegate the authority for a block of network addresses to the organization. The term *delegate* refers here to the assigning of the *IN-ADDR* (Internet-Address) domain for the block of addresses to the organization. In this instance, the organization now has the freedom to set up its network, build its name servers, and publish the domain names it wants to register. If the organization is large enough, it may need to receive a network number assignment from *American Registry for Internet Numbers* (ARIN) and to complete the IN-ADDR domain registration without the involvement of the ISP.

All the previously mentioned scenarios also have some problems, however. The simple fact is, if your ISP hosts your DNS servers, what safeguards will the ISP put in place to protect your zone data? What host information needs to be published? Even if you host your own DNS servers, how do you limit the amount of information that the outside world has access to? Well, it turns out, with Windows 2000, you have to publish a *lot* of sensitive information via DNS. The names and addresses of your Active Directory and domain controllers just for starters. Is this really the kind of information you want anyone to be able to gain access to? Not if it were my network! Chapters 9, "Designing Your DNS Services," and 10, "Security Issues," answer many of these questions.

All this is. . . of course, depends on the organizational structure and the policies established by the ISP. My advice is, if you have the resources to manage it, take as much control of your network services as you can. If you control your network, you have little difficulty deploying changes and can enforce your own policies regarding security and allowable content. You may find resistance from your ISP; some are unwilling to delegate a block of IPs and allow you to run your own DNS. If this is the case, it's time to start shopping around.

Getting Online and Setting Up Your Servers

So, now that you've registered your domain, you have your Internet connection, and you've made some basic decisions about the architecture of your network, it's time to start setting up your servers. Hopefully you've arranged everything with your ISP to provide your own name service, which means setting up your primary (or master) server. You also need to determine whether you need to set up local secondaries (or slaves) or remote secondaries. The first step in determining these requirements is to review the organizational structure and the network architecture that has been employed to provide data communications. The questions of how many name servers and where they will be located may also be complicated by the network security policies in place. Do the name servers need to work through firewalls? How many routers or wide area network (WAN) links will be used in the network? What are the speeds of the WAN links that will be used? Are any of the WAN links dial-on-demand? Also, how big is the organization, and how many subdomains should be established?

The following checklist can help you along the way:

1. Establish service contract with an ISP.
   - Get your Internet connection online.
   - Get IP addresses assigned.
2. Set up your network and test basic connectivity (routing and the protocols).
   - Make sure that you can reach the Internet by pinging IP addresses.
   - Make sure that you can telnet/ftp to remote sites and check throughput for downloads.
3. Establish your name service with a primary DNS server and at least one secondary (or with AD, multiple primaries)
4. Complete a host registration for the new name servers you want to register.
5. Complete the domain registration for your organization, including the newly registered hosts.
6. Populate your DNS server's databases (zones) with the required/desired data.
7. Test it all out to make sure that it works, preferably via a remote site. (Using lookup, select a remote name server to run queries for your domain.)
8. Worry about security now that you are "on the Net."

For a small company just starting out, a single domain may be perfectly suitable and would certainly be easier to manage. If an organization is larger and geographically diverse, subdomains may be a good idea, either departmentally or by region. Sites with firewalls must consider design issues. Should there be a "hole" punched in the firewall to allow the name server traffic to pass directly through? Should two separate name servers be set up and maintained (one internal and one external to the firewall), or should the external name server be a secondary for the domain? With split-brain DNS (so-called because primary name servers exist on both sides of the firewall), the external primary server publishes only the hosts that the organization wants the public to see. The internal primary server has mappings for all the hosts in the domain, but is configured to forward to the external DNS server for hosts external to the name server's domain (zones). The internal primary can also be configured to slave to the external primary, thereby remaining hidden from the rest of the Internet. If you decide to have your ISP host some portion of your DNS, it might be advisable to have the ISP primary for your domain, but only publish your publicly known hosts, and thus alleviate the need for maintaining multiple separate primaries onsite.

Geographically diverse organizations will often have multiple routed connections to different offices. If Windows 2000 is deployed across the enterprise, remote domain controllers are likely to provide name server service. The use of Active Directory makes the management of the remote name servers quite simple, because the name servers will all publish the same shared information available from the Active Directory. If Windows 2000 is not deployed across the enterprise, the traffic patterns for the organization should be examined to determine what percentage of network traffic is bound for internal hosts as opposed to external hosts. If the majority of the traffic is bound for internal hosts, secondaries are a wise choice for the remote offices. With secondaries in each remote office, most of the name service queries can be localized to the servers located in the office. Chapters 9 and 10 discuss specifics on these issues and their implementation.

Making Changes to Your Name Server

A name server should not have its IP address changed. Once in a while, however, it might be necessary. The ISP used for your public DNS might be changed, for example. The actual changing of the host's IP address is simple, but proper planning must precede the change to avoid service disruptions. Should you have to change the IP of a name server, you should follow some simple but extremely significant steps. If the name server is registered with the InterNIC, the new IP address information must be submitted to the InterNIC via a host-modification template. If the name server is a primary, the modification template becomes that much more important. If you are moving to a new location, you need to update your NIC Handle (contact information) as well as your host information. If your are just changing ISPs, the host-modification template is the only form required, which will appropriately update the whois database as well. Refer to Chapter 13, "Best Practices and Maintenance Tasks," for information on changing the name server's IP address and Appendix D for the forms and details regarding InterNIC registrations and modifications.

Fortunately, the primary and secondary name servers are the only real critical part of the whole process, and you may be able to take some steps to make your life easier. If at all possible, you should have your new IP addresses (and possibly new connection) set up well in advance of having to submit your changes to InterNIC. Having a new site or new connection available gives you plenty of time to test your new setup before committing any serious changes. If you are moving to a new site, with Windows 2000 Active Directory integration, bringing up the new name server is as simple as adding the machine as a replicated primary. If you are just changing ISPs, it would be advisable to assign a second IP address to your name server and run both IP networks concurrently. Again, this gives you the opportunity to test your services, and then to commit your changes. When everything is working, submit your modification templates and wait for the change confirmation. After you have received the change confirmation, you can just shut down the interface or remove the IP address for your old network.

This following checklist can also assist you with the task of changing IP addresses for your name server(s):

1. Is (are) the name server(s) registered with InterNIC?
   - If no, you can just change the IP addresses, update your local zone data, and then you're done.
   - If yes, go to step 2.
2. Is this a simple IP change or an ISP change?
   - If an ISP change, schedule some overlap where both providers are simultaneously active.
3. Assign the new IP address(es) to the affected name server(s).
   - This is most easily done by assigning a secondary address to the network interface.
4. Update the zone data for your name server to reflect the new IP addresses.
5. Update the host registration for the affected name servers.
6. Verify the changes and test the name server resolution.
7. Remove/shut down old IP addresses and ISP connection.

Of course, the content of your domain files (zones) is completely under your control and may be modified at any time. The only tricks for dealing with content changes are the *time-to-live* (TTL) values given to resolvers when making queries for your domain. These values can sometimes be quite large. If you plan to migrate a bunch of machines or make a large amount of changes in your network architecture, it is often advisable to decrease the default TTL prior to making the changes. This increases the amount of traffic on your name servers for the duration of the changes; however, it helps tremendously in transitioning to new IP addresses and so on without losing too many visitors to your site during the transition. Many sites that do business on the Internet cannot afford to lose potential customers because the customers can't reach the site. Maintaining connectivity and ensuring that hosts are resolvable and reachable are large tasks under normal conditions. Under change conditions, these tasks become immense.

Summary

This chapter showed once again that planning plays an important part in the success of any DNS installation or modification. By working with an ISP, you can ensure that everyone on the Internet can access hosts in your domain and that migrations and zone transfers are done in the most efficient manner possible.

II

Using the Windows 2000 DNS Server

7

Dynamic DNS and the Active Directory

THIS CHAPTER REVIEWS THE FOLLOWING:

- **Dynamic DNS (DDNS).** Provides a brief overview of the newer dynamic update feature of DNS, from the perspective of the Windows and DNS administrator. The conjoined issues of security and zone file cleanup are outlined, and the scavenging in Windows 2000 is discussed in detail.
- **Active Directory Integration of DNS Zones.** Covers the use of the Active Directory as a store for DNS zone data, the reasons this feature is made available, what it provides, and the considerations one faces in deciding whether to use this optional capability. The dynamic update security that this provides is discussed in detail.
- **Active Directory Dependence on Service (SRV) Records.** Looks at SRV record usage by the Windows 2000 domain environment. Of all the new DNS features leveraged by Windows 2000, this is the one that must be used to support the Active Directory.
- **Bringing Active Directory and DNS Together (or Not).** Serves to collect together a number of factors, an awareness of which is needed for making informed decisions on the use of this technology.

The Active Directory in Windows 2000 implements a *Lightweight Directory Access Protocol* (LDAP) directory service. However, a little history helps clarify just what that means. The original X.500 directory services specification languished without full commercial implementations for a number of reasons. One in particular, that it is such a thorough complex specification, led to the implementation of subsets. Out of these efforts came LDAP.

Although the character of LDAP is still evolving, one fact that Windows 2000 leverages is that existing implementations of LDAP have usually not provided a fully global scale locator service, in the sense that the DNS is one. The original concept in X.500 was to create just such a capability, providing the ability to locate directory structures and to then navigate within them. LDAP implementations have to date however focused on working with directory structures much more than on finding them.

The design of the Active Directory leverages the existing DNS locator capabilities, and accomplishes this through a tight coupling of the Active Directory and the DNS name spaces. As a result, the uppermost tiers of objects in the Active Directory appear in name to be DNS domains. This is precisely because the domain controller (DC) objects used there represent Windows 2000 domain boundaries, and for the initial release of Windows 2000 these are intended to be named after identically structured DNS domains and subdomains.

The implications from this are many. This chapter examines some of the capabilities, interactions, and vulnerabilities stemming from this design and from using some of the newest features of DNS in support of that design.

DDNS

The DDNS RFC 2136 details an Update operation (defining a new DNS opcode) and message format that can be used by a DNS client to request that changes be made in DNS domains. As we have seen, domain content must originate at the primary server for the domain, and so DDNS defines that an Update request when received by a secondary will be forwarded to the primary master for processing. If you are thinking this all sounds straightforward and simple, just wait a little; there is much more. The Update is very straightforward, but the implications do get involved.

Using dynamic updates a client, by locating an authoritative name server (querying for Name Server [NS] records) for its domain, can advertise its presence by requesting registration of an Address (A), and optionally a Pointer (PTR), record(s). Windows 2000 clients actually query for *Start of Authority* (SOA) rather than NS records and then register directly to the primary for their domain. After a machine has done this, it becomes resolvable by name, and optionally verifiable by Internet Protocol (IP) address, just as if the *resource records* (RRs) had been entered manually.

Now if this were painless, any DNS administrator would be as thrilled as a child with a new bicycle. As we all know, few new things bring large gains without cost or risk. Otherwise they would have been done long ago.

What Is DDNS?

The dynamic update capability in DNS is specified in RFC 2136, which introduces the Update message into the language of DNS. Using the Update message format, clients can delete an RR, add an RR, or test and assert preconditions.

The RFC details the use of RR sets—for example, sets of records with the same name like multiple A records for WWW in a DNS domain. Updates may deal with an individual RR, an RR set, or with RR sets. RRs are added, and RRs or RR sets may be deleted by dynamic update.

Tests that certain criteria are met—for example, that there is no A record for fs2.hq.example.net—can be used. These tests may be either as prerequisites that must be met for an Update request to be processed, or else as simple assertions without dependent actions. These assertions, exploiting the capability to use an Update message that has a test but no dependent update actions, provides a simple means to query the DNS database for the presence or absence of RRs or RR sets.

The DNS server informs the client of the outcome of an asserted test or update. If there are associated update actions and the prerequisites are met, the DNS server carries out those updates. In this case, the update is done in an all-or-none fashion—that is, the update is atomic.

Update messages are not limited to requesting simple additions or deletions of single records. Update requests can delete entire RR sets. Because of limitations on the use of wildcards, update actions do need to be fairly specific.

The RFC 2136 provides for implementation-specific or Request for Comment (RFC)-standard security to be enforced over the update process, but does not define a mechanism for this. The RFC 2137 presents the first specification for Secure DNS Dynamic Update. Dynamic update security has continued to develop, with most RFC-standard methods now requiring a public key infrastructure for support. In the initial release of Windows 2000, a security method that leverages Kerberos has been implemented (as discussed later in this chapter).

Windows 2000 Client's Use of DDNS

It was just said that Windows 2000 clients will go directly to the primary DNS server with DNS updates, which makes sense because the Start of Authority (SOA) server is where any changes to a domain's data must be made. The default for the first release of Windows 2000 is that clients configured to issue DDNS updates will attempt to refresh their DNS entries every 24 hours.

As later sections make clear, useless updates cause overheads that the entire system would be better off without. So Windows 2000 clients actually do behave more intelligently than has yet been indicated When they are registering, they first send an assertion-only update, testing to see whether what is known by DNS is, from the client's point of view, correct. If it is, no update is issued. If the client does need to issue an update, it will on registration failure try any other primaries that might exist if the zone is Active Directory integrated. If the client is not successful still, the process is retried after 5-, and then after 10-minute waits. If still unsuccessful a 50-minute wait is used before retrying. A Windows 2000 machine, when configured to dynamically update DNS, is persistent about making itself known.

In Chapter 15, "Windows DHCP Services," discusses the capability of a Windows 2000 DHCP server to register on the client's behalf. This can be configured in different ways, but the default is for a Windows 2000 client to handle the A records and for the Dynamic Host Configuration Protocol (DHCP) server to handle the PTR record. The Windows NT DHCP server does not have this capability. DHCP can be configured to register both record types, and also to perform these registrations for clients that are not Windows 2000. This all comes into play through an update security and registration cleanup (as discussed later).

What Are the Issues?

If DDNS can free DNS administrators from the labors of zone file maintenance, and has been a defined RFC since April 1997, why is it still used so little? Or, another way around, of what does one need to be aware before stepping on this train?

Security

The answer to the preceding question, in a word, is *security*. Many variations on spoofing and hijack hacks are made nearly trivial if anyone can register—for example, the A record for www.example.net, or even more boldly for the name server ns.example.net. Without some control over who, or what machine, is allowed to update which records, DDNS is like an extreme sport—only for the brave.

Microsoft has addressed securing the dynamic update process through the integration of zones with the Active Directory. The character of this integration is a subject in the next major section of this chapter.

Service Advertisement

After enabling dynamic update on a zone, you may notice new Service (SRV) records starting to appear. The Active Directory depends on the use of SRV records for locating its essential services. For example, _http._tcp, _ftp._tcp are expected be registered by their services in the future. This might be an issue for your environment, so be aware that Windows 2000 ships fully ready and able to utilize the SRV record to its fullest.

Zone Cleanliness

The other side of the secure update coin is update conflicts and zone cleanliness. If updates are rejected, including delete updates that really should be allowed, records can become orphaned. If a client fails to remove records it has registered while it is permitted to do so, and then later is disallowed by the security mechanisms, for example, who will ever remove the records?

Suppose the DNS server implementation rejects A record registration updates for a name if it, or the associated Internet Protocol (IP), is already in use in the domain. Then consider the experience of a DHCP client attempting to register when its name is already present, or when some other name will resolve to the IP it is registering.

These are just a couple conceptual examples of the problems caused by stale records. If there is no security over the update process, these problems disappear. When a client attempts an update, it would succeed. The client could then perform queries and updates to clean up potentially conflicting, and presumably old, records to ensure its proper operation.

The obvious choice made by the DNS community is security at the expense of cleanliness. But the problems of stale records can act as a glue that freezes up the usability of the whole machine.

In the Windows 2000 default implementation, record deletion is allowed to administrators and the client machine that originally added the RR. Therefore, if the client that registers a record abandons it, the record remains in the DNS database until some other action is taken to clean it out This is one of the incentives in the use of DHCP for registration: The cleanup responsibility can be moved to the more reliably behaved DHCP server. After all, clients can and often do change their behaviors.

Service Impacts

The use of DDNS also presents new impacts on zone behavior. It also allows new ways of accomplishing things. For example, registering DHCP clients with DNS records provides a standards-based replacement for the earlier DNS integration of Windows Internet Naming Service (WINS). For another example, when combined with the SRV record type, DDNS provides the service advertisement capabilities previously only available to Windows systems through NetBIOS names.

A dynamic zone is, at least potentially, in constant change. This not only loads the zone transfer mechanism, but also raises some new issues. How can zone transfers provide a consistent copy of a zone? How is an administrator to manually edit a zone file and load it when it is impossible to anticipate the version serial? You may say, "But why manually edit? DDNS was supposed to free us from those mass change methods." Well, yes. But what about zone cleanup?

Windows 2000 tries to anticipate issues such as these. The DNS server locks the zone against change during a transfer. For transfers, however, the first line of defense is to use the Notify option with incremental (IXFR) transfers. Another is to design your zones with their size in mind so that when full transfers do happen, they are as brief as possible (because of this locking). The Change log of DNS server is only so deep, so some IXFR requests can result in AXFR (full) transfers when the incremental change requested exceeds the changes recorded in the log. Active Directory–integrated zones avoid this possible problem between primaries, but not in the transfers to secondaries.

And for the administrator's new concerns, your first approach should be learning the capabilities of the new tools shipped with Windows 2000. You especially want to become familiar with DNSCMD.EXE (see Chapter 12, "Troubleshooting Tools and Utilities," and Chapter 13, "Best Practices and Maintenance Tasks"). The System Monitor's DNS object contains many new counters that you should be watching (see Chapter 11, "Configuring Windows DNS Servers"); these counters enable you to get a handle on how well the dynamic update features are working. And in the DNS management interface itself, there is the logging feature for when you really do want to spend the overhead, and time, digging into some of the details.

DNS RR Scavenging Features

Windows 2000 employs scavenging features to combat the tendency of dynamic zones to become, well, junky. Without Active Directory integration, there is no security available over the DDNS update capability in Windows 2000. Active Directory integration enables securing updates, and this creates the need for cleanup. The section later in this chapter titled "Active Directory Integration of DNS Zones," discusses security features. This section looks at the scavenging features provided to control the aftermath.

The Windows 2000 scavenging strategy is not the simplest of topics to understand. It is, however, one feature that is vitally import to understand well before using. You would be wise to refrain from enabling scavenging until you have a good understanding of its behaviors and its effects within your particular server configuration.

What Does Scavenging Do?

Scavenging can remove stale records, whether they were added dynamically or statically, according to the tuning intervals. This is done whether the record is actually stale or vitally needed, provided only that it meets the criteria to be considered stale. Understand what you do before you do it. Having vital RRs deleted obviously causes problems. After a record has been deleted, dynamic update can allow any machine to register the record, usurping it.

Scavenging acts to remove records that are not current, as determined by how recently they have been refreshed. A refresh is caused by a DDNS Update request in which there is no change specified in the subject RR data as compared to the existing RR. This means that statically entered RRs can be deleted by scavenging because they are not refreshed. As mentioned before, Windows 2000 when configured to dynamically update DNS attempts to refresh on a 24-hour interval schedule.

Primary zones may be enabled for scavenging, whether they are standard or Active Directory integrated. When enabled, there must be a way to track how recently a record has been refreshed. When Active Directory integrated, attributes of the objects storing the RRs are used to hold the time stamp information. When a zone is standard, the zone file format is modified to provide for the time stamp. The time stamp is updated when the record is modified or refreshed. The time stamp is scrubbed from DNS answers and transfers, so this change in RR content is a DNS server internal modification. When manually editing or moving a zone file, however, this difference must be considered.

Records added to a standard zone, when scavenging is not enabled, do not have a time stamp. Resultingly, these records are not scavenged, even after a zone holding them has been moved to Active Directory storage and enabled for scavenging. The DNSCMD.EXE tool provides a way to put a time stamp on such records.

How, and When, Does Scavenging Happen?

Scavenging works by using a number of time interval parameters. Two at the server level have default values of seven days. Notice that seven days is also the default lease period for DHCP, and this is not by accident. There are also two intervals at the zone level, and the server level values are used as the defaults for the zone level settings. The server level settings are located by selecting Set Aging/Scavenging for all zones from the server context or Action menu. At the zone level, these are located by using the Aging button on the General tab of the zone properties. Chapter 11 discusses locating these menus and the available options. Figure 7.1 shows the Zone Aging/Scavenging Properties dialog for the zone level settings. The server level dialog is named Server Aging/Scavenging Properties and has no zone scavenging date/time but is otherwise identical.

These intervals are as follows:

- **The No-Refresh Interval.** This sets the time during which refresh requests for an RR are refused. An RR may be updated, but a no-change update (a refresh) is not preformed. This prohibition has the effect of acting as a limiter on otherwise useless work that would be spent in replicating zone data, and makes it possible to not rely on client behavior to reduce this overhead. Reducing this value can have negative impacts of zone transfer and Active Directory replication overhead.

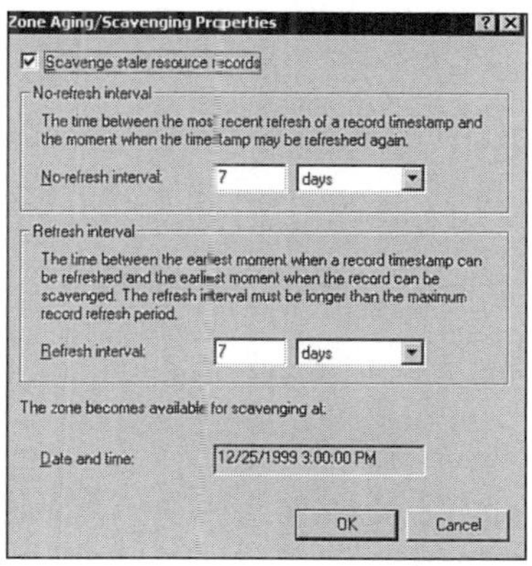

Figure 7.1 Scavenging settings in a zone's Properties dialog box.

- **The Refresh Interval.** This sets the length of time following the No-Refresh Interval during which a record is allowed to refresh but during which it will not be scavenged. A record may be refreshed any time after its time stamp shows it to be older than the No-Refresh Interval. After the time stamp shows a record is older than the sum of these two intervals, it becomes available for scavenging.

When a record is refreshed or changed, it receives a new time stamp. In zones enabled for scavenging on records that are not created by dynamic update (that is, manually created records), no time stamp seems to be used, although the Microsoft documentation states that a time stamp of zero is used. The scavenging algorithm will not touch RRs with a zero time stamp. There is, however, a check box on the properties of individual RRs labeled Delete This Record When It Becomes Stale, which can be used to enable scavenging them.

Scavenging never occurs until a grace period has passed. This is in addition to the logic of the intervals. A zone must have been continuously available for dynamic update for a time equal to the Refresh Interval before scavenging may start. This guarantees that clients have had a full measure of opportunity to refresh before they are scavenged. Scavenging can be started on schedule by using the Advanced tab of the server properties (refer to the bottom of Figure 11.4), or it may be started manually from the server context menu.

Scavenging will happen at some point after the grace period, if it is enabled at the server level. Scavenging will happen on primary zones enabled both for scavenging and for dynamic update. Within such zones, records subject to aging with non-zero timestamps showing they have not been refreshed sufficiently recently (per the two tuning intervals) may be deleted by the scavenging.

Active Directory Integration of DNS Zones

Listening to marketing evangelists can lead one to believe that the Active Directory is the cure-all elixir bringing all things good everywhere. Maybe it was that mindset, but more likely it was timing, that resulted in the Windows 2000 strategy for securing dynamic updates. The Secure DNS Dynamic Update specification (RFC 2137) has the same date as the dynamic update specification. But research has continued, and new efforts are clarifying the nature of how public key encryption can be used within DNS. At any rate, Microsoft has chosen to use a technique for securing dynamic DNS behaviors that leverages what design work they had in place for the Active Directory. If you check in Appendix B, "RFCs Related to DNS," draft proposals are listed which detail the approach taken to evolve the security features the earlier GSS-API (RFC 2078) codified.

As it turns out, Active Directory integration of zone data does not only provide a usable, if imperfect, solution to the security versus cleanliness dilemma discussed in the preceding section, but it also provides some further leverage points in the bargain.

How It Works

The way that zone data is integrated into the Active Directory is, from one point of view, simplicity itself. Zone data is merely converted into directory objects. Everything in the directory is an object, so this just had to be in order to use the directory store. After a zone has been integrated, it is visible in Read-Only (except for the Write-enabled security descriptors) mode to an administrator within the Active Directory Users and Computers console (you must have the Advanced mode enabled), where the RRs are listed within the MicrosoftDNS node (see Figure 7.2).

To cause this integration, one merely flips a switch on the properties of the server. This switch is shown in Figure 11.4, where changing storage from file to Active Directory is briefly discussed in Chapter 11. Individual primary zones may have their storage mode changed by using the Change button on the General tab of the zone's Properties dialog box (see Figure 11.7). The first primary zone changed to Active Directory storage triggers the server properties to change. There is nothing else to changing storage modes, at least that an administrator is expected to, or can, do.

Features Enabled

After the zone data has been stored as directory objects, there are a few immediate consequences. Some result directly from the nature of the persistent storage used for the Active Directory, such as having security attributes, and some are consequences from the data now being in a form with which the support services used for the Active Directory can work, such as the replication technology. This discussion briefly

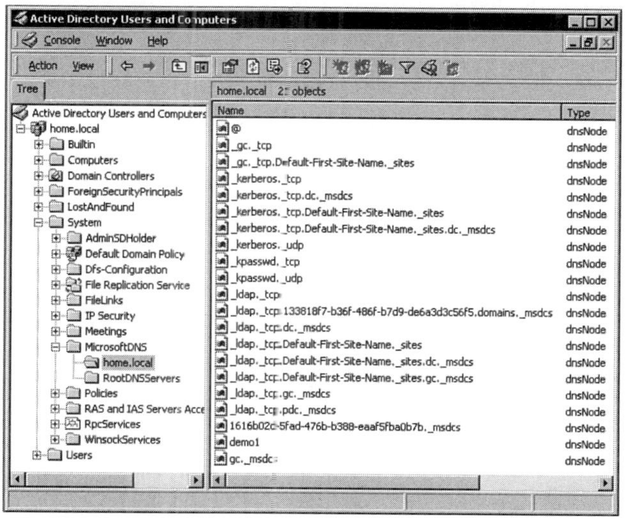

Figure 7.2 Zone data listed within the Active Directory.

reviews two of these "leveraged" extras, and then launches into a fairly long and involved explanation on zone data security, including securing the dynamic update process and its defaults.

Replication

The Active Directory uses a multimaster design in which, for much of its responsibilities, any DC is a peer to all others in the domain. Because DCs are remote from each other, a communications latency is inherent in propagation of changes to the object stored in the directory. The default installation limits the total delay to 15 minutes within a site; between sites, however, it is mostly a function of how the sites are linked.

This latency means that updates at two DCs might be in conflict because the changes are not transacted in a distributed fashion, but rather with each DC believing its data to be current. This design is supported by a replication technology that uses a "last write wins" algorithm with tie-breaking strategies for conflict resolution. In essence, one has a tightly coupled system that is loosely convergent. The DCs in the system act not just as peers, but in most cases as if they were identical clones, effecting the tight coupling. Because of independent change and the replication algorithms, however, the Active Directory content is continuously converging; because any particular change might be rolled back, however, it is a loose convergence. Anything stored in the Active Directory is automatically replicated to all DCs for the domain by using this technology. Hence, just as with standard zone transfers, with Active Directory–integrated zones there is a period during which two different DNS servers authoritative for a zone may give different answers to queries against the zone.

Multimaster Primary

It was only natural, because all zone data is merely content in the Active Directory (and so replicated to all DCs), that small changes be made to the DNS server to make the most of the opportunity. The result is that DNS also operates in a multimaster mode when its storage is integrated with the Active Directory. A zone may be present on multiple, equally primary DNS installations, each of which is on a DC (because only DCs contain the Active Directory).

It is still possible for there to be standard secondaries. It is just that there are multiple primaries. Of these, of course, for some things one specific server is selected as "primary." For example, how does the world know *the* primary? Or, when scavenging, it would be very foolish and inefficient for all DNS servers to scrub stale records (unless they divided the task), so which one initiates deletions that are then propagated to others?

Some of these types of questions are premature, relative to the available information. Others are internally managed, such as the initiator of scavenging, with related Registry settings. Suffice it to say that one gains multimaster primary zones when using the Active Directory store for DNS. The main result is that a vulnerability in the standard DNS architecture—that the primary server is a single point of failure—has been eliminated. It would take the DNS service on all DCs hosting a zone to go on the blink for secondaries of the zone to experience expired zone data, provided the secondaries are configured to use multiple primary masters. A further benefit is that dynamic updates, which must be processed by a DNS server primary for the zone, do not have to be routed to a single, sometimes distant, machine.

Security

Before jumping into this topic, recall that there is no security over dynamic update available in Windows 2000 unless the DNS zone is Active Directory integrated. Securing of DDNS updates is, in general in any environment, a fairly complicated affair. And this is also true of how the Secure Dynamic Updates capability, as it is termed in the Windows 2000 interfaces, is implemented and used. The goal is control of who, or what computer, is allowed to register with DNS or to modify and delete existing registrations.

The Secured DDNS Process

A Windows 2000 client uses a negotiation to establish a security context with the DNS server. In turn the DNS server uses this security context when it attempts to write to the DNS database. The client establishes this security context with the DNS server by use of a TKEY exchange, which attempts to negotiate the use of Kerberos as the security provider. If successful, TSIG is used to actually send the signed update request to the DNS server and the results back to the client. The DNS server itself uses LDAP methods to attempt the update, based on the established security context.

Windows 2000 clients may be configured to always attempt only nonsecured updates, to always attempt only secured updates, or to first try nonsecured and then if needed try secured updates. This last is their default configuration. The default dynamic update thus follows a sequence of stages, logically as follows:

1. Client attempts nonsecured update.
2. If not successful, client negotiates a security method.
3. After Kerberos security provider is agreed to, client establishes its credentials with DNS server.
4. Using these credentials, client requests update.
5. DNS server establishes a LDAP session using these credentials to impersonate the client.
6. DNS server uses LDAP methods to attempt requested update of the DNS database.

TSIG and TKEY

You will not find TSIG and TKEY in the RFCs, but should refer to the draft draft-skwan-gss-tsig-0*.txt for information on this and their relationship to RFC 2078, and differences from RFC 2535. References are provided at the end of Appendix B.

7. LDAP provider returns results to DNS server.
8. DNS server returns results to client.

The specific details are more involved, including signing of the Update request and the returned results to provide for authenticity. What is of interest is the use of Kerberos as the security provider, and the fact that DNS server uses normal LDAP methods to update the Active Directory. The LDAP update is performed as the client, allowing the existing Active Directory security mechanisms to enforce security as appropriate for that client.

Because Windows 2000 clients expect to use this Secure Dynamic Updates method, they can only negotiate secure DDNS updates with Windows 2000 DNS servers. If you are using other DNS servers to support Windows 2000, it is very likely that you will not have a DNS server that supports this Secure Dynamic Updates method. There is no provision in the initial release of Windows 2000 to configure clients to use methods compliant with RFC 2137 and 2535. Use of DDNS without using the Windows 2000 DNS Server, for the moment, means that updates cannot be secured within the update process but only outside of it by using technologies such as IPsec communications.

Access Control Level Security Settings

For DNS administration, the real issue in using Windows 2000 DNS for secured update is in the success or failure of the LDAP update of the DNS records. You must understand how standard Windows security permissions and ownership function, because these are what govern the success or failure of the update. Then if you understand what the default settings are for the security on zones and zone data and how these defaults can be adjusted, you are positioned to manage dynamic update security beyond the default configuration. This chapter attempts to make this as simple as possible, and assumes that you have a background in the aforementioned areas, a general understanding of Windows security concepts, including a general knowledge of *access control lists* (ACLs) and ownership.

The default out-of-the-box configuration enables any member of the Authenticated Users group to create records, such as A or PTR, in any zone. When a record exists, it can be read by any member of the Everyone group, but may only be modified by the Owner account that originally created it, or by various categories of Administrators, or by the System itself. In many cases, this post-creation restriction on changing and deleting existing records provides a desirable behavior, but in cases it can also cause problems and stale records. Figure 7.3 shows the default security settings on an integrated zone. Notice that Figure 7.3 shows a zone, not an RR.

The group Everyone is highlighted, showing this group is granted a specially configured permission, and just above that the Authenticated Users group shows that it is granted the permission to create all child objects (which in this case means RRs). The special permission granted to the Everyone group confers Read access on the zone itself, including list permission. Figure 7.4 shows the same zone, this time using the

DNS Server management console rather than the Active Directory Users and Computers console used in Figure 7.3. In Figure 7.4 the editor has been opened on the security assigned for the group Everyone to show the details. This granularity is available through either management interface.

Before delving too deeply into this, notice the group named DnsAdmins in Figure 7.3. This is a preconfigured group in the Active Directory. By making a general user a member of this group, an administrator grants that user the permissions needed to be a DNS administrator, as one might guess. A DnsAdmins member has sufficient power to configure and run DNS on all DNS servers in the domain residing on domain controllers, but does not have administrative power over other features of the enterprise unless these have been independently granted through other groups.

Therefore, what the preceding paragraph is saying is that any client that can negotiate a secure session with DNS as a recognized account (Authenticated Users member) can create RRs. When a nonsecured update is negotiated, the DNS server provides a context for the update. Figure 7.5 shows the security on an A record created with the defaults, showing that the group Everyone is granted Read permissions. If we were to look two levels deeper, as was done in Figure 7.4, we would find the same set of Read permissions are being granted, but in this case to an RR.

One thing that should be pointed out, by what has been shown already, an Authenticated User can create objects within a zone. Although there are limitations on the kinds of objects these might be, there is no limitation on how this might be done. It would seem that the DNS server does not have to be involved at all, if the users make use of direct LDAP methods as an Authenticated User. In other words, any valid user in the domain can create records, even by direct means.

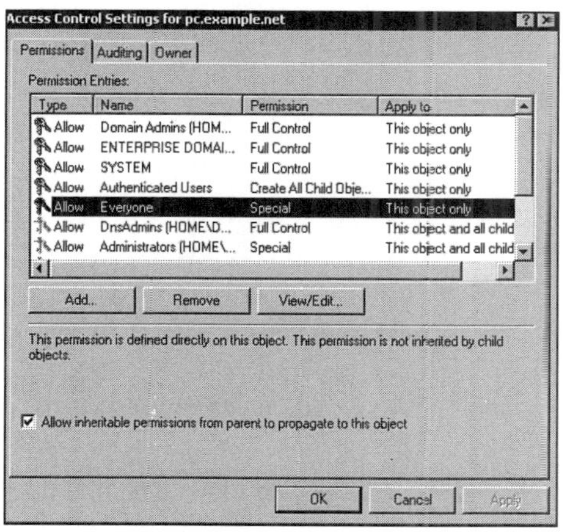

Figure 7.3 Advanced ACL security on a zone in Active Directory.

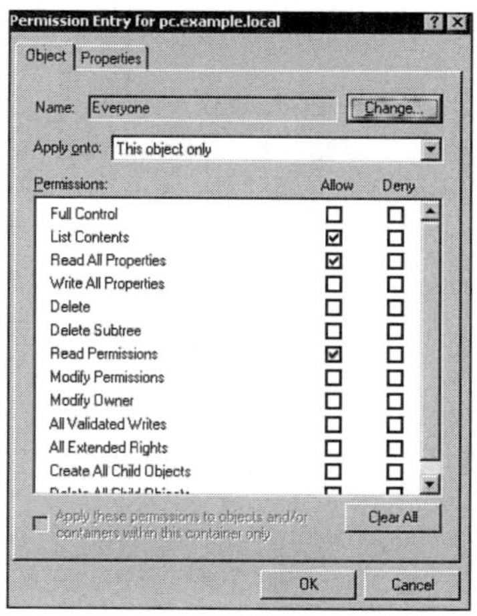

Figure 7.4 Security detail for Everyone on a zone.

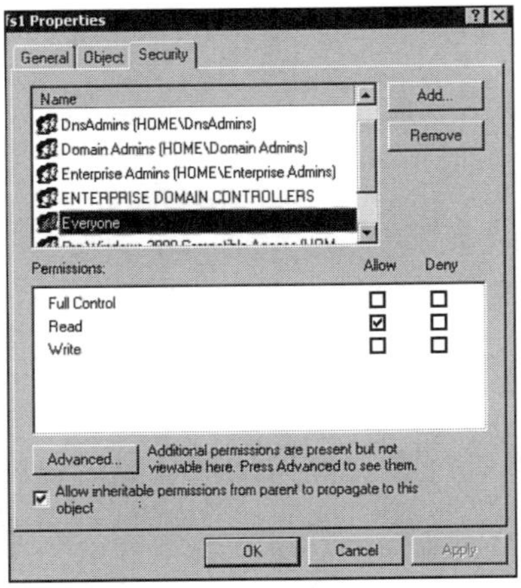

Figure 7.5 The security on an A record.

To change how permissions are set on new records when created, the inheritable permissions on the Active Directory container, the zone, can be changed. The actual requirements are, in general, quite involved; there are also permissions of the prototype, or object class in the schema for the type of object being created, that might also be applied when a new object is created from it. In the case of both zones and RRs, the schema classes dnsZone and dnsNode do, in the out-of-the-box configuration, provide permissions to newly created instances. Figure 7.6 shows the default security descriptor for the dnsNode class that is used for RRs. The dnsZone class is similar, except that it also confers the Authenticated Users permission to create child objects.

If we were to drill down here, and in Figure 7.4 (which is of an RR), we would find that the Everyone Read permissions are an exact match, appearing just as those in Figure 7.3. And they should match because this is where they came from. This permission was not inherited from the zone ACL, and most changes to the ACL on the zone will not change the fact that the Everyone group has Read on new RRs in the zone.

So, what have we seen so far? A negotiation defines the security context a DNS server uses when making DDNS updates. Any Authenticated User can create new records. Any member of Everyone can read a record. Any member of Everyone can list a zone. After being created, a record can only be changed administratively, or by the System, or by the account that created the record. Changing the default permissions that will be given to new RRs is possible by manipulation of the permissions on the containing zone or on the dnsNode schema object. Let's expand on this last part, how to predetermine the security ACL used for a new RR resulting from DDNS.

When any new Active Directory object is created without an explicitly provided ACL, it receives for an ACL a merging of inheritable permissions from its container and the default security descriptor of the object's prototype, unless there is on the container at least one rather specific permission. When such a specific permission is

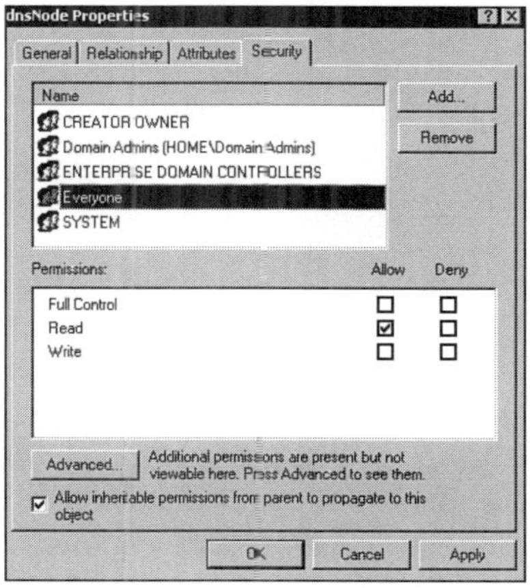

Figure 7.6 The default security for new RRs.

present on the container, the permissions from the prototype are not used. Therefore, when not inhibiting permissions from the prototype and a new RR is created, it receives the permissions on dnsNode plus any applicable inheritable permissions on the zone where it is created. Now let's look at the specific permissions needed to inhibit use of the prototype's permission. If the container has any inheritable permissions specific to the object class being created, the default security descriptor of the prototype for the class is not merged in and the new object receives only the inheritable permissions from the container. So, if the zone had a permission placed on it which was inheritable and which applied to RRs (objects of the dnsNode class), new RRs within that zone would only receive the permissions inheritable from the zone.

The method just described for overriding the default security received by an Active Directory object from its class is documented in the Microsoft-provided *Active Directory Programmer's Guide*, which is available in the current MSDN library. Inhibiting the default security from dnsNode and dnsZone is not presently possible, however, because the key prerequisite has not been made available in the administrative interfaces in the initial release of Windows 2000. No permissions are available that are specific to the zone or RR objects. If inhibiting the prototype security were or later becomes possible, you need to be aware of this issue, both in case you wish to use it and to avoid using it where you do not want to. So here is the precaution: After a zone has been created, changing permissions on it could prevent the default security descriptor (on the dnsNode prototype) from being added on to new RRs. This may or may not be desired. With the prototype's default security not being applied, it is necessary to make sure that there are inheritable permissions on the containing zone that will provide the desired parts of the (then inhibited) defaults from the prototype.

So you have seen that the permissions on the container (the zone) control the security placed on new contained objects (RRs), that this must be accomplished with care, and that there are two aspects to consider: inheritable permissions on the container (zone) and default permissions from the prototype (dnsNode). Not mentioned yet is that changing the security on the dnsNode prototype—for example, if Everyone being able to read is too permissive—is an action that impacts every domain in the Active Directory. Not only may this be too severe, but one must understand why it is that Everyone has been granted this permission, and why in a way that is so difficult to override. If the accesses that will be broken are acceptable, changing dnsNode permissions is the simplest way to accomplish a change such as this. But no schema level change should be undertaken lightly or without deliberation.

After a zone has been created, adding permissions inheritable by all child objects changes the permissions on future RRs created in the zone. Because the dnsZone and dnsNode classes provide for the Everyone and the Authenticated Users groups to have the permissions to read zone data and to create new records, respectively, as was shown earlier, there is really very little that could be added in the way of permissions. So again, changing the security on the prototypes seems to be indicated if the out-of-the-box settings are not suited to your environment. This in turn means fully understanding the permissions changed on the schema classes, and of providing for the desired parts to still be supplied either from the prototype or by permissions placed on the zones.

If you are raising your hands, pleading for this to stop, do not worry. With some experimentation, this can become well understood. So why then did we even cover this, you might be asking. If Microsoft, or a third party through extensions, does make available a qualifying RR object-specific permission ACE that can be applied on zones, you are ready.

The method described to inhibit application of the default security descriptor from the schema class has worked throughout the beta cycle leading up to the final released version of Windows 2000. With the gold code, however, it seems that something has been changed that is not yet documented. Instances of object classes for which this was previously a working alternative are now not following this behavior. Because security is a big issue, and the complexity level is not small, it is likely that revised information, and hopefully methods, will be available as deployments of Windows 2000 are undertaken. You need to watch for improved information from Microsoft on how to change security of zone data. For now, at the last possible moment before this goes to print, when the default from the prototype needs to be trimmed, changing the default on the prototypes to a least common set of permissions and adding inheritable permissions on zones where more than the least common set is needed is the one available approach. The change to the schema classes can be accomplished through the Active Directory Schema management console (SCHMMGMT.MSC); the change to the zones can be done through the Active Directory Users and Computers management console (DSA.MSC) or through the DNS Server management console (DNSMGMT.MSC).

Let's now look at another side of DNS data security, auditing. Figure 7.7 shows that the defaults also configure the records created in a zone so that they are enabled for auditing.

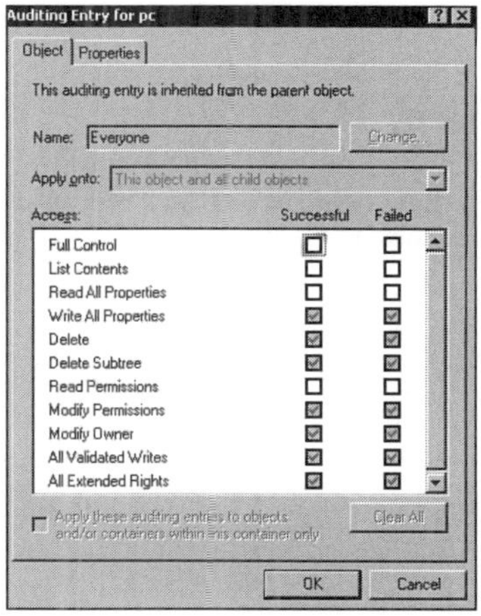

Figure 7.7 The auditing ACL on an A record.

The check boxes in this figure show what actions will trigger auditing. They are grayed out because these settings have been inherited from a higher level. These settings will, when auditing is turned on, cause all access except reading of the record to cause an audit record to be logged.

If you return to Figure 7.4, you will notice that the Read permissions for Everyone were shown with white boxes. This is because the permission was applied directly onto the RR, originating from the dnsZone class. What this comes down to is that if one wants to change a permission granted in this way, which does not use inheritance, the best thing to do is to change the controlling settings before any objects have been created. After they exist, changing this, but only this, permission requires visiting every RR object individually.

DHCP and the DnsUpdateProxy Group

To reduce the complexity of all this, Microsoft has mapped a preconfigured route for use with DHCP. Instead of letting clients obtain ownership of the RRs, and so becoming dependent on their behavior about cleaning up, one can let DHCP perform the registrations. When this happens, DHCP would then be the owner, and so also be able to modify them and clean them up. This is all good, but there are some small problems.

If default DHCP behaviors are used, Windows 2000 clients end up owning their A records, and DHCP owns the PTR records for its IPs. This is reasonable because the client owns the name and DHCP owns the Internet Protocols (IPs). If the client has its name changed or is rejoined to the domain, however, it then has abandoned a record in the zone. For non-Windows 2000 clients, DHCP may be registering both the name and the IP, and so would own both records. This causes a problem when DHCP servers are configured to share responsibility for a subnet because only one of the servers can change the A record, whereas any of them might have issued the lease. (Note that normally each has a uniquely owned IP pool, so the PTR does not have this problem.)

To solve these problems, a special group has been predefined in Windows 2000, the DnsUpdateProxy group. When a machine is made a member of this group, and it then creates a fresh DNS record, that record will have slightly different semantics than what has thus far been discussed. Instead of the creator automatically becoming the record owner, a record created by a DnsUpdateProxy member becomes owned by the first account that successfully does an update or refresh on the record.

Although this does tend to solve some issues, it opens up others. One very important thing to notice is that machines, such as those running DHCP, would be in this group; and so all records created dynamically by those machines would behave by these new semantics. If a machine so configured registers any records, whether by DHCP for a client or by the machine itself for itself, this applies to those records. This is not a small consideration when a machine, such as a domain controller, performs many dynamic updates. (See the next section for a discussion of Netlogon in this regard.)

The DnsUpdateProxy group is intended to have DHCP servers as members. This allows them to register A records for clients and have ownership of those records pass to the clients when they attempt to update the records. Any records registered dynamically by the machine running DHCP, including its own records, or SVR records created by Netlogon if it is also a domain controller, are subject to hijacking when the machine is a DnsUpdateProxy member. The solution is, of course, to not use this for domain controllers and to use manual DNS entries for DnsUpdateProxy members.

Summarizing DNS Security

This section has covered some ground. Active Directory integration enables the use of security methods to control access to DNS data, and also updates to it. Without this integration, Windows 2000 provides for no DNS security.

Updates are secured through a Microsoft variation of the methods provided for in RFC 2078. These methods are, today, Microsoft specific. Windows 2000 clients need to be extended to use third-party DNS servers using security based on RFC 2137 and 2535. The secured dynamic update process leverages the Kerberos support in Windows 2000 as a security provider. The DNS server itself uses LDAP methods when updating the DNS data on behalf of the client.

When stored in the Active Directory, DNS data is subject to normal ACL permissions validation. The defaults provide the Authenticated Users group the ability to create RRs, and the Everyone group the ability to list zones and read RRs. These permissions originate in the dnsZone and dnsNode schema objects, and with what is provided in the initial release of Windows 2000 can only be changed there, or on the RRs after they have been created.

After being created, an RR is owned by the creating account, unless that account is a member of the DnsUpdateProxy group. In this case, the first account succeeding in updating or refreshing the newly created record becomes its owner.

Well, there you have it. The initial framework of the Microsoft strategy for Secure Dynamic Update, as configurable for Active Directory–integrated DNS zones. It has good points, and it has some warts. Before criticizing too harshly, consider that this is a front-runner, pioneering the new ground of DDNS. It is probably true to say that no other commercial operating system today has stepped so far down the road of secure, DDNS implementation. Much of what is implemented had to balance product timelines and needed functionality with the then evolving RFCs, some of which are now, and some not yet if ever, standards track. The most recent RFCs for securing DNS data and updates rely on a public key infrastructure that is only now being built, but in which Windows 2000 is quite ready to participate. How you use DDNS in Windows 2000 and exert security over it must be well considered.

Active Directory Dependence on SRV Records

The efficient operation of the Active Directory depends in part on the ability of clients and of server services to rapidly locate key services in the domains composing the Active Directory. DNS is the means used for much of this.

When a domain member machine boots, for example, it must contact a domain controller for its domain, and possibly another domain controller if the first does not host the Global Catalog. Or for another example, when a client on one machine issues a request for a resource in a different domain within the Active Directory forest, a DC for that domain is involved in deciding whether the client request should be permitted or denied.

When resources within domains that have already been located are needed, such as a client opening a shared folder within the client's own domain, there is no need for the services of DNS. Very often, however, the first steps do need these location-finding services, and DNS is heavily used for this in the Windows 2000 architecture.

To make this as efficient as possible, Windows 2000 maintains a fairly involved set of SRV and CNAME records. The Netlogon process on DCs has responsibility for this, using dynamic updates to build it, and to clean it of records determined to be invalid.

The Domain Locator Service

A Windows 2000 client can attempt to find a DC by using three types of information about a domain: the domain name (and hence the DNS domain in the initial release); a *globally unique ID* (GUID) which is an internal and unique name for a domain; and also a site identifier. In attempting to locate a DC (and as you will see most of the key services are on DCs), the client hands these, in so far as it knows them, to the Domain

Locator Service.

The Active Directory can be partitioned by sites that are used to represent the network topology. A single domain may be present in multiple sites, and a site may be included in multiple domains—that is, there may be machines from multiple domains within a site. Sites are used to facilitate network communication being directed to "local" machines when possible for a requested service.

The Windows 2000 domain locator uses all the information, of these three types, that the client can provide, to obtain an IP address as efficiently as possible for the request. If the client knows what site it is in, and requests a particular service such as LDAP services in a specific domain, for example, the first attempt may be to query for _ldap._tcp SRV records specific to the requested domain and site. If the locator already knows of a DC for the domain, it can also send LDAP queries to the DC to verify information that is then returned to the client.

The locator service makes use of knowledge about names expected to be present in the DNS database. As said, the Netlogon service on DCs builds and maintains these registrations using dynamic update. When dynamic update is disabled, this becomes impossible, and the efficient operation of this lookup process becomes the responsibility of some unfortunate person. If the DC and site topology is static and highly available, however, this is not quite as awesome a task as it may seem.

The Structure of SRV Entries

Netlogon registers many different layers of records. Figure 7.8 shows an expanded portion of this structure for a very small single domain Active Directory when there

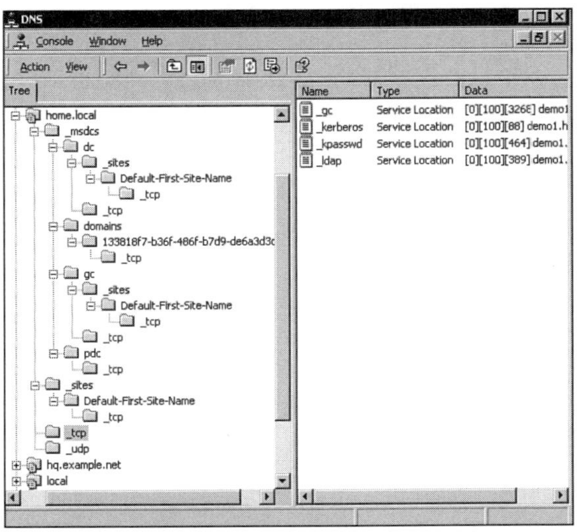

is only one DC. In other words, this is about as simple as it gets.

Figure 7.8 A simple Netlogon maintained SRV recordset.

The first thing to remember is that in a larger environment there would be multiple records with different IP addresses but otherwise the same for a number of these registrations. When a client queries for a particular name, all matching records are used to determine the IP addresses returned. In a larger environment, you would also see more entries for each domain, and a larger set of entries built out under the domain that is at the Active Directory root (the forest root domain).

The view in Figure 7.8, within the DNS Server management console, gives the impression of a subdomain structure. In fact, this structure is logically created in the Name rather than the Domain field of the SRV records (see Listing 7.1).

Next, notice that there are records for LDAP, GC, Kerberos, and Kpasswd services. LDAP is used for LDAP services, which in Windows 2000 are always on DCs. GC is for Global Catalog services, also always on domain controllers, just not all of them. In Windows 2000, Kerberos servers and Kerberos password change servers (Ktpasswd) also happen to always be on domain controllers.

All the records specify the TCP protocol, except that the two Kerberos-related services are also available over the User Datagram Protocol (UDP). This can be seen by the _TCP and _UDP in the protocol part of the SRV records.

The entries with a qualifier of site within the name are used to classify services by their location in the Active Directory topology. Because a particular DC is listed for a specific site does not necessarily mean that the machine is physically within that site, however, or even logically defined in the Active Directory site topology as a member of that site. When a site does not have a local provider of a particular service, Netlogon registers its belief of the best domain controller that a member in that site should first try for the service. How Netlogon makes its determination based on site topology is not a DNS issue, and so is not covered in this book. What is important is to keep in mind that the Active Directory functions more optimally when Netlogon can use dynamic DNS updates to tune the SRV records.

This structure further elaborates available services by records having an _msdcs qualification. Within this set are certain special advertisements, such as one qualified as pdc representing the one DC in a domain acting as the NT 4 PDC emulator for down-level clients. The entire set is repeated for each domain. Also, entries for locating within the Active Directory when only the root domain of the Active Directory is known are elaborated under the DNS domain at the top of the Active Directory hierarchy.

If you need to manually maintain this structure, you are advised to seek out all the current information available. Your overall performance will benefit from having this structure accurately reflect your Active Directory.

SRV Entries Without DDNS

When DDNS updates are not allowed, one must use manual methods of zone data management. This includes not only the expected record types—A, PTR, CNAME, NS, and so on—but also SRV and CNAME records that Netlogon would otherwise provide. As has been described, SRV records are at the heart of the Domain Locator Service in the Active Directory architecture, and are required.

Although a minimum list of SRV records is created as NETLOGON.DNS (see Listing 7.1) and stored in %windir%\System32\config when **dcpromo** is run to form a domain controller, just looking at the flat listing does not convey the full impact of manual maintenance of SRV records.

Listing 7.1 **An example NETLOGON.DNS file**

```
hq.example.net. 600 IN A 169.254.101.113
_ldap._tcp.hq.example.net. 600 IN SRV 0 100 389 dc1.hq.example.net.
_ldap._tcp.pdc._msdcs.hq.example.net. 600 IN SRV 0 100 389 dc1.hq.example.net.
_ldap._tcp.855aa338-2137-4ad5-9fdc-790814150512.domains._msdcs.hq.example.net. 600
IN SRV 0 100 389 dc1.hq.example.net.
d3506455-5459-4564-a4f1-cbb484c2fc3c._msdcs.hq.example.net. 600 IN CNAME
dc1.hq.example.net.
_kerberos._tcp.dc._msdcs.hq.example.net. 600 IN SRV 0 100 88 dc1.hq.example.net.
_ldap._tcp.dc._msdcs.hq.example.net. 600 IN SRV 0 100 389 dc1.hq.example.net.
_kerberos._tcp.hq.example.net. 600 IN SRV 0 100 88 dc1.hq.example.net.
_kerberos._udp.hq.example.net. 600 IN SRV 0 100 88 dc1.hq.example.net.
_kpasswd._tcp.hq.example.net. 600 IN SRV 0 100 464 dc1.hq.example.net.
_kpasswd._udp.hq.example.net. 600 IN SRV 0 100 464 dc1.hq.example.net.
_ldap._tcp.HQ-Site._sites.hq.example.net. 600 IN SRV 0 100 389 dc1.hq.example.net.
_kerberos._tcp.HQ-Site._sites.dc._msdcs.hq.example.net. 600 IN SRV 0 100 88
dc1.hq.example.net.
_ldap._tcp.HQ-Site._sites.dc._msdcs.hq.example.net. 600 IN SRV 0 100 389
dc1.hq.example.net.
_kerberos._tcp.HQ-Site._sites.hq.example.net. 600 IN SRV 0 100 88
dc1.hq.example.net.
_ldap._tcp.gc._msdcs.hq.example.net. 600 IN SRV 0 100 3268 dc1.hq.example.net.
gc._msdcs.hq.example.net. 600 IN A 169.254.101.113
_gc._tcp.hq.example.net. 600 IN SRV 0 100 3268 dc1.hq.example.net.
_ldap._tcp.HQ-Site._sites.gc._msdcs.hq.example.net. 600 IN SRV 0 100 3268
dc1.hq.example.net.
_gc._tcp.HQ-Site._sites.hq.example.net. 600 IN SRV 0 100 3268 dc1.hq.example.net.
_ldap._tcp.Remote1-Site._sites.hq.example.net. 600 IN SRV 0 100 389
dc1.hq.example.net.
_ldap._tcp.Remote1-Site._sites.gc._msdcs.hq.example.net. 600 IN SRV 0 100 3268
dc1.hq.example.net.
_kerberos._tcp.Remote1-Site._sites.dc._msdcs.hq.example.net. 600 IN SRV 0 100 88
dc1.hq.example.net.
_ldap._tcp.Remote1-Site._sites.dc._msdcs.hq.example.net. 600 IN SRV 0 100 389
dc1.hq.example.net.
_kerberos._tcp.Remote1-Site._sites.hq.example.net. 600 IN SRV 0 100 88
dc1.hq.example.net.
_gc._tcp.Remote1-Site._sites.hq.example.net. 600 IN SRV 0 100 3268
dc1.hq.example.net.
```

First, if you study this example of a file you will come to notice that it builds a logical structure, which will need to be correctly created. That part is minor, because these records provide the full specification and can be pasted directly into a zone file.

What does not show up at all is the impact on overall performance that results from not allowing the Netlogon service to maintain the SRV structure in DNS. This structure is used to aid clients, and for that matter to aid services at the core of the design, to rapidly and efficiently locate key services. This SRV structure allows more direct queries rather than sequences of chained queries. The structure also is used to provide pointers to the "best" or "most local" provider for different services based on a client's knowledge of what domain and especially what site they are within.

Without dynamic updates enabled, this structure needs constant adjustment as a deployment changes; otherwise, it will be inadequate for optimal performance. This comment likely applies especially to the records that have GUIDs (the long 128-bit undecipherable label) for names and are used by services for optimal, direct location queries. Where a shop's politics allow, delegating zones to DNS on Windows 2000 enabled for dynamic update to maintain these structures is recommended, as is use of update security. When entire DNS domains cannot be delegated to list the hosts and clients as well as these SRV-related structures, consider delegating _msdcs, _sites, _tcp and _udp if your preexisting DNS can be configured to accept the underscore (_) characters.

Bringing Active Directory and DNS Together (or Not)

So far in this chapter very select topics have been covered in some detail. If you are thinking that this has been long on information but coming up short on simple answers, you have likely read this information well. The out-of-the-box deployment of a Windows 2000 domain environment is aimed at a design point in which Microsoft DNS is primary for all the domain environment—where DDNS is enabled with Active Directory integration, where DHCP is used to service clients, where Secure Dynamic Update is used, and where the Active Directory is secured behind a firewall. As one begins walking away from this design point along any of these vectors, one assumes new issues to be resolved.

To aid in these evaluations, this section collects observations, some newly mentioned and a few previously discussed, within an ordering that brings related factors together for at least a couple of these vectors.

Topology of the Active Directory and of DNS

With the first release of Windows 2000, virtually all public documentation is written from the point of view that there will be a one-to-one correspondence between the domain structure of the Active Directory and that used for DNS. In fact, Microsoft and a number of partners have been working to make this strict isomorphism between the two namespaces more of a convenience for new deployments than a requirement for all deployments.

It is possible to have the DNS identity of clients and servers differ from the dotted Active Directory name of a domain. Although much normal operation is possible, it is not necessarily problem free. In the period between the emergence of the Beta 2 release and the final code freeze for the retail release, a fair number of changes were made to assist with this namespace independence. Just as with NetBIOS independence, however, there is more to be done.

Another factor that comes into the picture here is that immediately before the code freeze, RFC 2672, "Non-Terminal DNS Name Redirection" (defining the DNAME record), attained standards track. This record permits the substitution of a branch of the DNS namespace so that it is known under a different DNS domain name. This creates an alias for domain branches akin to how CNAME allows aliases for common host names. With DNAME it will be possible to remap xyz.com to an existing DNS branch such as corp.com so that its leaves and children, such as cowpoke.corp.com, can be known under remapped names (cowpoke.xyz.com, in this example).

Over the next year, we expect to see much change in the documented choices available. For the moment, the straight-and-narrow path with name pace isomorphism is the one that has received the most deployment testing and for which there is documented guidance. What is easily possible, problem free, and documented by the vendor is very likely to adjust to the realities of deploying Windows 2000 Active Directory into large-scale preexisting Transmission Control Protocol/Internet Protocol (TCP/IP) infrastructures. For the present, if you want or need to follow this route, you should be in touch with your Microsoft Consulting Services contacts and be prepared to do some custom hand holding in places.

DNS Server Topology Matched to DC Placement

With the exception of network loading in transfers, and machine load, integration of DNS with the Active Directory seems to leverage some hard design work that should have gone into deciding where in an enterprise DC placement is needed. The considerations in this decision are highly parallel to the considerations in placing DNS services.

Whether one or another of the modes of caching servers (see Chapter 11) would be sufficient at a location is still a valid inquiry, even when it has been determined that the site needs a DC. If DC placement relied on a requirement for availability of the Windows 2000 domain environment even under conditions of network interruption, however, locating zone copies there would also be indicated.

It is very important to consider where clients or DHCP will be sending updates. When DNS is not integrated, these are all funneled to the one primary for the zone, wherever that might be. With primaries available on DCs that have been locally placed, this becomes merely an issue of replication load. Because DCs already have a hefty workload—hosting LDAP and Kerberos as well as replication—and with DNS the dynamic update load, however, it is worth considering local secondaries or caching-only servers to which clients are then directed. With these local secondaries obtaining transfers from their local DC, the primary DNS zones on the DCs automatically act as bridgehead servers between sites. These DCs handle only added load from DNS resulting from registrations and refreshes and change replication and transfers to secondaries. The local secondaries handle the DNS load from client queries, and caching of answers received from forwarders.

Domain Environment Predefined Groups

When running the Windows 2000 networking service within a domain, the server machine is a participant in the Active Directory. This means that a number of predefined groups are available for use. With the initial release of Windows 2000, not too many of these are directly tied to networking services, as can be seen from the listing in Table 7.1. You should consider using these groups to facilitate your delegation of administrative responsibility, or in the case of DnsUpdateProxy to mitigate issues that arise when using DHCP to dynamically update DNS.

Table 7.1 **Predefined Network Services Groups in Active Directory**

Group Name	Description
DnsUpdateProxy	Members of this group do not automatically become owners of RRs that they create through dynamic DNS.
DnsAdmins	A domain local group, members of which can administer DNS servers in the domain.
DHCP Administrators	A domain local group, members of which can administer DHCP servers in the domain. Note that Enterprise Administrator membership is needed to authorize a DHCP server.
DHCP Users	A domain local group, members of which can examine DHCP server configuration in the domain.
WINS Users	A domain local group, members of which can examine WINS server configuration in the domain.

DNS Zone Data Availability

In integrating zone data into the Active Directory, that information becomes available to LDAP queries. Only one security mechanism is native to the Active Directory, and it is used to control update and also to control read access. Because by its very nature zone data must be available, RRs have Everyone Read allowed. There appears to be nothing currently implemented that would prevent anyone who can obtain a security context allowing an LDAP session from enumerating the entire set of zone data. The extent that this is available with a null security context depends on the limits imposed on the group Everyone and on null, or anonymous, LDAP connections. This last item has been the subject of some shifting in the implementations leading up to the initial release version. For the moment, the firewall solution is the most well-defined approach, but this appears to leave the zone data exposed for enumeration to all valid users of the Active Directory. Although off-topic here, the ability of any Authenticated User to create and then own RRs has similar concerns associated.

Directory Services Navigation and DNS Load

The opening of this chapter mentioned how DNS was designed into the top levels in the Active Directory topology. What was not mentioned is that traditional LDAP navigates within a directory services structure through a process of referrals. If a client at a level four tiers deep is trying to access a resource at a level two deep in a different branch of the directory structure, the client iteratively walks up the tree, node by node, to the root, and then back down the branch holding the resource. At each step there is a round trip, LDAP query, and referral reply, with each successive LDAP server. This is in the traditional LDAP referral process, in which each node knows and can refer a client to its neighbors, where the client then goes asking, and so on.

To leverage the fact that DNS information is available, and that the directory structure is conformant to the DNS structure, Microsoft changed the way this locating is done. In the released version of Windows 2000, clients (as soon as they have sufficient information, such as by a lookup in the Global Catalog, to know in what domain a resource resides) go directly to DNS asking for a reference. If a client needed LDAP services in the domain, for example, it would query DNS for _ldap._tcp SRV records in the domain. This gives the client a direct path to the LDAP services for the target domain, potentially cutting out much LDAP tree walking. This also will increase the use (and usefulness) of DNS.

You saw previously how Netlogon uses DNS and SRV records. And one can anticipate increased use of SRV for locating services such as _http._tcp in the future. All these factors add up to heavily used DNS services.

DDNS Update Load

This topic mostly collects in one place reminders and observations on the impact of DDNS on server performance. Any specific deployment must be analyzed by measuring actual behavior in the field.

With DDNS enabled, zone files can be in constant change. The different Microsoft systems differ in their defaults, from attempting to update DNS registration three or four times per hour for clusters, to once per day for Windows 2000 Professional, to once every seven days for DHCP leases. The scavenging parameter, the NoRefreshInterval discussed earlier in this chapter, has an all-important impact in reducing the churn and needless replication or zone transfer overhead.

But the fact remains, zones in change will be triggering transfers. If everything goes well with standard zones, the Notify option is used and slaves request IXFR incremental transfers, the load in minimized. When storage is in the Active Directory, these changes will propagate incrementally. But small attributes have a relatively large wrapper overhead in the Active Directory replication technology.

The Active Directory, because it is loosely convergent, provides much opportunity with DDNS for different simultaneous authoritative answers from different servers. However, this is possibly at least as likely with standard zone transfers.

Of course, this is all a moot point because the one alternative is to not use dynamic updates. But keep these factors in mind when planning a DNS deployment. Where caching servers are sufficient, there is now a little extra to recommend their use, because with them the constant zone transfer overhead is avoided.

Summary

In this chapter, the high points that fall out of the, at times natural and at times unnatural, tangency between Active Directory and DNS have been discussed. The most prominent of the players in this are DDNS and the consequences flowing from the properties of the Active Directory. This tangency has been leveraged by Microsoft to address concerns over the use of SRV records and of dynamic updates. How well this has been accomplished has been left to the reader for consideration.

8

Working with BIND Servers

THIS CHAPTER REVIEWS THE FOLLOWING:

- **Communication Between Name Servers.** Although compliant when a name server communicates with early BIND-based name servers, problems can arise. This section provides some precautionary measures for communication with these types of name servers.
- **Migrating from BIND to Windows 2000 DNS.** This section covers the required operations necessary when integrating or replacing BIND-based name servers (version 4 or 8) with Microsoft DNS.
- **Running the BIND Pport on Windows.** This section, although not an option yet available for supporting a Windows 2000 domain environment, warns of the currently limited BIND port on Windows.
- **Other Boot and Zone File Differences.** Migration from and integration of BIND with Microsoft DNS requires attention to a few zone and configuration file details mentioned here.

Communication Between Name Servers

All name servers must be able to communicate with each other. If they didn't (or couldn't), Internet host names would never get resolved and the World Wide Web would be as useful as the Commodore VIC 20 in my parents' attic. Microsoft's DNS is Request for Comment (RFC) compliant in terms of how it talks to other name servers. The types of communications that name servers must be able to understand are queries, answers to queries, and zone transfers. The queries and responses are pretty self-explanatory as the basic components of name resolution. Clients make queries, which may in turn cause servers to make additional queries until a response is found and returned to the client. Zone transfers are the mechanisms that allow master servers to propagate information to slave servers, and thus enhance the capabilities of the "distributed" system. The message format and query packets have the same structure and bit alignment. The Windows 2000 DNS Server accepts and responds appropriately to both iterative and recursive queries. Even though the Windows 2000 DNS Server is standards compliant, one must watch out for issues with features offered by some of the alternatives.

The use of Active Directory places certain restriction on one's choice of DNS services. Support for the *Service* (SRV) *record* type is required. If dynamic updates are supported, it is very advisable to use incremental transfers and the Notify option. The earliest BIND version known to successfully support this combination is 8.1.2.

Before getting into specific versions, it should be mentioned that using the Microsoft proprietary Windows Internet Naming Service (WINS) and Windows Internet Naming Service-Reverse (WINS-R) records and forgetting to exclude them from zone transfers to non-Microsoft DNS servers will cause problems.

Communicating with BIND Version 4.9.4 and Earlier

In general, using BIND 4.x will prove unsatisfactory for all purposes except some very specific cases. If a domain environment is being used, Active Directory requires that DNS support the SRV record. You may need to interoperate in some cases, if so these issues need to be considered.

The one thing to watch out for with the Windows 2000 DNS Server, with regard to versions of name server binaries based on BIND 4.9.4 and earlier, is the messages sent during zone transfers. Although written into the RFC, the older versions of BIND and its derivatives can have problems with messages that contain multiple RRs. If this situation should occur, the administrator should take care to set the Windows 2000 DNS Server to send only single RR messages to BIND secondary servers during zone transfers. This eliminates a number of problems related to the zone transfers themselves, as well as protects the health and well-being of the other name servers in the network.

This can be accomplished in NT 4.0 by uncommenting the BindSecondaries line in the boot file, or in all versions by editing the value of the BindSecondaries key in the Registry, or in Windows 2000 by setting the Bind Secondaries option in the

Advanced tab of the server properties. In Windows 2000, this option has no effect on transfers between two Windows 2000 DNS Servers. The setting is serverwide, affecting all zone transfers to secondaries.

In NT 4.0 if the administrator wants to effect the change by editing the boot file, and the name server system is running from the Registry, the administrator must follow these steps:

1. Change the Registry keys to boot from a file rather than the Registry.
2. Create a boot file that matches the current configuration.
3. Reset the name server so that it boots from the file.
4. Start the DNS manager and perform an Update Server Data Files from the DNS menu.

The key in the Registry that affects this operation contains a binary operator. The value of the BindSecondaries key is just set to one or zero. The binary value of one represents a true state, implying that BIND secondaries will be used, and zero represents a false state.

The drawback in NT 4.0, that DNS lacked a tool to generate a boot file matching the Registry settings, has been fixed for the Windows 2000 release. It used to be that switching back and forth between boot files and the Registry could cause problems in and of itself by the sheer fact that configuration settings may be lost in transitions. So, the administrator needed to pay very close attention to every detail when making these changes or, for that matter, any others. Windows 2000 has remedied these issues, with the Registry and file boot files being kept synchronized when the server is started from file.

Communicating with BIND 8

When dealing with BIND 8, one no longer needs to worry about the number of RRs per message, but BIND 8 has a number of new features that can make life rather interesting. If BIND 8 is used for the master server, the Microsoft DNS administrator must take care to query the master appropriately. That is to say, BIND 8 can filter requests made to or from specific addresses and ports. Say a system running BIND 8 is dual homed, and provides zone information for both external and internal networks. The BIND 8 server can be configured to give different responses to queries, based on the interface the query was received on or even the port number used for the communication. BIND 8 enables administrators to define who may perform zone transfers, as well as who may query the system, and even the port numbers that are allowed when clients make queries to the server. If running Microsoft DNS as a secondary, make sure that the access controls are set appropriately to allow the zone transfers by the secondary and make sure that the secondary is pointed to the correct interface.

As said previously, BIND 8.1.2 supports the minimum requirements for Active Directory. So, using a BIND implementation at or above 8.1.2 as a secondary is not only possible, it can be problem free. It is likely, however, that BIND 8.1.2 or higher will be entrenched in many environments, and even delegation of source authority to a Windows 2000 DNS Server may be out of the realm of possibility. In this case, a number of issues must be overcome.

When BIND is used as the primary, one must address the fact that there is no way to secure the dynamic update process that the Windows 2000 client implementation understands and uses, at least in the initial release. This means that you cannot use the security mechanisms that might otherwise be available. The net result is that one may well select to not use dynamic updates. This in turn means that one will be manually maintaining not just the normal *Address* (A), *Pointer* (PTR), and so forth record types, but also the SRV records and their structures. Chapter 7, "Dynamic DNS and the Active Directory," offered some insight into this. If only the original NETLOGON.DNS records are added, the Windows 2000 Active Directory will not have its access paths optimized, as it would if netlogon could update SRV records for such as _Sites.

Migrating from BIND to Windows 2000 DNS

An administrator already running BIND who wants to implement the Windows 2000 DNS solution must answer a couple of questions first:

- Will the Windows 2000 DNS be used in conjunction with BIND? If so, will it be the primary or the secondary? And what version of BIND is being used?
- Will the Windows 2000 DNS be used to replace the BIND server outright, or will it function for only a delegated portion (subdomain) of the domain?

If the Windows 2000 DNS Server will be used in conjunction with BIND, you need to know which version of BIND is being used. If BIND 8 and Windows 2000 DNS are to be used together, the issues of building the Windows 2000 DNS are minimal if the Windows 2000 DNS will be a secondary, and if the DNS domains are not used for Active Directory. The administrator needs to set up the Windows 2000 DNS for the secondary domains only. There is little else to do unless the Windows 2000 DNS machine will also be a secondary master, meaning that other secondaries will pull their zones from it. For a primary, the issues really relate only to the setup of the server. BIND 8 configuration files will not load on Windows 2000 DNS server. This means that the configuration of the Windows 2000 DNS must be performed manually or by using a stripped-down configuration file. For more information about manual configuration, see Chapter 11, "Configuring Windows DNS Servers."

It is hoped that now, as the DNSSEC and DNSIND working groups have consolidated, that their efforts to reach a consensus on standards revisions for supporting secure updates will bear fruit that wins wide industry implementation. Until then, DNS servers using proprietary means for securing the use of the Update opcode will remain of limited interoperability. That RFC 2137 is not supported in the Windows 2000 DNS implementation and does limit ones choices, but it is not as though there are many DNS implementations that do support this RFC.

If the Active Directory does need to be supported, the issues covered in the preceding section must be studied and decided. The easiest coexistence approach is to delegate source authority to Windows 2000 for its use within its DNS services.

If the Microsoft DNS Server is going to be a primary, the sources for the zone files will also be needed. The zone files, if coming from an existing server, can just be copied over. Because they are just formatted text files, no special warnings need be given. The only potential problem might be a resource record type not supported by the Microsoft DNS and that has been added recently. Microsoft says that such records will just be skipped, and the support of RR types in Windows 2000 is close to complete.

In actually making the transition, consider the case of the Windows 2000 DNS taking over the role of primary for a BIND host. For argument sake, the Windows 2000 DNS is being set up to participate in an Active Directory, within which the DNS records will be integrated. To begin, you need to install the OS and DNS server for the Windows 2000 Server (refer to Chapter 11). After this has been accomplished, the next step is to migrate the zone data to the new server. The easiest and recommended way to perform this task is to follow these steps:

1. Initially set the Windows 2000 DNS Server up as a secondary by creating the secondary zones in the DNS management interface.
2. Verify that the new "slave" has the access rights to perform the zone transfers from BIND.
3. Start the new server, or manually force transfer using the Transfer from Master selection in the context menu of the secondary zone(s). Within seconds (normally), the zone files transfer to the new server.
4. Verify that the new server is configured to boot from file (in the server properties Advanced tab).
5. Take the new name server off the network to be reconfigured as the primary, by following steps 6 to 8.
6. Delete the zone configuration (boot file) entries for the secondary zones just transferred; be careful, however, this is not saying to delete the zone files themselves.
7. Create new configuration entries using primary directives and using the transferred zone files as the sources for the domains.
8. Change the Internet Protocol (IP) address of the new server to match the existing, prior primary server.
9. Shut down the existing primary server and bring the new Windows 2000 DNS Server online.
10. Change the storage mode to Active Directory integrated when desired.

Running BIND on Windows

One other possibility when building a name server on NT is the BIND port to NT. The downside to this approach is the fact that the port of BIND for NT is based on BIND version 4.9.7. This now is a deprecated version, and no effort will be put forth to support this version. Another factor that would discourage users of this port is that it was intended for NT 4.0. The software is problematic at best under the Windows 2000 edition. If your intention is to run BIND, you should stay away from this option, choosing instead to implement a UNIX-based solution.

Other Boot and Zone File Differences

One major thing to remember when configuring the Microsoft DNS Server is the WINS integration. Because WINS is not supported as part of the RFCs for DNS, and WINS is becoming deprecated and will primarily be used for supporting legacy operating systems and applications, this will be an issue for a few years yet. If you are supporting NetBIOS clients using WINS (refer to Chapter 16, "WINS: Legacy Name Services and Resolution") and use the WINS pseudo-RR, remember to strip the record out in all zone transfers to non-Microsoft DNS servers.

Windows 2000 DNS Server processes only cache, primary, and secondary directives in its boot file. Other information may cause problems or be ignored.

The last difference worth mentioning is the BIND XFRNETS directive. Essentially, this directive is not supported under the Microsoft DNS, and it will generate an error message in the Event log, but will not hinder the operation of the name server. It just remarks on the invalid directive, and moves on.

Summary

This chapter has collected together an assessment of the options available for BIND and Microsoft DNS interoperation. It was shown that the range of choices depends on one's objectives and especially on the supported DNS features that are either required or recommended for using Active Directory. When Active Directory support is not needed, BIND 8.1.2 and Windows 2000 DNS were said to be fully interchangeable and interoperable, with the exception of some BIND-specific configuration extensions.

9

Designing Your DNS Services

THIS CHAPTER REVIEWS THE FOLLOWING:

- **DNS Server Capacities.** This section explains some of the factors that determine the capacity of a DNS server.
- **Deciding How Many Domains and Zones to Have.** This section helps you think through the issues you face when you consider how many domains to have, how these are partitioned into zones, and where these are placed.
- **Deciding How Many DNS Servers to Have.** This section describes the role DNS servers play serving multiple and single domains to help you decide how many DNS servers you'll need for your situation.
- **Practical Design Examples.** This section provides several illustrative DNS design examples to give you ideas for use in composing your own DNS installation.
- **Windows 2000 and Active Directory Considerations.** This section provides an overview of the added issues resulting from the use of a Windows 2000 domain environment. This section also mentions features available in the Windows 2000 server that can be effectively employed as design elements.

This chapter provides information that you can use to make key decisions, such as deciding how many DNS servers and how many domains you will need. When the Active Directory domain environment is used, much of the domain decision becomes no longer a DNS administration issue. But placement of these domains on different servers, or in different locations through the zones partitioning of the domains, is still a DNS administration decision. The "Practical Design Examples" section provides design illustrations to help you see clearly what the issues are and how various design alternatives can affect the results of the decisions you make. Because the Windows 2000 DNS implementation is quite usable outside of Active Directory support roles, and is an alternative to any Request for Comment (RFC)-standard DNS server, its use can be in highly varied situations. It can be used within an NT 4.0 domain, or on an isolated standalone server, on a member server in a Windows 2000 domain, or integrated with Active Directory on domain controllers. This makes covering design a complicated issue, without some specific requirements a design is to meet. So in the following section, you will find first a discussion of server selection criteria. Then, you'll find a number of frequently encountered design options suited for the small office or as elements in a larger organization. These are presented mostly in their traditional form, appropriate to UNIX, NT 4.0, or any standard Transmission Control Protocol/Internet Protocol (TCP/IP) deployment before the special requirements of the planned deployment are folded into the mix. Some observations specific to the Windows 2000 DNS Server or domain environment are made along the way, but most are reserved until the end, after the design elements have been examined.

DNS Server Capacities

The capacity of a server to handle the queries it receives (both internal and external) varies depending on the following factors:

- The number of domains for which the server is expected to be authoritative
- The number and speed of subnets to which the server is directly attached with either virtual Internet Protocol (IPs) or actual separate interfaces
- The number of client requests the server will actually serve
- The amount of dynamic update activity and volume of zone transfers triggered
- The hardware that has been selected for the server

The best way to determine the capacity of the servers at a given site is to use the System Monitor (or Performance Monitor if one prefers the NT 4.0 name). System Monitor can provide a record of the overall performance of the underlying server and many measures specifically of the DNS server as well. The most important things to look at are network performance, disk performance, memory allocation, and CPU utilization to understand the hardware and how it is being driven. For the DNS server, one can look at more than 60 measures (refer to Table 11.3) in real-time, some as rates, such as updates per second or queries per second, and some as cumulative values. System Monitor can be used to log activity over a time period, and can then later analyze the counters recorded, which can take some disk space. Doing this on a periodic basis is a good idea to track usage against an initially established baseline.

Although the DNS service itself is not a heavily taxing process, the number of requests that come in that generate a load on a DNS server can take a toll. If the server is used for other services as well, you should be concerned about the response times of the DNS service. In general, a single DNS server can handle a fair number of DNS domains and keep up with the flow of requests. If a DNS server takes too long to respond, the requesting client or recursive server process may give up, thus negating the value of having a DNS server. When it is appropriate, Windows DNS Server can be configured to refuse recursive queries, which extends capacity. In large environments, when dynamic update and notify-driven transfers are significant factors, leaving the primary to this task with slave secondaries for clients is an option. For these reasons, when a site served by a *domain controller* (DC) has many clients and that DC is hosting Active Directory–integrated DNS, it is best to provide local secondaries for the client's use. In general the underlying hardware system should not show high disk activity, short of updates.

The next issue is managing the zone information on a single server. For *Internet service providers* (ISPs) that offer domain hosting, the servers should be fairly hefty in terms of processor performance. Windows 2000 provides support for ATM and Gigabit Ethernet if the existing network bandwidth at the interface is constraining. DNS servers should be loaded with as much memory as possible, and need only a modest amount of disk space. The disk capacity needs to accommodate only the OS and the zone files for the domains. When the zone files are text, the size of the individual zones is generally not large, and similarly when Active Directory storage is used the impact on the disk subsystem provided for NTDS.DIT is not great. Many times it is necessary to place multiple IP addresses on an interface card, but at times this is done when it is not actually necessary. If there is no real requirement necessitating such virtual presence in a network, all that is accomplished is an increase of overhead for the TCP/IP protocol stack.

Memory is a big factor, because the caching operations of the name servers use the system memory. Having plenty of memory ensures a snappy performance from the name server, and enables some fairly large caches. For an average organization that will need to serve only its own domain information, very modest machines can go quite far. For most implementations, having enough memory in the system is probably the biggest issue and the key to improving name server performance.

Resource Record and Zone Limits

If you are using the NT 4.0 DNS Server, you should be aware that it experienced the following problem. A DNS server with 65,553 resource records in each of 1,000 zones can support more than 65 million records! There are limits, however: DNS Manager hangs if more than 65,553 records are in one zone or if there are more than 1,000 zones. These limits are documented in Microsoft Knowledge Base articles Q172477 and Q170518, respectively. The latter of these is noted as fixed with NT 4.0 Service Pack 4; the former was an issue with the NT 4.0 DNS Manager.

Here are some guidelines to help you build a system based on recommended DNS server resource requirements. Use at least the minimum hardware for your version of Windows 2000 Server, and then add 8MB of RAM for every 64KB (65,536) resource records that will be published, including domain and host records. This assumes that no other services will be running on the same computer to compete for resources. However, scale up from the minimum hardware recommendation for CPU, both in speed and number, how far depending on the number of client requests. If additional services are going to run on the system, increase resources to meet requirements of the additional software. Also consider the speed of the network interface and the bandwidth available for queries and answers. The speed of the hard disk is not terribly important if there's enough RAM to keep the server from paging.

Deciding How Many Domains and Zones to Have

The number of domains that will be established on a single server is really just a matter of management. The typical name server can, theoretically, handle an almost infinite number of domains, but who would want to manage such a beast? Having the sole responsibility for thousands (or hundreds of thousands) of domains would not be a task to take lightly. Remember, too, that one DNS server can handle many domains, and that one domain can be served by multiple DNS servers.

Organizations with several thousand computers in only one location, or in a single metropolitan area network, can easily use only one domain. Geographically dispersed organizations can have one domain to top their tree, with one subdomain under it for each city or region.

In practice, the DNS domain plan is often determined by the architecture defined for the Active Directory when it is used. In this case, the same DNS services management flexibility can be achieved by how the domain structure is carved into zones, and how these are then placed on servers. Zones define the units of DNS data transfer, and are the parts of the domain space assignable to different servers. For the smaller environments, this can easily come down to a single zone; for large organizations, this distribution is a balance of numerous requirements, not the least of which is geography. As Windows 2000 begins to mature, divorcing strict DNS domain conformance to the Active Directory domain boundaries will become less problematic. Most initial implementations will align the two domain boundaries, but many will not have this freedom because of preexisting deployments. Initial experiences show that although this separation is possible, it is not yet problem free, and does require some agility and hand-crafting.

ISPs that provide domain hosting have a lot of responsibility for commercial clients that rely on email and Web presence for their livelihood. If the ISP fails to provide quality name service for even one day, the results could be catastrophic for a business waiting for an all-important email to close a deal, or losing business through customers being unable to reach their Web site and make purchases.

For the average DNS administrator or IS manager, decisions about the number of domains or zones are usually matters of company politics or geographic limitations.

These considerations become very clear when the Windows 2000 domain environment is involved. For many technology-oriented companies, the engineering departments usually have their own domains for the simple reason that they can't wait for a corporate bureaucracy to get around to making changes. Engineers often need to move more quickly than that for testing new products. The responsibility for maintaining these domains is then dispersed among different departments so that they will not impede each other with conflicting requests based on their respective missions.

In terms of geographic limitations, many companies have a global presence in the physical location of their offices. It's generally easier for local administrators to be responsible for subdomains that they can touch and feel, instead of having to email another person halfway around the world to make a host record change. Other than the amount of client access throughout the distributed organization, as compared to local, and link type and speed, central or outlying placement of primaries in Windows 2000 will also depend on whether dynamic DNS (DDNS) is used, on whether Active Directory storage is used, and on where the Active Directory design has placed DCs. Much of this is decided on the basis of efficiency, and it can significantly affect email delivery as well.

You must consider delivery issues when a mail system is used that does not leverage the Active Directory. Because email addresses are associated with domain names, it's a good idea to make your mail services match the domain structure. DNS domains can be broken up along political, organizational, or geographical boundaries, often mirroring the IT support structure. Problems may arise when a potential mail recipient works for a company in the United States, but lives and works out of an office on another side of the world. Instead of having email go to a single large company server, subdomains and mail aliases are usually set up to redirect mail to servers that are distributed around the company (and, often, the world) to provide better access to the recipient, and to decrease the load on a single machine.

Deciding How Many DNS Servers to Have

The number of name servers that an organization may need is a judgment call. No rules of thumb cover all cases, and recommendations are advisory at best. Still, you'll find some general rules of thumb a little later in this chapter to provide a modicum of guidance.

If you want to set up a number of subdomains to match the hierarchy of your organization, you'll surely need to place each domain on a primary and at least one secondary server. It's not that two machines couldn't handle everything; they can. But there are always issues of accessibility, reliability, and redundancy to consider.

Accessibility, Reliability, and Redundancy

Accessibility refers to whether the clients who need the service are being delivered the services that they need, where they are. Access from the clients really means network connectivity. Reliability means that the provided access is stable—always available.

A single server, set up to handle queries for a domain, could easily be saturated by a high request load. This saturation could easily result in a denial of service—that is, names not getting resolved before a timeout occurs.

Having multiple machines for a single domain means that other hosts will service some of the requests. The issues of redundancy and reliability are pretty straightforward. What happens if a name server crashes (or the hard disk fails, or memory error occurs, or major service is to be installed, and so on)? The loss of a host supporting a domain by itself essentially means the loss of the domain until the service is restored. With multiple machines serving the domain, the administrator can be assured that
the queries for the domain are being answered. You may want to use some sort of hardware load-balancing solution to increase your uptime and reliability.

Having multiple machines means that the query load can be spread among the machines. If one goes down, there can be problems getting names resolved, such as delays or timeouts. Aged cached information pointing to a downed machine can also cause some short-term resolution failures. But operations do continue, if at a reduced level. Also, it is at times possible to temporarily shift an IP address to a remaining server from the one out of service, immediately relieving the clients' experience of the problem while it is being fixed. Redundancy is the easiest approach to contribute much to reliability. Reliability has more involved than machine outage contingencies— for example, avoidance of mismanagement that affects all machines.

Another redundancy issue involves service location. If all the name servers are in one physical location and that site is impacted so that your ISP connection is lost, the domain becomes inaccessible. By default, the greater the number of servers providing name service and the better geographic distribution, the better the availability and reliability of the name service. Each system that is truly multihomed on completely different networks can count as two servers in terms of presence, but not for all aspects of redundancy. If one of the network paths fails, the other remains available; if the machine fails, however, both are lost.

General considerations to take into account when deciding on a name server architecture include the number of locations that need support, the type of network communications that will be established among the locations, the number of clients at each location, the character of ongoing operations between locations, and the nature and type of connectivity the organization has to the Internet.

Rules of Thumb for Selecting the Number of DNS Servers

All organizations need two DNS servers. If an ISP handles name service for you, however, neither of these need to be yours to set up or manage. Small organizations often let the ISP manage the whole thing, but some choose to manage one DNS server, either the primary or secondary, letting the ISP keep the other. For reasons discussed earlier, this is a good, safe practice. A small organization with the Active Directory in use internally will most often implement an internal, and private, namespace and contract the public namespace in one of these ways with their ISP. When selecting the ISP services, use the availability, reliability, and redundancy factors to determine the quality of service being offered.

Mid-sized organizations need only two DNS servers, and they can add one site server for every geographical location to facilitate outbound queries. (These could be caching only.) Alternatively, they could turn geographically dispersed DNS servers into secondaries to add independence for local queries. If dynamic updates are used, the site local servers would forward the updates to the primary if they are secondaries. In some cases, this will be undesirable; and in others, desirable depending on Windows 2000 DC distribution and other factors.

Large organizations can have very complex DNS setups involving multiple domains and subdomains. The next section, "Practical Design Examples," illustrates some of the many options for composing them that can make large systems complex, as well as necessary. Tradeoffs among capacity, responsiveness, and reliability make simple rules of thumb useless for designing DNS services for a large organization.

Practical Design Examples

This section provides several illustrations that you can use to help you determine what kind of design best suits your installation.

Setting Up a Domain with One or More Subdomains

Engineering organizations are often very dynamic environments where experiments occur, so it's a good idea to separate them from the main corporate domain. The goal is to give an engineering department control over its own subdomain and the ability to handle changes independent of the rest of the company. Figure 9.1 shows a DNS setup that could be used for a domain named xyz.com.

A corporate domain with primary and secondary DNS servers, delegating to a subdomain. xyz.com, the main corporate domain, delegates primary authority for the engineering subdomain to the DNS servers in eng.xyz.com. In this scenario, changes made in eng.xyz.com will not affect the corporate domain, xyz.com., and engineering can make changes themselves for all their own hosts without having to bother corporate system administrators. The only case in which engineering will need to contact corporate services is if the IP address(es) of their name server(s) change.

Using an ISP to Provide Primary DNS Service

In very small organizations or even homes, it is often advisable to have the ISP provide the primary DNS service, as illustrated in Figure 9.2.

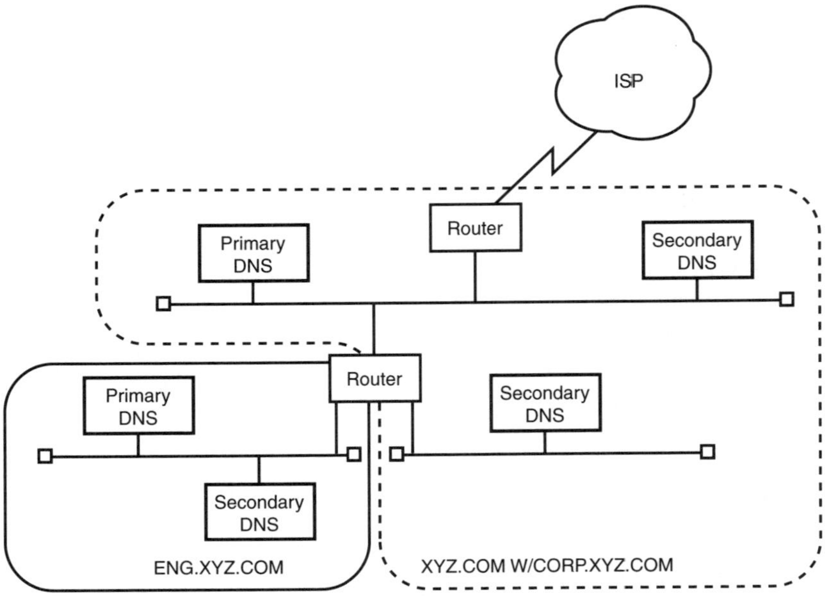

Figure 9.1 A corporate domain with primary and secondary DNS servers, delegating to a subdomain.

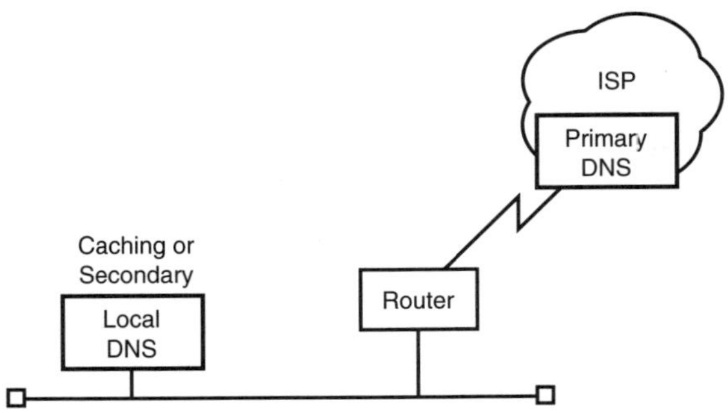

Figure 9.2 The ISP provides primary DNS services for this domain.

You can have your own caching server to improve performance, or a secondary server for redundancy. If you don't have a secondary server, the ISP can easily provide one. In this scenario, your public DNS namespace is managed by the ISP and your organization doesn't need to bother except to initiate changes with the ISP. For your internal use, a simple DNS services configuration can suffice if Active Directory is used. In this design, every change in public names requires communication with the ISP and they'll have to edit the zone file for you. One disadvantage of this method is that changes can sometimes take a long time to be performed. Sometimes the delay can be 72 hours or more, depending on holidays and such. Your internal name services can be easily set to forward to the ISP-provided DNS servers for resolution. For small organizations, installing Active Directory can provide default template DNS services with local name and IP addresses appropriate for this design after the forwarding DNS server has been configured an access route to the ISP.

If the connection to your ISP is persistent, for resolution of the public names a forwarding or even a caching-only server is fine. If the link is a dial-up or an on-demand line of some kind, installing a secondary DNS server might be better because you can then do local lookups without having to connect to the ISP for each query. Having a secondary also means that you can easily verify changes by examining the local copy of the zone file, which is periodically updated by transfer from the ISP's primary server.

Using an ISP to Provide Secondary DNS Service

In Figure 9.3, the organization is hosting its own primary DNS server, but the ISP or some other external organization is hosting the secondary. Remember, two servers, one primary and one secondary or two secondaries must be registered with InterNIC.

This scenario can help the performance of the whole system by distributing DNS query processing to several machines in different places. It also provides redundancy. If xyz.com loses connectivity, for example, a timeout would occur trying to connect, but its hosts could still be resolved by external systems. It is important to always have DNS for your domain, which is one reason why you shouldn't ever put all primary and secondary DNS servers for a domain on a nondedicated link (such as a dial-up link).

If primary authority is kept in-house, there is risk that the public secondaries could stop resolving names for your domain. This would occur in an outage situation where

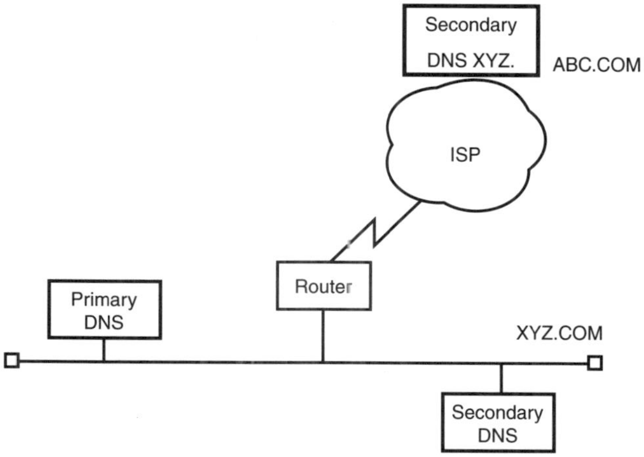

Figure 9.3 The ISP provides secondary DNS service for this domain.

the secondaries are unable to receive transfers and then eventually expire the zone. For this reason, good connectivity is needed, and optionally the zone expiration settings can be adjusted.

Protecting a Primary DNS Server from Unauthorized Access

You can improve security by registering two secondaries with the InterNIC rather than a primary, as shown in Figure 9.4.

This setup hides the machine hosting the zone data files from hackers. While the primary provides the zone data for the domain, it feeds the secondaries with authoritative data by transfers. Although all the servers can answer with authority, then, only the secondaries will respond to requests from external sources.

Additionally, the option to allow only secondaries in the Notify list to perform zone transfers can prevent unscrupulous people from dumping the contents of the zones. This setup prevents hackers from accessing the machine with the zone source. Routers can also be used to block access to the primary from outside the organization.

How a Large Site Can Create a Large Cache of Queries

If you want to reduce the number of name queries that must be resolved outside your organization, such as by ISP DNS servers, you can create a sitewide cache, as illustrated in Figure 9.5.

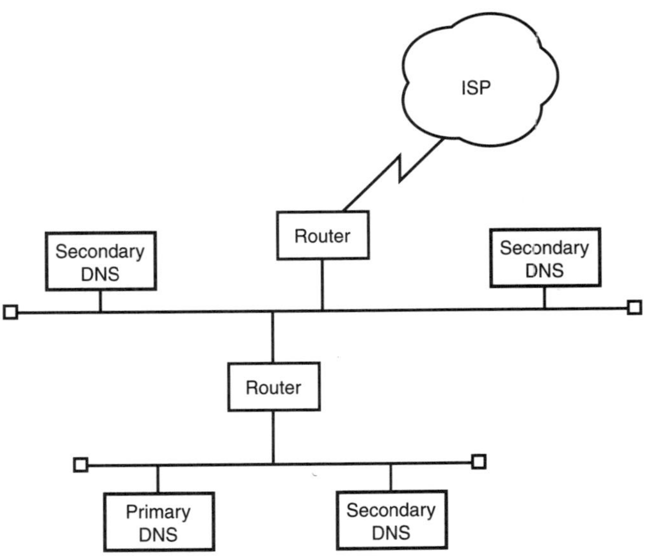

Figure 9.4 Secondaries serve outside queries into the domain, hiding the primary name server.

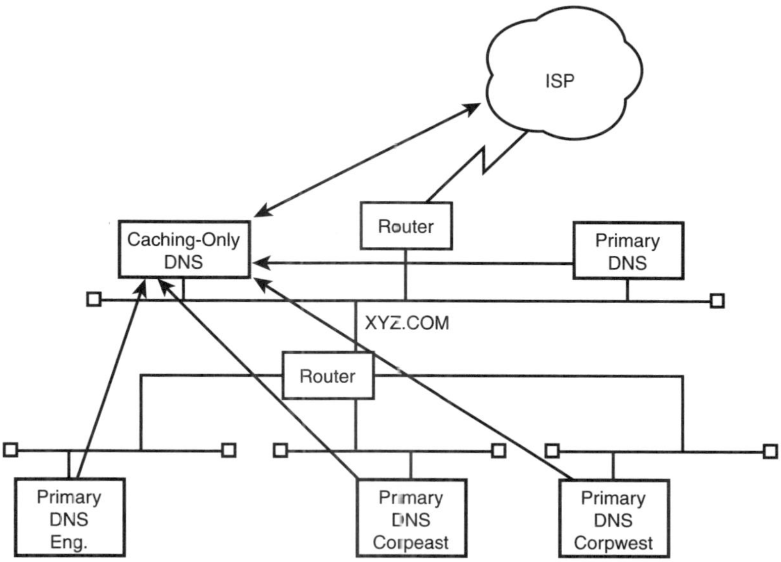

Figure 9.5 A sitewide caching-only DNS server can respond more quickly than individual queries going to outside servers.

You install a sitewide caching-only server by having all the name servers forward queries to one or more caching servers. Notice that it is the DNS servers that access the caching-only server, not the clients directly. This way all requests and answers get cached on one or more machines that will be queried by all other name servers in the company. This eliminates the need for the corpwest name server to go outside for any queries that have already been cached by any clients anywhere in the company.

Establishing an Organization-Only DNS That's Coordinated with External DNS

Split-brain DNS, as it is sometimes called, uses multiple primaries to increase security for a domain (see Figure 9.6). Usually one of these namespaces is outside and one is inside the firewall, with the public namespace having a primary often placed outside in the demilitarized zone (DMZ). The practical value of this setup for large organizations is profound. Split-brain DNS enables you to provide DNS service to internal clients for internal addresses, without having to post all addresses where outside DNS clients can see them. Administrators can decide precisely which internal hosts will be listed in outside DNS servers and which ones will be listed only in internal DNS servers.

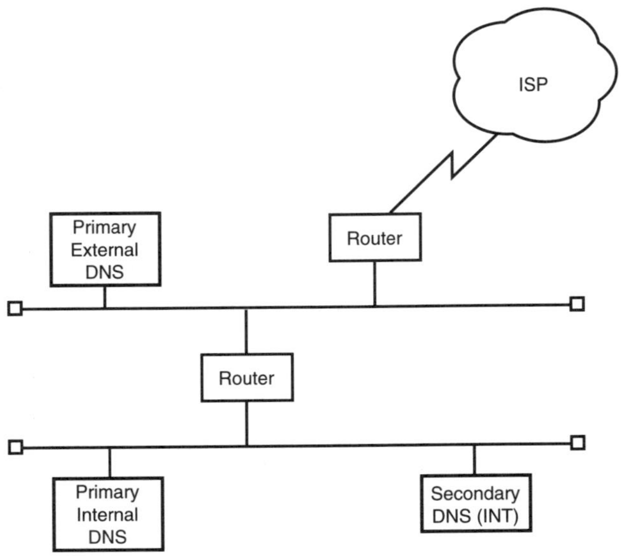

Figure 9.6 Split-brain DNS provides a measured degree of security for zone data.

The primary external server contains only entries in its zone file that you want the outside world to know about; the internal primary contains entries for all hosts in the domain. The internal name servers are set up to forward to the external primary name server all requests that they cannot answer directly, where they can be cached. The internals are also slaves to the externals, so they cannot attempt resolutions on their own. This keeps the internal servers hidden from the outside world, giving hackers fewer targets. Most often the connection between the internal and the external networks is through a firewall, which might be a filtering router, rather than just a router as shown here.

Security is a big concern of large corporations, and DNS servers contain significant data: knowledge of every machine in your domain! For this reason, it's a good idea to employ some scheme that prevents access to primary DNS servers because they're designed to transfer authoritative data to secondary servers. Hackers know this and they know how to exploit this feature for their own purposes. You can do this with the ISP providing the "outside" services as well. This design is discussed further in relation to firewalls in Chapter 10, "Security Issues."

Windows 2000 and Active Directory Considerations

Windows 2000 brings a number of further design needs and alternatives to the table. These are in cases supporting features included in the operating system, not characteristics of DNS itself, which can be used effectively in meeting DNS design needs.

Private Networking

The services available with the Windows 2000 Server for fine-tuning network connectivity are extensive. Features gathered together in the Routing and Remote Access services can be used to provide intelligent control over first-hop connectivity for multihomed machines. Also, TCP/IP properties can be used to filter packets by protocol and by Transmission Control Protocol (TCP) and User Datagram Protocol (UDP) ports, restricting availability of the services bound to a machine's interfaces, as shown in Figure 9.7, in an unconfigured state permitting all TCP/IP connectivity.

If you look at the Options tab of the Advanced TCP/IP properties, you will see that Windows 2000 includes an implementation of IPsec security. Using this requires defining a security policy by domain and does require a fair amount of preparation work for the public key infrastructure needed. Where extranet type connectivity, or high security applications are involved, however, you will quite probably want to give this alternative consideration. IPsec can be used with software encryption, or better with hardware on the interface cards to reduce the CPU load, which could be even more important for the DNS and other servers than it is for the clients.

Namespace Protection and Sharing

When the Active Directory is used, the nature of the information available from DNS by queries on Service (SRV) and other record types will be a concern to most systems managers. For this, and all the well-accustomed reasons, placement of the Active Directory behind a firewall or otherwise outside of the public Internet namespace is recommended. One variation of the split-brain design or another is typically used to accomplish this, tying the two namespaces together through forwarders and modifications of the root hints entries.

The public domain name and the internal domain name do not need to be the same. The internal can be dependent as a child name under the officially registered

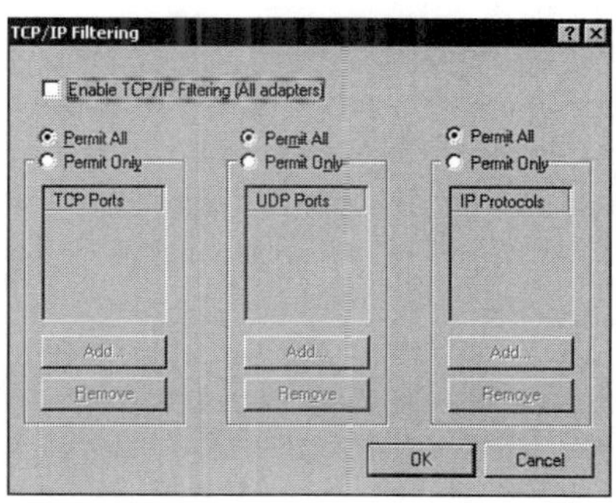

Figure 9.7 Security OPTIONS in TCP/IP Properties dialog box of Windows 2000.

name, or it can be a separate, private name, perhaps not even registered. In the last case, one will be assuming that the chosen name will never be made public. If this is an uncomfortable assumption, obtain control over the internal name as if it were to be a public name.

In some cases, likely to increase in number over time, use of the Active Directory technologies in the public network are desired. For example, a company providing services through a directory-enabled application to their clients would need a public Windows 2000 domain structure. In this case, the company will likely make this a "for-public-consumption-only" structure and keep the internal Active Directory isolated as has been discussed. Over time, metadirectory services—which provide users a unified access to multiple directory services, and in some cases provide administrators a unified management of them—will make situations like this more convenient and manageable.

The variety of *virtual private networking* (VPN) support in Windows 2000 can be used effectively in supporting extranet-type capabilities and in conjunction with remote access services in supporting small outlying offices using the Internet. Although the character of the extranet interactions your organization undertakes with other companies is beyond of the scope of DNS design and services, this might involve supporting more zones. It is possible that your company has a main Active Directory for purely internal purposes walled in, and yet another used with interbusiness processes. This second will likely have presence in the DMZ, and of course it will have a distinct DNS domain namespace, but otherwise the DNS support considerations are much the same.

DNS Service Placement

When the Active Directory is used in a multisite, or even just larger campus situation, much design work has already gone into placement of DCs. This design work can be leveraged for DNS. This is true using standard zones, but especially so when Active Directory–integrated DNS zones are used. When zones are standard, the placement of DCs will indicate where local DNS resolution is probably needed. The connectivity issues considered for DCs, bandwidth, continuous nature, and so on are relevant to supporting DNS transfers. Issues of the number of clients, the need for independent operation through network outages, and so on indicate a location should have both DC and DNS service presence.

With the zones integrated, their data will automatically be propagated onto all DCs on a per-domain basis. This happens whether the data is used or not. So using this zone data by installing another DNS server is more of a DNS server overhead issue than anything else. Doing so provides for local primaries.

Because a site with a secure internal network may opt to use dynamic updates using the Microsoft-provided Secure Dynamic Update capability, the primary DNS zones on the DCs would be used for registering updates. If dynamic update is used but Active Directory integration is not, registrations and refresh updates will be directed to the single zone primary. Placement of primary zones then becomes a priority design consideration.

The Use of Secondaries

The use of Active Directory integration places some extra load on DCs and their replication engine. The updates to the DNS database place load on the replication engine. This can be dampered by using the NoUpdateInterval scavenging parameter (refer to Chapter 7, "Dynamic DNS and the Active Directory," for information). Where site size warrants, it is good to consider providing sites with local secondaries for use by the clients, reserving the DNS service on the DC to handle updates.

Although for most purposes these DNS secondaries would only need zones for the local site and any other high-use domains, there are further issues to consider. If these secondaries use their root hints for external resolution services, the variety of addresses permitted through the firewall is less well controlled. If on the other hand these secondaries are configured to use forwarders, such as specifically designated DNS servers in the DMZ or at the ISP, these secondaries should have all the internal zones. A DNS server will forward a query when it cannot provide an authoritative answer. If all the internal zones are not present, the secondary can provide a referral or work the query recursively, but it will not have the authoritative answer in its data. Before working the query recursively, it will forward it, which for internal names would be undesirable. Very large sites can afford to funnel clients into the Internet access through slave secondaries. But all size sites should keep in mind that such use of forwarders is not just a convenient choke-point for security policy, but it is also a potential bottleneck and point of failure.

Summary

This chapter has shown, even without Active Directory considerations, that there are as many designs for DNS services as there are requirements. Carefully mapping out requirements and load factors, link characteristics, connectivity needs, and security policies is the first step for a larger design. Then applying design elements that satisfy these in the numerous alternatives will assist in rapidly narrowing the number of suitable designs. Thoroughly examining these for their operational characteristics, the routes taken, the placement of loads, and so forth will further refine the designs.

This chapter provided practical information that you can use to help design your own DNS installation. Chapter 11, "Configuring Windows DNS Servers," takes you to the next step, getting your DNS server up and running.

10

Security Issues

THIS CHAPTER REVIEWS THE FOLLOWING:

- **Spoofing Name Queries.** Spoofing can make your DNS server trust an untrustworthy host that's impersonating a valid secondary server. Unscrupulous hackers use this technique to get copies of zone files; and when your internal computer addresses are known, they're vulnerable to direct attacks.
- **Denial of Service.** Flooding a machine to prevent it from performing as intended can be the first step in some forms of attack. Protection in this situation is an exercise in maintaining high availability of services. A few DNS-specific configurations can assist in reaching this goal.
- **Using DNS with Firewalls.** Firewalls are dedicated devices or computers running special software to limit what can pass through them to protect one or more networks from unwanted access. Firewalls vary from special hardware, router solutions, and multiple machine configurations down to only one machine using two or more network cards. Where connection to the Internet and an internal network or *demilitarized zone* (DMZ) is needed, DNS requires special configuration depending on resolution and public presence needs.
- **Service Advertisement.** Knowing more about a target generally assists an attacker probing for weak points. Issues related to the protection of computer host and service advertisement in the namespaces published by modern systems

are usually addressed by restricting access to such publication. Here the DNS and NetBIOS namespaces are known concerns, but the added factors of *Service* (SRV) *records* and Lightweight Directory Access Protocol (LDAP) services are new.

- **Dynamic DNS (DDNS).** This new capability holds much promise, and much danger. Issues specific to the Windows 2000 operating system when using this dynamic update capability are briefly recapped in this section.
- **Mail Security: SMTP, POP, IMAP, and Exchange.** Mail servers are subject to a variety of attacks. This section describes a few potential security holes and suggests how you can use DNS Mail Exchanger (MX) records and mail relays to reduce exposure.
- **WWW Security.** As Web servers and browsers become more powerful and popular, they also become more capable of creating holes that can breach security. This section describes some Web security issues and techniques that you can use for protection.
- **FTP Security.** FTP servers are useful for posting software and electronic documents for download, and are used to compliment Web servers both for downloads and for publishing. They present some security problems that this section describes.

This chapter doesn't cover all the security issues you should consider when setting up a network connected to the Internet. The intention here is to help you understand some of the issues most closely related to DNS services. It has been said that security begins, or should, with design. Unless designed in from the start, security is often patchwork layered on vulnerabilities, or it is accomplished by redesign. The truth is that security in networking is no one thing, but results from contributions on all corners in a deployment. This chapter focuses on DNS when addressing the need for public network connectivity and its risks. Many risks must be addressed internally. It does little good to filter out all but selected ports if an insider may bring up an FTP or Telnet server on those ports, for example. Large environments can benefit from internal, logical segmentation by realms of security, and in these cases some of the issues faced when dealing with the public network can be applied internally.

As always, in dealing with security issues, you should make sure that you keep up on all new security announcements, patches, and bug fixes. Besides remaining in touch with your vendors, a number of organizations, not necessarily DNS focused, issue alerts and advisories. Two of these, CERT and SANS (`www.cert.org` and `www.sans.org`), are excellent, vendor-neutral sources of timely information.

Spoofing Name Queries

DNS spoofing—the process by which hackers penetrate the system and alter the host Internet Protocol (IP) mappings to point to bogus servers—is possible, but fairly difficult to accomplish. The biggest issue with an attack on the DNS server is the integrity of the zone information, and the possible redirection of requests to alternative hosts. The bright side is that this sort of attack is fairly easy to detect and correct.

nslookup, ping, and tracert (traceroute) can identify machines that have been altered (especially to an IP address that does not belong to the site or domain). If there seems to be a problem, query other authoritative servers and check the results. If the attack happened some time ago, the information may be cached around the Net, but will expire allowing return to normal operation. If you are unsure whether your server is showing bad information, examine its answers using nslookup with iterative queries. To determine whether the corrupt data is from cache or has been committed to the zone data, you can examine both within the DNS management console using the Advanced mode, or you can use DNSCMD.EXE. If the cache is the problem, you can flush the server's cache, again through either tool. You can stop and restart a zone or the server, forcing it to read the zone information from its store. You should only do something after you have diagnosed the point of the corruption.

Of course, these are the situations that should not happen. If they do, they need to be corrected immediately. Putting a form of monitoring in place, especially for large zones, is nontrivial. If it is possible to have early detection, however, the trail of attack is fresh and the chances of preventing future attack increases. Monitoring can be more successfully accomplished, in some cases, by watching for abnormal measures of the server performance and its networking more easily than by watching for zone data corruption or bad answers. Do not overlook that DNSCMD.EXE allows for scripted transfer of zone data, at which point it could be periodically compared to a standard defined dataset.

The difficulty lies in determining how and where the hacker gained access to the system to make changes in the first place. Intrusion detection packages and auditing can aid in tracking down a suspected hacker. A number of other books and resources that deal specifically with these topics are available.

The benefit to a hacker manipulating zones is that the hacker can use redirections to point users to machines under his/her own control. The hacker can then use this setup to capture information from unsuspecting users regarding logons or mail accounts, and even gain access to other hosts on the remote network. When a hacker can pose a false machine as an authoritative server for a domain, he pollutes the cache for other name servers on the Internet by intercepting and answering queries. Remember that Windows 2000 DNS Server can be configured to secure its cache, as some measure of protection against this.

One way that servers in your environment can reduce the risks from this sort of attack is to use reverse lookups as validation. If a host is impersonating another server, the reverse lookup can be used to make sure that the IP address maps back to the same host name. This is actually done by some FTP and HTTP servers before they allow downloads or connections. To assist using this for your environment, your DNS service must have reverse lookup zone(s) configured.

The best policy for setting up a name server is to try to make it as secure as possible. Don't use a machine that has a lot of user logon activity or provides other interactive services. Many security experts suggest a single service run on a single machine if the traffic levels warrant it. Some go so far as to suggest all remote access either be removed or tightly controlled with only encrypted access via encrypted private networking or some other mechanism of this sort for allowed access.

Another concern is a hacker performing a zone transfer from your name server to get addresses. The best way to reduce the risk of transferring data to any illegitimate secondary server is to list the legitimate DNS servers in the DNS management console under the Zone Transfers tab. Select the Allow Zone Transfers as shown in Figure 10.1, and then select the Only to the Following Servers item and add the servers by IP. You would then use the Notify tab to configure use of the Notify option to servers that support it (see Figure 11.8). This is a good idea even in environments where you don't consider this information to be at risk. It provides a performance efficiency, and protects even in the internal network where there can be the disgruntled and the transient disreputable consultant. It is truly too bad that security so often entails looking at the worst side of people, or rather, entails needing to assume its possibility.

Denial of Service

Denial of service attacks are sometimes used in spoofing efforts, and sometimes just out of maliciousness. The method is to exploit known problems with a server's Transmission Control Protocol/Internet Protocol (TCP/IP) stack implementation, or even to just exploit a machine's limited capacity. By sending malformed, specially formed, or just floods of packets, a server is rendered unresponsive, or is crashed entirely. This then leaves the opening for spoofing through substitution if routers or a machine on the appropriate subnet have been compromised.

The most obvious prevention is maintenance, and use of only the minimum complement of services. With DNS servers, there are some specific actions that in some cases can be used. When there is no reason not to, make the DNS service refuse

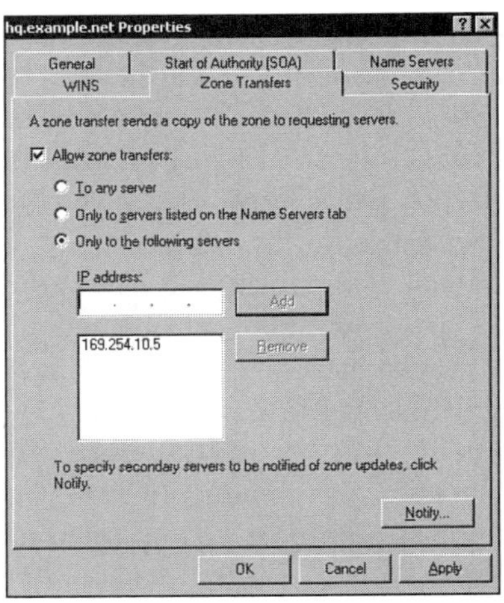

Figure 10.1 Controlling zone transfers to defined machines only.

recursive queries (see Chapter 11, "Configuring Windows DNS Servers"), as can usually be done with your DNS servers used to provide the public namespace. This not only extends the capacity of the machine, but also limits the paths in the DNS server code that are used. Denial of service attacks that leverage knowledge of the operating system and level of services installed are not easy to detect when they require only one or a few specially formed packets. If the signatures of these attacks were known for monitoring, the holes would be plugged. Flood-based attack, on the other hand, has a distinctive signature.

Other things related to DNS servers to remember here are that the primary does not need to be in the public space to provide presence, and is better placed internally or in the DMZ. Monitoring can easily be set up which periodically checks that the DNS services are healthy. Pinging a machine is of course not a valid test for continuity of DNS services. A capability like that available in the Monitoring tab of the DNS server's properties pages is used, except that it needs to be able to target specific remote servers, through the public interfaces, and then issue alerts as needed.

Using DNS with Firewalls

When using DNS with or through firewalls, you must consider two things: the security policies of the site or organization, and the type of firewall that is going to be used. You must examine the security policies to determine what traffic will be allowed to go through the firewall. Also, the type of firewall being used will determine how data is handled between the private network, the DMZ, and the Internet.

Firewalls can have several capabilities, including packet filtering and proxying, with caveats concerning stateful inspection. *Stateful inspection* is a mechanism that examines information on packets going in and out of the firewall to determine the state of a session. The state is used by the inspection agent to determine whether packets should be allowed through the firewall.

Combinations of authentication, encryption, and high levels of auditing give you several powerful tools. Many firewall solutions provide DNS support directly, or have templates for easily setting up a configuration to pass, or proxy name service requests from one side to another. For the administrator who has to design the security policy for a site, at least two schools of thought apply:

- Make everything accessible and be sure that there are good backups.
- Restrict access to every machine, and allow only that traffic into your network that is absolutely necessary.

In the first scenario, a site may not even use basic filters on the router that acts as their gateway to the Internet. In the second situation, only certain ports and protocols are allowed, and then, for only a few specifically named machines, and these machines would be further protected from each other on the same network. The restriction by specifying permitted machines is a vital feature.

Protecting machines from each other necessitates, at a minimum, that you set up separate administrator accounts with different passwords on each. The goal is to make the machines as independent as possible so that a hacker who has managed to gain access to one machine cannot use its accounts to also access other systems in the DMZ. By analogy, this is like separating airplanes and volatile fuels on a military airfield to minimize the damage caused when any one target is destroyed. Using separate accounts makes it much harder to exploit many machines at once like dominos. The trust relationships between these machines should be severely limited as well, if not totally removed. This means that the perimeter would reside outside of the Active Directory forest, which in turn limits its friendliness to valid users. Remember that a trusting machine, if compromised, may be used to examine the group and account structure of the trusted domain.

DNS can be handled in as many different ways as firewalls can be configured. The key thing to remember is that an authoritative name server must be reachable for the outside world to resolve any public hosts at the local site, and external name servers must be reachable (through some mechanism, such as forwarders and proxies) by internal hosts for lookups on other domains.

The best protection for the name server is to make sure that you back up the zone and configuration information regularly and maintain the level of the code base. You should also ensure that this information is accessible in the event that the files need to be recovered. The concept of completely hiding a domain from the outside world is certainly good protection, but in itself offers little to the users inside the network who want to reach the outside world.

One method of backing up the zone information is to make a specific backup DNS server that is listed as a valid secondary on the primary for every zone the primary has and snapshotting that secondary to get domains. You would typically use this method on a high-load primary server to reduce the time needed to back it up. Also, with some UNIX solutions, this technique enables you to repopulate the zones from the secondary without having to manually move files and such.

You can set up a domain such that the primary name server is kept inside the firewall (where it is safe) and a secondary is put outside to handle lookups by external hosts. This is a good solution if the administrator doesn't mind letting the outside world see the entire domain. It is a rare administrator who wants to expose his entire domain to the Internet. Then there is the concept of the split-brain DNS, with two versions of a domain—one for public consumption and the other for the organization's internal use. This can be taken one step further and you can actually run two sets of DNS servers, with public consumption secondaries on the exposed network. Remember to go over the configuration of these secondaries carefully to identify any removable risk factors, such as by disabling Telnet, or their capability to master zone transfers.

In most organizations today, the users of hosts in the domain need Internet access for the Web and email, at the very minimum. In these situations, the idea of totally hiding a domain is not a viable solution. If security is needed, and the administrator wants to limit what the outside world sees of the domain, a split-brain DNS, or some other method of limiting the hosts that are published to the world, is probably the best solution. Chapter 9, "Designing Your DNS Services," has a description and drawing depicting a split-brain setup.

A traditional split-brain DNS uses two primary servers: one inside the firewall and the other outside. The external primary name server that resides outside the firewall will be furnished with a minimum number of entries for its zone files, typically the MX records for the domain, WWW and FTP hosts, and, depending on the type of firewall, some entries may be used for reverse lookups by outside hosts to sessions established from inside the firewall.

Some firewalls use address translation to reassign a predetermined list of IP addresses. For these IP addresses to be useful for certain transactions, a reverse lookup that maps to a valid host name may be required. These host names would be handled by the external primary name server, because there could be no resolution by the internal name server. The internal primary DNS server would be populated with the entries for every host in the domain (including the external hosts). The internal DNS would also be set up to forward to external DNS services, as well as slave from them for external names. The external forwarders could be your external public presence DNS servers, or separate servers specifically provided to be your forwarders, all depending on capacity, budget, and extent of your security concerns and policies.

This will result in internal name services that, when queried by a client resolver for information that they cannot answer, forward the query to the external name server. Because the internal name server is configured to slave from the external, the internal name server will not attempt to resolve the query itself, but must wait for the external server to provide an answer. The firewall, configured to allow name server queries to be passed only between these hosts, would then prevent queries from outside hosts from reaching the internal name server. Whether the internal forwarding machine is purely a caching-only slave or contains internal zone data is a consideration. If it has no internal information, no clients, but only your other DNS servers, should use it directly. If it has internal zone data, it should have all internal zone data to slave only for Internet names. The forwarding machine will forward all queries for which it cannot provide an authoritative answer, even when it could provide a direct referral to another internal DNS server. For this reason, it should be provided with complete zone data, which also leads to a desire to place it in a more protected placement. Again, budget, network size and load, and degree of concern will define your alternatives. Remember that forwarders function as choke-points as well as bottlenecks in a design.

Because the internal and external name servers use different zone data, no zone transfers need to go through the firewall. The difficulty with this arrangement is that the administrator has to maintain two separate sets of zone files, not to mention the additional maintenance that's needed if there are also additional, secondary servers on each side of the firewall. This also presents the possibility of human error and name conflicts from confusing names, because internal and external domains appear the same. Using distinct internal and external domain names is a minor variation that can resolve this, but that also places limits on the future evolution of namespaces.

The key steps to remember when setting up a DNS server to work through a firewall are as follows:

1. Build primary internal namespace DNS and secondaries.
2. Build primary external namespace DNS and secondaries.
3. Decide which hosts to publish in zones.
4. Decide how internal clients will resolve external names and configure the internal services to provide this.
5. Register the external hosts with the InterNIC (because these are the ones that will be "seen").
6. Allow name service through the firewall for designated hosts only.
7. Test the design and make sure that it works as expected.

The last step should be obvious, but it's always wise to make sure that the design works (especially from an external site) to confirm that only the information that the administrator wants published is available. Also, testing from the inside is required to make sure that the firewall is properly configured and external domains are resolvable by users inside the firewall. Scaling resolution of external domains to the needed capacity and reliability may require providing parallel paths.

One nice setup for DNS through firewalls is to have a primary for the external namespace inside the firewall or in the DMZ and a secondary outside it. As far as the world is concerned, the outside server can be primary, because the distinction is only relevant when you are considering who has the master zone files. You can perform all maintenance on the internal server, and the external will update the zones as required. This may require running three servers, but it is definitely more secure than allowing access from the outside to the primary. Also, if the zones become corrupted, you still maintain control of the primary zone internally. Make sure that if you are going to use this technique you open the firewall for only the secondary-to-primary communications (and the converse of course). Some experts also maintain that you should limit that communication to an unused high port number instead of using the standard DNS port 53 for an additional contribution to security. This has only touched on some DNS design alternatives and some firewall product characteristics. This is a very large topic and additional resources having direct application to the firewall type and capabilities in use should be consulted.

Service Advertisement

The Windows community has for some time recognized and accepted that it is a good precaution to filter the NetBIOS ports in and out of a network campus. The underlying concern is very similar to the reason most DNS administrators see no need for everyone to be able to receive zone transfers. Knowledge is power, or at least in this case, it is a map of where one might get power. The information available from a DNS zone file has previously qualitatively differed from that available from a WINS database. Both provide a pretty good mapping of the machines existing at a site, and something of their organization and structure. But NetBIOS names can carry information about what types of services are running on different machines, which are domain controllers, which host Web services, which host databases, and so on. This is even more "power" to place into just anyone's hands.

With the introduction of the use of SRV records, the DNS data is now equal to, if not advanced beyond, NetBIOS in the capability to widely advertise services by location on their hosts. This is how many aspects of Windows 2000 function, with aid from the Domain Locator Service (which understands the Windows 2000 SRV record structuring).

SRV record usage is not inherently bad, nor is use of the NetBIOS namespace. The difficulty is that the advertisement puts the burden on systems administrators to harden their machines. Security is achieved through additive efforts. Sometimes it is enhanced by obscuring things which otherwise need not be widely known. Although hiding is no real security, hardening is difficult. The bottom line is that if the SRV record structure does not need to be public, do not make it so. This leads to the dual name and split-brain designs. Just because the external world has been walled off, however, the internal network is still alive with this information.

Not related directly to DNS, but on the subject of namespaces, the capability of LDAP utilities to gather much information about the configuration of a Windows machine and its services, groups, accounts, and so on, whether it is an upgraded NT 4.0 or a Windows 2000 machine, should not be overlooked. The Active Directory then adds its own level on to this with its directory services, which by design are intended to assist a qualified client in discovering and so accessing resources. Here again, this accessibility is not bad in itself. It all comes down to guarding what is a "qualified client." And the approaches range from hardening through hiding, with all combinations in between.

Dynamic DNS (DDNS)

Providing for security is always an exercise in balancing the capabilities provided with the degree of lockdown desired. The dynamic update capability in DNS presents an unprecedented opportunity for name hijacking, which in turn can enable spoofing and man-in-the-middle, as well as plain malicious disruption attacks. This is not how it has to be, just how it can be. As industry DNS providers enable this technology, and the underlying key exchange support comes into place, using this technology in the public namespace will become increasingly safe. One should know the limits of the security features available in the Windows 2000 implementation of dynamic update, and the limits of the provided client relative to using differing security methods. The discussion in Chapter 7, "Dynamic DNS and the Active Directory," dealing with the configurations available in the initial release of Windows 2000 should be consulted. For most environments, there is no need for the dynamic update capability in the publicly published namespace. If your deployment intends to leverage directory-enabled applications and services to the public network, you need to examine the alternatives, using dynamic update or not and for securing it when used, very fully and relative to the then current developments.

For most purposes, when providing public access points dynamic update capability is wholly unneeded. Alternatives for extranet capabilities with private networking technologies, including over the open network, can enable extending Active Directory technologies outside of the walled environment and should be explored. What has gone unsaid, but is implied here is that until the strategies for locking down dynamic update to the degree desired while yet enabling its use and benefits, this technology is best treated as a "for-internal-consumption-only" item, and then when one has a trusted user base.

In the Windows 2000 implementation at release, dynamic DNS updates cannot be secured unless the zone data is integrated into the Active Directory. Windows clients off-the-shelf cannot issue secure update requests to Request for Comment (RFC)-compliant non-Microsoft DNS servers. When using secured updates with the Windows 2000 DNS Server, the defaults allow a new record to be created by any member of the Authenticated Users group. After having been created, the creating account becomes the owner, and it alone can change or delete the record, with the exception of administrative and system privilege. There is a specially defined group, the DnsUpdateProxy group, which has different behavior. When a DNS record is created by a machine that is a member of this group, the record does not become owned by the creating account, but instead by the first account that modifies or refreshes the record. Use of the Windows 2000 security mechanisms as defined for any Active Directory object can modify these default behaviors, but the defaults are a reasonable compromise between crippling, or clogging, the dynamic update process and securing it.

Mail Security: SMTP, POP, IMAP, and Exchange

The security advisories are full of warnings about exploits against Sendmail™, Exchange, IMAP servers, and so on. How mail is handled by a domain can largely depend on the setup of the name servers and firewalls. In general, POP and IMAP services should be kept behind the firewall to protect the users' mail, directories, and especially passwords from external entities that could use this information to invade the site. Bear in mind that POP (unless it is APOP) sends passwords in the clear, so anyone capable of subverting a router between the user and the server can monitor this traffic and get usernames and passwords. It is best to use some sort of authenticating server process that does not send passwords as clear text.

It is actually best to relay mail to the main server from a server that sits outside the firewall. This enables you to trust a server that is outside the wall that you can get a feed from. You will probably want either a simple server outside or an exchange server.

If you really want to be careful, you can maintain a monitoring program to verify that nothing major has changed on the external server, and in the case that it has changed you should replicate it from sources/CD/some uncontaminated source.

You should not have to take any more than normal precautions with an Exchange server because it is like any mail server. You may want to monitor connections to port 25 if you are concerned about who is connecting to your server.

Generally speaking, you should use some host in the DMZ as a relay for both inbound and outbound mail. Using the relay for inbound mail, the actual mail spool can be placed on the inside of the firewall, which would be configured to allow mail connections from the DMZ host only. In the same manner, the relay would be used for outbound mail to hide the internal machines, and could include special rules for the addressing to have all outbound mail addressed just by the user@the.domain. This simplifies the ability of recipients to be able to respond to mail addressed to a domain, and helps protect the identity of the originating machine.

Of course, a display of the full headers will reveal the path that a mail message has traversed, but if the originating host is hidden behind a firewall and is not resolvable through the external DNS server for an organization, and then its passage in is guarded, this is not an issue. This can be overcome with remailing programs as well, if this is an issue. The best type of remailing program is a self-written one that is particular to your environment. You need to strip all headers before remailing the message, if you want to hide the originating source.

MX records on the internal name servers can be used to direct mail from internal hosts to the relay for any addresses that are not local. The relay, upon receiving the mail messages, would perform another lookup (using the external name servers) to send the mail on to its Internet destination. The relay would also be set up to forward any inbound mail for the domain to a specific host inside the firewall, which would then be responsible for distributing mail to internal users and subdomains via mail aliases. Again, MX records would be used for distribution to hosts inside the domain.

WWW Security

When it comes to the World Wide Web, just about everyone seems to have a Web site these days. The trick is to make the Web server secure and protect its content. The problem is that having a Web presence means hanging a machine out for everyone to see. (After all, if they can't see the machine, there's not much point in having a Web server on it, is there?) The exception to that rule is the intranet site targeted to the internal staff of an organization.

A number of products and technologies are available to help secure the information on your machines. The solution that has been around probably the longest is packet filtering. An administrator can protect the Web server by putting a filter in front of the machine that allows only Web traffic to hit the server, and nothing else. Blocking access to such things as Telnet, FTP, and mail from this machine will limit the types of attacks that can be made on it.

Proxies also can be valuable for protecting a Web site because the remote users never actually get to the real Web server. Remote user requests are intercepted by the proxy servers, which then query the Web server. The proxy servers then pass the information back to the remote user requesting the data.

A number of redirection schemes can also be employed, in which the Web server's name resolves to a virtual IP through DNS. When HTTP requests come to the virtual IP, the requests can be redirected to the actual server. In this situation, the remote user does get the information from the actual Web server, but the real IP address of the Web server is hidden from the requestor. These redirection schemes can also provide a great deal of flexibility for load balancing and high-availability solutions.

DNS is often called on to load balance or at least randomize the traffic to a farm, either of Web servers or their proxies. A number of difficulties are encountered when more stateful service is to be delivered, and more direct access to component and data services is needed. These tend to lead away from the purely packet-filtering solutions, but all do need coordination among the DNS, the Web farm, and the firewall administrators.

In combination with previously mentioned DNS attacks, you can be subject to a "man-in-the-middle" attack. If a hacker can redirect all requests for a specific Web address to his own machine and has a modified server on his machine, the hacker can use his machine to service the requests your Web clients' are making and monitor everything that is done with the site. This is one of the reasons that having a secure server that is not subject to DNS attacks is important.

FTP Security

FTP servers have their own vulnerabilities, but one way to help secure the FTP server is through the use of reverse lookups. Many FTP servers log connections made by remote hosts, capturing the host name and IP address. Reverse lookups are used to verify that the host name and IP address used to establish the connection match. Although this may not seem like much in terms of security, the logs at least indicate a true IP address and host name, should a break-in occur via the FTP server. Many HTTP servers, by the way, have their logs mined for information discovered by reverse lookup also.

The purpose of the reverse lookup is to make sure that the IP address and the host name match either way. If the host name and IP address do not match, the connection is refused by the FTP server when the download is attempted. Along with the use of reverse lookups, filters can also be applied to prevent other types of traffic from reaching the FTP host. Securing even your friendly, in-house FTP servers in this way is well worth considering, and requires only the DNS support of the reverse resolution and a capable FTP server.

One mistake administrators too often make when setting up an anonymous FTP site is allowing anonymous users to write to directories. This can create vulnerability to problems such as hackers attempting to fill a file system and create instability in the system, or generating numerous logon requests that can lead to high levels of CPU and memory utilization. This sort of attack can create a denial of service for both the server and the network segment to which the server is attached.

Having anonymous FTP is very useful and, in some situations, a necessity; however, putting limits on the number of connections that the FTP server will allow and disallowing anonymous writes can prevent a lot of hardship for the administrator. Anonymous FTP also presents the problem of passwords passing in clear, readable text that anyone with a network-traffic snooping or tracing tool can capture.

One major point you may want to consider is that you should run the FTP server on a totally separate box in the DMZ. Also make sure that your passwords for the box are *not* the same as passwords on other machines on the network. This way if a password is compromised, it will only affect the FTP server and not the rest of the machines on the network. The box, as any other in the DMZ, should have no, or as little as possible, trust relationship with your network host environment.

Summary

This chapter did not cover all the security issues you'll consider when setting up a network connected to the Internet. It only describes some of those most closely related to DNS services. The following are a few good books on security that you can consult to help you establish a secure site for DNS and other services:

- *Firewalls Complete*, Marcus Goncalves, McGraw-Hill. ISBN: 0-0702-4645-9.
- *Windows NT Security: A Practical Guide to Security Windows NT Servers and Workstations*, Charles B. Rutstein, McGraw-Hill. ISBN: 0-0705-7833-8.
- *Internet Firewalls and Network Security*, Karanjit S. Siyan and Chris Hare, New Riders Publishing. ISBN: 1-5620-5437-6.
- *Internet Security: Professional Reference, Second Edition*, Derek Atkins, et al. Tom Sheldon, Tim Petro, Joel Snyder, Chris Hare, New Riders Publishing. ISBN: 1-5620-5760-X.
- *Maximum Security: A Hacker's Guide to Protecting your Internet Site and Network*, Anonymous (an experienced hacker), Sams Publishing. ISBN: 0-6723-1341-3.
- *NT Network Security*, Matthew Strebe, Charles Perkins, and Michael G. Moncur, Sybex. ISBN: 0-7821-2006-7.
- *Windows NT Security Guide*, Stephen A. Sutton, Addison-Wesley. ISBN: 0-201-41969-6.
- *Windows NT Security Handbook*, Tom Sheldon, Osborne McGraw-Hill. ISBN: 0-07-882240-8.

11

Configuring Windows DNS Servers

THIS CHAPTER COVERS INSTALLING AND CONFIGURING the Windows 2000 DNS server. Some discussion is provided on when and why different features should or would be used, but the focus is on getting to know the server with the assumption that the design and planning has taken place prior to use.

This chapter reviews the following:

- **Before You Begin.** Provides a brief reminder of the preparation steps that make setting up DNS services much more direct.
- **Installing the Windows DNS Server.** Covers the steps required to minimally set up DNS in Windows 2000.
- **DNS Server Configuration.** Looks at server properties.
- **Zone, Subdomain, and Manual Resource Record (RR) Creation.** Briefly covers how to populate your local server.
- **Active Directory Integration.** Looks at the settings and effects of using Active Directory storage.
- **Types of Servers.** Looks at configuring the server in relation to other servers.
- **Zone Cleanliness.** Briefly discusses scavenging.
- **Support Features.** Points out some of the handles provided for managing and understanding server operations.

This chapter is designed to augment and build on the information presented to you in the previous chapters. The DNS is by far the most popularly used namespace management service. DNS is placed into a more significant role by Windows 2000 than, perhaps, it has ever been called on to fill, certainly more so than in any prior Windows version.

Early on, one of the main reasons for the DNS service was just to make it simpler for a user or an administrator to be able to identify his system individually. Back when DNS first came into play, it was because the old method (a single HOST.TXT file) was becoming too large, and it was getting more difficult to find names for machines, and more inefficient. Before DNS, the HOST.TXT file method had a flat namespace and therefore could only have one host with a particular name, and quickly the popular names were being taken.

Imagine that you have 300 unnamed machines on several different subnets and you'll quickly understand why name services make sense. It would be like remembering three hundred phone numbers without any address book. Today many services fully expect and in some cases demand a name; therefore, it is only logical that there is a namespace management tool.

Imagine that you have 300 sophisticated client systems in a distributed security, client/server environment, each of which is regularly locating and accessing resources. Imagine resources that come and go, advertising their presence while available, and taking down the shingle when not. This begins to show how central DNS service is to the new Windows architecture.

Before You Begin

By this time you should have a very strong understanding of your network and your goals for your network. You should also have your Active Directory structure mapped out both logically by namespace boundaries, and physically by server placement and zone assignments to those servers. Configuring the Microsoft DNS service is reasonably straightforward. Installation is so easy it is deceptive. But don't be fooled. If you fail to design or configure your use of the service correctly, you'll be forced to return and do it over again if you are lucky, else patch over the mistakes if not.

You should know quite a bit about not only your network and your goals, but also such things as your connectivity and how that will impact you. The reasons are infinitely large, but some of them include the use of firewalls, special bridged and/or routed networks, remote site links, and client load and access patterns. Other areas that you need to be clear on by this time should include whether you use the Active Directory and where, whether dynamic DNS will be used, and how you will configure both.

This chapter has been written for those individuals who have prepared, who have a clear plan. This chapter covers setting up the Windows 2000 DNS in an environment of unrestricted network access, whether that means having available full connectivity to the Internet or to the parts of your internal site. The considerations for planning and design, for protection of your namespace, and others that come into play have been treated in Chapters 7, "Dynamic DNS and the Active Directory," 9, "Designing Your DNS Services," and 10, "Security Issues." Your biggest challenge will be, or rather has been, planning appropriately your domain in terms of delegation, or the lack thereof, and server and zone placement. For this exercise, you should have completely mapped out somewhere other than your brain roughly where every server and client will reside on your network.

As for installing DNS, now is the time to do it.

Installing the Windows DNS Server

If anything in Windows 2000 has been made into a mindless experience, it is installation of networking services of the different sorts. It has been made so simple, that one can be lulled into believing that running these services is as simple. Although not hard, running the installed result takes a good understanding of what is installed, as well as a well-configured installation.

The prerequisites are similar to those for installing most service software. You need to have Windows 2000 Server installed with the Transmission Control Protocol/Internet Protocol (TCP/IP) protocol configured. If the server is not yet using a statically assigned Internet Protocol (IP) address, this should be done. The name used for the host should be stable; previously after advertising to clients, changing this or the IP address can be less than convenient and simple. You need to log on with administrative privileges; other than that, however, there is little else to consider. The software itself is small, and you have already selected the server. Your choice should prefer large amounts of memory, because DNS will try to cache its database for performance, taking advantage of the RAM you can give it. This scales with zone size of course, as does the storage space you will need on the boot partition; or if Active Directory storage is to be used, wherever you have NTDS.DIT stored.

Installation Procedure

The installation process, as said previously, is very similar to other networking services, and the effort is actually in the post-install configuration. Figure 11.1 shows the Network Components configuration dialog box, where a simple check box controls installation of DNS. You can use the Configure Your Server Wizard, or follow these few required steps:

> **DNS Server Service a Must**
>
> Any computer running a DNS Server service *must* have a statically assigned IP address. The name and address used for the machine should be chosen so that there will be only rare need for these to be changed, if at all.

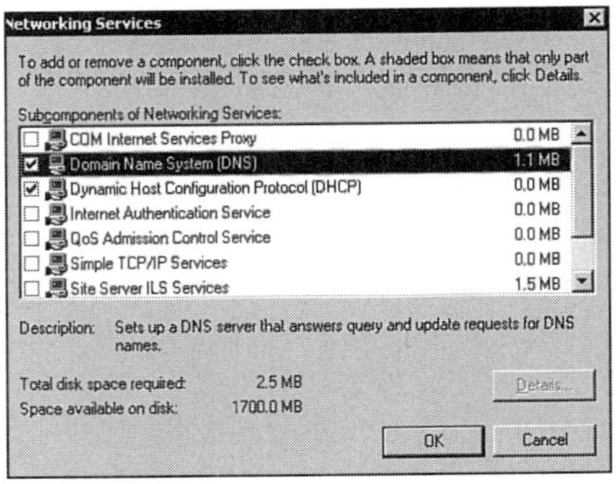

Figure 11.1 Selecting DNS in the Networking Components dialog box.

1. Open the Control Panel.
2. Start the Add/Remove Programs applet.
3. Use the Add/Remove Windows Components icon on the left to start the Windows Component Wizard.
4. Scroll to and select Networking Services.
5. Use the Details button to get to the list of Networking Services.
6. Scroll down and check the box beside Domain Name System (DNS).
7. At this point, just finish the execution of the Windows Component Wizard using the Next and/or Finish buttons as needed based on whatever other options may have been selected while in the wizard.

As with so many things in Windows 2000, you can navigate the interface in a number of ways. In this case, in place of the preceding steps 1 through 3, a quick alternative is as follows:

1. Use the context menu (right-click) of My Network Places and select Properties. This opens an Explorer window with the focus set on Network and Dial-up Connection.
2. In the main menu bar, expand the Advanced drop-down menu and select Optional Networking Components.

With DNS installed, the work is ready to begin. This of course means your work. Only if you are installing a caching-only server is your work nearly complete.

So, what just happened? Well, of course, DNS Server was installed and should now be running. But a number of other things also happened. You received a new selection on the Start menu, and entries in a couple of Microsoft management console snap-ins. You now have a subdirectory structure at %windir%\system32\dns, which is the default file storage location used by DNS Server. And, you now have information for

DNS Server stored at HKLM\System\CurrentControlSet\Services\DNS in the Registry. Finally, some new counter support was loaded for the System Monitor, and probably a number of other adjustments were made to your system behind the scenes.

DNS Server Management Console

First, you need to get access to the main tool, the DNS Server management console. You can find this on the Start menu in the Administrative Tool folder. Just look for the DNS selection. You can start this from the Run box or at the command line by using **"dnsmgmt.msc"**. This tool is your home for most DNS administration, although you should not overlook DNSCMD.EXE for scripted management (see Chapters 12, "Troubleshooting Tools and Utilities," and 13, "Best Practices and Maintenance Tasks").

In the management console, you can manage multiple DNS servers, whether one local and the rest remote, or all remote. The installation of the Windows 2000 administrative tools at your workstation (oops, at your professional workstation) will enable you to manage these services without being at the server. This can be done by locating ADMINPAK.MSI either on a Windows 2000 Server version CD in .\i386 or in %windir%\system32 of an installed server, and then installing it on the management machine.

To register a DNS server for management, first click on the topmost node named DNS. Then use either the context menu of that node or the Action menu, and select Connect to Computer. You may find the experience in the management console a little erratic at first. Notice that actions are sensitive to the focus of the tool. You very often need to first click a node, causing it to expand in the right, or details, pane and then you will have menu options adjusted for the new focus.

With the DNS management console open, select the View menu. Within this View menu, you may want to adjust the Custom options, but you likely should click on Advanced to enable the extended display features. This Advanced View mode also enables you to examine the cached records in the newly visible node named Cached Lookups.

Two of the more popular ways to access the DNS management interface are through the use of custom consoles, and from within the Computer Management console. You must create the first. To access the second, either use the context menu of My Computer and select Manage or use Run to fire off **compmgmt.msc**. When the console opens, DNS is found under the Services and Applications node. This management console has the convenience of collecting Event log access and related services, such as DHCP, WINS, and DNS into a single interface.

Before you feel at home, you should take a look around in the management interface. We are about to take a tour of the features for DNS, but first would like to bring a few switches and commands to your attention. Take a look at Figure 11.2; it shows the context menu of the server node.

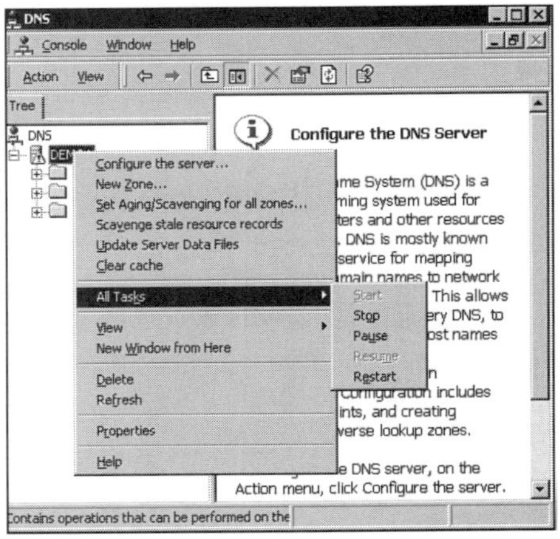

Figure 11.2 DNS server menu for a server node.

The All Tasks option has been extended out to show the ability to Stop, Start, Pause, and Resume the server. In the main list, the Clear Cache option provides the ability to clear the DNS caching resolver's cache. Because the Windows 2000 DNS Server implements the NCACHE specification, caching negative responses, being able to flush the cache might be needed a little more often, particularly in predeployment test environments. Also on this menu is the Update Server Data Files option that provides the ability to force the configuration and zone data to persistent storage so that the in-memory version is synchronized with the stored version. The two options relating to scavenging (Set Aging/Scavenging for All Zones, and, Scavenge Stale Resource Records) should give you a hint that the console intends to make supporting dynamic DNS (DDNS) as painless as possible. The option to Configure the Server fires up a wizard (discussed later), and the topic of zone creation hiding under the New Zone option will be first in line after we have a look at server configuration options.

DNS Server Configuration

Before going any further it is time to become familiar with the server-level controls available in Windows 2000 DNS Server. Figure 11.3 provides a view of the DNS Server Properties dialog box, with the Forwarders tab selected.

To get to the DNS Server Properties dialog box, follow these steps:

1. Open the DNS Server management interface.
2. Click the desired server from the server nodes listed under the top node named DNS.
3. Use either the Action menu or the context (highlight and right-click) menu of the selected server.
4. Select Properties.

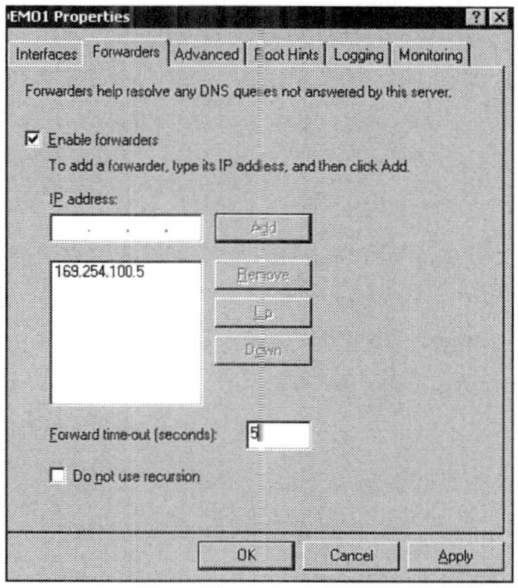

Figure 11.3 Forwarders tab in Windows 2000 DNS Server Properties dialog box.

We need to take a small tour of the options and settings available here. These are server-level settings, meaning that they affect the server overall. The zone- and resource record–level properties are discussed later.

DNS Server Properties: Interfaces

If you look at the Interfaces tab, you will see that you can control the network interfaces on which the DNS server will listen and respond. Your choices are either all interfaces, or a manually configured list of IP addresses. Because this is a server setting, this is telling you that the default behavior of the DNS server is to make all zones available on all permitted interfaces.

DNS server needs to be stopped and restarted for changes here to become effective. To do so, look under All Tasks in the server's context menu.

DNS Server Properties: Forwarders

With the Forwarders tab, you can enable the use of forwarders (refer back to Figure 11.3). You will recall that a *forwarder* is a DNS server to which the forwarding (the one you are managing) DNS server will send queries that it has received from client resolvers. The forwarding server first checks whether it can answer the query, and forwards those that it cannot. This is an easily overlooked aspect about using forwarders: Anything that cannot be answered completely is forwarded. When using forwarders to bridge from the internal to the public DNS namespaces, the forwarding machine should have authority for all internal zones to prevent queries for internal names from being forwarded to the external DNS server.

You configure forwarders by enabling the feature with the Enable Forwarders check box and then building a list of DNS servers by repeatedly entering an IP address and clicking Add. Notice that you can order the listed forwarders so that the best performing and most available DNS servers are listed at the top.

Your DNS server sends queries to the listed machines. The configuration option Forward Time-out (seconds) is setting how long your DNS server waits for a response before it attempts other means to satisfy the client query.

At the bottom, when forwarders are enabled, there is a Do Not Use Recursion selection. Notice that this option is mutually exclusive with the Forward Time-out. This option needs some explanation. If Do Not Use Recursion is selected, your DNS server is a slave to the forwarders. It is not allowed to initiate its own attempts to recursively resolve a query, but is restricted to the services of the forwarders. This option might seem a little misnamed, as one could wonder, what about using iterative queries starting with the root servers in the root hints? Maybe it should have been Do Not Initiate Resolution. Do Not Use Recursion makes your DNS server a forwarding-only slave to the forwarders you have specified.

DNS Server Properties: Advanced

Figure 11.4 shows the DNS Server Advanced Properties tab. Although we are not spending the space on shots of all these configuration options, there is a lot going on here.

If you compare Figure 11.3 with Figure 11.4, you will notice an extra tab named Security. Figure 11.3 shows from a member server; Figure 11.4 shows a DNS server on a domain controller for a domain and configured to use the Active Directory for zone data storage.

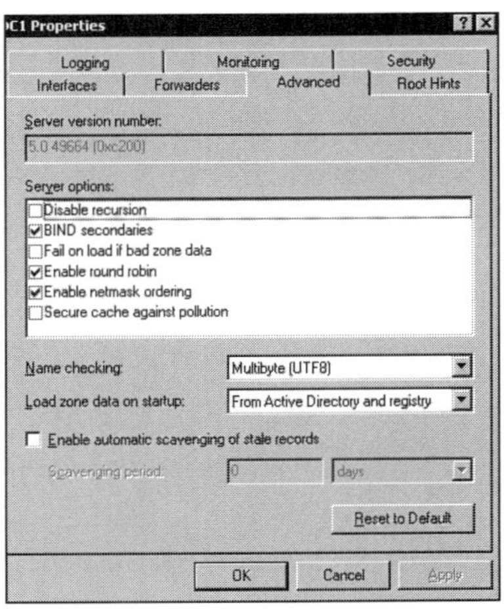

Figure 11.4 Advanced tab in Windows 2000 DNS Server Properties dialog box.

Name Checking

The Name Checking drop box on the Advanced tab controls the algorithm used to parse labels in DNS names for validity. The setting Strict RFC (ANSI) forces names to be fully Request for Comment (RFC) compliant. The default is Multibyte (UTF-8), which is an evolving option for internationalization support (see Appendix B, "RFCs Related to DNS," for references). The other two options, Non RFC (ANSI) and All Names, provide for looser name checking, and differ in that the last shuts off checking and the former requires only that labels be composed from the ANSI character set. For complete interoperation with the worldwide DNS, you should use Strict RFC (ANSI).

Configuration and Zone File Storage

Possibly the first thing that should be pointed out is the ability to configure how the server will Load Zone Data on Startup. Three choices are available: From File, From Registry, or From Active Directory and Registry.

This is the place where Active Directory integration of DNS is configured. It does a lot, but it is a simple switch. As my reviewer so accurately phrased it, this is "A simple change with many consequences." Because Chapter 7, "Dynamic DNS and the Active Directory," is devoted to examining the most significant of these consequences, the discussion here is restricted to DNS server configuration.

When From File is selected, the boot file stored at %windir%\system32\dns is used to define the zones loaded. It does not seem possible to change the storage location; use of the directory directive in the boot file is ignored, and use of full paths for zone files also leads to no joy. Presently, no documented Registry key information has been found that allows relocating this storage.

When From Registry is selected, the zones loaded are as defined in the Registry key but the zone data is still in the zone files as used for the From File option, provided the filenames have not been changed in the Registry keys for the zones. It is only with Active Directory storage that these zone files cease being used.

When switching from file to Registry, the existing boot file is copied to a subdirectory (.\backup) that will be created if needed. When switching back to file storage, a new boot file is created from the information in the Registry. When set to use file storage, the boot configuration information in the Registry and the boot file is kept synchronized.

When this setting is From Active Directory and Registry, the boot configuration information is stored in the Registry, and the zone data is in the Active Directory. Upon switching to this setting, zone data is transferred into storage as Active Directory objects, and is accessible through Lightweight Directory Access Protocol (LDAP) tools, including being present in the Users and Computers Active Directory console, **"dsa.msc"**, for Read access. On making this change, the boot file is again moved to .\backup and a BOOT.TXT file is left with a message to let you know this.

Table 11.1 summarizes the storage locations used under the different settings.

Table 11.1 **DNS Configuration and Zone Data Storage**

Option	Configuration	Zone Data
From File	Text file and Registry	Text file
From Registry	Registry	Text file
Active Directory	Registry	Active Directory

While on the topic of files, it would be good to make sure that using the Update Server Data Files option is not overlooked. Before editing a file, boot or zone, this option forces the DNS server to flush out any cached changes to the on-disk configuration. Figure 11.2 shows this option.

Disable Recursion

This Disable Recursion switch should not be confused with the similar setting on the Forwarders tab. Here, the switch controls the types of queries that will be accepted.

When Disable Recursion is enabled (checked), the DNS server acts like a root server, accepting only iterative queries. By default the Windows 2000 DNS Server installs configured to accept recursive queries.

Bind Secondaries

This switch does not affect how two Windows 2000 DNS Servers perform zone transfers between themselves. If a zone transfer is being made to a BIND server or a server not recognized, this forces the use of less-efficient but more fully compatible zone transfer. This switch was in NT 4 DNS Server. Make sure that this option is enabled if there will be transfers to BIND versions earlier than 4.9.4 so that these servers are not sent multiple RRs in a transfer message. By default this option is enabled.

Fail on Load If Bad Zone Data

This is a fairly self-describing option. If the zone file contains bad data, it fails to load when this option is enabled. When not enabled, which is the default, the DNS server merely logs error messages but loads the zone with some data ignored. It can prove useful to remember what you have this set to, before you start editing, in case you have made syntax errors during manual edit jobs!

While on the topic of files, be careful: As Figure 11.5 shows, editing zone and data files does not always lead to happy results. And again, do not forget to update files first and to be aware of whether dynamic updates are enabled.

Enable Round Robin

This switch allows the DNS server to cycle between the IP addresses on multiple A records for a host name. There is nothing intelligent, in a load-balancing sense, but this is a free load-distribution capability. DNS server tracks which IP was listed first in the response to the last query, and rotates the IP list in successive answers.

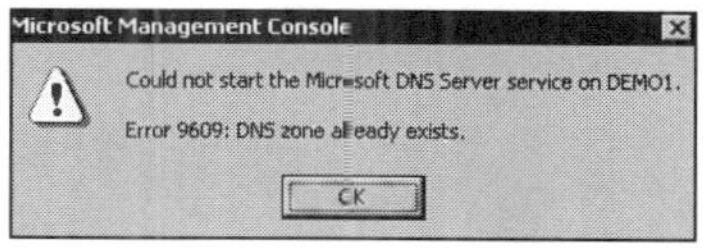

Figure 11.5 A friendly message letting you know your boot or zone file editing was less than perfect.

Enable Netmask Ordering

This is a feature of the Windows 2000 DNS Server that permits a server to prioritize the IP addresses in answers returned to queries. When a host has multiple A records, if the DNS server can determine that any of them are matches to the local subnet of the requesting client, those are placed first in the answer. This defaults to enabled.

Secure Cache Against Pollution

This feature controls how the Windows 2000 DNS Server handles adding referral replies to its cache. If this option is enabled, referrals are only added to cache if the referred-to host is of the same parent domain as that sought in the query. When querying a host in hq.example.net, for example, if the DNS server returned a referral to a name server in example.net this would be cached; if a referral to bad.hack.com is returned, however, it will not be cached, and so not used from cache in future resolutions. This is not enabled by default. Before enabling this, you should consider the value compared to the overhead of the extra lookups used in verification.

DNS Server Properties: Root Hints

This tab shows the current cache, or root hints, file. This was shown earlier in Figure 4.11, in which the default set of Internet root servers is being used. This is a quick place to check a DNS server's root hints configuration. Remember that manipulation of this file is a key to configuring internal namespace servers, and so troubleshooting can entail verifying that the correct root hints are in use.

DNS Server Properties: Logging

This tab enables you to select what will be logged to the debug log file. On a heavily used DNS server, you need to walk softly with the check marks. You can find the log file at %windir%\system32\dns\dns.log; it is an ASCII text file.

Table 11.2 provides a little more information on the choices. This could prove helpful, because there is none on the selection screen.

Table 11.2 **DNS Server Logging Options**

Option	Explanation
Query	Logs inbound queries
Notify	Logs inbound Notify option messages
Update	Logs inbound dynamic updates
Questions	Logs question part of inbound queries
Answers	Logs the answer part of messages sent in response to queries
Send	Tracks number of queries sent by the server
Receive	Tracks number of queries inbound to the server
UDP	Tracks number of inbound requests over User Datagram Protocol (UDP)
TCP	Tracks number of inbound requests over Transmission Control Protocol (TCP)
Full packets	Tracks number of full packets sent
Write through	Tracks number of packets written through to the zone

This logging capability, especially when combined with the other available tools, monitoring (System Monitor, that is), and event logging make for a powerful information resource. Hopefully you will rarely need to use this logging capability, beyond understanding your capacity planning requirements or some less-than-aboveboard attempts. When you do enable this logging, remember that this degrades the performance of a production server and also generates large amounts of file data rather quickly.

DNS Server Properties: Monitoring

This tab enables you to send a test recursive query to a remote DNS server, or to perform a simple test on a local system. This is done by just checking the desired test and clicking on the Test Now button. The Remote option is more interesting but still, even with recurrence scheduling, this does only verify that two servers are in touch and speaking the same language. You can also perform recurring tests at a defined interval.

DNS Server Properties: Security

This tab is only available with Active Directory integration enabled for at least one zone. The simpler form of the Security tab is shown in Figure 11.6 and is the familiar Security dialog box used to edit Access Control Lists (ACLs) throughout Windows 2000. It is looking at the security configuration of the MicrosoftDNS object in the Active Directory.

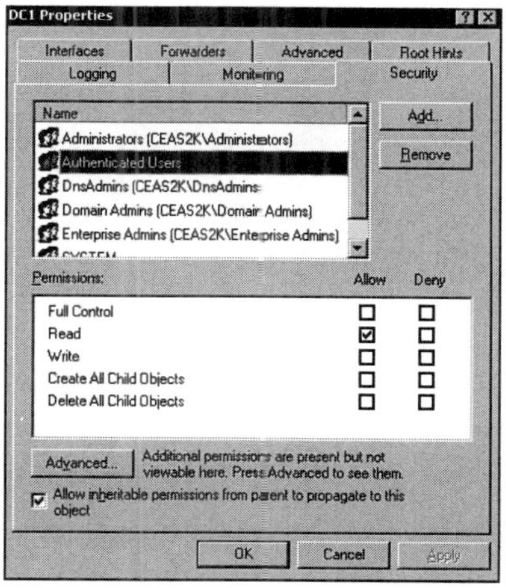

Figure 11.6 The Security Editor focused on the DNS server.

The highlighted entry for Authenticated Users shows that this pervasive group can read this container. Chapter 7 covers the security through the use of Active Directory integration in detail.

Zone, Subdomain, and Manual Resource Record Creation

To put your local server to use, at this point you have two options. If you are installing a caching-only server, and the root hints file for the Internet is desired, you are done. Just point clients at this machine. You may possibly want to define some forwarders, but it will work as it is. If your need is for a caching-only server for your internal namespace, adjust the root hints file and specify your forwarders (if any).

Creating Zones

More likely, you need to support a delegated part of the DNS namespace, internal or public. We will assume that you need a primary server for your test.example.net domain. Here is what you need to do, assuming you are just starting to configure the server and so need to first create a zone:

1. Open the DNS Server management interface.
2. Click the desired server node to give it focus.
3. Use either the Action menu or the context menu of the selected server and select New Zone to start the New Zone Wizard.

4. Click Next, and then tell the wizard that you are creating a standard primary zone. This can be Active Directory integrated later, but this way you can examine the zone files. Click Next.
5. Choose to create a forward lookup zone. Click Next.
6. Enter the name for the DNS domain. In real life, this is a name that you officially have rights to use, if you are connecting to the world. Click Next.
7. For the zone file, you have the option of using a name other than the suggested default (in this example, test.example.net.dns). Notice that you also are given the option to import using an existing zone file. Just accept the default, click Next, and then click Finish.

That should not have taken very long. If you expand the Forward Lookup Zone node, you will see your new zone. Creating secondary zones are just as easy, except that some extra information is collected, such as where to get the zone information.

1. Start the New Zone Wizard, as was done earlier.
2. Click Next, and then tell it you are creating a standard secondary zone. Click Next.
3. Choose to create a standard secondary zone. Click Next.
4. Enter the name for the DNS domain. Because this is a secondary zone, this will be the same as used by the primary. Click Next.
5. Either enter IP address(es) for the DNS servers that will be primary for transfers to this secondary zone; or if they are DNS servers configured in the DNS Server management console, browse to and select them. After you have entered all primaries, verify that their order is as desired.
6. Click Next, and then click Finish. The wizard does not allow for selection of a filename, which must be changed later if something other than the default is wanted.

Creating reverse lookup zones are equally painless, except that these are specified by a network's reversed IP address.

To create one, follow these steps:

1. Start the New Zone Wizard, as was done earlier.
2. Click Next, and then tell it you are creating a standard primary zone. Click Next.
3. Choose to create a reverse lookup zone. Click Next.
4. Enter the IP address as is done in naming a network. 10.10 would be using part of a Class A IP range, for example, because it is used in a 10.10.0.0/16 network. Notice that it generates a zone name for you. Click Next.
5. You again have the option of using another name for the file, but just click Next and then click Finish.

You now have a reverse lookup zone to handle IP addresses from 10.10.0.0 through 10.10.255.255 that should appear under the Reverse Lookup Zones node.

If you click either of the new zones so that the RRs are shown in the details pane, you will see the zones each have two records. There is an Start of Authority (SOA) and a Name Server (NS) record, both identifying your server. The SOA identifies as the responsible party the account you have been using.

If you look in the %windir%\system32\dns directory, you will see the new zone files. If you look in the Registry key HKLM\System\CurrentControlSet\Services\DNS\Zones, you will see entries for these zones, including ones providing the zone filenames. Finally, if you open the boot file in%windir%\system32\dns, you will see that it is a minimally configured NAMED.BOOT file, except that it has no directory directive.

Secondary zones differ a little, because the wizard asks that you provide the IP address(s) of the master DNS server(s). These machines are used to provide zone transfer data. Before creating a secondary, and populating it with a transfer, first delegate or at a minimum guarantee that the server hosting the new secondary will be allowed by its designated master(s)to pull the transfer. You might not want to formally delegate to the server if you want to keep the new secondary from being discovered by queries. As will be seen when looking at zone properties, Windows 2000 fully implements the Notify option and the IXFR incremental transfer. You will probably want to configure the Notify option for your secondary on the master. If the zone is enabled for dynamic update, the advantages of this are quite important.

Zones Transfers and Other Properties

Bring up the properties for your forward lookup zone, and you will see the Properties sheets shown in Figure 11.7. The two tabs titled SOA and Name Servers were shown and discussed earlier in Chapter 4, "Domain Information Details."

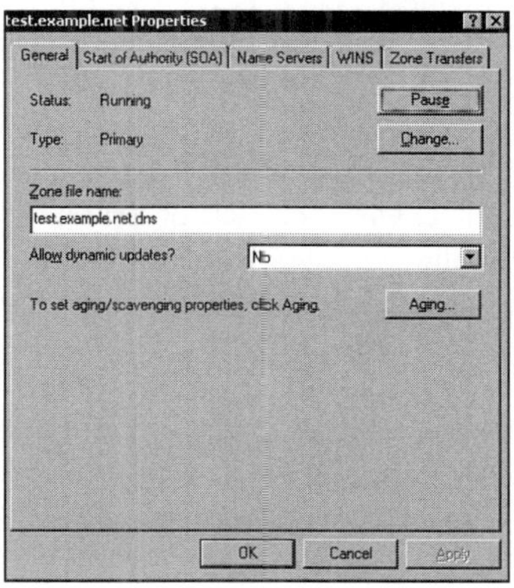

Figure 11.7 The General Forward Zone Properties dialog box.

The tab Windows Internet Naming Service (WINS) (and Windows Internet Naming Service Reverse [WINS-R] on reverse zones) was also covered in Chapter 4 and the implications for DNS services are covered in detail in Chapter 16, "WINS: Legacy Name Services and Resolution." These three are each pretty much tied to single RR types. So, it's important to look at the two remaining tabs now.

General Settings

Standard zones are, by default, created with dynamic DNS updates disabled. Enabling the feature is as simple as changing No to Yes for Allow Dynamic Updates? and applying the change. When you create an Active Directory–integrated zone, this defaults to Only Secure Updates, which is not available without integration. Chapter 7 discusses the issues involved in using Active Directory–integrated storage at some length.

On this General page, you can see the current status of the zone and pause and resume the zone, providing a finer grain of control than the server-level pause and resume of the server node. The value beside Type tells whether the zone is a standard primary or secondary or is Active Directory integrated; the Change button opens a dialog box in which the type can be changed. Notice the Aging button. Figure 7.1 showed the configuration settings available for scavenging stale records for the zone revealed by this button.

When DDNS is in use, and security is also in use, it is very likely that RRs that are otherwise useless will be left in the zone files. These records can be detrimental, preventing registrations that should happen from being allowed and also needlessly slowing queries by increasing zone size. Chapter 7 discusses scavenging at length.

Zone Transfers

The Zone Transfers tab is where you can configure the characteristics of both the type and the security for zone transfers. Figure 11.8 shows this tab with the Notify button (it is covered by the upper window shown) having been used to show the setting to enable the update notification feature. NT 4.0 had the Notify option, but because its zone transfers were not incremental, it was not made conveniently available.

On the main tab, zone transfers can be disabled by unchecking Allow Zone Transfers. When enabled, you can provide a list of servers by IP address that are allowed to pull transfers, or allow transfers to any server, or allow transfers (as shown here) to only machines represented by NS records in the zone. Figure 11.8 shows the Notify button covered by the Notify dialog box. The Notify configuration is used to disable notifications, or when enabled to target DNS Notify messages either to NS-represented machines, or to a specifically entered list of machines.

The Windows 2000 DNS Server can always perform incremental zone transfers. Whether it does depends on whether it has received an AXFR (a full zone transfer) or an IXFR (an incremental zone transfer) request. When IXFR has requested incremental transfer, the DNS server does so unless the version difference is too great. When the DNS server Change log cannot support an IXFR request because some changes have "flushed off the end," a full transfer is negotiated and performed using AXFR directives.

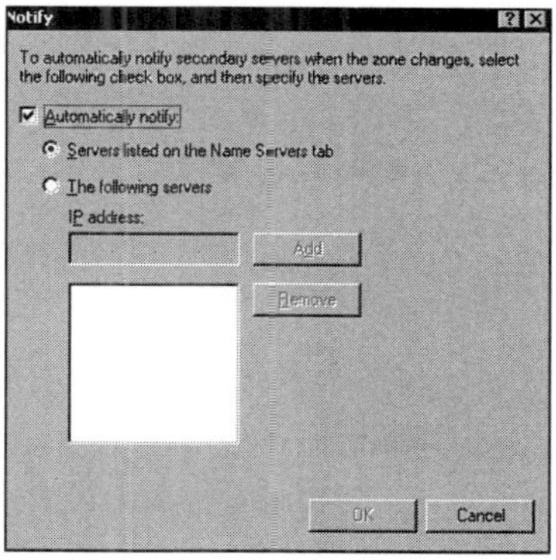

Figure 11.8 The Zone Transfer's tab and the Notify dialog box.

Using these optimizations for the zone transfer process is quite important with zones enabled for dynamic update. When configuring the Notify option, remember to permit (that is, to list) your servers so that they may receive zone transfers and to configure notification at each server acting as a master.

Delegation and Subdomains

Using the DNS management console to delegate is almost the same process as was used to create a zone. Now that you have the DNS server running with primary authority for test.example.net, it is time to see what can be done with it. Figure 11.9 shows the context menu on a primary zone. The context menu on a secondary zone differs quite a bit, because the server does not have source authority, and so the options to create records are not provided in a secondary zone, but instead the option to pull a transfer (send an IXFR request) is provided.

In Figure 11.9, the domain example.net has been expanded to show the presence of glue records. Because you did not create an example.net zone, your server will differ. Here example.net and a number of dependent DNS domain names have been created.

If you examine the context menu, you will see a number of options to create new records, and then two options labeled New Domain and New Delegation. The following sections discuss what these do and how they differ.

New DNS Domain

Using the New Domain selection causes a prompt for a new domain name, and that is all. In the discussion in Chapter 4, this was at times referred to as creating a subdomain. This option creates a namespace division without any delegation involved.

1. Open the DNS Server management console and expand the server where the new domain will be defined.

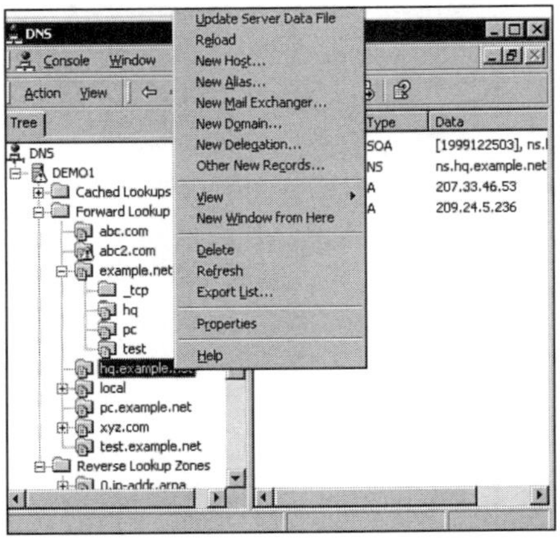

Figure 11.9 The menu options on a primary zone.

2. Set the focus on the primary zone where the domain will be defined (for example, example.net to define west.example.net), and in the context menu (right-click) of the zone select New Domain.
3. In the New Domain dialog box, enter the name for the new domain. In the example of the preceding step, this would be west with no trailing period.
4. Click OK and the new folder should appear as a node under the zone.

When you select New Domain, you must enter a valid single label without a trailing period—for example, west, but not west., nor west.example.net—for the OK button to become enabled. When you click OK, a new folder by the name is created within the zone node. The icon is a simple folder, and it is empty. If you were to now create an A record for a machine in the west.example.net subdomain that was just created, giving it the name Bld12-r1023, the record will be shown within the west folder under example.net. If you update the server file on disk and then check the zone file for example.net, you will see a new A record with Bld12-r1023.west as the name registered.

New DNS Delegation

The New Delegation selection is used to create a delegated subdomain, including a NS record designated to answer queries for it. This option fires up the New Delegation Wizard. Your first dialog box asks, just as in the case of a New Domain, for a single label, without trailing period, that will be the name of the new subdomain within the node where you selected to delegate.

1. Open the DNS Server management console and expand the server where the new delegation will be defined.

2. Set the focus on the primary zone where the domain will be delegated—for example, example.net to define east.example.net—and in the context menu (right-click) of the zone, select New Delegation.
3. In the New Delegation Wizard, first click Next to enter. In the Delegated Domain Name dialog box, enter the name for the new domain in the Delegated Domain text box. In the example of the preceding step, this would be east with no trailing period. Notice that the fully qualified domain name (FQDN) for the domain being delegated is shown in the grayed-out text box. Click Next.
4. You now need to specify the name servers that will handle the domain. Click Add to open the New Resource Record dialog box for creating NS records.
5. Browse to the A or CNAME records for the machine(s) or enter them by IP one at a time. For each machine entered, a new NS record results in the delegated domain.
6. Click Next and then click Finish to close the wizard. The new domain node should appear under the node where New Delegation was selected.

After you provided the subdomain name, you were allowed to enter any number of servers to which authority (not source authority) is to be delegated. Add your servers either by FQDN or IP address, but most easily by using browse if the DNS server(s) A or CNAME records in the DNS database of servers connected to the management console. Each server added receives NS records in the new domain. After you have finished the wizard, you have a new subfolder with a distinctive icon, expanding which shows the NS records. Updating the server's files and examining the zone file also show the NS records. The DNS Server management console does not enable you to add records within the new node. The delegation has created the glue records within the parenting zone, with the assumption that a zone will exist at one of the delegated servers.

Resource Records

Chapter 4 discussed the main resource record types in some detail, and you can find information on the rest in Appendix F, "Resource Records and the InterNIC Cache File." Because Chapter 4 included screenshots, and the information entered is so predictable, this chapter does not cover the manual creation of resource records within your primary zones. Most selections to create a record take you to a simple dialog box that collects the essential details, and makes some usually reasonable assumptions, ending with creation of an RR, leaving you in the dialog box ready to create another.

A number of frequently used RRs have selections on the context menu when focus is on or within a primary zone. The one selection, Other New Records, enables you to select almost any RFC-specified RR type (DNAME seems to be missing in the initial Windows 2000 version available as we go to press) and a few not specified by the RFCs (at least not yet, such as for ATM support). Remember that you can always stop a zone that uses zone file storage and directly edit it. Just make sure that you force out any cached updates first and that you increment the version before you restart so that the changes transfer—all pretty standard stuff for the experienced administrator.

Active Directory Integration

The use of the Active Directory for zone storage has a number of implications, which were covered in Chapter 7 in some detail. Because it is so easy to change a zone to this storage mode, using the Change button on the General tab of the zone's properties (refer to Figure 11.7), it is also equally easy to overlook many implications and subsequent new options that can, and probably should, be used.

After having been integrated, zone data is stored in the Active Directory, as can be seen in Figure 11.10. This figure shows the Active Directory Users and Computers management console with the MicrosoftDNS container expanded. (Advanced mode needs to be enabled.)

The presentation in this console is flattened rather than structured by domain, as can be seen. This is a Read-only view, except that security descriptors can be modified. What this visibility illustrates is that the zone data is available to LDAP queries. This LDAP availability can provide a circumventing route around all your attempts to secure zone data and transfers, if you are not careful.

Refer to Chapter 7 for a discussion of other aspects of integrating your zones into this storage mode. A couple of the main considerations not covered there are load on the replication engine and network and DNS server placement on domain controllers,

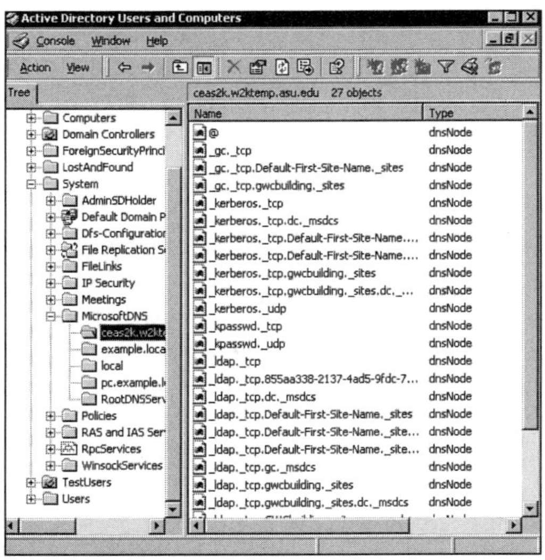

Figure 11.10 Zone data enumerated in the Active Directory.

which were instead touched on in Chapter 9. With that said, we will end with this reminder that the simple switch is not so simple.

Types of Servers

Because the information is otherwise scattered over the earlier sections, this topic very briefly lists the settings needed to configure a server for the different types of operation.

Using Forwarders

As discussed earlier, forwarders are configured at the server level in the server properties. The Windows 2000 DNS Server sends recursive queries to these machines. Other than to forwarders, the Windows 2000 DNS Server always sends iterative queries to other DNS servers.

You can use forwarders in a number of the configurations that follow. When defined, the forwarding DNS server may or may not also start its own efforts to resolve a query it has received, after it has forwarded it. If not disallowed from doing so, the Windows 2000 DNS Server begins working the query itself after a period waiting for forwarder(s) to reply has expired.

Caching Only

A caching-only DNS server has no primary or secondary zones. It relies solely on the services of other DNS servers, and caches the results for use in providing nonauthoritative answers to later queries. The Windows 2000 DNS Server in its initial installation configuration is without any zones and has a root hints file appropriate for Internet use. As such, the initial install is configured as a caching-only server.

You may want to do two things to complete the configuration as a caching-only server. First, if you are using the DNS server in an internal DNS services design, you certainly want to adjust the root hints file. And second, it is a good idea to set the server to use specific forwarders chosen in all events for proximity and in the internal design for the namespace to be resolvable.

Slave

Slave servers, as meant here, are not zone transfer slaves, but are DNS servers configured to only use forwarders. These differ from caching-only servers in that they cannot initiate any efforts to resolve the received queries other than to forward them. To make a DNS server into a slave, first provide it with forwarders. Then set the Do Not Use Recursion option on the Forwarders tab of the server properties. A similar, although likely less-efficient, result can be accomplished by adjusting its root hints file so that it knows of only itself, as is done with some UNIX servers.

Authoritative Slave

For want of a better term, this configuration is called an authoritative slave. The configuration is much the same as for a slave as just outlined. The difference is that the DNS server also has primary and or secondary zones delegated to it. In this configuration, the forwarders are used, and their results cached. If the query is for a host in the authority of the server, however, the query is answered authoritatively from the zone data. Otherwise, the query is only answered if the forwarders can resolve the query. This is worth restating: When the Do Not Use Recursion option is enabled, the DNS server can still provide authoritative answers.

Iterative

The Windows 2000 DNS server by default will accept both iterative and recursive queries. This can be changed so that it will only accept iterative queries. This is done by checking "Disable recursion" in the Advanced tab of the server properties. An iterative server has a reduced workload, and hence an extended capacity. Iterative servers are worth your consideration for such purposes as your public presence DNS server, as this configuration hardens the server from attacks based on overloading the server processes.

Zone Cleanliness

Using dynamic update brings issues. Perhaps the biggest after security concerns is zone content management. It's important to note here that the scavenging capability built in to the Windows 2000 DNS Server has the power to cause you some very real grief, if you attempt to use it without having fully considered the consequences first. Refer to the discussion in Chapter 7 before venturing too far into the Aging and Scavenging options you have seen in this chapter.

Support Features

The DNS server in Windows 2000 is quite capable of running on its own, in a quite problem-free manner, for extended periods. Nevertheless, services stand some oversight, and your main options for doing so have yet to be discussed.

Logging

Keeping an eye on your server is an ongoing task. When first setting up your DNS services, this is especially important, and should be done to get a feel for how heavily loaded your servers are and to discover any minor or major problems.

You have seen already the Logging tab of the server properties. It is perhaps unfortunate that this tool cannot be enabled on a per-zone basis, but it can still provide you with valuable information. Again, go gently into the use of this tool on heavily loaded production servers. Not only does it take cycles, but it can also generate large files fairly fast.

We have not yet pointed out the Windows Event log, which in Windows 2000 has a new DNS log. Figure 11.11 shows the Computer Management console opened. The DNS Event log is a good place over which to keep watch, because any serious problems surface here. Just do not rely on it as a source of capacity and performance-tuning information.

The Computer Management console is most easily located in the context menu of My Computer as the Manage selection or one can Run **compmgmt.msc**. Notice that the System Tools and the Event Log nodes are expanded in Figure 11.11, with the DNS Event log having the focus to show the logged events in the detail pane. At the bottom, Services and Applications has been expanded to show that full access to the DNS management interface is loaded as a snap-in within the Computer Management console.

Statistics and Monitoring

If you are new to Windows NT and 2000, you may not have discovered the value of the System Monitor. Pull up this tool by selecting Performance in the Administrative Tools folder, or Run **perfmon.msc**. In NT 4.0, this tool was called the Performance Monitor, and the name persists. The monitor works in three modes: Live Viewing, Logging, and Alerting. If you click on the big plus icon (+) to add counters to the chart, a dialog box appears in which you first need to select the object of interest, in this case it is DNS, and then the counters within the object that are to be used.

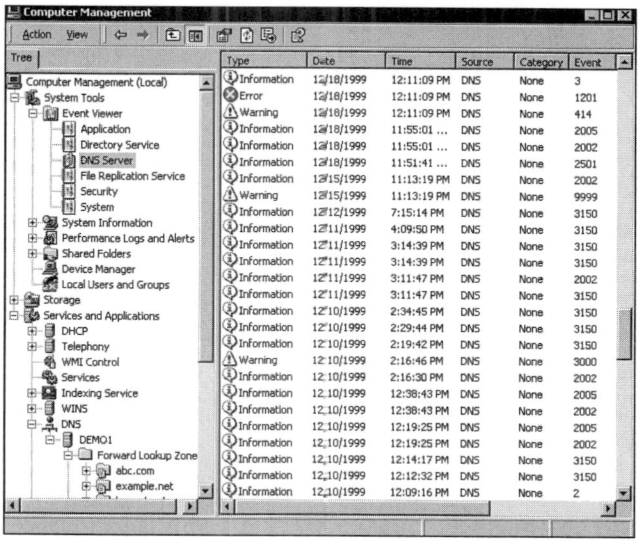

Figure 11.11 The DNS server Event log.

You can record entire objects to log files for later viewing. What is very, very nice is that you can also program conditions on counters that will trigger Event log messages. If you then have a tool such as *System Management Server* (SMS) provides, these Event log messages can then trigger programmed actions, email messages, and so forth.

To entice you into exploring just how extensive the information is that the DNS object makes available, Table 11.3 lists these counters. Looking into the list of objects, you will see that the use of memory is easily monitored, enabling you to determine how well endowed your server is with this, to a DNS server, most critical resource. The Notify, IXFR, AXFR, and Transfer sets of counters provide a view into the zone transfer load and whether incremental (IXFR) transfers are resulting in full (AXFR) transfers—assuming that only IXFR should be happening. The Dynamic Update and the Secure Update counters provide information on dynamic zone management activity of the server. Other combinations can be used to observe the server load from queries, and so forth.

Table 11.3 **Counters of the DNS Object in System Monitor**

AXFR Request Received
AXFR Request Sent
AXFR Response Received
AXFR Success Received
AXFR Success Sent
Cache Memory
Database Node Memory
Dynamic Update NoOperation
Dynamic Update NoOperation/sec
Dynamic Update Queued
Dynamic Update Received
Dynamic Update Received/sec
Dynamic Update Rejected
Dynamic Update TimeOuts
Dynamic Update Written to Database
Dynamic Update Written to Database/sec
IXFR Request Received
IXFR Request Sent
IXFR Response Received
IXFR Success Received
IXFR Success Sent
IXFR TCP Success Received

IXFR UDP Success Received
Nbtstat Memory
Notify Received
Notify Sent
Record Flow Memory
Recursive Queries
Recursive Queries/sec
Recursive Query Failures
Recursive Query Failures/sec
Recursive Send TimeOuts
Recursive TimeOuts/sec
Secure Update Failure
Secure Update Received
Secure Update Received/sec
TCP Message Memory
TCP Query Received
TCP Query Received/sec
TCP Response Sent
TCP Response Sent/sec
Total Query Received
Total Query Received/sec
Total Response Sent
Total Response Sent/sec
UDP Message Memory
UDP Query Received
UDP Query Received/sec
UDP Response Sent
UDP Response Sent/sec
WINS Lookup Received
WINS Lookup Received/sec
WINS Response Sent
WINS Response Sent/sec
WINS Reverse Lookup Received
WINS Reverse Lookup Received/sec
WINS Reverse Response Sent

continues

Table 11.3 **Continued**

WINS Reverse Response Sent/sec
Zone Transfer Failure
Zone Transfer Request Received
Zone Transfer SOA Request Sent
Zone Transfer Success

DNS Server Registry Entries

The DNS server in Windows 2000 has a number of Registry keys, most of which store values that can be configured through the DNS Server management console. The root location in the Registry is HKLM\System\CurrentControlSet\Services\DNS and below this are subkeys, \Parameters, where global settings, shown in Table 11.5, are configured, and \Zones, where zone configurations, shown in Table 11.4, are stored divided by the FQDN for the zone.

Table 11.4 **Zone-Specific DNS Registry Keys**

Value	Type	Explanation
Aging	Reg_Dword	0 disabled, 1 enabled
AllowUpdate	Reg_Dword	0 disabled, 1 enabled, 2 secure update only
DatabaseFile	Reg_Sz	Zone filename within %windir%\system32\dns
DSintegrated	Reg_Dword	0 disabled, 1 enabled
MasterServers	Reg_Sz	Space-separated IP list
NoRefreshInterval	Reg_Dword	Hours in hex
NotifyLevel	Reg_Dword	0 Notify disabled, 1 Notify NS servers, 2 Use NotifyServers
NotifyServers	Reg_Sz	Space-separated IP list
RefreshInterval	Reg_Dword	Hours in hex
SecureSecondaries	Reg_Dword	0 disabled, 1 NS servers, 2 Use SecondaryServers
SecondaryServers	Reg_Sz	Space-separated IP list
Type	Reg_Dword	0 is cache zone, 1 is primary, 2 is secondary

Table 11.5 **DNS Server Global Registry Keys**

Value	Type	Explanation
BindSecondaries	Reg_Dword	0 disabled, 1 enabled
BootMethod	Reg_Dword	1 File, 2 Registry, 3 AD and Registry
CleanupInterval	Reg_Dword	Seconds between cache purges (900 default)
DisableAutoReverseZones	Reg_Dword	0 F = enabled, 1 T = disabled (0., 127., 255.inaddr.arp)
Forwarders	Reg_Sz	Space-separated IP list
ForwardingTimeout	Reg_Dword	Seconds in hex
IsSlave	Reg_Dword	0 disabled, 1 enabled
ListenAddresses	Reg_Sz	Space-separated IP list
NoRecursion	Reg_Dword	0 = accept recursive, 1 = accept interative
RecursionRetry	Reg_Dword	Seconds in hex (per try)
RecursionTimeout	Reg_Dword	Seconds in hex (total)
PreviousLocalHostname	Reg_Sz	String host name
ScavengingInterval	Reg_Dword	Hours in hex, the enable automatic period
SecureResponses	Reg_Dword	0 disabled, 1 enabled

Summary

The options available in Windows 2000 DNS Server have been examined, along with some discussion of the importance to post-installation configuration. With this chapter, you should be able to step through a problem-free installation of DNS server, and begin populating zone data. Where issues need extended treatment, references have been provided to the relevant chapters.

III

Supporting DNS Services in Windows

12

Troubleshooting Tools and Utilities

THIS CHAPTER REVIEWS THE FOLLOWING:

- **nslookup.** The nslookup tool is included with Windows NT and 2000 and always comes with the BIND software package. This powerful diagnostic tool offers many options and provides a way to trace DNS queries from start to finish. This section explains how to use it.
- **dig.** The dig tool is less intimidating than nslookup. It comes with BIND and provides more information than nslookup provides.
- **dnscmd.** This Resource Kit tool, new with Windows 2000, provides a command-line interface for accomplishing DNS server management tasks otherwise only available through the DNS Server Management snap-in.
- **ping.** The ping tool provides the simplest method to find out whether another host can be reached over the network. This is probably the most-used diagnostic tool for Transmission Control Protocol/Internet Protocol (TCP/IP).
- **pathping.** This new, Windows 2000-specific command provides tracert-like information in a ping package.
- **tracert.** As its name implies, the tracert tool indicates what route through the network a packet will take to go from one computer to another. This command is similar to the UNIX command **traceroute**.

- **NetLab.** NetLab is a Swiss Army Knife of network tools. You can download this freeware product at no cost; it provides some of the same functionality of several standalone tools in a simple, friendly, graphical user interface.
- **Host.** Host is the second of two freeware utilities chosen for this chapter. This command-line tool allows a number of sophisticated queries that otherwise would require a sequence of **nslookup** commands.
- **ipconfig.** A built-in command-line tool for Windows NT and 2000, ipconfig provides basic information about how each TCP/IP network interface is configured and provides control over a client Dynamic Host Configuration Protocol (DHCP) lease.
- **winipcfg.** A built-in tool for Windows 95 and 98, winipcfg provides basic information about how each TCP/IP network interface is configured in a windowed interface.
- **netdiag.** This Resource Kit tool, new with Windows 2000, provides an all-and-everything type, command-line interface to networking settings. It is of most power in diagnosing Active Directory support problems, many of which are rooted in DNS.
- **netsh.** This NetShell tool, new with Windows 2000, provides a shell with a rich set of provided command context and has the capability to host context extensions. Although not providing a DNS context, the network interface, DHCP, and Windows Internet Naming Service (WINS) contexts along with the scriptability, for starters, make this a "must-know" tool for Windows 2000 network management.
- **netstat.** A built-in command-line tool for Windows 95, Windows 98, Windows NT, and Windows 2000, netstat reveals more than basic configuration about each TCP/IP interface; it shows routes, connections, ports, and connection statistics.
- **nbtstat.** A built-in command-line tool for Windows 95, Windows 98, Windows NT, and Windows 2000, nbtstat reveals NetBIOS information, including connections and statistics, and in some platforms provides settings controls.
- **System Monitor.** This standard Windows NT and 2000 tool has a DNS object with useful counters covering many key area of DNS server operational statistics.
- **netmon.** This Windows 2000 and NT tool is the standard for getting down to the packet level and seeing what is actually happening.

nslookup

The nslookup tool has traditionally been one of the most commonly used tools for manually performing DNS queries. This particular tool is somewhat unique in that it can emulate both a standard client resolver and a server. Used as a client resolver, nslookup can directly query a server for information. Used as a server, nslookup can perform zone transfers from a primary or master server. This tool can be used in two modes: noninteractive (which is typically typed from the command line as **nslookup www.example.net**), and interactive (which is entered by typing **nslookup** and pressing Enter with no arguments). Options can be passed to nslookup in either mode, but interactive mode is more often used in times of trouble with the name server. In interactive mode, you can obtain help by typing **help** or **?** at the > prompt. Doing so provides basic information on the commands covered in the sections that follow. Note that most command examples in this chapter are performed from the interactive nslookup prompt.

A noninteractive use of nslookup looks something like the following, if you perform nslookup on your machine with a default name server of `ns.win2000dns.com`. (Note that the win2000dns.com address is just for example purposes.) Notice the line stating "Non-authoritative answer," because this is the only indication one ever receives indicating whether a query was answered from cached resolutions. If the server is authoritative for the name, this line does not appear.

```
C:\>nslookup www.example.net
Server:  ns.win2000dns.com
Address:  10.10.10.1

Non-authoritative answer:
Name:    VENERA.ISI.EDU
Address:  128.9.176.32
Aliases:  www.example.net
```

You could have used **nslookup www.example.net venera.isi.edu**, where the second host name is the DNS server to use in place of the default. Notice that the response is now authoritative.

```
C:\>nslookup www.example.net  venera.isi.edu
Server:  venera.isi.edu
Address:  128.9.176.32

Name:    VENERA.ISI.EDU
Address:  128.9.176.32
Aliases:  www.example.net
```

If you are using the command-line mode, and want to use some of the arguments discussed later, remember to place them first, and that they may be abbreviated to the point of remaining unique. If you want to see all the traffic generated by the resolution, for example, you could use **nslookup –d2 www.example.net venera.isi.edu**, although **–d** is often quite sufficient.

Before beginning a detailed examination of the options available in nslookup, you may want to keep in mind a few pointers when using this tool. As previously said, nslookup has an internal resolver. You should control the query type that the resolver is using, because it can be set to send requests for iterative or for recursive resolution. Quite often when debugging your DNS servers, you will want to change from the recursive default to iterative to be sure that you are examining what is known by your DNS server. It is often very handy to limit the type of resource records (RRs) that should be returned by using the **set type=any** option, or if all types are not wanted using something other than **any**, the default being Address (A) records. The resolver may be pointed at your server, or others, by using the **server Name** and **lserver Name** options, which differ in how the **Name** is itself resolved. If you have used the **server x.y.z** to point the resolver at an invalid machine, attempting to use **server some.good.nameserver** will fail because **x.y.z** cannot be used to resolve **some.good.nameserver**. In this case one must either use an Internet Protocol (IP) or use **lserver some.good.nameserver**, assuming the local server (**lserver**) is a valid name server. You should manage the resolution process of appending domains with the **set** options **defname**, **domain**, **search**, and **srchlist** options, or by using Fully Qualified Domain Names (FQDNs) with the trailing period (.). When in doubt, issue the interactive command **set all** to see the current configuration. Finally, one thing not apparent to the Windows users is that **^C** as a command terminator can be used. If you have started a zone transfer with the **ls** command and see the need to stop it, for example, **^C** will do just that, returning to the nslookup > prompt.

help (?) Command

The **help** or **?** command displays the help information with a very brief summary of the commands. The syntax for this command is as follows:

```
> help
```

or

```
> ?
```

You will get the results as follows:

```
Commands:       (identifiers are shown in uppercase, [] means optional)
NAME                    - print info about the host/domain NAME using default
server
NAME1 NAME2             - as above, but use NAME2 as server
help or ?               - print info on common commands
set OPTION              - set an option
      all                       - print options, current server and host
      [no]debug                 - print debugging information
      [no]d2                    - print exhaustive debugging information
      [no]defname       - append domain name to each query
      [no]recurse               - ask for recursive answer to query
      [no]search                - use domain search list
      [no]vc                    - always use a virtual circuit
      domain=NAME       - set default domain name to NAME
      srchlist=N1[/N2/.../N6]   - set domain to N1 and search list to N1,N2, etc.
      root=NAME         - set root server to NAME
      retry=X                   - set number of retries to X
      timeout=X                 - set initial time-out interval to X seconds
type=X                  - set query type (ex. A,ANY,CNAME,MX,NS,PTR,SOA,SRV)
```

```
querytype=X              - same as type
      class=X                     - set query class (ex.  IN (Internet), ANY)
[no]msxfr                - use MS fast zone transfer
      ixfrver=X                   - current version to use in IXFR transfer request
server NAME              - set default server to NAME, using current default server
lserver NAME             - set default server to NAME, using initial server
finger [USER]            - finger the optional USER at the current default host
root                     - set current default server to the root
ls [opt] DOMAIN [> FILE] - list addresses in DOMAIN (optional: output to FILE)
      -a                 -  list canonical names and aliases
      -d                 -  list all records
       -t TYPE           -  list records of the given type (e.g., A,CNAME,
                            MX,NS,PTR etc.)
view FILE                 - sort an 'ls' output file and view it with pg
exit                      - exit the program
```

The following options were listed in earlier versions of the Windows nslookup help information or provide information on further options accepted by nslookup in the Windows 2000 version available as we go to press:

```
set OPTION                - set an option
      [no]ignoretc                - controls whether truncation of communication
                                    packets is ignored
      port=X                      - set port number to send query on
ls [opt] DOMAIN [> FILE] - list addresses in DOMAIN (optional: output to FILE)
      -h                 -  list HINFO (CPU type and operating system)
      -s                 -  list well-known services
```

exit Command

The **exit** command enables you to quit nslookup. If you type **quit**, nslookup treats it as a host name and tries to resolve it, as it will any other string that is not a valid command. You can also exit by using **^C** at the nslookup prompt. The syntax for the exit command is as follows:

```
> exit
```

finger Command

The standard **finger** command applies to the current host. The term *current* refers to the most recent successful lookup performed. If the last command was for an A record query for machine.example.net that returned an IP address and then the **finger <username>** command was entered, this would basically be the same as entering at a command prompt **finger <username>@machine.example.net**. The syntax for the **finger** command is as follows:

```
> finger <username> [> filename]
```

The following shows part of an nslookup session, in which the account "user" is fingered on the UNIX machine www.example.net that is running the fingered daemon. A Windows server would need to have the Simple TCP/IP Services installed and enabled to respond in this way.

```
> machine.example.net
Server:  ns.win2000dns.com
Address:  10.10.10.1

Name:    machine.example.net
Address:  192.168.1.1

> finger user
[machine.example.net]
Login: user                             Name:
Directory: /home/user                   Shell: /bin/bash
On since Thu Sep  2 19:32 (PDT) on ttyp2 from www.example.net
   1 second idle
New mail received Wed Jul 28 00:25 1999 (PDT)
     Unread since Sat May 15 14:24 1999 (PDT)
No Plan.
```

server Command

The **server** command, which is very similar to the **lserver** command, resolves another name server and sets that server as the default. The difference is that the **server** command uses the current default server to resolve the new server <host name>. The syntax for the **server** command is as follows:

```
> server <host name>
```

An example of its use to change the nslookup resolver to use ns.win2000dns.com is as follows:

```
>server ns.win2000dns.com
Default Server: ns.win2000dns.com
Address: 10.10.10.1
```

lserver Command

The **lserver** command first uses the local name server to perform a lookup on another name server, and then sets the name server that was just resolved as the default. This operation can be useful when you have reset the default server to a host that is not responding or is not a DNS server. Using the **lserver** command, the default name server can be reset without having to rely on the current default name server. The syntax for this command is as follows:

```
> lserver <host name>
```

The **lserver** command is quite useful when one needs to recover in this situation.

```
>lserver ns.win2000dns.com
Default Server: ns.win2000dns.com
Address: 10.10.10.1
```

root Command

The **root** command enables the user to change the default name server for a given session to the root server listed by the **set all** command. The default root server is a.root-servers.net. The default name server is set to a.root-servers.net. by issuing the **root** command. The syntax for this command is as follows:

```
> rootc
```

The following example shows that a.root-servers.net was the root server and has been set as the default server. The root server being used can be controlled by use of the set **root=Name** option.

```
> root
Default Server: a.root-servers.net
Address: 198.41.0.4
```

ls Command

The **ls** command, with its associated options, enables the user to view the contents of zone files for DNS domains. With no options specified, the default displays the host names and IP addresses for a domain. If zone transfers are restricted on the server, a denial message is returned. Other options can be specified to vary the scope of the listing. Output redirection to a file is available to capture information. In fact, using the **ls** command is one way to perform a manual zone transfer to a client or secondary name server. The syntax for this command is as follows:

```
> ls [option] <domain name> [> filename]
```

The options available for the **ls** command are as follows:

-t **<RR>**	Lists all records of the specified type
-a	Lists all aliases of computers in the domain (same as **-t CNAME**)
-d	Lists *all* records for the domain (same as **-t ANY**)
-h	Lists the CPU and OS information about the hosts in the domain (same as **-t HINFO**)
-s	Lists the well-known services of hosts in the domain (same as **-t WKS**)

Note that when using the **-t <RR>** option to filter by type, previously in NT 4.0 the entire list would transfer and the filtering would be local. As discussed previously, the **–h** and **–s** options are no longer documented in the online help, but were still parsed in the final Windows 2000 versions before the code was frozen for release. Be sure to notice that the **<domain name>** is not optional or you may have a bewildering time. Also, **filename** does not allow a path.

set Command

The **set** command modifies operating parameters for nslookup and is essentially a prefix used for a number of subcommands. The first subcommand to become familiar with is the **set all** command, which displays the current operating parameters with which the queries will be executed. The **set** commands can be abbreviated provided that each command is unique, so completing the command is not necessary. The commands are illustrated using brackets to indicate the point of completion. Some versions of the commands include an implicit **[no]** to turn off a feature as well. An example of the **set all** command is as follows:

```
> set all
Default Server:  ns.win2000dns.com
Address:  10.10.10.1
Set Options:
nodebug
defname
search
recurse
nod2
novc
noignoretc
port=53
type=A
class=IN
timeout=2
retry=1
root=a.root-servers.net.
domain=win2000dns.com
MSxfr
IXFRversion=1
srchlist=
```

Other subcommands that fall under the set command, most of which had their values listed in the prior output, are as follows:

set class *or* **set cl**

set [no]debug *or* **set [no]deb**

set [no]d2

set [no]defname *or* **set [no]def**

set domain *or* **set do**

set [no]ignoretc *or* **set [no]ig**

set IXFRversion *or* **set ixfr**

set [no]msxfr *or* **set noms but set msxfr**

set port *or* **set po**

set querytype *or* **set q**

set [no]rec[urse] *or* **set [no]rec**

set ret[ry] *or* **set ret**

set ro[ot] *or* **set ro**

set [no]sea[rch] *or* **set [no]sea**

set srch[list] *or* **set srch**

set ti[meout] *or* **set ti**

set ty[pe] *or* **set ty**

set [no]v[c] *or* **set [no]v**

Using the set commands can require some experimentation to obtain the desired effect. The sections that follow provide some hints as to the functional purpose of each option.

set class Command Option

The **set class** option is used to set the appropriate protocol for the class of the query. The default is the Internet class; other options are **Chaos**, **Hesiod**, and **ANY**. Curiously, **HS** and **Hesiod** are accepted for Hesiod, and **IN** for Internet, but Internet is not accepted. The class names are not case sensitive, so **IN** and **in** work equally well. The syntax for this command option is as follows:

```
>set class=<class name>
```

set [no]debug Command Option

The **set [no]debug** option turns on (or off) standard debugging. In debug mode, information about the query sent to the server and the answer is printed in a formatted text display. Default operation is nodebug. Turning debug level off also turns the d2 level off if it is on. The syntax for this command option is as follows:

```
> set debug
> set nodebug
```

set [no]d2 Command Option

The **set [no]d2** option turns on (or off) the exhaustive debugging, in which every packet for the query and answer that are sent to or received from the server is printed. The default mode of operation is nod2. Turning this level of debugging on also sets debug on, but turning the d2 level off leaves debug level on. The syntax for this command option is as follows:

```
>set d2
>set nod2
```

set [no]defname Command Option

Setting the **defname** option enables the default domain name to be appended to any query for a name that does not contain dots (.) in the name. The **defname** option set to on is the default mode of operation, although it can be disabled. No arguments exist, because the default domain name is set elsewhere in the domain option (see also the **search** and **srchlist** options of **set**). The syntax for this command option is as follows:

```
set defname
set nodefname
```

set domain Command Option

The **set domain** command option actually sets the default domain name that will be used by **defname**. The default is the local host domain, if one is assigned, but it can be changed to match any domain. The syntax for this command option is as follows:

```
set domain=<domain name>
```

set [no]ignoretc Command Option

The **set [no]ignoretc** option enables nslookup to ignore received packets with the truncation errors flag set during a query, although the default is noignoretc. This option is familiar as noignore in UNIX nslookup implementations. When nslookup receives a truncated packet (usually a User Datagram Protocol [UDP] packet), it means that all the information could not be put into the packet. With noignoretc, nslookup retries the query using TCP. TCP responses can be larger, thereby allowing more information to be received and hopefully completing the answer. The syntax for this command option is as follows:

```
>set ignoretc
>set noignoretc
```

set IXFRversion=<version> Command Option

The **set IXFRversion** option enables you to set the version number reported to the server when performing an incremental (IXFR-type) transfer. This value is compared to the version number on the Start of Authority (SOA) record, and is used to determine what records need to be transferred. The syntax for this command option is as follows:

```
>set IXFR=5555
```

set [no]msxfr Command Option

The **set msxfr** command option activates Microsoft's fast zone transfer method; the **set nomsxfr** returns it to the normal method. Some DNS servers, such as BIND servers prior to 4.9.4, do not support the transfer of a zone by compressing multiple resource records into each packet. Windows 2000 DNS Servers will always do so with each other. This option allows nslookup to appear as an equally capable peer in this regard (the default), and enables one to test the transfers needed for a server not using compressed transfers. The syntax for this command option is as follows:

```
>set msxfr
>set nomsxfr
```

set port Command Option

The default port number assignment for DNS is 53 (TCP and UDP). Note that ports can be higher and are negotiated for determination of which port will be used under BIND 8 or higher; this behavior is the default behavior for the later versions of BIND. Using the **set port** option, nslookup can query a DNS server that is configured to use another port. This is generally done when debugging. The syntax for this command option is as follows:

```
set port=<number>
```

set querytype Command Option

The **set querytype** (or **set type**) command option changes the type of information for which the query looks. Changing the query type modifies the question asked of the name server to reflect the information required. If the user wants to see the *mail exchange* (MX) records for a given domain, for example, the query type would be set to MX. By default, the query would look for an A record to match a host/domain name. If the query is sent with an IP address in the question, the resolver reverses the address, adds the in-addr.arpa. domain, and looks for a Pointer (PTR) record. The syntax for this command option is as follows:

```
>set querytype=<value>
```

The values that you can set for this option in Windows 2000 are as follows:

A	Finds an IP address for the host/domain
AAAA	Finds an IP version 6 address for the host/domain
AFSDB	Finds AFS or Distributed Computing Environment (DCE) records
ANY	Finds all information about the host/domain
CNAME	Finds canonical name for an alias
DNAME*	Finds domain redirection alias
GID	Finds a group identifier for a group name
HINFO	Finds host CPU and OS type
ISDN	Finds ISDN phone number records
KEY	Finds encryption key records
MB	Finds mailbox domain name
MG	Finds mail group member
MINFO	Finds mailbox information
MR	Finds mail rename information

MX	Finds mail exchange information
NS	Finds name servers for the host/domain
NSAP	Finds Open Systen Interconnect (OSI) (CLNP) access point records
PTR	Finds a host name that matches the IP address
PX	Finds records used for X.500 address mappings
RP	Finds the responsible person records for the domain
RT	Finds any route through records
SIG	Finds digitally signed records in the domain
SOA	Displays the domain's SOA
SRV	Finds the service resources advertised in the domain
TXT	Displays any text information about the host/domain
UID	Finds a user ID for the host/domain
UINFO	Finds the user's information
WKS	Displays well-known services information
X25	Displays records for X25 network support

** DNAME is not in the current version of Windows 20000 as this goes to press.*

set [no]recurse Command Option

The **set [no]recurse** option enables nslookup to send recursive or iterative queries to another host. The default mode is recurse, which means that a name server that accepts the query should query other name servers if it does not have the answer. By setting norecurse, nslookup can emulate another name server sending an interactive query looking for hints about a domain. The option is quite important to remember when debugging one of your DNS servers, permitting you to see either what information it has in cache, or is able to obtain, depending on the setting. The syntax for this command option is as follows:

```
>set recurse
>set norecurse
```

set retry Command Option

The **set retry** option specifies the number of times a query will be sent before giving up the search. Typically, when a query is made, the client sends the query to the name server. If no response is received, the client resends the query up to the number of retries set. Each time the query is sent on a retry, the timeout value is doubled. This grants the name server a longer window in which to find the answer. The default value is typically 4 but is set to 1 in the current Windows 2000 version. The syntax for this command option is as follows:

```
>set retry=<number>
```

set root Command Option

The **set root** option enables the default root server to be changed to another root server. The default root server is a.root-servers.net but could be changed to another InterNIC root server such as e.root-servers.net or to any server of choice. This sets the server that becomes the default local server if the **root** command (not the **set root** option) is issued. The syntax for this command option is as follows:

```
>set root=<server name>
```

set [no]search Command Option

The **set [no]search** option provides for a search of the entries in the domain search list. If a query is received that contains at least one dot (.) in the name but that is not terminated with a dot, the domain names listed in the search are appended to the query until an answer can be found. One caveat here is that defname is disabled if search is on. Because search is the default, defname is not used unless the **set nosearch** command is given. The syntax for this command option is as follows:

```
>set search
>set nosearch
```

set srchlist Command Option

The **set srchlist** option permits a list of domain names to be specified that will be used with the **search** option. The domain names are added to any query not terminated with a dot. Unless otherwise set, the default search list contains the local host's domain name. This command also overrides the **set domain** command. The search list can contain up to six different domain names, separated by slashes. The syntax for this command option is as follows:

```
set srchlist=<domain 1>/<domain 2>/.../<domain 6>
```

set timeout Command Option

The **set timeout** option specifies the initial timeout period that the resolver will wait for a reply. If no reply is received before the timeout, the request is sent again and the timeout is doubled. Each time a reply is not received, the request is re-sent, up to the number of retries, and the timeout period is doubled. The default timeout is two seconds. The syntax for this command option is as follows:

```
set timeout=<number of seconds>
```

set type Command Option

See the equivalent **set querytype** option which also happens to have the shorter abbreviation.

set [no]vc Command Option

The **set vc**, or virtual circuit, option enables the user to specify whether UDP (novc) or TCP (vc) should be used for the query This could be used in conjunction with the

ignoretc option. If the user wanted all the queries to be handled with TCP, the **ignore** option could be used. The syntax for this command option is as follows:

```
>set vc
>set novc
```

nslookup Error Messages

The user should pay attention to a couple of error messages when using nslookup. The error messages (as described in the list that follows) can provide insight into the nature of a problem on the server.

- **Timed out.** This typically means that the server did not respond in the allocated time. Check to see that the server is alive and well, and review the Event logs to see whether any errors have occurred that may be affecting the service.
- **No response from server.** This means that DNS is not accepting queries at all. Check the Service and Event log for errors.
- **No records.** This would typically occur if, for example, the user requested an Host Information (HINFO) record for a domain, but no HINFO records are published in the domain.
- **Format error.** The name server is rejecting the query because of the format. This could be caused by an old version of some name server binary, or it might indicate corruption of the data on the network.
- **Server failure.** This typically occurs when there is a problem in a zone file. A misplaced semicolon or some other typo is usually the cause of this kind of failure. Check the Event log for more detail, or contact the mailbox listing in the SOA if this error is coming from a remote machine.
- **Connection refused, or Network unreachable.** This could mean a couple of things. First, make sure that the name server can be pinged. If not, some kind of network failure has occurred. If the name server can be pinged, the error may be caused by the type of query you are sending. If you try to do an ls on a domain using some level of security (for example, if the option to allow transfers to hosts in the Notify list only is set), the error may indicate that the user does not have permission to get a copy of the zone.
- **Refused.** This could be very similar to the preceding case, or it may mean that the query went to an interface not configured to answer name service queries. Check the configuration of the name server.

dig

The dig tool is another utility that can be used for querying name servers for information. This tool isn't built in to Windows NT or Windows 2000, but it does come free with the BIND distribution, and there's also an online interface to dig run by one of the computing centers at Berkeley (see Appendix A, "The LMHOSTS and HOST Files"). The dig tool does not offer an interactive mode, but it has a number of options that can be specified from the command line. Typically, the syntax used with dig is as follows:

```
> dig [@server][domain][q-type][q-class]{q-opt}{d-opt}[%comment]
```

The following list defines the options for the dig utility:

[@server] — The name server at which the query is pointed. This enables the user to change the name server just as the **server <name>** option does with nslookup. The default value for this option is the first name server in resolver list.

[domain] — A name in the domain name system. Essentially, this is what the user is seeking.

[q-class] or **[query-class]** — Sets the class for the query; is one of (**in**, **any**, **hs**, and so on). The default value for this option is **in**.

[q-type] or **[query-type]** — Sets the type of resource record that the query is requesting. Just as nslookup uses the **set querytype=<type>**, the type will be one of (**a**, **any**, **mx**, **ns**, **soa**, **hinfo**, **axfr**, **txt**, and so on). The default value for this option is **a**.

{q-opt} or **{query-option}** — Defined as one of the following values:

-x dot-notation-address — For resolution of dot notation addresses without having to specify PTR **query-type**.

-f file — For batch operations to resolve multiple addresses.

-T time — To specify a time interval between queries when operating in batch mode.

-p port — To specify an alternate port. The default value for this option is 53.

-P ping-string — After a successful query returns; also performs a ping for response time comparisons, and may specify a string to send in the ping packet.

-t query-type — Same as the **q-type**.

-c query-class — Same as **q-class**.

-envsav,-envset	Allows for modifying or setting environment variables. The dig tool can use a DIG.ENV file for preset parameters.
-[no]stick	Determines whether environment settings stick between successive queries. The default value is nostick.
{d-opt} or {dig-option}	Is of the form +keyword=value, where the keyword is defined by the options in Table 17.1.

Table 17.1 **Keywords for the {d-opt} and {dig-option} Options**

[no]debug	**[no]d2**	**[no]recurse**
retry=#	**time=#**	**[no]ko**
[no]vc	**[no]defname**	**[no]search**
domain=NAME	**[no]ignore**	**[no]primary**
[no]aaonly	**[no]sort**	**[no]cmd**
[no]stats	**[no]Header**	**[no]header**
[no]ttlid	**[no]cl**	**[no]qr**
[no]reply	**[no]ques**	**[no]answer**
[no]author	**[no]addit**	**pfdef**
pfmin	**pfset=#**	**pfand=#**
pfor=#		

Most of these dig options are quite similar to the nslookup options, but these options are activated by **a +** if the option takes a value as part of its operation. Detailed help files are available with the distribution.

The **defname** and **search** options for the resolver don't work with dig, so the user should remember to use fully qualified domain names for queries.

The dig utility can be a very useful tool for testing and troubleshooting a name server. One very effective use of dig is to obtain a current copy of the root cache. By just typing **dig > cache** at the command prompt, one can capture a complete root cache that can be compared to the existing file to see whether changes or updates need to be made. If dig is being used to test the local system, typing **dig domain.name** dumps the entire message from the server with the appropriate labels for the fields. The following example shows a typical implementation of the dig utility.

```
C:\> dig company.com

; <<>> DiG 2.2 <<>> company.com
;; res options: init recurs defnam dnsrch
;; got answer:
```

```
;; ->>HEADER<<- opcode: QUERY, status: NOERROR, id: 6
;; flags: qr aa rd ra; Ques: 1, Ans: 1, Auth: 1, Addit: 1
;; QUESTIONS:
;;      company.com, type = A, class = IN

;; ANSWERS:
company.com.     36000     A     10.188.112.62

;; AUTHORITY RECORDS:
company.com.     36000     NS     ns.compnay.com.

;; ADDITIONAL RECORDS:
ns.company.com.     36000     A     10.188.112.62

;; Total query time: 10 msec
;; FROM: ws-hknief to SERVER: default — 206.14.194.74
;; WHEN: Mon Apr 27 13:12:07 1998
;; MSG SIZE  sent: 26  rcvd: 79
```

dnscmd

This command-line tool is provided in the Resource Kit that ships with Windows 2000 Server versions. It offers a command for many situations that would otherwise have you digging into the DNS management console. This tool has been designed to work with DNS zones whether they have been integrated into the Active Directory or not. Some of the capabilities are the creation/deletion of records and even zones, the ability view zones, to pause and restart zones, to manipulate the server cache, to view and clear its statistics, to force scavenging, and more. Although it is true that one can add many DNS servers into the DNS management console on a work machine and manage them remotely, some would say that there is nothing like a command prompt. If that is your style, you definitely will be using dnscmd. Even if that does not describe you, notice that this provides a way to do some zone management without so many mouse clicks, such as adding many hosts to a zone. Without doubt, this tool is valuable for its DNS server cache management capabilities alone, but there is much more. To get an idea of the possibilities, review the following help information:

```
C:\:> dnscmd /?
USAGE:  DnsCmd <ServerName> <Command> [<Command Parameters>]

    <ServerName>:
      .                          — local machine using LPC
      IP address                 — RPC over TCP/IP
      DNS name                   — RPC over TCP/IP
      other server name          — RPC over named pipes
    <Command>:
      /Info                      — Get server information
      /Config                    — Reset server or zone configuration
      /EnumZones                 — Enumerate zones
```

```
    /Statistics                 — Query/clear server statistics data
    /ClearCache                 — Clear DNS server cache
    /WriteBackFiles             — Write back all zone or root-hint datafile(s)
    /StartScavenging            — Initiates server scavenging
    /ResetListenAddresses       — Select server IP address(es) to serve DNS
                                  requests
    /ResetForwarders            — Set DNS servers to forward recursive queries
                                  to
    /ZoneInfo                   — View zone information
    /ZoneAdd                    — Create a new zone on the DNS server
    /ZoneDelete                 — Delete a zone from DNS server or DS
    /ZonePause                  — Pause a zone
    /ZoneResume                 — Resume a zone
    /ZoneReload                 — Reload zone from its database (file or DS)
    /ZoneWriteBack              — Write back zone to file
    /ZoneRefresh                — Force refresh of secondary zone from master
    /ZoneUpdateFromDs           — Update a DS integrated zone by data from DS
    /ZoneResetType              — Change zone type Primary/Secondary/DSintegrated
    /ZoneResetSecondaries       — Reset secondary\notify information for a zone
    /ZoneResetScavengeServers   — Reset scavenging servers for a zone
    /ZoneResetMasters           — Reset secondary zone's master servers
    /EnumRecords                — Enumerate records at a name
    /RecordAdd                  — Create a record in zone or RootHints
    /RecordDelete               — Delete a record from zone, RootHints or Cache
                                  data
    /NodeDelete                 — Delete all records at a name
    /AgeAllRecords              — Force aging on node(s) in zone
  <Command Parameters>:
    — parameters specific to each Command
    dnscmd <CommandName> /?     — For help info on specific Command.
```

ping

The ping utility is not really a DNS tool but rather a TCP/IP tool for determining whether a host is connected to a network. This tool also provides some level of functionality for answering network requests. The ping tool actually uses the *Internet Control Message Protocol* (ICMP) to send an echo request message to the remote host, and then it waits for a reply. If the reply is received before the timeout period (which can be set by the user), the round-trip time for the message and reply is displayed for the user. With the ping utility provided with Windows 95, Windows 98, Windows NT, and Windows 2000, a series of four requests is sent to the remote host by default. ping provides reply echo followed by short summary statistics such as that shown immediately here. Notice that when the destination is provided as a host name, ping provides the corresponding IP. The reverse can be conveniently accomplished by using the **-a** option.

```
Ping statistics for 10.10.10.100:
    Packets: Sent = 4, Received = 4, Lost = 0 (0% loss),
Approximate round trip times in milli-seconds:
    Minimum = 10ms, Maximum =  50ms, Average =  30ms
```

A variety of command-line options can be used with ping, using a general syntax as the following:

```
ping [-taf] [-n count] [-l length] [-i ttl] [-v tos] [-r count] [-s count]
[[-j host-list] ¦ [-k host-list]] [-w timeout] destination
```

In this syntax, the following holds true:

-t sets ping to work continuously until interrupted.

-a is used to resolve addresses to host names.

-f tells ping not to fragment packets. (If **-l** is set to a value that requires fragmentation, the message is not sent and a message is displayed concerning the DF [Don't Fragment] flag.)

-n specifies a count for the number of ping requests to send.

-l specifies a length for the echo request.

-i specifies a time-to-live (TTL). (Values from 1 to 255 are accepted.)

-v enables the user to change the *Type of Service* (TOS) field in the IP datagram.

-r records the route for the requests and replies. A minimum of one and maximum of nine hosts can be recorded as specified by the value.

-s produces time stamps for the number of hops specified by the value.

-j specifies loose source route hosts with a maximum of nine host names. (Loose source routes provide for intermediate routers between hosts.) Notice that **-j** and **-k** are mutually exclusive.

-k specifies strict source route hosts with a maximum of nine hosts. (Strict source routes do not allow for intermediate routers between hosts.) Notice that **-j** and **-k** are mutually exclusive.

-w enables the user to specify a timeout interval for the replies, in milliseconds. Destination can be a host name or an IP address.

pathping

Although the ping utility is a time-honored TCP/IP tool, this new, somewhat similar utility comes with the Windows 2000 Resource Kit. This tool gives the route taken and more complete information on the line quality. As compared to tracert, this tool provides more immediate output of the route, but as compared to ping it requires more time to execute because of the statistics compiled.

The syntax available is as follows:

```
C:\>pathping /?
Usage: pathping        [-n] [-h maximum_hops] [-g host-list] [-p period]
      [-q num_queries] [-w timeout] [-t] [-R] [-r] target_name
```

Options are as follows:

-n	Do not resolve addresses to host names
-h maximum_hops	Maximum number of hops to search for target

-g host-list	Loose source route along host-list
-p period	Wait period milliseconds between pings
-q num_queries	Number of queries per hop
-w timeout	Wait timeout milliseconds for each reply
-T	Test connectivity to each hop with Layer-2 priority tags
-R	Test whether each hop is RSVP aware

Using our old friend of earlier examples, a pathping trace to www.example.net follows to give you an idea of the information available:

```
C:\>pathping www.example.net
Tracing route to VENERA.ISI.EDU [128.9.176.32]
over a maximum of 30 hops:
      0  ns.win2000dns.com [10.10.10.1]
      1  prxy.win2000dns.com [10.10.10.253]
      2  209.217.25.11
      3  USC—abilene.ATM.calren2.net [198.32.248.85]
      4  ISI—USC.POS.calren2.net [198.32.248.26]
      5  128.9.16.17
      6  128.9.32.7
      7  venera.isi.edu [128.9.176.32]

Computing statistics for 225 seconds...
                    Source to Here   This Node/Link
Hop  RTT    Lost/Sent = Pct  Lost/Sent = Pct  Address
  0                                   dc1.ceas2k.w2ktemp.asu.edu [129.219.113.113]
                          0/ 100 =  0%
  1     0ms      0/ 100 =  0%     0/ 100 =  0%  prxy.win2000dns.com [10.10.10.253]
                         0/ 100 =  0%
  2    10ms     0/ 100 =  0%     0/ 100 =  0%  209.217.25.11
                          0/ 100 =  0%
  3    10ms     0/ 100 =  0%     0/ 100 =  0%  USC—abilene.ATM.calren2.net
[198.32.248.85]
                          0/ 100 =  0%
  4    10ms     0/ 100 =  0%     0/ 100 =  0%      ISI—USC.POS.calren2.net
[198.32.248.26]
                          0/ 100 =  0%
  5    15ms     0/ 100 =  0%     0/ 100 =  0%      128.9.16.17
                          0/ 100 =  0%
  6    12ms     0/ 100 =  0%     0/ 100 =  0%      128.9.32.7
                          0/ 100 =  0%
  7    10ms     0/ 100 =  0%     0/ 100 =  0%      venera.isi.edu [128.9.176.32]
Trace complete.
```

tracert (traceroute)

The traceroute utility or tracert (the command is more familiar as **traceroute** on UNIX) establishes the relative path that packets must travel to get to the destination. A series of ICMP packets (note that most UNIX varieties of traceroute actually send

UDP packets) is sent to the destination, but the TTL is set to one for the first three packets and is incremented by one on each subsequent set of three packets. Because routers are required to decrement the TTL by one, the first packet will make it only to the first router. The router then sends an ICMP reply to the originator that the TTL has expired. This allows the **tracert** command to log the IP address of the first router. Hence, the second set of packets with a TTL of two will make it to the second router in the path when the TTL expires Then another ICMP reply is sent to the originator. This process of incrementing the TTL continues until the destination answers, or until the maximum TTL (255) is reached.

Command-line syntax and options for tracert are as follows:

```
tracert [-d] [-h maxhops] [-j hostlist] [-w timeout] destination
```

In this syntax, the following holds true:

-d tells tracert not to resolve IP addresses to host names.

-h specifies the maximum number of hops to try. (This essentially sets the max TTL.)

-j enables the user to specify loose source route hosts. (Again the maximum number is nine, just as with ping.)

-w specifies the timeout interval, in milliseconds. Destination can be a host name or an IP address.

Again using www.example.net, it is possible to see that tracert does not provide any information advantage over pathping, but it is faster overall but slower in initial output, but at the cost of the decreased accuracy of a single time measurement:

```
C:\>pathping www.example.net
Tracing route to VENERA.ISI.EDU [128.9.176.32]
over a maximum of 30 hops:
  1   <10 ms   <10 ms   <10 ms prxy.win2000dns.com [10.10.10.253]
  2   <10 ms   <10 ms   <10 ms  209.217.25.11
  3     10 ms     10 ms     10 ms  USC—abilene.ATM.calren2.net [198.32.248.85]
  4     10 ms     10 ms     20 ms  ISI—USC.POS.calren2.net [198.32.248.26]
  5     10 ms     10 ms     20 ms  128.9.16.17
  6     10 ms     10 ms     20 ms  128.9.32.7
  7     10 ms     10 ms     20 ms  venera.isi.edu [128.9.176.32]
Trace complete.
```

NetLab

NetLab (current version is 1.4) is a freeware utility written by Alexander Danileiko. You can download it from a number of mirror sites. The easiest way to find a good download site is by searching on `http://soft-seek.com` or `www.shareware.com`. Although NetLab could use a little update for Windows 2000 and it does not offer the broadest choice of configuration options, it does combine a nice set of tools in a single graphical user interface as Figure 12 1 shows.

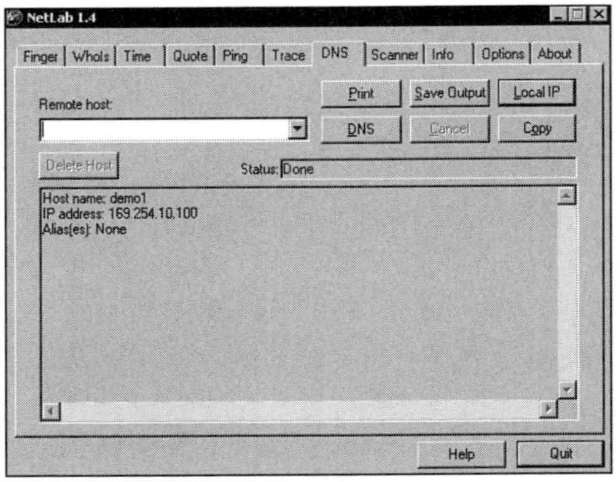

Figure 12.1 NetLab 1.4 interface with DNS selected.

The basic tool set that NetLab provides includes Finger, WhoIs, Time, Quote, Ping, Traceroute, DNS, and a Port Scan. NetLab doesn't take a lot of disk space and seems to be fairly efficient in terms of memory use. This tool can be configured to work through a firewall and gives rudimentary info about the Winsock. The downside to this tool for DNS queries is its inability to set a query type. NetLab performs A record and PTR record queries, but there is no way to select an MX record—or anything else, for that matter. Among the features in NetLab, security conscious administrators will be interested in knowing of the scanner availability which Figure 12.2 shows in the process of scanning ports on the one configured IP address.

Host

Host is a freeware utility that you can obtain by anonymous FTP from `ftp.nikhef.nl` in the /pub/network directory. The capability of this tool to conveniently perform some DNS inquiries that otherwise require sequences of nslookup commands has won it a place as one of the two freeware programs listed in this chapter. The current distribution includes the source that for Windows needs to be compiled with the BIND 4.9.x files available. An earlier, more limited version is available in binary executable form for Windows. Host has been ported to most UNIX systems, and in its most recent version supports most all the newest DNS features and resource records, including SRV and the DNSsec-related KEY, Digital Signature (SIG), and Non Existence (NXT) resource records. You can use Host to check zone delegation, to obtain record listings by type, and much, much more.

There is a Web interface to some features of the newest version of Host and access to the main page at `www.nikhef.nl/user/e07/tools/host.html` (hosted by the Dutch National Institute for Nuclear and High-Energy Physics, which provides Host).

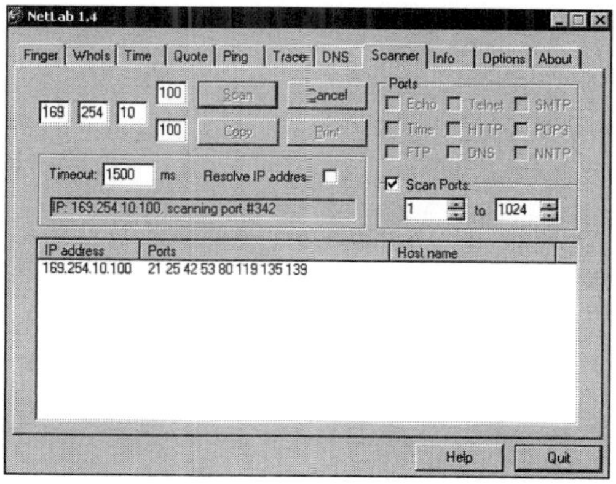

Figure 12.2 NetLab 1.4 shown in process of a limited port scan.

But because many administrators will not have access to the newer version until it is available in a binary executable, the command syntax of the prior version is provided here to give some idea of the capabilities of this version.

```
C:\>host
Usage:      host [-v] [-a] [-t querytype] [options]  name  [server]
Listing:    host [-v] [-a] [-t querytype] [options]  -l zone  [server]
Hostcount:  host [-v] [options] -H [-D] [-E] [-G] zone
Check soa:  host [-v] [options] -C zone
Addrcheck:  host [-v] [options] -A host
Listing options: [-L level] [-S] [-A] [-p] [-P prefserver] [-N skipzone]
Common options:  [-d] [-f|-F filename] [-I chars] [-i|-n] [-q] [-T] [-Z]
Other options:   [-c class] [-e] [-m] [-o] [-r] [-R] [-s secs] [-u] [-w]
```

Extended usage: [-x [name ...]] [-X server [name ...]

ipconfig

The ipconfig utility is a diagnostic command-line tool for Windows NT and Windows 2000. This tool has been enhanced in important ways for Windows 2000 as is pointed out after what is common in both platforms. Previously, in Windows NT it could show how the computer's IP stack is configured and cause a DHCP client to release or renew its IP lease. The Windows NT syntax for the ipconfig tool is as follows:

```
ipconfig
ipconfig /all
ipconfig /release [adapter]
ipconfig /renew [adapter]
```

If you use ipconfig without arguments, it reveals the basic network configuration, as shown in the following example:

```
C:\> ipconfig
Windows NT IP ConfigurationEthernet adapter E190x1:

      IP Address. . . . . . . . . : 192.168.1.2
      Subnet Mask . . . . . . . . : 255.255.255.0
      Default Gateway . . . . . . : 192.168.1.1
```

If DHCP is enabled, you can use the optional **/release** switch with ipconfig to release the IP lease. Likewise, the **/renew** switch reconfigures the IP stack directly from the DHCP server through the lease process. The **/release** and **/renew** switches can also be used with an optional adapter name so that you can specify the adapter to change. This is important when the computer is multihomed.

For Windows 2000 the basic output is much the same, and in either version an output listing is provided for each configured interface. For Windows 2000, however, this tool has been enhanced to allow management of the client resolver cache and also of the DHCP client class. The added options for Windows 2000 are as follows:

```
ipconfig /flushdns
```

As it sounds, **/flushdns** is used to purge the DNS resolver cache on the client.

```
ipconfig /registerdns
```

With **/registerdns** the client is caused to reregister using DNS dynamic updates, after having refreshed its DHCP lease if applicable.

```
ipconfig /displaydns
```

The **/displaydns** option can be used to look at the content of the client's DNS resolver cache.

```
ipconfig /showclassid adapter
```

The **/showclassid** option can be used to list all class IDs allowed on the adapter. Note that adapter is required.

```
ipconfig /setclassid adapter [ClassidToSet]
```

The **/setclassid** option can be used to set class IDs; and when none is given, the class ID is removed from the adapter. Note that adapter is required.

These last two options are a little vague in the documentation. As we go to press, the code is frozen; but the Request for Comment (RFCs) defining the DHCP Option 81 are still subject to revision, which no doubt explains this.

Additionally, Windows 2000 permits adapter name patterns using an asterisk (*) to match any and a question mark (?) to match one character.

When you use the optional **/all** switch, ipconfig reveals a good bit more than basic configuration information. It shows the IP host domain name, the DNS and WINS servers, the NetBIOS node type, the NetBIOS scope ID (if any), and other things. The tool also shows information for every network adapter, if more than one is installed. The following example is typical of the ipconfig tool using the **/all** switch.

```
C:\> ipconfig /all
Windows 2000 IP Configuration

        Host Name . . . . . . . . . . : machine.example.net
        Primary DNS Suffix . . . . . . : .example.net
        Node Type . . . . . . . . . . : Hybrid
        NetBIOS Scope ID. . . . . . . :
        IP Routing Enabled. . . . . . : No
        WINS Proxy Enabled. . . . . . : No

Ethernet adapter Local Area Connection:

        Connection-specific DNS Suffix. :
        Description . . . . . . . . . : 3Com EtherLink XL 10/100 PCI TX NIC (3C905B)
        Physical Address. . . . . . . : 00-A0-B9-68-B1-60
        DHCP Enabled. . . . . . . . . : No
        IP Address. . . . . . . . . . : 192.168.1.2
        Subnet Mask . . . . . . . . . : 255.255.255.0
        Default Gateway . . . . . . . : 192.168.1.1
        DNS Servers . . . . . . . . . : 192.168.1.1
        Primary WINS Server . . . . . : 192.168.1.1
        Secondary WINS Server . . . . : 192.168.1.254
```

winipcfg

The winipcfg utility is a graphical diagnostic tool for Windows 95 and 98 that, like ipconfig, shows how the computer's IP stack is configured. You can invoke winipcfg from a command window or from the Run menu, or you can create a shortcut for the WINIPCFG.EXE program itself. The syntax for the winipcfg tool is as follows:

```
winipcfg
winipcfg /all
```

Figure 12.3 shows the dialog box that appears when you type **winipcfg**. OK closes the tool, and Release releases the current adapter's configuration information. Renew renews the current adapter's configuration information.

The More Info button expands the dialog box to reveal additional information, as shown in Figure 12.4. If you type **winipcfg /all**, the same expanded dialog box appears immediately.

netdiag

The netdiag tool is new and very Windows 2000 specific and helpful. Actually, it might be considered as not a tool in itself so much as a wrapper over almost every networking-related test in Windows 2000. The easiest way to introduce netdiag is to

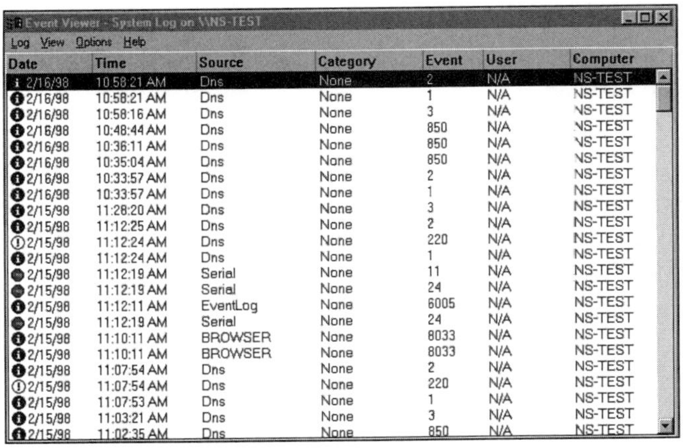

Figure 12.3 The main winipcfg interface.

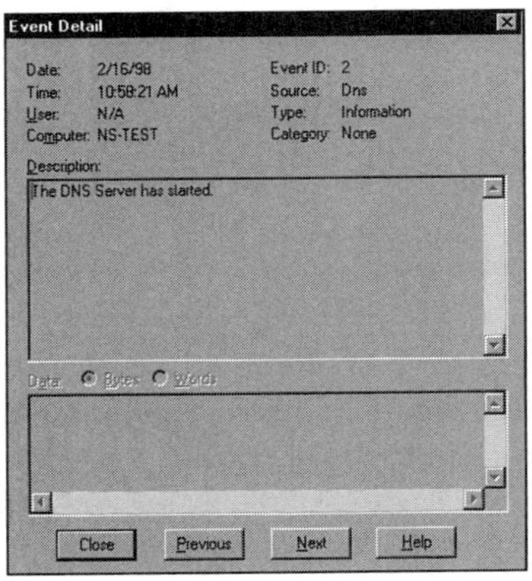

Figure 12.4 The winipcfg /all extended dialog box.

show the help syntax, because it gives a good overview of both how to use this tool and of what it can do.

```
C:\>netdiag /?
Usage: netdiag [/Options]>
   /q - Quiet output (errors only)
   /v - Verbose output
   /l - Log output to NetDiag.log
   /debug - Even more verbose.
   /d:<DomainName> - Find a DC in the specified domain.
   /fix - fix trivial problems.
   /DcAccountEnum - Enumerate DC machine accounts.
   /test:<test name>  - tests only this test. Non - skippable tests will still be
run
```

```
Valid tests are :-
     Ndis - Netcard queries Test
     IpConfig - IP config Test
     Member - Domain membership Test
     NetBTTransports - NetBT transports Test
     Autonet - Autonet address Test
     IpLoopBk - IP loopback ping Test
     DefGw - Default gateway Test
     NbtNm - NetBT name Test
     WINS - WINS service Test
     Winsock - Winsock Test
     DNS - DNS Test
     Browser - Redir and Browser Test
     DsGetDc - DC discovery Test
     DcList - DC list Test
     Trust - Trust relationship Test
     Kerberos - Kerberos Test
     Ldap - LDAP Test
     Route - Routing table Test
     Netstat - Netstat information Test
     Bindings - Bindings Test
     WAN - WAN configuration Test
     Modem - Modem diagnostics Test
     Netware - Netware Test
     IPX - IPX Test
     IPSec - IP Security Test
/skip:<TestName> - skip the named test.  Valid tests are:
     IpConfig - IP config Test
     Autonet - Autonet address Test
     IpLoopBk - IP loopback ping Test
     DefGw - Default gateway Test
     NbtNm - NetBT name Test
     WINS - WINS service Test
     Winsock - Winsock Test
     DNS - DNS Test
     Browser - Redir and Browser Test
     DsGetDc - DC discovery Test
     DcList - DC list Test
     Trust - Trust relationship Test
     Kerberos - Kerberos Test
     Ldap - LDAP Test
     Route - Routing table Test
     Netstat - Netstat information Test
     Bindings - Bindings Test
     WAN - WAN configuration Test
     Modem - Modem diagnostics Test
     Netware - Netware Test
     IPX - IPX Test
     IPSec - IP Security Test
```

netsh

The netsh tool is called NetShell in the Windows 2000 documentation. NetShell provides a shell, or command prompt, environment that is configurable. The power and usefulness of NetShell in part comes from its design based on contexts and that new contexts can be provided using custom DLLs, in part from the provided contexts, and in part from the ability to script netsh use. The netsh utility can be used in online, offline, and script modes. To use it in script mode, netsh is invoked specifying a script file with the **–f** option, or a script may be executed within netsh by using the **exec** command at the netsh prompt. The invocation syntax for netsh is as follows:

```
Netsh  [-a <AliasFile>] [-c <Context>] [-r <RemoteMachine>]
[-f <ScriptFile> ¦ NetshCommand]
```

Within the NetShell interface, all commands can be abbreviated to their point of uniqueness. The two command modes called online and offline are basically controlling live execution or queuing of entered commands. Commands entered while in offline mode may then be executed using the **Commit** command. Scripts may be created within netsh in offline mode and then written out with the **Dump** command. There is much more available in netsh than can be touched on in this chapter. The interested reader should refer to the Windows 2000 online help documentation where a search for "netsh" will provide a long list, including much information on its use with routing and remote access services that is not touched on in what follows.

The following listing shows starting netsh and listing out the main commands, which include the built-in contexts:

```
C:\>netsh
netsh>?
```

The following commands are available:

```
Commands in this context:
..                          - Goes up one context level.
?                           - Displays a list of commands.
aaaa                        - Changes to the `aaaa' context.
abort                       - Discards changes made while in offline mode.
add                         - Adds a configuration entry to a list of entries.
alias                       - Adds an alias.
bye                         - Exits the program.
commit                      - Commits changes made while in offline mode.
delete                      - Deletes a configuration entry from a list of entries.
dhcp                        - Changes to the `dhcp' context.
dump                        - Displays a configuration script.
exec                        - Runs a script file.
exit                        - Exits the program.
help                        - Displays a list of commands.
interface                   - Changes to the `interface' context.
offline                     - Sets the current mode to offline.
online                      - Sets the current mode to online.
```

```
popd                          - Pops a context from the stack.
pushd                         - Pushes current context on stack.
quit                          - Exits the program.
ras                           - Changes to the `ras' context.
routing                       - Changes to the `routing' context.
set                           - Updates configuration settings.
show                          - Displays information.
unalias                       - Deletes an alias.
wins                          - Changes to the `wins' context.

The following subcontexts are available:
 routing interface ras dhcp wins aaaa

To view help for a command, type the command, followed by a space, and then
 type ?.
```

Notice the listed, built-in contexts: routing, interface, ras, dhcp, wins, and aaa. To give some idea of navigation in netsh and of the rich set of capabilities, the following shows changing to the interface, the dhcp, and then the wins contexts and in each getting to the full subcommand **help**.

First, the netsh interface context is as follows:

```
netsh> interface
interface>/?

The following commands are available:

Global commands:
<<  the list here exactly  repeats the top level context commands already shown
and has been deleted >>

Commands in this context:
?                             - Displays help.
add                           - Adds a configuration entry to a table.
delete                        - Deletes a configuration entry from a table.
dump                          - Dumps a configuration script.
help                          - Displays help.
ip                            - Changes to the 'interface ip' context.
reset                         - Resets information.
set                           - Sets configuration information.
show                          - Displays information.

The following subcontexts are available:
 ip

To view help for a command, type the command, followed by a space, and then
 type ?.

interface> show
```

```
The following commands are available:

Commands in this context:
show credentials - Shows the credentials used to connect an interface.
show interface - Displays interfaces.
interface>show int

Admin State    State          Type             Interface Name
-------------------------------------------------------------------------
Enabled                       Dedicated        Local Area Connection
Enabled                       Internal         Internal
Enabled                       Loopback         Loopback

interface>ip
interface ip> show

The following commands are available:

Commands in this context:
show address             - Displays IP addresses.
show config              - Displays IP address and other information.
show dns                 - Displays the DNS server addresses.
show icmp                - Displays ICMP statistics
show interface           - Displays IP interface statistics
show ipaddress           - Displays IP addresses
show ipnet               - Displays IP net-to-media mappings
show ipstats             - Displays IP statistics
show joins               - Displays multicast groups joined
show offload             - Displays the offload information.
show tcpconn             - Displays TCP connections
show tcpstats            - Displays TCP statistics
show udpconn             - Displays UDP connections
show udpstats            - Displays UDP statistics
show wins                - Displays the WINS server addresses.
interface ip>
```

You will probably already be convinced that this is a tool to learn and use. But now consider server support by this look at the netsh dhcp context:

```
netsh> dhcp
dhcp>?
list  - Lists all the commands available.
dump    - Dumps configuration to a text file.
help    - Displays help.
?       -Displays help.
add     - Adds a configuration entry to a table.
delete         - Deletes a configuration entry from a table.
show           - Displays information.
server [\\servername/ipaddress]        - To switch the context to the server
specified.
                                         A Null implies the local machine.
```

```
dhcp>server 169.254.10.100
dhcp server>/?
list                            - Lists all the commands available.
dump                            - Dumps configuration to a text file.
help                             - Displays help.
?                               - Displays help.
add                             - Adds a configuration entry to a table.
delete                          - Deletes a configuration entry from a table.
initiate                        - Initiates an operation.
set                             - Sets configuration information.
show                             - Displays information.
scope <scope-ip-address>        - To switch to the scope identified by
                                  the IP Address.
mscope <mscope-name>            - To switch to the mscope identified by
                                  the MScope name.

dhcp server>show all

MIBCounts:
        Discovers = 7.
        Offers = 7.
        Requests = 7.
        Acks = 7128.
        Naks = 0.
        Declines = 0.
        Releases = 4.
        ServerStartTime = Saturday, November 27, 1999 3:19:09 PM
        Scopes = 1.
        Subnet = 10.0.10.0.
                No. of Addresses in use = 3.
                No. of free Addresses = 250.
                No. of pending offers = 0.

Server Database Properties :

        DatabaseName                    = dhcp.mdb
        DatabasePath                    = C:\WINNT\System32\dhcp
        DatabaseBackupPath              = C:\WINNT\System32\dhcp\backup
        DatabaseBackupInterval          = 60 mins.
        DatabaseLoggingFlag             = 1
        DatabaseRestoreFlag             = 0
        DatabaseCleanupInterval          = 1440 mins.

Server Status:
        Server Attrib - Server Servicing Clients            :TRUE
        Server Attrib - Dynamic BootP Support Enabled       :TRUE
        Server Attrib - DHCP Server Part Of DS              :FALSE
        Server Attrib - DHCP Server Bindings Aware          :TRUE
        Server Attrib - Administrative Rights               :TRUE
dhcp server>list
list                            - Lists all the commands available.
```

```
dump                          - Dumps configuration to a text file.
help                          - Displays help.
?                             - Displays help.

add class                     - Adds a class to the server.
add mscope                    - Adds a multicast scope to the server.
add optiondef                 - Adds a new option to the server.
add scope                     - Adds a scope to the Server.

delete class                  - Deletes a specific class from the server.
delete mscope                 - Deletes a multicast scope from the Server.
delete optiondef              - Deletes an option from the Server.
delete optionvalue            - Deletes an option value from the server.
delete scope                  - Deletes a scope from the Server.
delete superscope             - Deletes a superscope from the Server.

initiate auth                 - Initiates retry authorization with the server.
initiate reconcile            - Checks and reconciles the database for all
                                scopes under the server.

set auditlog                  - Sets the audit log parameters for the server.
set databasebackupinterval    - Sets the database backup interval of the
                                current server.
set databasebackuppath        - Sets the database backup path for the Server.
set databasecleanupinterval   - Sets the database clean up interval.
set databaseloggingflag       - Sets/resets the database logging flag.
set databasename              - Sets the name of the server database file.
set databasepath              - Sets the path of the server database file.
set databaserestoreflag       - Sets/Resets the database restore flag.
set detectconflictretry       - Sets the number of conflict detection attempts
                                by the DHCP server.
set dnsconfig                 - Sets the Dynamic DNS configuration for the
                                Server.
set optionvalue               - Sets the global option value for the Server.
set server                    - Sets the current server in the Server mode.
set userclass                 - Sets the global user class name for
                                subsequent operation.
set vendorclass               - Sets the global vendor class name for
                                subsequent operation.

show all                      - Displays all information for the Server.
show auditlog                 - Displays the Audit log settings for the server.
show bindings                 - Displays Binding information for the server.
show class                    - Displays all available classes for the Server.
show detectconflictretry      - Displays the detect conflict retry settings.
show dnsconfig                - Displays the dynamic DNS configuration for the
                                server.
show mibinfo                  - Displays MIBInfo for the Server.
show mscope                   - Displays all multicast scopes for the Server.
show optiondef                - Displays all options for the Server.
```

```
show optionvalue              - Displays all optionvalues that are set for the
                                server.
show scope                    - Displays all available scopes under the Server.
show server                    - Displays the current Server.
show dbproperties             - Displays server database configuration
                                information.
show serverstatus             - Displays the current status for the Server.
show userclass                - Displays the currently set user class name.
show vendorclass              - Displays the currently set vendor class name.
show version                  - Displays the current version of the Server.

scope <scope-ip-address>      - To switch to the scope identified by
                                the IP Address.
mscope <mscope-name>          - To switch to the mscope identified by
                                the MScope name.

dhcp server>
```

To shorten things up, the following shows only the commands within the WINS server context:

```
wins server>list
list                              - Lists all the commands available.
dump                              - Dumps configuration to the output.
help                              - Displays help.
?                                 - Displays help.
Add Name                          - Adds a name record to the server.
Add Partner                       - Adds a replication partner to the server.
Add PNGServer                     - Adds a list of Persona Non Grata Servers for
                                    the current server.

Check Database                    - Checks the consistency of the database.
Check Name                        - Checks a list of name records against a set
                                    of WINS servers.
Check Version                     - Checks the consistency of the version
                                    number.

Delete Name                       - Deletes a registered name from the server
                                    database.
Delete Partner                    - Deletes a replication partner from the
                                    list of replication partners.
Delete Records                    - Deletes or tombstones all or a set of
                                    records from the server.
Delete Owners                     - Deletes a list of owners and their records.
Delete PNGServer                  - Deletes all or selected Persona Non Grata
                                    Servers from the list

Init Backup                       - Initiates backup of WINS database.
Init Import                       - Initiates import from an LMHOSTS file.
Init Pull                         - Initiates and send a pull trigger to
                                    another WINS server.
```

```
Init PullRange               - Initiates and pull a range of records
                               from another WINS server.
Init Push                    - Initiates and send a push trigger to
                               another WINS server.
Init Replicate               - Initiates replication of database with
                               replication partners.
Init Restore                 - Initiates restoring of database from a file.
Init Scavenge                - Initiates scavenging of WINS database
                               for the server.
Init Search                  - Initiates search on the WINS server
                               database for the specified record.

Reset Statistics             - Resets the server statistics.

Set AutoPartnerConfig        - Sets the automatic replication partner
                               configuration info for the server.
Set BackupPath               - Sets the backup parameters for the server.
Set Burstparam               - Sets the burst handling parameters for the
                               server.
Set DefaultParam             - Sets the default values for the WINS Server
                               configuration parameters.
Set Logparam                 - Sets the database and event logging options.
Set MigrateFlag              - Sets the migration flag for the server.
Set NameRecord               - Sets Intervals and Timeout values for the
                               server.
Set PeriodicDBChecking       - Sets periodic database checking parameters
                               for the server.
Set Pullpartnerconfig        - Sets the configuration parameters for the
                               specified pull partner.
Set Pushpartnerconfig        - Sets the configuration parameter for the
                               specified push partner.
Set PullParam                - Sets the default pull partner parameters for
                               the server.
Set PushParam                - Sets the default push partner parameters for
                               the server.
Set ReplicateFlag            - Sets the replication flag for the server.
Set Startversion             - Sets the start version ID for the database.
Show Browser                 - Displays all active domain master browser
                               [1Bh] records.
Show Database                - Displays the database and records for all or
                               a list of specified owner servers.
Show Info                    - Displays server configuration information.
Show Name                    - Displays the detail information for a
                               particular record in the server.
Show Partner                 - Displays all or pull or push partners for
                               the server.
Show Partnerproperties       - Displays default partner configuration.
Show Pullpartnerconfig       - Displays configuration information for a
                               pull partner.
Show Pushpartnerconfig       - Displays configuration information for a
                               push partner.
```

```
Show Reccount                      - Displays no of records owned by a specific
                                     owner server.
Show Recbyversion                  - Displays records owned by a specific server.
Show Server                        - Displays the currently selected server.
Show Statistics                    - Displays the statistics for the WINS server.
Show Version                       - Displays the current maximum version
                                     counter value for the WINS Server.
Show Versionmap                    - Displays the owner Id to Maximum Version
                                     Number mappings.

wins server>
```

netstat

The netstat tool displays protocol statistics and the state of current TCP/IP connections. Note the difference: Netstat works for TCP/IP connections, and nbtstat works for NetBIOS connections. The syntax for the netstat utility is as follows:

```
C:\>netstat /?

Displays protocol statistics and current TCP/IP network connections.

NETSTAT [-a] [-e] [-n] [-s] [-p proto] [-r] [interval]

  -a            Displays all connections and listening ports.
                (Server-side connections are normally not shown).
  -e            Displays Ethernet statistics. This may be combined
                with the -s option.
  -n             Displays addresses and port numbers in numerical form.
  -p proto      Shows connections for the protocol specified by proto; proto
                may be TCP or UDP. If used with the -s option to display
                per-protocol statistics, proto may be TCP, UDP, or IP..
  -r            Displays the routing table.
  -s            Displays per-protocol statistics. By default, statistics are
                shown for TCP, UDP and IP; the -p option may be
                used to specify a subset of the default.
  interval      Redisplays selected statistics, pausing interval seconds
                between each display. Press CTRL+C to stop redisplaying
                statistics. If omitted, netstat will print the current
                configuration information once.
```

nbtstat

The nbtstat tool checks the state of *NetBIOS over TCP*/IP (NetBT) connections and also returns NetBIOS session and name-resolution statistics. In addition, this tool can be used to force an update of the local NetBIOS name cache. This tool is mostly unchanged from NT, but it should be pointed out that the **–RR** switch was added beginning at Service Pack 4 and is much welcome because it allows an alternative to rebooting to reregister with WINS. The syntax for the nbtstat utility is as follows:

```
C:\>nbtstat /?
Displays protocol statistics and current TCP/IP connections using NBT
(NetBIOS over TCP/IP).
NBTSTAT [ [-a RemoteName] [-A IP address] [-c] [-n] [-r] [-R] [-RR] [-s] [-S]
[interval] ]

  -a   (adapter status)   Lists the remote machine's name table given its name
  -A   (Adapter status)   Lists the remote machine's name table given its IP
                          address.
  -c   (cache)            Lists NBT's cache of remote [machine] names and their
                          IP addresses
  -n   (names)            Lists local NetBIOS names.
  -r   (resolved)         Lists names resolved by broadcast and via WINS
  -R   (Reload)           Purges and reloads the remote cache name table
  -S   (Sessions)         Lists sessions table with the destination IP addresses
  -s   (sessions)         Lists sessions table converting destination IP
                          addresses to computer NETBIOS names.
  -RR  (ReleaseRefresh)   Sends Name Release packets to WINs and then, starts
                          Refresh

  RemoteName              Remote host machine name.
  IP address              Dotted decimal representation of the IP address.
  interval                Redisplays selected statistics, pausing interval
                          seconds
                          between each display. Press Ctrl+C to stop
                          redisplaying statistics.
```

System Monitor

The System Monitor may be started by **perfmon.msc** in Run or at a command prompt, or by selecting Performance in the Administrative tools part of the Start menu. The System Monitor node is what will be familiar from Windows NT, where its precursor was called the Performance Monitor. After the DNS object has been selected in Add Counters (use the button with the big plus sign [+], however, it will be apparent that this is a new implementation indeed. There are more than 50 counters for the DNS server object, which should provide for monitoring most of the aspects of the DNS server that might be of interest. While in the Add Counters window, it is worth noticing that objects are available for the other services that are discussed in this book, such as DHCP and WINS.

The best any Windows administrator can do is to become fully familiar with the use of Performance Monitor, and its logging and alerting capabilities, and then to make a practice of using these. It is all too easy to overlook the power of this tool in understanding machine operations. The counters provide statistics on many aspects of the following and more:

```
AXFR and IXFR transfers
Caching and memory use
Dynamic updates
Notify
```

```
Recursive queries
Secure updates
Total query and response volume
TCP and UDP processing
WINS
Zone transfers
```

netmon

A listing of tools related to networking in Windows 2000 or NT would do an injustice by failing to mention the Network Monitor. This tool permits the capture and examination of communication packets. Although a little too low level for routine use, this tool can be invaluable both in troubleshooting and also in understandin what is happening as compared to what is said to be happening.

This is an optionally installed component on server versions of Windows, so one may need to use the Add/Remove Programs applet of the Control Panel; where, by selecting Add/Remove Windows Components to bring up the Windows Components Wizard, one can find it under the Details of Management and Monitoring Tools under the name Network Monitoring Tools. Just as with NT 4.0, this is a version of the tool is restricted from putting the NIC into promiscuous mode. One needs the System Management Server version or a third-party tool if trapping more than packets from and to the server where the tool is installed is needed.

Summary

Windows 2000 has a large networking substructure, and a heavy reliance on healthy DNS services. It is not surprising then to find the number of tools provided has increased, as well as their capability. This chapter has reviewed the main tools provided by Microsoft as well as a couple of others. For the main tools, discussion has been provided to help one start to use them effectively.

13

Best Practices and Maintenance Tasks

THIS CHAPTER REVIEWS THE FOLLOWING:

- **Design-Tweaking DNS Servers.** This section covers a number of issues related to the evolution of more complex DNS server hierarchies, and recommends some design objectives that can be used. A number of the topics of the other sections provide input to the overarching considerations of this section.
- **Ongoing Monitoring of DNS Servers.** This section explains how you can use tools provided in Windows 2000 to remain informed about your DNS Servers, their configuration, and their operational quality.
- **Changing a Registered DNS Server's Internet Protocol (IP) address.** This section helps you consider some important aspects when changing a DNS server's IP address, including its registration with InterNIC.
- **Adding Capacity with a New DNS Server.** This section summarizes the steps and reasons for building a new DNS server within an existing DNS services architecture.
- **Zone Data Maintenance.** The various tasks involved in maintaining the zones on, and moving zones between, DNS servers are considered in this section.

Many decisions determining how well DNS services work are made at the design stage, or when adapting the design as its performance and reliability are observed over time. To maintain the services at their peak, and to pace their capacity to changing requirements placed on them, the DNS administrator needs continually take the pulse of the installed DNS servers, including separately understanding the performance of the machines on which the DNS servers are installed. The service level of the software and, especially security-related, patches must be kept current. And then, of course, there is maintenance of the DNS database. This includes the day-to-day management of resource record changes, the occasional moving of zones to different machines, replacement and rebuilding of machines, and now also cleaning of dynamic zones to remove stale records and keep their size in check.

Design-Tweaking DNS Servers

This section looks at some ways to monitor DNS servers. For this to be of most use, you need a feel for your services. You need to have established baselines of performance and of load within the "normal" operations window. You also need a good understanding of the services design, of what it should be capable. Then, when monitoring shows some deviation, going over to the great chart on the wall will not be a hunting expedition, but merely a taking of bearings to confirm the places to be tested that could be the cause. This chart of your services architecture should make clear to you what types of queries are passing where, and from whom. It should also help you to see the path a client is taking for an internal and an external resolution as well as the alternatives available to the client.

Watching performance of your DNS servers is important, and can show the need to adjust how your services are set up; but this only goes so far. The performance as experienced by the end user, or resolvers in other DNS servers, is the real measure, and this information is not captured by looking at the measures a server logs about itself. One needs to have a way to evaluate the whole system, network latencies included, that affect the delivered service. This could be automated spot checks at times of normal load; and less reliably or usefully, a simple attentiveness to customer feedback.

When bottlenecks or heavy loading of points are indicated, see whether there is an easy way to shift load. Or, is another server needed to split the load? Why is a server spending so many cycles responding to AXFR transfers when all should be IXFR?

Security policies were taken into account in the initial design. Are they still being implemented correctly? Does there need to be a testing process? Or, does the change control and configuration change monitoring provide sufficient insurance?

Over time, a design will be changed. You may find that having clients configured to use primary servers directly, rather than secondaries, is too confining of your options to perform manual zone or software maintenance, for example. Or use of the Internet in business processes may have increased the amount of resolution of external names.

Or any number of forces will change the system over time. As this happens, keep the design criteria in mind and try to adjust your deployment so that it meets the requirements you have found best for your use of the services.

Recommended criteria for this include the following:

- Easy to maintain at current service and security patch level without client service degradation or interruption.
- Minimum distance, as measured by network quality, from clients to servers authoritative for the clients' own, and most frequently used, zone data.
- Minimum network bandwidth consumed for zone transfers, but minimum time for convergence of zone data at all authoritative servers.
- Every client configurable with at least two truly independent, resolution paths that can provide all and only resolution access within the security policy of the site

When translating these into some of the available configuration choices, follow these recommendations:

- Use incremental transfers (IXFR) with the Notify option configured for use.
- Restrict transfers from occurring between any except the intended DNS servers.
- Provide parallel servers, by server type and zone content, for all resolution needs.
- Distribute servers to be local, in terms of network quality, to the clients using them.
- Use secondaries for redundancy, load distribution, and to free primaries from client burden especially when storage is Active Directory integrated.
- Understand and accept the lack of security over dynamic updates, or use Active Directory storage with only secured updates allowed, if dynamic updates are enabled. Understand how record ownership is assigned and monitor membership in the DnsUpdateProxy group (possibly making it a Restricted group) so that no machines are mistakenly made members.
- Restrict queries on zones used to support the Active Directory to only trusted clients.
- Keep zone data cleaned of excess, unnecessary resource records. For any zone this means such things as unneeded CNAME records; for dynamic zones, however, this means cleaning out stale records.
- Use forwarding and caching servers appropriately; and where zone data is not needed locally, do not provide it.
- Use bridgehead transfers between major sites, with site-local secondaries mastering from their site bridgehead server.
- Understand dynamic zone change rates and the dampening effected with the NoUpdateInterval parameter.

- Align Dynamic Host Configuration Protocol (DHCP) lease duration with scavenging parameters (and possibly even adjust time-to-live [TTL] values) when dynamic updates are enabled. Also know how record ownership works if the DHCP server is and is not made a member of the DnsUpdateProxy group.
- Divide larger zones with multiple subdomains into separate zones when localized distribution to secondaries can be minimized.
- Configure servers to refuse recursive queries where this makes sense, such as your public presence servers.
- Minimize overheads imposed on the server—by disabling subnet mask ordering where this provides no benefit, for example, or by reducing caching memory consumption by cleaning zones.

This list could be continued, especially by looking at specific DNS server hierarchies or server types. For some servers with vulnerable placement, for example, it makes sense to restrict Transmission Control Protocol/Internet Protocol (TCP/IP) (and also User Datagram Protocol [UDP]) to only the needed ports. Be willing to go to the chart and assess alternatives for reconfiguration over time.

Ongoing Monitoring of DNS Servers

In a small business–sized system, DNS is fairly maintenance free. As the system grows more complex in its hierarchy of transfers and site distribution, the number of places where less-than-ideal behavior can develop increases. To determine whether a larger system is performing as at optimum levels, you must monitor and measure it.

Using the Microsoft Management Console Effectively

This book to this point has introduced you to most every switch and setting in the DNS server management console. With some time to explore further, the ability to start and stop the server or individual zones, to cause a zone to reload, to force synchronizing of the on disk zone storage, and a host of other options will be second nature. We have noted that within the console, many DNS servers can be connected for a "one-stop shop" to manage a group of servers conveniently. You by now have probably discovered how easy it is to forget to set the console mode to Advanced under the View menu.

You have also seen that the Computer Management console is preconfigured to allow access to the Event log, DNS, DHCP, Windows Internet Naming Service (WINS) servers, and much else. What you have not seen yet is how to make a custom console.

While defining a custom console, you can select and add any of the available Microsoft Management Console snap-ins and their extensions, so you will want to make sure these are available on your machine. The easiest way to build up the collection of available snap-ins is to make sure that the Windows 2000 Resource Kit and the Administrative Tools package have been installed. Your licensed copy of the Resource Kit launches into installation when the CD is loaded. The Administrative

Tools package is shipped on the Windows 2000 Server CDs. You can find a Windows Installer package named ADMINPAK.MSI in the .\i386 directory of the CD or in the %windir%\system32 directory of an installed server. As with any MSI package, it is better to install this through the Add/Remove Programs applet; but you can use the Install option of the MSI file's context menu. Either of these can be installed on a Professional build you will be using for remote management of your servers.

To define a custom console, just follow these very simple steps:

1. Using the Start menu, run **"mmc"** to bring up an empty management console.
2. From the Console pull-down menu, select Add/Remove Snap-in.
3. Click the Add button under the list box.
4. In the Add Standalone Snap-in dialog box, you need to add and select snap-ins in the order that they will be listed in the resulting console. Start with DNS, highlighting it and clicking Add.
5. As in step 4, select and add DHCP and WINS if these are used, select and add Event Viewer and also Performance Logs and Alerts. Very possibly you may find Routing and Remote Access desirable Some snap-ins, such as Event Viewer, can be added separately for the local machine and for each remote machine. If these are added for the local machine, their focus can later be changed to another machine from their context menus.
6. After you have finished making selections, click Close.
7. Some snap-ins have registered extensions. Use the Extensions tab of the Add/Remove Snap-in dialog box and select Routing and Remote Access in the drop box, if you added it. Select the check box beside the IP Routing extension. Doing this updates the list in the drop box, where you can now select the newly added IP Routing choice.
8. After you have configured the desired snap-ins, click OK to return to the new console.
9. Use the Console pull-down menu and select Save As to store the console, giving it a name with the .MSC extension and a location (such as the desktop).

This configures a tool customized to what you do. At this point, just configure each snap-in added, DNS, DHCP, WINS to connect to the servers that will be managed. In building this, we let the mode default to Author mode, which means that when opened, the snap-ins configured in the console can be modified in the future. Consoles may also be saved in a number of restricted User modes by first setting choices by using the Options dialog box listed in the Console drop-down menu. You can use restricted consoles to provide task-oriented interfaces to those who have been delegated management tasks.

A nice feature of the management capabilities in Windows 2000 is the addition of the **runas** command, which provides something much like **su** does for UNIX. This enables you to follow good practices by using a normal account and then running management tasks with elevated privileges when needed without logging off and back on as the privileged user. You can issue **runas /?** on the command line for full syntax options. For example, you could use **runas /user:topdomain\schmadmin "mmc %windir%\system32\schmmgmt.msc"** to execute the Schema Management console as the account schmadmin defined in domain topdomain.

An easier way to use the **runas** capability is to just create a shortcut in the Start menu for your new custom console. Then navigate to the new shortcut in the Start menu, right-click, and edit its properties (found in the shortcut's context menu). On the Shortcut tab of the properties, just check the box labeled Run as Different User. Having done this, whenever the shortcut is used you will be presented with a dialog box for logging on with an alternative account, which is then used while in the execution session. Restricted custom consoles with this **runas** setting configured are an effective way to delegate tasks and the power to perform those tasks.

DNS Server Statistics and Configuration Information

DNS server has a huge number of internal statistics. We will not even try to show the many pages of output available from the command line using the **dnscmd <server> /statistics** command, where a period (.) is used for the local <server> or a DNS host name or IP address can be provided. You can clear the server statistics with **dnscmd <server> /statistics /clear**, and you can filter the view to provide only a specified selection of statistics output. Listing 13.1 provides information on the categories of statistics available, and the filtering of them. Much of the information available with this command is not otherwise normally available, although some is surfaced in other tools. In the future, new interfaces to management information and live management of DNS Server may become available as vendors or Microsoft develop on the fact that the Windows 2000 DNS Server is fully instrumented using the underlying *Windows Management Instrumentation* (WMI) services.

Listing 13.1 **The Available dnscmd Statistics Options**

```
C:\>dnscmd /statistics /?
USAGE:  DnsCmd <ServerName> /Statistics [ <Filter> ¦ /Clear ]
        <Filter> -- combination of desired stats: (ALL is the default)
                00000001    -- Time
                00000002    -- Query
                00000004    -- Query2
                00000008    -- Recurse
                00000010    -- Master
                00000020    -- Secondary
                00000040    -- Wins
                00000100    -- Update
                00000200    -- SkwanSec
                00000400    -- Ds
                00010000    -- Memory
                00100000    -- PacketMem
```

```
                00040000     -- Dbase
                00080000     -- Records
                00200000     -- NbstatMem
        /Clear   -- clear statistics data
Command completed successfully.
```

The use of **dnscmd <server> /info** is a very quick way to examine the settings controlling server operations. Listing 13.2 is the output from this command issued against the local server, in which you will recognize most of the switches that have been discussed in the previous chapters.

Listing 13.2 **Settings Information as Presented by DNSCMD.EXE**

```
C:\>dnscmd . /info
Query result:
Server info:
        ptr                         = 00075AE0
        server name                 = demo1.home.local
        version                     = C2000005
        DS container                = c
  Configuration:
        dwLogLevel                           = 00000000
        dwDebugLevel                         = 00000000
        dwRpcProtocol                        = FFFFFFFF
        dwNameCheckFlag                      = 00000002
        cAddressAnswerLimit                  = 0
        dwRecursionRetry                     = 3
        dwRecursionTimeout                   = 15
        dwDsPollingInterval                  = 300
  Configuration Flags:
        fBootMethod                          = 3
        fAdminConfigured                     = 0
        fAllowUpdate                         = 1
        fDsAvailable                         = 1
        fAutoReverseZones                    = 1
        fAutoCacheUpdate                     = 0
        fSlave                               = 0
        fNoRecursion                         = 0
        fRoundRobin                          = 1
        fLocalNetPriority                    = 1
        fStrictFileParsing                   = 0
        fLooseWildcarding                    = 0
        fBindSecondaries                     = 0
        fWriteAuthorityNs                    = 0
  Aging Configuration:
        ScavengingInterval                   = 0
        DefaultAgingState                    = 0
        DefaultRefreshInterval               = 168
        DefaultNoRefreshInterval             = 168
```

continues

Listing 13.2 **Continued**

```
  ServerAddresses:
        Addr Count = 2
                Addr[0] => 169.254.10.100
                Addr[1] => 169.254.10.101
  ListenAddresses:
        NULL IP Array.
  Forwarders:
        Addr Count = 1
                Addr[0] => 10.10.9.9
        forward timeout         = 5
        slave                   = 0
Command completed successfully.
```

Monitoring the DNS Server Performance

DNS server has an extensive set of counters in the DNS object used by System Monitor, as were listed in Table 11.1 earlier. The Windows 2000 System Monitor is used in tandem with the Performance Logs and Alerts management console snap-in. Together System Monitor and Performance Logs and Alerts provide the capabilities available in NT 4 as Performance Monitor (which, by the way, can be found in the Resource Kit as PERFMON4.EXE). Figure 13.1 shows using Performance Logs and Alerts to set an alert on AXFR zone transfers, assuming all servers have been configured so that only incremental transfers should occur.

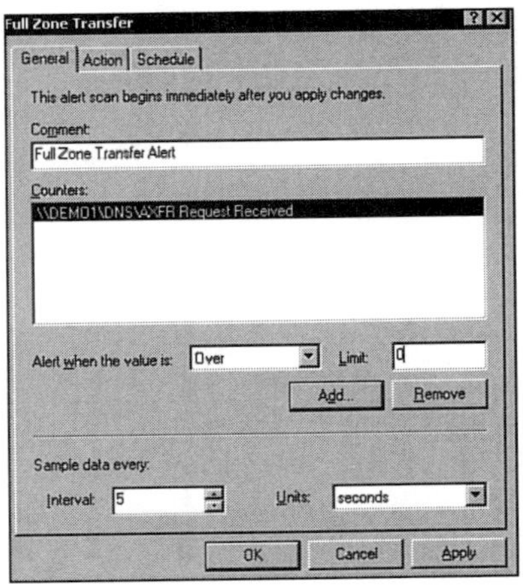

Figure 13.1 Configuring an alert using DNS server object counters.

The flexibility of this system-provided service is quite large. When an alert is triggered, it is possible to start Performance Monitor logging, write to the Event log, send a message, or fire up a command. Scanning for alertable conditions can be scheduled to happen only during defined time windows, with the schedule being set per alert.

Logging is the ability to have the counters recorded to file on a per-object basis, such as for all counters of the DNS object. This log file may then be analyzed later. Periodic logging is an excellent way to build up a library of data from which trends may be extracted for capacity analysis.

The System Monitor itself can be used to play log files or to view live statistics in one of a few charting/graphing modes. One feature not to overlook is the use of the System Monitor Properties dialog box. Somehow there ended up being two different dialog boxes by this name in the first release of Windows 2000. The properties accessed in the Action or context menu when the System Monitor node has focus is of little use. Rather, in the toolbar above the charting area, click on the icon having the image of a hand pointing into a sheet of paper, just to the left beside the red circle with a white "X" icon. Most settings are for visual presentation, but here is where the display refresh rate interval is found.

This book doesn't cover this tool in any further detail. But, as a final word, this capability is an essential one with which one should become well familiar.

Watching the DNS Event Log for Problems

DNS services are so important to Windows 2000 that DNS has been given its own Event log. For a small business, for example, it is one thing to plan and execute an agreement to share DNS data and duties with an Internet Sevice Provider (ISP). Yet it's another thing altogether to make sure everything is working properly. The Event log provides valuable clues you can use (for example, to verify that transfers are happening as they should).

This is usually accessed within the Computer Management console using the **compmgmt.msc** command, or the Manage selection of the My Computer context menu, or it is also accessed directly by selecting Event Viewer from the Administrative Tools folder of the Start menu. The Event log contains entries for any severe DNS server problems and also informative entries for such things as zone transfers. The value of keeping a watch on the Event log cannot be understated. Small problems surfacing here can explain, and help one to cure, problems in many aspects of a Windows 2000 Active Directory environment. Tools available to issue alerts, such as by email, when specific events are logged are available to make watching the Event log an easier task with multiple systems and to many other, better things to do.

Event logs are records of system messages written in Windows 2000. Event log entries generally have the following format:

```
<TYPE> <DATE> <TIME> <SOURCE> <CATEGORY> <EVENT> <USER> <COMPUTER> <DATA>
```

The Event Viewer displays different logs for the various services: System, Security, Application, Directory Service, File Replication Service, DNS server, and so on. The <DATA> associated with an event provides extended diagnostic information. For monitoring the DNS service, just select the DNS server log in the appropriate view (see Figure 13.2). The other items listed above—<TYPE>, <CATEGORY>, and so on—can be arranged by dragging on the separation bars in the right-pane heading. The online help in Windows 2000 contains a listing with explanations for the commonly seen DNS Event log messages.

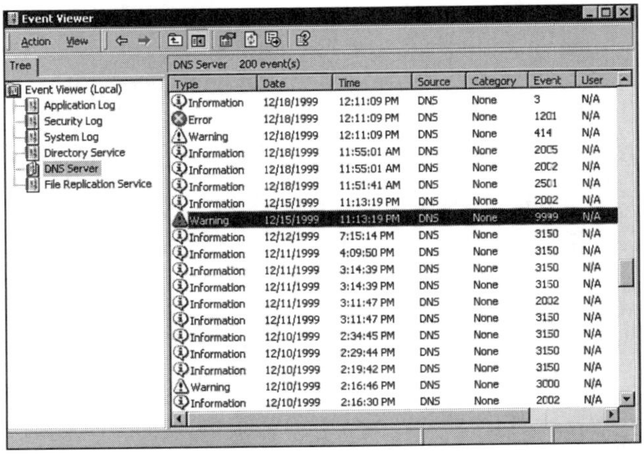

Figure 13.2 The DNS server Event log.

Figure 13.2 shows the format of the typical Event log. Notice the leftmost column of the Events window, which displays the type of entry. The white "bubble" with the "i" denotes that this is an informational message and that no error condition exists. The yellow triangle with the "!" denotes that this is a warning message. Some condition requiring the administrator's attention has been noted, but the system continues to function. The third symbol, a red circle with a white "X," tells the administrator that a severe error has occurred and that some aspect of the configured system is probably left in a nonfunctional state. This could have resulted from a zone failing to load or from a failed piece of hardware. Double-clicking on an item of interest brings up a window with further details, as illustrated in Figure 13.3.

The event shown in Figure 13.3 indicates that the DNS service has encountered erratic communications. This often seen message does not necessarily indicate a problem with the server; because a high collision rate on inbound messages, such as during a transfer, may cause this. However, this message can also be triggered by someone mounting a denial attack based on malformed packets. Another set of events to watch for are startup initialization messages that should occur any time the DNS server is started. Other messages display when zone transfers occur or if the service stops. If any other messages appear in the Event log regarding DNS, they should be evaluated to see what has happened. Warnings occur if the administrator has started the service via a boot file and then issued an unsupported directive. Generally, warnings indicate a problem, but they do not necessarily stop the DNS server from answering queries. If a fatal error has occurred and the red "X" icon appears in the Event log, the DNS server is not functioning as configured and the administrator must correct some problem.

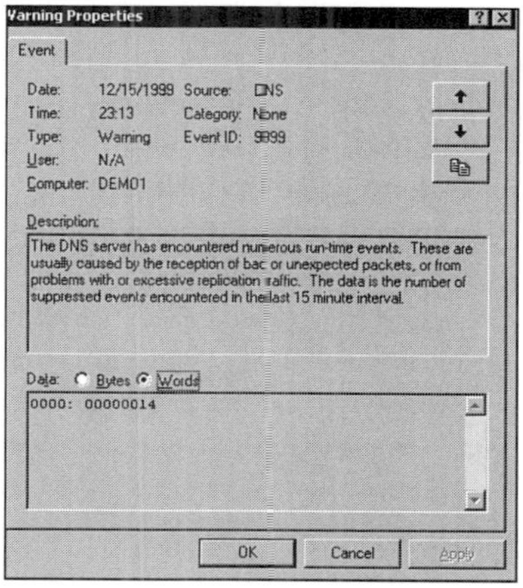

Figure 13.3 An event with data as recorded in the DNS server log.

Preventing Configuration Drift

Configuration drift is really only an issue in an environment with shared administration. After a server has been tuned through the server and zone configurations, it is worth having a method in place to check that these settings are not unintentionally changed, as can often happen when one administrator adjusts a setting without having a full understanding of all design issues and service impacts. One of the easiest ways to accomplish this in the Windows 2000 DNS Server is to have on file extracts of the Registry structure at HKLM\System\CurrentControlSet\Services\DNS because this does include current values for all these settings. For Windows 2000 it seems that for this key the NT 4 Resource Kit utilities REG.EXE and REGDMP.EXE do work, and a version of REGDMP.EXE is provided with the Windows 2000 Resource Kit. The first of these saves the key in a binary form suited for restoring and the second dumps the key into an ASCII file suited to reading and automated comparing.

In NT 4 or (although unsupported) in Windows 2000, the commands to store these into files at C:\bkup \DNScfg\Srv1 are as follows:

```
reg save HKLM\System\CurrentControlSet\Services\DNS  C:\bkup\DNScfg\Srv1\DNSkey-bin

regdmp HKEY_LOCAL_MACHINE\System\CurrentControlSet\Services\DNS  >
C:\bkup\DNScfg\Srv1\DNSkey.txt
```

With these files in reserve, one can easily monitor the server and zone configuration. One can obtain a saved key directly from REGEDT32.EXE by selecting the DNS key and using the Registry, Save Key menu selection, but this is not an automated solution. The biggest problem encountered in using a practice like this is maintaining the saved information in a current state. A change control method that includes updating this information when machines are reconfigured, or an automated process that periodically dumps and compares to the saved ASCII for differences and sends an email when difference are found, is effective in this regard.

Listing 13.3 is an example output from a small DNS server illustrating the format, which does contain all configuration information about the DNS server. If all settings in these files for all DNS servers remain unchanged, the zone placement, the zone transfer topology and security, and the server types including forwarders used and slaves—in short, everything except the zone data itself—are unchanged. What has not been said yet is that the **–m** switch of the **regdmp** command and an optional machine specification in **reg save** can be used to obtain information from a remote machine whose Registry is accessed and to which the executing account must be able to connect with sufficient privilege.

Listing 13.3 **DNS Server Registry Settings Via REGDMP.EXE**

```
C:\>regdmp  HKEY_LOCAL_MACHINE\System\currentcontrolset\services\dns
HKEY_LOCAL_MACHINE\System\currentcontrolset\services\dns
    Type = REG_DWORD 0x00000010
    Start = REG_DWORD 0x00000002
    ErrorControl = REG_DWORD 0x00000001
    ImagePath = REG_EXPAND_SZ %SystemRoot%\System32\dns.exe
    DisplayName = DNS Server
    DependOnService = REG_MULTI_SZ "Tcpip"  \
                                   "Afd"  \
                                   "NetBT"  \
                                   "RpcSs"  \
                                   "NTLmSsp"
    DependOnGroup = REG_MULTI_SZ
    ObjectName = LocalSystem
    Description = Answers query and update requests for Domain Name System \
                  (DNS) \
                  names.
    Parameters
        PreviousLocalHostname = demo1.home.local
        BootMethod = REG_DWORD 0x00000003
        ScavengingInterval = REG_DWORD 0x00000000
        NoRecursion = REG_DWORD 0x00000000
        Forwarders = 10.10.9.9
        ForwardingTimeout = REG_DWORD 0x00000005
        IsSlave = REG_DWORD 0x00000000
        BindSecondaries = REG_DWORD 0x00000000
        SecureResponses = REG_DWORD 0x00000001
```

```
Performance
    Library = dnsperf.dll
    Open = OpenDnsPerformanceData
    Close = CloseDnsPerformanceData
    Collect = CollectDnsPerformanceData
    Last Counter = REG_DWORD 0x00000c7e
    Last Help = REG_DWORD 0x00000c7f
    First Counter = REG_DWORD 0x00000c02
    First Help = REG_DWORD 0x00000c03
    Object List = 3074
    WbemAdapFileTime = REG_BINARY 0x00000008 0x5c030000 0x01bf2efc
    WbemAdapFileSize = REG_DWORD 0x00008110
    WbemAdapStatus = REG_DWORD 0x00000000
Security
    Security = REG_BINARY 0x000000b8 0x80140001 0x000000a0 0x000000ac \
               0x00000014 0x00000030 0x001c0002 0x00000001 0x00148002 \
               0x000f01ff 0x00000101 0x01000000 0x00000000 0x00700002 \
               0x00000004 0x00180000 0x000201fd 0x00000101 0x05000000 \
               0x00000012 0x00000220 0x001c0000 0x000f01ff 0x00000201 \
               0x05000000 0x00000020 0x00000220 0x00730072 0x00180000 \
               0x0002018d 0x00000101 0x05000000 0x0000000b 0x00000220 \
               0x001c0000 0x000201fd 0x00000201 0x05000000 0x00000020 \
               0x00000223 0x00730072 0x00000101 0x05000000 0x00000012 \
               0x00000101 0x05000000 0x00000012
Zones
    1.168.192.in-addr.arpa
        Type = REG_DWORD 0x00000001
        DatabaseFile = 1.168.192.in-addr.arpa.dns
        SecureSecondaries = REG_DWORD 0x00000000
        NotifyLevel = REG_DWORD 0x00000001
        AllowUpdate = REG_DWORD 0x00000000
    10.10.in-addr.arpa
        Type = REG_DWORD 0x00000001
        DatabaseFile = 10.10.in-addr.arpa.dns
        SecureSecondaries = REG_DWORD 0x00000000
        NotifyLevel = REG_DWORD 0x00000001
        AllowUpdate = REG_DWORD 0x00000000
    example.net
        Type = REG_DWORD 0x00000001
        DatabaseFile = example.net.dns
        SecureSecondaries = REG_DWORD 0x00000000
        NotifyLevel = REG_DWORD 0x00000001
        AllowUpdate = REG_DWORD 0x00000001
        NoRefreshInterval = REG_DWORD 0x000000a8
        RefreshInterval = REG_DWORD 0x000000a8
        Aging = REG_DWORD 0x00000000
    hq.example.net
        Type = REG_DWORD 0x00000001
        SecureSecondaries = REG_DWORD 0x00000002
        NotifyLevel = REG_DWORD 0x00000002
```

continues

Listing 13.3 **Continued**

```
            AllowUpdate = REG_DWORD 0x00000001
            NoRefreshInterval = REG_DWORD 0x000000a8
            RefreshInterval = REG_DWORD 0x000000a8
            Aging = REG_DWORD 0x00000000
            DsIntegrated = REG_DWORD 0x00000001
            NotifyServers = 169.254.10.10 10.10.10.10
            SecondaryServers = 169.254.10.10 10.10.10.10
        pc.example.net
            Type = REG_DWORD 0x00000002
            MasterServers = 207.32.154.3 209.132.35.3
            DatabaseFile = west.demo.net.dns
            SecureSecondaries = REG_DWORD 0x00000003
            NotifyLevel = REG_DWORD 0x00000002
    Enum
        0 = Root\LEGACY_DNS\0000
        Count = REG_DWORD 0x00000001
        NextInstance = REG_DWORD 0x00000001
```

Changing a Registered DNS Server's IP Address

An administrator should not have to change the IP address of a server very often. Once in a while, however, it might be necessary. Here we are not talking about changing a machine's IP address as when replacing one server with a new swap-out replacement. Rather, this deals with situations where the IP address for an existing, delegated server must be changed.

The act of changing the IP address itself is relatively straightforward and simple. The loss of service that might occur if proper planning does not precede such a change, however, can be distressing. It is inevitable that during the changeover, some clients will continue for a time to use the old address if it is cached around the network. Planning for this by specifying the TTL for the machine is the best way to limit this impact.

Before changing an IP address, first verify whether this name server is registered with InterNIC. (InterNIC registration services are provided by Network Solutions, Inc; you may also have another registration service other than InterNIC, especially if you are located outside the United States.) Then, if the name server is registered with the InterNIC, is it a primary or a secondary server? If the machine is registered with the InterNIC, the registration information must be entered on a modification template, which is submitted to InterNIC. If the name server is a primary, the modification template becomes that much more important.

Changing the Registration

The modification template is called the Host template and should be used to update the IP address and/or the host name of a name server. Versions of the Domain Name Registration Agreement to date do not allow changes to the IP address or name of a host. The Domain Name Registration Agreement does, however, allow the appropriate party to replace the current name server for a domain with a different existing name server. In other words, the Domain Name Registration Agreement can be used to switch a domain to a new service provider, but an ISP or a server administrator cannot use it to alter the IP address or name of a host.

The Host template is used to register, delete, and modify information associated with a name server. To see information currently associated with a name server, search WHOIS for the NIC Handle. If you have a name server already associated with certain domain names but don't know the name server's NIC handle, search WHOIS for that server's domain name or IP address. The WHOIS program verifies that the domain is available. To use WHOIS, connect to www.internic.net/ through a Web browser. A NIC Handle is a unique identifier, which can be up to 10 alphanumeric characters, that is assigned to each domain name record, contact record, and network record in Network Solutions' domain name database. NIC Handles should be used on registration forms whenever possible, because they save time and help to ensure accuracy in the records.

Fortunately, if the IP address or host name of a name server must be changed, all the domain records associated with the host do not need to be updated. When the IP address or host name of a server is updated, all domain records associated with the host are automatically updated. This occurs because both the name and the IP address of a name server are associated with the NIC Handle, and all domain records are associated with the host by its NIC Handle.

The registration forms are used to submit and process registration requests. These forms, which include the Domain Name Registration Agreement, are used to register new domain names, new contacts for domain names, and new hosts (name servers) as well as to update domain name, contact, and host records. Both Web versions and Plain Text (ASCII) versions of the forms exist.

Before actually submitting the modification request, make sure that a new server has been built to take the place of the old one, and make sure that the name server is configured to answer on the new address. InterNIC does not process requests that it cannot verify. If the machine claimed as primary does not answer requests, InterNIC will not make the changes. If the change is just a new IP address, make sure that a secondary address is configured and accessible. If the change entails building a new server, the machine should be built and should run the DNS server with a complete set of zones. If the name server to be changed is the primary or a master secondary, the other consideration involves making sure that the secondaries that perform zone transfers from this host are updated as well. If not, the administrator will be in for quite a surprise when all the secondaries' zones expire and they stop answering queries sometime after the changeover.

The final thing to remember is the clients. Any clients that were pointed to the changing name server need to have their resolver configurations changed. For hosts using DHCP, this may be a trivial matter of making the changes in the DHCP options and setting an appropriate lease time. The key to changing any active service is to plan the changes and to ensure attention to all the details.

Changing the IP Configuration of DNS in Windows 2000

If you have not already changed the computer's IP address, you need to perform the following steps:

1. Add a new IP address to the network adapter.
2. Run DNS server management console.
3. Update the DNS server information for the new interface.
4. Remove the retired IP address (possibly not immediately).

The following subsections summarize the steps involved in carrying out these four processes.

Adding a Second IP Address to the Network Adapter

Figure 13.4 shows the area in the Advanced tab of a Windows 2000 Server's TCP/IP properties being used to add a new IP address for the computer. (To find the TCP/IP properties, refer to the opening section of Chapter 14, "Windows Client Configuration and Resolution.")

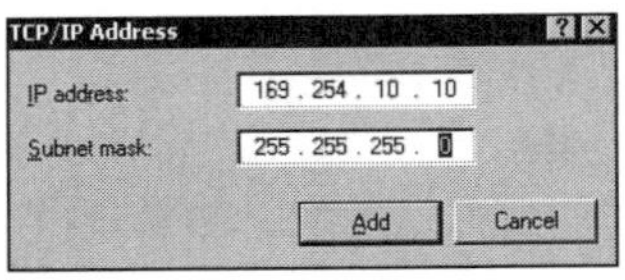

Figure 13.4 Adding a New IP address in Windows 2000 TCP/IP properties.

To add a second IP address to the network adapter, follow these steps:

1. Open the TCP/IP properties for the adapter and select the Advanced tab (see procedure in Chapter 14).
2. On the IP Settings tab, click the Add button under the IP Addresses text box.
3. In the TCP/IP Address pop-up, enter the new IP and mask as shown in Figure 13.4.
4. Click Add and verify that correct information has been added to the IP Addresses text box.
5. Click OK to return to the General tab of TCP/IP properties, and then close up with two OKs.

The Windows 2000 Server should become immediately responsive on the newly added IP address. At this point, you should verify that the DNS server uses the new interface.

Configuring DNS Server with the New Interface

If you have not modified the default settings, the DNS server will be configured to respond on all interfaces. When changing interfaces, however, it is necessary to stop and restart the DNS server; so verify the settings that enable DNS services on the new IP address as follows:

1. Open the DNS server properties from the context or the Actions menu in the DNS management console. (If you have multiple DNS servers connected, be sure to set the focus to the correct server by clicking the icon for it.)
2. On the Interfaces tab, either verify that All IP Addresses is selected or, depending on need, whether Only the Following IP Addresses is selected, and then enter the new IP address and click the Add button.
3. Close the DNS server properties.
4. For the appropriate DNS server, use either the Action or the context menu to select Restart under All Tasks.

After all changes to the DNS services infrastructure have been completed and accepted, if needed reverse the previous steps to remove the old IP address from the machine.

Changing the IP Configuration of DNS in Windows NT 4

In Windows NT 4, this was a much more elaborate process. Figure 13.5 shows the Windows NT 4 Network Control Panel applet opened to the TCP/IP properties (again, refer to Chapter 14), where you'll need to make a change of address for the computer itself.

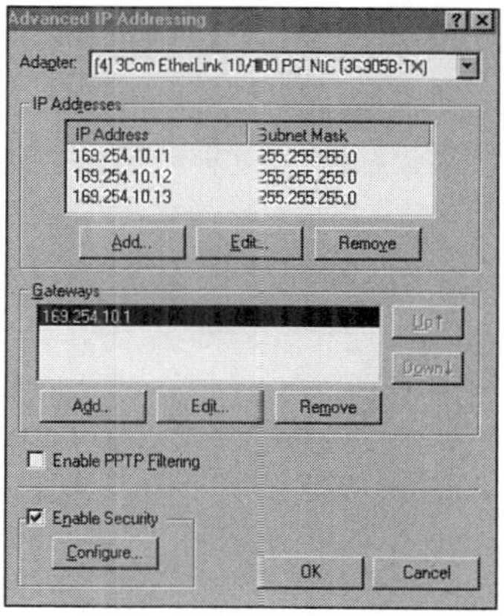

Figure 13.5 Adding a new IP address in Windows NT 4 TCP/IP properties.

Adding a Second IP Address to the Network Adapter in NT 4

For NT 4 to add a second IP address to the network adapter, follow these steps:

1. Open the Network Control Panel and select the Protocol tab.
2. Select TCP/IP, and click on the Properties tab.
3. Click Advanced, and then click the Add button under the IP Address list box, being sure that the correct adapter is selected in the drop-down list at the top of the dialog box.
4. Enter the IP address and subnet mask, and click Add.
5. If needed, as with a new adapter, add a new gateway address.
6. Close the Control Panel, and reboot the computer.

Configuring the NT 4 DNS Manager with the New IP Address

The DNS Manager in NT 4 listed DNS servers by establishing connections to them by IP. Figure 13.6 shows the NT 4 DNS Manager where the connection will be defined for the new IP.

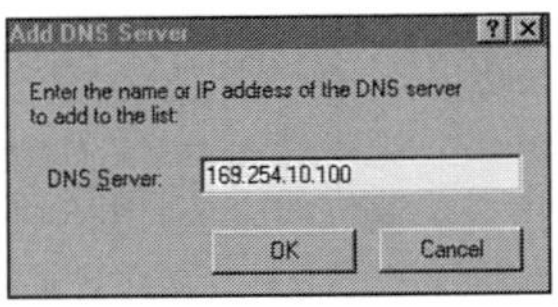

Figure 13.6 Adding a new DNS server in Windows NT 4 DNS Manager.

Next you need to run NT 4 DNS Manager and register the server at the new IP address, as follows:

1. From the Start menu's Program, Administrative Tools folder, select DNS Manager.
2. Right-click the Server List, and select New Server.
3. Enter the new IP address, and click OK.
4. If appropriate at this time, select the old IP address and right-click, and then select Delete Server from the menu and confirm.

Updating NT 4 DNS Server Information

After registering the server on the new IP address in DNS Manager, you must update the DNS server information, as follows:

1. Select the newly added IP address in the left pane of the DNS Manager.
2. In the DNS menu, select Update Server Data Files or locate this in the context menu of the IP for the server.

At this point the server on the new IP address is ready for adjustment of zone files and their content as needed.

Removing the Old IP Address in NT 4

Finally, eventually you may need to remove the retired IP address, as follows:

1. If the old DNS server was left registered in the DNS Manager, remove it there.
2. In the Network Control Panel applet, click the Protocol tab.
3. Select TCP/IP, and click Properties.
4. Click Advanced, and select the correct adapter and then the old address; then click Remove.
5. Close the Control Panel, and reboot the computer.

Adding Capacity with a New DNS Server

Invariably there comes a time when an old build needs to be refreshed, or a new server needs to be added. Chapter 11, "Configuring Windows DNS Servers," presented the steps for installing and configuring Windows 2000 DNS Server, but a short recap of the steps is provided here for reference.

1. Install the Windows 2000 Server, if not yet done.
2. Configure the server with the static IP address(es) to be used.
3. Use Add/Remove Programs, Windows Components to select DNS in the Networking Services details.
4. Start the DNS management console, connect to the local server, and configure the server interfaces and properties as needed for server type and use.
5. Configure the zones to be hosted by the server.

In practice, a machine is sometimes built with a temporary IP address, with the actual IP address being configured as a last step in swapping out a previously used machine. Similarly, configuring the zones can take different forms, depending on whether zones are being moved from a prior server or whether the server is being brought up for new purposes. The next section covers some of these variations.

When adding new servers, replacing servers, moving zones, adding new zones to servers, and so forth, it is common to need to create new zones on the receiving server first. The following provides a short recap of these procedures, and the all-too-easily forgotten zone configuration that should always be done before starting to load and use a zone.

Adding a Primary Zone

If a Windows 2000 DNS Server is configured to load its configuration from file, the direct editing of the boot configuration file to add a new primary directive and restarting or reloading the server can be used to add a new primary zone. This requires that the zone data file be available, and is a nice method when multiple zones are being moved, but this is more effort for new zones. An easier way, that works in all cases, whether booting by any of the options, and that includes using existing zone data, is to use the management console. This makes adding a new zone fast because it creates the initial zone data when needed.

To add a primary zone, in the DNS Server management console, follow these steps:

1. Click the correct DNS server icon, to place the focus on it.
2. Right-click the same server icon, and select New Zone to start the Zone Wizard.
3. Click Standard Primary, and then click Next. The zone may later be changed to Active Directory integrated.
4. Select whether a forward zone or a reverse inaddr.arpa zone is being created.
5. For forward zones, provide the full DNS domain name; for reverse zones, provide the network IP set (the easier choice) or enter the correctly named inaddr.arpa domain name.
6. If a zone is being migrated, and the data file has been prepared with any needed small edit changes, select to Use this Existing File option and specify the correct filename (in the %windir%\system32\dns directory). Otherwise, either accept the default filename for the new file or provide one based on your naming conventions.
7. Click Next, verify the entered information, and then click Finish.

The Zone Wizard finishes up and then automatically creates the zone and zone file and adds *Start Of Authority* (SOA) and *Name Server* (NS) records to the zone file. Verify that the SOA and NS records are correct on zones imported from existing files. If boot is from file, the boot file should have received a new primary directive also.

Whenever possible, create a reverse-lookup zone for each range of IP addresses used before adding A records for computers. By doing so, you can use the automatic Create Associated Pointer (PTR) Record option in the Add Host dialog box. As stated previously, reverse lookup can prove of value, even in an internal network. It's much easier to provide for reverse lookup to begin with than to have to go back and define and load all the needed reverse zones later.

Adding a Secondary Zone

Adding secondaries is very similar, except that one needs to specify from what master DNS server(s) the zone data will be obtained. To add a secondary zone, follow these steps:

1. Click the correct DNS server icon, to place the focus on it.
2. Right-click the same server icon, and select New Zone to start the Zone Wizard.
3. Click Standard Secondary, and then click Next. Secondary zones are never Active Directory integrated.

4. Select whether a forward zone or a reverse inaddr.arpa zone is being created.
5. For forward zones, provide the full DNS domain name; for reverse, provide the network IP set or enter the correctly named inaddr.arpa domain name. In either case, you can browse to the primary and select it, if it is on a server currently connected in the management console.
6. In the next screen, you are allowed to enter a number of DNS servers by IP address that will server to master the zone—that is, from which zone transfers will originate. They will be tried in the order listed. Again, you have the option of browsing to select connected DNS servers.
7. Click Next, verify the entered information, and then click Finish.

Changing Zone Properties

After you have successfully added a zone, you should perform additional configuration by changing the zone properties. Chapter 11 discussed these many configuration options extensively, and should be consulted. Be sure to set the dynamic update capability on a primary if this feature is being used, and to take control over zone transfers for both primary and secondary zones. Although only two options have just been mentioned, a number of other options need attention before using a newly created zone.

If a new primary was created using an existing zone data file, be sure to check the SOA and the NS tabs. Make sure that these have been corrected for the new server and that all NS records listed are still valid for a moved zone.

When making changes to the zones with the DNS server management console, the administrator should be aware of the Update Server Data Files selection under the context menu. Selecting this menu item writes the new data to the appropriate database immediately, and pushes it to disk when file storage is used. The data will also be written out upon normal shutdown of the DNS server. There is also a Reload option in this menu for a zone; this option causes the zone to immediately reload its data from whatever persistent store it is configured to use.

Zone Data Maintenance

There was a time when maintaining zone data meant opening an ASCII file and editing it to change resource records, modifying the version serial number on the SOA record, and then restarting the server to load the newly updated zone. Although that is still done, less so in Windows than elsewhere, a number of other aspects to maintaining zone data now exist. In this section, methods of use in Windows 2000 and, because the issues are so different, in NT 4 are treated, showing how data may be moved between servers and how a replacement server can be prepared and "plugged in," replacing a retiring server.

You should keep a few things in mind when moving zone files between servers. First, the Windows 2000 boot configuration file is very limited in what directives are supported. As a result, BIND will have no problem with a boot configuration file from Windows, although a directory statement will likely need to be added; but the reverse is not the case. Because the boot file is a BIND extension to DNS, and not an RFC specification, Microsoft has chosen to provide only limited support, namely the cache, primary, and secondary directives. Anything else will be ignored. Zone data files are completely standard, and mutually portable between Windows 2000 DNS and BIND, with two exceptions. One is if WINS and Windows Internet Naming Service-Reverse (WINS-R) records are used, they need to be deleted. The other is the added time stamp that is present when scavenging is enabled. If you are planning to move a zone from being primary in Windows DNS to being primary in BIND, it would be easiest to first disable scavenging on the zone and then update the file before the move. If you were looking to move a zone to create a secondary, the simplest thing is of course to just use a zone transfer; this automatically removes the extra time stamp information that is of value only on the primary.

If the purpose of moving the zones is a precursor to replacing the primary name server, an easy way to transfer a lot of the information is to set up the new machine as a secondary. After the zones have been transferred, the DNS service can be altered to change the host from a secondary to a primary. The new host can now be put on the network in place of the old host and can begin serving the DNS information.

Scavenging in Dynamically Updated Zones

Managing dynamic zones involves providing acceptable levels of security over the updates firstly, and then management of zone file size. Without something, or someone, removing resource records (RRs), dynamically updated zones will grow without bound over time. This consumes valuable memory the DNS server could put to better use and slows queries. More importantly, this also tends to create conflicts when new registrations are requested. Chapter 7, "Dynamic DNS and the Active Directory," describes in some detail the configuration of the scavenger that ships with Windows 2000 to automate this process. Because scavenging can be overaggressive, one should use caution by preparing fully before enabling this feature and when adjusting its parameters or enabling further zones for aging.

Even with scavenging enabled, there is likely to be a point when intervention is needed to clean up the zones. Periodically checking zone size is a recommended practice. Because most of the time when dynamic updates are enabled storage will, or should, be in the Active Directory, however, this is not as simple as checking the zone file sizes on the primaries. If a secondary is configured, the file storage can be checked there. Otherwise, manual inspection of the zone in the DNS management console, or a scripted transfer to a file would provide alternatives. One traditional method for doing this is by using the **nslookup** command, but Windows 2000 also provides this through the new **dnscmd** command-line tool as shown in Listing 13.4. The following shows the syntax for the **dnscmd <server> /EnumRecords** command, and then an example of its use to list a small test zone.

Listing 13.4 **Listing Zone Data with DNSCMD.EXE**

```
C:\>dnscmd /EnumRecords /?
USAGE:  DnsCmd <ServerName> /EnumRecords <ZoneName> <NodeName> [<DataOptions>]
[<ViewOptions>]
      <ZoneName>        -- FQDN of zone node to enumerate
             /RootHints for roots-hints enumeration
             /Cache for cache enumeration
      <NodeName>        -- name of node to enumerate
             - "@" for zone root                            OR
             - FQDN of a node  (name with a '.' at the end) OR
             - node name relative to the <ZoneName>
      <DataOptions>:  (All data is the default)
                        /Type    <RRType> -- enumerate RRs of specific type
                         <RRType> is standard type name;  eg. A, NS, SOA, ...
                        /Authority        -- include authoritative data
                        /Glue             -- include glue data
                        /Additional       -- include additional data when
enumerating
                        /Node             -- only enumerate RRs of the given node
                        /Child            -- only enumerate RRs of children of the
given node
                        /StartChild <ChildName> -- child name, after which to
start enumeration
      <ViewOptions>:
                        /Continue         -- on full buffer condition, continue
enum until end of records
                                 default is to retrieve only first buffer of data
                        /Detail           -- print detailed record node
information
                                 default is view of records similar to zone file

Command completed successfully.

C:\>dnscmd /EnumRecords example.net. @
Returned records:
@ 86400 NS      ns.example.net.
                 86400 NS               demo1.home.local.
                 86400 SOA              ns.example.net. administrator.
1999122544 10800 3600 604800 86400
                 86400 MX       10 mailhub.example.net.
                 0 WINS LOCAL   2 900 192.168.1.10 192.168.16.10
fs1 86400 A                     192.168.1.2
mailhub 86400 A                 192.168.1.126
ns 86400 A                      192.168.1.1
ws1 86400 A                     192.168.1.21
ws2 86400 A                     192.168.1.22
ws3 86400 A                     192.168.1.23
ws4 86400 A                     192.168.1.24
Command completed successfully.
```

Managing Multiple Zones

Managing multiple zones takes a little skill and a lot of attention to keeping the databases organized and easy to read. The administrator must be concerned with IP address allocations and must have a scheme for assigning addresses to hosts. Typically, an administrator will have at least two zones to maintain: one or more for the forward lookups of domain names to find IP addresses, and an in-addr zone for the lookups of IP addresses to find host names in reverse.

Within the Microsoft DNS management console, you can add multiple Windows 2000 DNS Servers and change the zones managed by those servers. It is important to note that when creating the primary and secondary servers required for Internet connectivity, you must first define and configure a server by using the DNS management console. You then define one or more zones managed by that server. No fixed limit exists for the maximum number of zones you can manage.

The generally used reference to primary and secondary DNS servers is actually misleading when applied to the actual configuration and operation of DNS name servers. Because each DNS server manages its portion of the domain name space using the administrative grouping of a zone, data on the server is stored in zone files. In the Microsoft DNS product, a zone is a contiguous branch of the domain name space, such as a domain and a number of its direct descendents, and a zone will have one SOA record.

When data is transferred between primary and secondary servers, it is actually the zones that are transferred. Microsoft DNS Server is designed to incorporate this operational characteristic by assigning the primary or secondary characteristic to the zones. In other words, the designation of the primary or secondary data source is configured on a zone-by-zone basis, not on a server-by-server basis.

Administrators fortunate enough to get experience with DNS from an ISP—especially one that performs domain hosting—may have to deal with thousands of zones on a single server. Although the number of in-addr domains may be relatively few, the zones for the standard domains can become a jumble of files that may or may not be easily identifiable by name alone. Careful management of zones and domains must be followed so that IP addresses don't get cross-referenced or, worse, assigned to the wrong domain altogether. It is perhaps regrettable that the default naming for zones in Windows 2000 is <domain_name>.dns rather than <reversed_domain_name>, because this would group domains and zones for their children domains naturally together in the directory listing. By using reversed names, a directory listing would naturally group like this:

```
com.corp
com.corp.asia
com.corp.hq
com.corp.west
net.example
net.example.advisory
net.example.communication
```

```
net.example.consult
net.example.training
```

With use of the default file naming convention, these organize themselves in a directory listing less conveniently as follows:

```
advisory.example.net.dns
asia.corp.com.dns
communication.example.net.dns
consult.example.net.dns
corp.com.dns
example.net.dns
hq.corp.com.dns
training.example.net.dns
west.corp.com.dns
```

If you need to manage large numbers of zones, a naming convention that enables you to see domain structure when looking at filenames in the directory is highly recommended.

An administrator thinking of restructuring the network of his company might run across this type of question: Is it possible to have two primary domain name servers, each serving a zone and having a domain such as example.net with the following subdomains?

```
consult.example.net
training.example.net
advisory.example.net
communication.example.net
```

The administrator would like, for example, to assign one name server "consult and training" and the other name server "advisory and communication."

No problem. You can do this, but you have to create five or three zones, depending on your preference:

```
primary: example.net
primary: consult.example.net
primary: training.example.net
```

and

```
primary: advisory.example.net
primary: communication.example.net
```

Here, example.net includes delegation to all subdomains of example.net, so there are five zones. You could also leave two of the subdomains in the same zone as example.net. That would leave you with the following configuration:

```
primary: example.net
```

with consult.example.net and training. example.net in the example.net zone; and

```
primary: advisory.example.net
primary: communication.example.net
```

The preceding examples show only two options for distributing primary zones for a domain with four subdomains among two servers. Of course, many other configurations are possible. Splitting large zones for distribution in ways appropriate to an Active Directory structure and a network topology can be a very important optimization for large, distributed organizations.

Moving Zone Files Between Servers

A zone is authoritative for all the DNS information within it. One zone may contain one or several domains, and the same given zone can also contain subdomains, but these must be contiguous in Windows 2000. To enhance performance and availability, each zone should have more than one authoritative name server. This can create the common data maintenance problems that arise when more than one master database must be kept accurate and timely. A master name server can initialize the database for each zone it maintains from either locally stored data or from another master name server. In the latter case, the secondary master can ask the primary master on which the database is maintained to transfer an entire zone's information via a Transmission Control Protocol (TCP) connection. The information is recorded and stored locally in a data file, to be used later in case a zone transfer cannot be completed. With some non-Microsoft DNS Servers, this local storage is optional; for Windows 2000 DNS Server, a secondary zone is always stored in a local file. It is probably a good idea to store the zone locally in a file in case both primary and secondaries go offline and then the primary does not come back. At least with the secondary storing zone files locally, you have a copy that may be good enough to use until the primary can be brought back online. This file can in a pinch also be used in rebuilding out of a worst-case failure of the primary. Some sites will use a DNS server that has the sole purpose of being secondary for all zones, using file storage, just for this type of backup purpose. Beyond this traditional arrangement, use of Active Directory storage and of the Registry to store configuration information adds new considerations. One of these is backup when file storage is not used. The way to accomplish this is with a Windows backup program, such as the light version bundled with Windows 2000, specifying to backup the system state.

Regardless of which DNS strategy is adopted for the primary DNS, at least one of the secondary DNS servers for your public names should be placed at an ISP connected by network paths as independent as possible from those used by the main site. Such arrangements can usually be made with ISPs, other groups within a large organization,

> **Note**
>
> As with any server of importance, the administrator must be sure to make backups routinely. If the server handles many different domains, the importance of good backups is intensified. No precautions are required when performing backups, because the zone files themselves are merely text files or are within the Active Directory store NTDS.DIT, and the configuration information will either reside in a text file or in the Registry. The Windows DNS Server does not lock the files in an open state. To back up the Registry and Active Directory, the administrator should be sure to specify that the system state should be backed up.

or other sites willing to arrange a secondary DNS swap (that is, to handle each other's secondary DNS servers). The farther away (networkwise) the offsite secondary is the better. The best case is where the secondary has completely different network connectivity than the provider that the primary is on. These considerations work well for the public presence DNS services, but for Active Directory support, the best arrangement allows placement of DNS server(s) at each remote internal site.

Zones are typically moved between name servers via zone transfers initiated by a secondary, either upon startup (especially the first time around, or if the secondary does not have a backup copy of the zone) or after the secondary detects a change in the serial number of its master. One way to decrease the time it takes to propagate changes is by implementing the Notify option (as shown in Figure 11.8) so that the primary or master tells the secondaries that a change has been made. Using the Notify option causes the primary to prompt the secondaries to verify that the serial number has been incremented. A secondary then requests a zone transfer if the serial on the SOA resource record indicates that it does not have the most recent zone data. Notification-driven transfers should be incremental (using IXFR requests). Using the Notify option in combination with restricting transfers to the Notify list servers is an essential part of zone data security.

In the earlier section on "Adding Capacity with a New DNS Server," the few steps for creating a new server were outlined. You also learned how to create a new primary or secondary zone. In the case of primary zones, you saw two ways to transfer a zone by using an existing zone data file, either with manual editing or through the management console. A few special cases are involved with moving zones that have not yet been covered.

Zone Transfers in DNS/WINS-Integrated Environments

If Microsoft's DNS Server is integrated with WINS, it must be explicitly configured to interoperate with non-Microsoft name servers (UNIX servers). Microsoft represents WINS information in DNS using a nonstandard resource record type. All the resource records are commonly used by DNS name servers on the Internet except for the WINS and WINS-R resource records. These records are specifically implemented for interoperability between Microsoft DNS Servers and WINS servers.

This can cause a name server to fail when attempting a zone transfer from a Microsoft server. Older BIND servers may actually terminate when receiving such resource records in a zone transfer. Because these records are unique to Microsoft DNS Servers, when transferring primary zone files to a secondary zone, these records should not be copied to a DNS name server running non-Microsoft DNS Server software.

If you are using WINS lookup or WINS-R reverse lookup and have a non-Microsoft DNS Server as secondary, you must prevent transfers from copying WINS or WINS-R records to the non-Microsoft DNS Server. Care must also be exercised to delete any such records from zone files when manually moving these to BIND.

For Windows NT 4, the following steps enable you to disable transfer of WINS or WINS-R pseudo-records:

1. Start the DNS Manager.
2. Right-click the folder for the appropriate zone.
3. Click Properties.
4. Click the WINS Lookup or WINS Reverse Lookup tab (see Figure 13.7).
5. Select the Settings Only Affect Local Server check box.
6. Click OK.

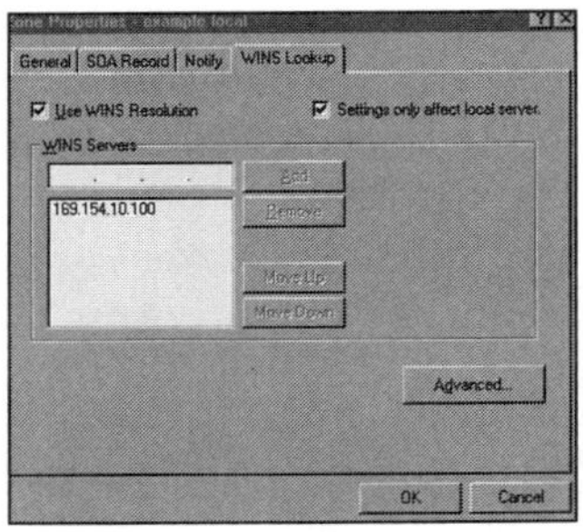

Figure 13.7 The WINS settings of DNS Server in Windows NT 4 DNS Manager.

In Windows 2000, this is controlled by a setting labeled Do Not Replicate This Record found on the WINS or the WINS-R tab of the forward or reverse lookup zone's properties, respectively.

For Windows 2000, perform the following steps:

1. Start the DNS Server management console.
2. Set the focus on the zone to be modified.
3. Right-click the appropriate zone and select Properties.
4. Click the WINS or WINS-R tab (see Figures 16.7 and 16.9).
5. Select the Do Not Replicate This Record check box.
6. Click OK.

Moving Zone Data Between UNIX and Windows

Between UNIX name servers and Windows name servers, you can perform manual zone transfers by using **nslookup**, which comes with Windows and UNIX servers. Start **nslookup**, and then type **server servername**, where *servername* is a name server authoritative for the zone you want to transfer. Then on Windows type **ls zonename > c:\outfile.txt**, where *c:\outfile.txt* should be substituted with the desired storage location provided as a full path and filename. On UNIX use a standard out redirection to a valid file location. Effectively, this transfers zone information from a one-name server to another. For this to work, the machine where this is executed must be permitted to pull transfers from the target server. Sometimes this is more convenient than using other means to move the file, such as FTP. This is also a good way to confirm that zone transfers are allowed, when troubleshooting, but you would probably want to first limit the records that will be listed rather than pull the whole zone.

Transfer All Zones to a New Windows 2000 DNS Server with Boot File Startup

When you use the Microsoft DNS Server to host one or more zones being moved from a prior DNS server to a new Windows DNS Server, you have some shortcut options. For this to work most easily for large numbers of zones, the option of starting the service using a boot file on the new server should be used. The option of using information stored in the Registry is discussed a little later.

If you are starting DNS using a boot file, follow these steps to move your zone file(s). These steps, of course, assume that you have installed the Microsoft DNS Server service on the new Windows 2000 Server.

1. Copy all zone files into the %windir%\System32\dns directory.
2. Edit each zone file to guarantee that any SOA and NS records, and the associated A records, are correct.
3. Open the Microsoft DNS Server management console, and verify that the server is set to boot from file.
4. Use the Action or server context menu to select Stop to stop the server.
5. Edit the boot file in the same directory to include primary or secondary directives for the new zones.
6. Use the Action or server context menu to select Start to start the server.
7. If the changes are not seen immediately, use the Reload selection on the menu; this should not be necessary.
8. If desired, set the server back to booting from Registry.
9. Use the properties of the zones to configure zone options, or use a Registry tool to load these settings en masse.

Alternatively, one can use the DNS Server management console to create zones, one by one, importing from the moved, edit-prepared zone files.

Transfer All Zones Between Two Windows NT 4 DNS Servers with Boot File Startup

Although the need for this procedure is now aged, experience has found this to be the best approach; so it is included here for information. If you are starting DNS using a boot file, follow these steps to move your zone file(s) from an old NT 4 to a new NT 4 build. This process completely replaces any other existing DNS configuration on the new machine.

1. From the Services applet in Control Panel, stop the Microsoft DNS Server on both Windows NT 4 machines. This should be done on the old before obtaining files being copied out to a new server, and this should also be done on the new Windows NT 4 Server before loading the moved zones.
2. Manually copy the entire contents (subfolders included) of the %Systemroot%\System32\DNS folder from the source server to the destination server (here the source is Windows NT 4).
3. Restart the Microsoft DNS Server on the new Windows NT 4 DNS Server.

After completing this, it will possibly be necessary to set the IP address of the new server so that it is a "drop-in-place" replacement for the old server; otherwise client reconfiguration is the next step.

Transfer All Zones to a New Windows 2000 DNS Server with Registry Startup

Windows 2000 has two settings for booting from the Registry, one used with file storage and the other with Active Directory storage of the zone data. If the Active Directory–integrated storage is not being used, one can easily change the server to use the Boot From File option. Then, after forcing the server to Update Data Files (just in case), the earlier methods for moving zones can be used. After the zones have been moved and have had their properties configured, you can set the server back to using the Boot From Registry setting. If Active Directory storage is used, this won't work for moving zone files. In this case, the shortest route is to use the management console to create new zones and during this process to import the existing zone data at the point provided for this purpose by the New Zone Wizard. One can also use this method conveniently whenever importing only a few zones in all storage configurations.

Transfer Zones Between Two Windows NT 4 DNS Servers with Registry Startup

If you are starting DNS Server in NT 4 using the Registry, you should follow these steps when you are moving a single zone file:

1. On the server being copied to, create the new zone using the DNS Manager. Configure the zone as it was configured on the source server, either as a primary or secondary zone. The new zone must be created using the same zone filename

as the original file. If PARADISE.COM.DNS was the original file on the source server, for example, PARADISE.COM.DNS must be the name of the new file.

2. From the Services applet in the Control Panel, stop the Microsoft DNS Server on both Windows NT 4 DNS Servers.
3. From the source DNS server, copy the desired zone file, <zone name>.dns, from the %Systemroot%\System32\DNS folder to the same folder on the destination Windows NT 4 DNS Server.
4. If necessary, edit the copied file to adjust SOA and NS and the associated A record to use the correct host name and IP address for the new machine.
5. Restart the Microsoft DNS Server on the new Windows NT 4 DNS Server.

The following procedure guides you through the process of moving all zones if you are starting Windows NT 4 DNS Server using the Registry. Perform steps 1 and 2 on the destination Windows NT DNS Server only. Perform steps 5 through 8 on the source server only. Perform steps 10 through 14 on the destination server only. In this procedure, a replacement server is built and any prior zones on the destination are lost.

1. Using the DNS Manager, create a sample primary zone called SAMPLE.COM. Creating the sample zone ensures that the DNS Server boot file information has been written to the Registry and that the DNS Server knows the location of the cache information.
2. Using DNS Manager, delete the sample zone that you just created in step 1.
3. From Services applet in Control Panel, stop the Microsoft DNS Server service on both Windows NT 4 DNS Servers.
4. From the source DNS Server, copy the entire %Systemroot%\System32\DNS folder to the same folder on the destination Windows NT 4 DNS Server.
5. Start Registry Editor (REGEDT32.EXE) on the source server.
6. Go to the following subkey:
   `HKEY_LOCAL_MACHINE\SYSTEM\CurrentControlSet\Services\DNS`
7. Click Zones, click Registry, and click Save Key.
8. Save this key to a location from which you can restore it to the destination server and close Registry Editor.
9. Move this saved Registry file to the destination server.
10. Start Registry Editor (REGEDT32.EXE) on the destination server.
11. Go to the following subkey:
    `HKEY_LOCAL_MACHINE\SYSTEM\CurrentControlSet\Services\DNS`
12. Click Zones to verify that it is selected, click Registry, and click Restore.
13. Locate the Registry key file that you exported from the destination server.
14. Click Yes in the confirmation dialog box, and close Registry Editor.
15. Restart the Microsoft DNS Server service on the new NT 4 DNS Server.

The information transferred in the Registry key maintains the names of the zones and keeps you from re-creating the zone names in the DNS Manager for every zone file that was copied. Optional server configuration settings are also transferred. Be aware, however, that using the Registry Editor incorrectly can cause serious systemwide problems that may require you to reinstall Windows NT 4 to correct them. Make sure to back up your Registry before using this tool.

After completing this procedure, it will most likely be necessary to adjust the host name and IP address of the new server. At that point, you should be ready to kill the old server and place the new machine on the live network. The only real "song and dance" is isolating the new server for some limited acceptance testing while at the new name and IP address, because it of course cannot be present on your network while the old machine is operating.

> **Note**
>
> Microsoft DNS in Windows NT 4 seems unable to manually push zones for testing purposes. An administrator must wait for the zone to transfer and then personally check the results. The **nslookup** utility can be used to view the contents of a zone and copy it to a file if the machine from which it is run has the authority to perform a zone transfer. One tool the administrator does have is the Event Viewer, which captures zone transfer requests and the zone transfers themselves. The Event Viewer reports on the status of the transfer, the date and time it occurred, the domain that was affected, and the name of the zone file that was written. Both **nslookup** and Event Viewer are the best troubles hooting tools for Windows NT 4 if your DNS does not run.

Issues When Manipulating DNS Servers in Windows NT 4

The process of manipulating zones, however, was not always so smooth in some cases in the Windows NT 4 DNS Server implementation. If you created a secondary zone and then changed that zone to primary, for example, the Registry was not updated to reflect the change. The next time you restarted the DNS Server, you received an error message stating that the primary DNS address was missing. In this instance, the DNS Server did not start. Also, the CACHE.DNS file may have been overwritten with a blank file, causing you to lose name resolution outside your zone of authority.

In Windows NT 4 upgraded to Service Pack 4, the Microsoft DNS Server has been fixed to correctly write back the Zone Type key to reflect the correct role of the zone. This is not a problem in Windows 2000.

Windows 2000 addresses some other problems that may occur with Windows NT. In particular, when a zone file contains a large number (approximately 100) of A records for a single host name (each mapped to a different IP address), the user interface appears to stop responding (hangs) when trying to display the zone information.

During this time, the amount of memory used by the NT 4 DNS Manager (DNSADMIN.EXE) progressively increases until the system displays a dialog box that says that the system is running low on virtual memory and that instructs the user to increase the size of the paging file. Several minutes later, the system displays another dialog box stating that there is not enough memory to get all the records. An Out of Memory message displays in the lower-right corner of DNS Manager, followed by another message stating that the system is running low on virtual memory. The DNS Manager hangs when there are a lot of records for a particular node because it is running out of the RPC buffer space.

To resolve this problem of NT 4, you need to edit the Registry to increase the default RPC buffer size for the DNS Admin (refer to the following procedure).

1. Run Registry Editor (REGEDT32.EXE).
2. Go to the following key:
   ```
   HKEY_LOCAL_MACHINE\Software\Microsoft\DNS Administrator
   ```
3. On the Edit menu, click Add Value and use the following information to create a RpcBufferAlloc with a value of 16384:
   ```
   Value name: RpcBufferAlloc
   Data type: REG_Dword
   Data: 0-FFFFFFFF
   Default: 800(2048)
   Description: This parameter determines the Size of the RPC Buffer Allocation
   used by the DNS Administrator.
   ```
4. Repeat steps 2 and 3 for the following key:
   ```
   HKEY_CURRENT_USER\Software\Microsoft\DNS Administrator
   ```
5. Close Registry Editor.

Another issue exists with the management interfaces to DNS Server, not DNS Server itself. In NT 4, if one or more of your zones contain more than 65,535 records, you may face another problem: When you view your DNS zones with DNS Manager, it may stop responding. If you check Performance Monitor or Task Manager, you may notice that DNS Manager or DNS Server management console is using up to 90% of the CPU utilization.

At the time of this writing, no resolution existed for this issue. Windows 2000 seems to be affected by something similar, possibly related to this problem. The DNS Server will start and continue to function correctly. Whereas in NT 4 the DNS Manager stops responding, however, in the Windows 2000 DNS Server management console you can access only about half of the resource records. So it seems that, for now, in both NT 4 and Windows 2000 if you have zones with more than 65,535 records, you need to edit these files using a text editor, such as WordPad or Edit.

Summary

This chapter presented a number of ideas and practices, as well as some more hard-won information, that relate to the actual running of a DNS server hierarchy. Some information has been included on the DNS server in Windows NT 4 because it was a different DNS implementation with different, and at times troublesome, issues.

14

Windows Client Configuration and Resolution

THIS CHAPTER REVIEWS THE FOLLOWING:

- **Client Transmission Control Protocol/Internet Protocol (TCP/IP) properties.** This shows, for the different client systems, where the starting point for the client configuration procedures can be found.
- **Configuring Clients to Use Dynamic Host Configuration Protocol (DHCP).** DHCP can be used to configure all TCP/IP settings on its clients. These can be used as the settings or as defaults when not explicitly overridden at the client.
- **Configuring Clients to Use DNS.** This shows how to configure Windows clients to use DNS.
- **Configuring Client to Use Windows Internet Naming Service (WINS).** This describes the options used to configure clients to use WINS.
- **Understanding Client Use of the Windows Resolver.** This discusses how the configuration settings affect the behavior of the Windows client when needing to obtain an Internet Protocol (IP) address from a name.
- **Other Client-Support Information.** This section addresses a few further issues: WINS proxies, the TCP/IP-32 upgrade for MS-DOS, and NetBT Registry settings.

A Windows computer can resolve names in several ways, depending entirely on how the computer is configured. This chapter shows how to configure clients to perform host name lookups on DNS servers and NetBIOS name lookups on WINS servers. Also described in this chapter is how and why you would configure clients to look up NetBIOS computer names via DNS. This chapter describes how these settings can be configured centrally when clients use a DHCP server. Client machines can use a variety of networking protocols, but this chapter focuses specifically on TCP/IP configuration because it is a requirement for the use of DNS.

Client TCP/IP Properties

The configurations covered in this chapter are found under the TCP/IP Properties page on the client system. To access the TCP/IP Properties page, use the following procedures.

On Windows NT 4.0 (note that Windows 95/98 are similar), follow these steps:

1. Open the Network dialog box. Either double-click on the Network applet in Control Panel, or right-click on the Network Neighborhood icon on the desktop and select Properties.
2. Select the Protocols tab, and then highlight the TCP/IP Protocol selection in the list box.
3. Click on the Properties button under the list box to open the Microsoft TCP/IP Properties dialog box, or a similar dialog box for the other down-level operating systems.

On Windows 2000 things have changed a little, so follow these steps:

1. Open the Network and Dial-up Connections dialog box. Either select this from the Start menu under Settings, or double-click on this applet in Control Panel, or right-click on the My Network Places icon on the desktop and select Properties.
2. Select the connection object with the default name of Local Area Connection and right-click to select its Properties, or double-click it and then use the Properties button. This opens the Local Area Connection properties (or whatever your connection object's name has been named).
3. In the Local Area Connection Properties dialog box, highlight the Internet Protocol (TCP/IP) entry in the list box.
4. Click on the Properties button under the list box to open the Internet Protocol (TCP/IP) Properties dialog box.

Figure 14.1 shows the Windows 2000 Internet Protocol (TCP/IP) Properties dialog box. Most of this chapter deals with settings in this dialog box and especially those accessed by clicking the Advanced button. For convenience, this dialog box is referred to as the TCP/IP Properties.

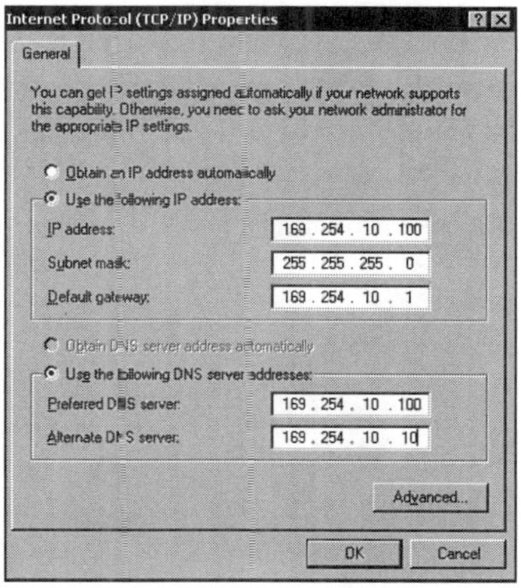

Figure 14.1 Most configurations settings are accessed through the Advanced button in the TCP/IP Properties of Windows 2000.

Configuring Clients to Use DHCP

Because many deployments use DHCP to deliver client IP addresses and configuration settings, this is where we start. Another good reason to start with DHCP client con-figuration is that when used, the settings received from the DHCP server are used unless they are specifically set at the client in the DNS and WINS settings covered next in this chapter. When troubleshooting a DHCP client, it is good to remember this and to check that the DCHP settings are not being overridden.

The only requirement that a DHCP client must meet to use DHCP is that the client computer have a DHCP-supported operating system. The following operating systems allow DHCP to be enabled for the client:

- Windows 2000 Server and Professional
- Windows NT Server 3.5, 3.51, and 4.0
- Windows NT Workstation 3.5, 3.51, and 4.0
- Windows 95 and 98
- Windows for Workgroups 3.11 with the Microsoft TCP/IP-32 for Windows for Workgroups installed
- MS Network Client 3.0 for MS-DOS with the real-mode TCP/IP-32 driver installed
- LAN Manager 2.2c (but not LAN Manager for OS/2)
- Solaris 2.x and 7
- Linux (all recent distributions)

To enable a Windows 2000 DHCP client, you must log on with administrator privileges at the client. Normally, you enable DHCP as part of the installation procedure for Microsoft TCP/IP. You can use the following procedure, however, if you have previously manually configured TCP/IP:

1. Open the TCP/IP Properties dialog box.
2. On NT 4.0 use the radio button labeled Obtain an IP Address from a DHCP Server and acknowledge the message box about the DHCP protocol. On Windows 2000 the option is labeled Obtain an Address Automatically.
3. The IP Address and Subnet Mask boxes are not available (grayed out), and the manually configured values are no longer displayed. On Windows 2000 the newly enabled radio button to Obtain DNS Server Address Automatically enables you to use the DHCP-provided value or to configure it manually.
4. Automatic settings configuration is normal; but if they are to be overridden, do so now. In Windows 2000, use the Advanced button to set the WINS and DNS server addresses. When changing a previously configured client to have all automatic settings, it is best to check that prior settings, especially the WINS settings, have been removed.
5. Choose OK to exit from TCP/IP Properties and return to the Network Settings in NT 4.0 or the dialog box.
6. Choose OK again. For Window 2000, one is now done. For down-level clients, shut down and restart the computer.

If a non-Microsoft DHCP server is used to supply an IP address and other configuration information to DHCP clients, the DHCP server will likely provide all the normal options, but might not handle a few things that Windows 2000 DHCP can. One is interfacing with DNS using dynamic updates, another is the Option 81 user class, and then finally the NetBIOS and WINS settings. The ability to update DNS is a server configuration, and the Option 81 is presently still being defined and so not likely to be found in other DHCP servers in a form that will interoperate with the initial release of the Windows 2000 DHCP client. To supply the necessary WINS configuration information to DHCP clients, the DHCP server must have the following DHCP options available:

- 044 WINS/NBNS servers configured with the IP address of one or more WINS servers
- 046 WINS/NBT node type set to 0x1 (b-node), 0x2 (p-node), 0x4 (m-node), or 0x8 (h-node)

Refer to Chapter 15, "Windows DHCP Servers," for more information on setting up the Microsoft DHCP Server to service Windows clients. For more information on the node types, see Chapter 17, "NetBIOS: Legacy Name Services and Resolution."

Configuring Clients to Use DNS

As you know from previous chapters, DNS provides a distributed database that contains a hierarchical naming system for identifying hosts on the Internet. The original specifications for DNS are defined in RFCs 1034 and 1035.

For down-level clients, DNS server requires static configuration of IP addresses for name-to-address mappings in its zones, unless the Windows 2000 DHCP server or DNS/WINS integration is used. Although DNS and WINS may seem similar as name services, WINS can provide name-to-address mapping dynamically, and so when DNS integrated can require far less administration than does DNS when used without dynamic update. Down-level clients, even in the absence of Windows 2000 DHCP, can be available through DNS when the DNS server is configured to use WINS. Windows 2000 clients can, of course, maintain their entries in DNS when dynamic updates are enabled. These issues affect the capability of other systems to locate a particular machine by using DNS in a standard fashion based on the machine's registrations.

In all these cases, the client must have settings pointing it to one or more DNS servers if it is to be able to locate machines and resources in the DNS namespace. This can be delivered by DHCP, or set manually. What these setting are doing is configuring the TCP/IP resolver used to locate resources on the TCP/IP network. If a Windows 2000 Server is running DHCP services, this also configures to where DHCP server sends dynamic DNS updates if this feature is enabled.

Setting the Host and Domain Name for DNS

To set the host and DNS domain name for down-level operating systems, you enter the names in the Host Name and Domain boxes of the DNS tab in TCP/IP Properties. The section titled "Enabling DNS" discusses this in more detail.

For Windows 2000, this setting differs a little, reflecting the important place DNS plays in this release of Windows. The machine as a whole has a primary DNS identity in Windows 2000 as is shown in Figure 14.2, and interfaces can have specific DNS identities as will be seen later in this chapter.

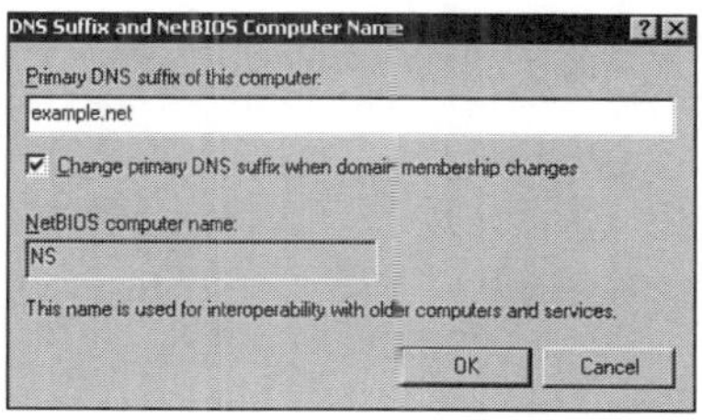

Figure 14.2 Setting the Windows 2000 primary DNS identity.

To set the machine's DNS identity in Windows 2000, follow these steps:

1. Right-click on the My Computer icon on the desktop and select Properties, or double-click on the System icon in the Control Panel to bring up the System Properties dialog box.
2. Select the Network Identification tab.
3. Enter the DNS name for the computer in the Computer Name area.
4. Use the Properties button to open the Identification Changes dialog box.
5. Use the More button to open the DNS Suffix and NetBIOS Name dialog box.
6. Enter the correct Primary DNS Suffix of This Computer.
7. For a machine in a domain, keeping Change Primary DNS Suffix When Domain Membership Changes enabled is a good idea when DNS domains are aligned with Windows 2000 domains.
8. Click OK as needed to close up, and reboot (one of the few reboots left in Windows 2000).

The DNS domain name is used with the host name to create a *fully qualified domain name* (FQDN) for the computer. When Windows 2000 is configured to update DNS dynamically, A and possibly Pointer (PTR) records will be created for this FQDN (unless other settings change this behavior). In down-level systems, the DNS domain very often differs from the Windows NT or LAN Manager domain. In Windows 2000, these can be different only with some effort in the initial release, and so most fresh deployments will likely follow the model in which the DNS and Windows 2000 domain names are synchronized. The DNS records in these down-level systems, and so the domains where they appear, are controlled by the DNS administrator, or the DHCP server configuration. The DNS records for Windows 2000 clients are controlled by the DNS administrator when registrations are static, or by these client DNS configuration settings when the client registers dynamically.

The DNS Suffix List

In addition to use when other machines query to locate a machine, the DNS name has a role in how the local resolver operates. During DNS queries, the local DNS domain name may control what is appended to short names. A short name is a name that is not a FQDN. When the TCP/IP resolver forms a query to DNS, it uses the DNS suffix list, appending the suffixes one at a time and attempting to resolve the result.

If no explicit DNS suffix list is configured, a default is used. This default consists of the machine's DNS domain, and all included parent domains that are not a top-level domain (TLD) name (that is, consist of at least two labels). If a machine is cowpoke.hq.example.net, for example, the default list will be hq.example.net, followed by example.net. It will not include just "net." If a DNS suffix list is configured, it will be used exactly as provided. So if the machine's own domain is to be used, it and any desired parent domains need to be included in the list.

If you look ahead to Figure 14.5, you will see the setting in the DNS configuration of Windows 2000 where one can impact this list. The lowest text entry box labeled DNS Suffix for This Connection is where one can configure a DNS domain associated with a specific adapter. The DNS domain you saw previously in the System Properties dialog box is the primary DNS suffix. You will notice that there is a mutually exclusive radio button choice between configuring the TCP/IP resolver to use the primary and connection-specific suffixes, and optionally parents of the primary, or configuring it to use the specified suffix list. Older versions of Windows do not have this degree of configuration.

Enabling DNS

With Windows 2000 you do not have a choice, but with down-level clients you can decide whether computers should be configured to use DNS. Usually, you will use DNS if you are using TCP/IP, whether to communicate over the Internet or if your private intranet uses DNS to distribute host information. If you choose to use DNS, you must configure the way in which the computer will use DNS. Use of the HOSTS file is then also automatically enabled. If DHCP is used for automatic IP configuration, these parameters can be provided by the DHCP server. DNS configuration is global for all network adapters installed on a down-level computer, but Windows 2000 allows some additional interface-specific settings. The following Figures 14.3, 14.4, and 14.5 and accompanying procedures show these interface configurations for Windows 95/98, Windows NT 4.0, and Windows 2000, respectively. The Windows 2000 global configuration was seen earlier with the server level primary DNS identity.

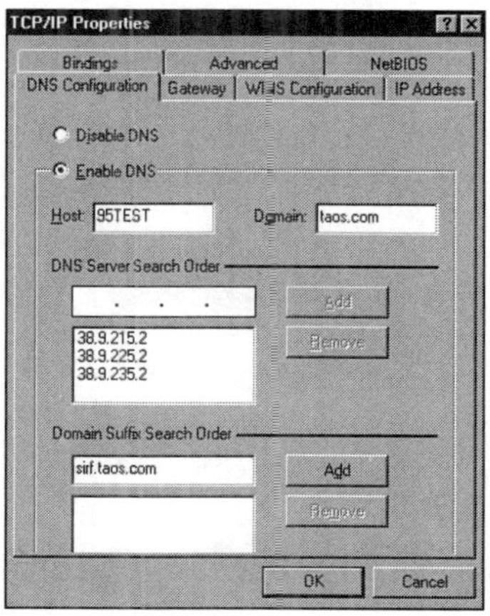

Figure 14.3 The process of enabling DNS in a Windows 95 client.

To configure a computer running Windows 95 to use DNS for name resolution, follow these steps:

1. In the TCP/IP Properties, click the DNS Configuration tab.
2. Click Enable DNS.
3. Specify a host and domain name, making sure you enter the DNS information that forms the FQDN for this machine.
4. Enter and add one or preferably more DNS servers by IP address in the DNS Service Search Order area.
5. In the Domain Suffix Search Order area, enter a custom DNS domain suffix list if one is to be used by the resolver.

To configure a computer running Windows NT 4.0 to use DNS for name resolution, the steps are as for Windows 95, they just look different.

1. In the TCP/IP Properties, click the tab labeled DNS.
2. Specify a host name and domain, making sure that you enter the DNS information that forms the FQDN for this machine.
3. Enter and add one or preferably more DNS servers by IP address in the DNS Service Search Order area.
4. In the Domain Suffix Search Order area, enter a custom DNS domain suffix list if one is to be used by the resolver.

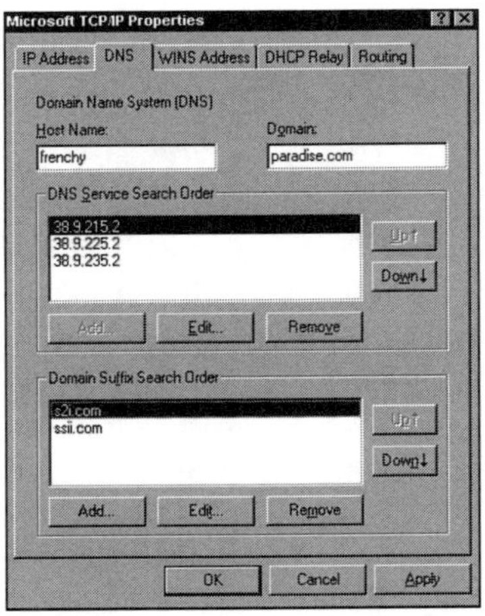

Figure 14.4 The process of enabling DNS in a Windows NT 4.0 client.

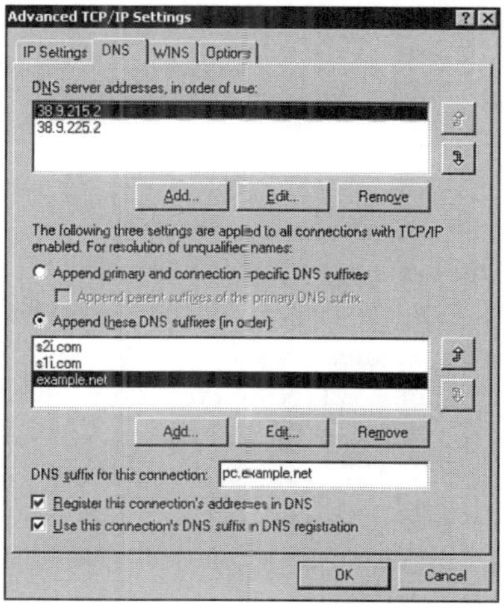

Figure 14.5 The process of enabling DNS in a Windows 2000 client.

To configure a computer running Windows 2000 to use DNS for name resolution, follow these steps:

1. In the TCP/IP Properties, click the Advanced button, and then select the tab labeled DNS.
2. Enter and add one or preferably more DNS servers by IP address in the DNS Server Addresses area.
3. Either select Append Primary and Connection Specific DNS Suffixes, or select Append these DNS Suffixes and then use the Add button to enter any DNS domain suffixes to be used by the resolver in the list box area.
4. Select the option for dynamic DNS update appropriate to your environment using the Options at the bottom.

In all these systems, as discussed earlier, please remember that a custom suffix list will be used as given. As is most obvious in the Windows 2000 configuration, a custom suffix list replaces the default based on the machine's own DNS domain.

Specifying DNS Configuration in the Registry

You can add up to three IP addresses for DNS servers in down-level systems and very many more than this in Windows 2000. For a given DNS query, the Windows resolver attempts to obtain DNS information from the first IP address in the list. If no response is received, it goes to the second server in the list, and so on. To change the order of the IP addresses in down-level clients, you must remove them and re-enter them in the order that you want the servers to be searched. One may use the much nicer reorder buttons in Windows 2000. This setting on a machine running DHCP server configures to which DNS server the DHCP server will send dynamic DNS (DDNS) update messages.

In Windows 2000, this list is stored in the Registry under HKLM\System\CurrentControlSet\Services in the specific interface keys under Tcpip\Parameters\Interfaces\<Interface Guid> as a string value named NameServer. This should clue you to the fact that in Windows 2000, each adapter can be configured independently from the others. Figure 14.6 shows this area of the Registry, listing some of the values that can be configured on a per-interface basis.

Obviously, any addresses added as DNS servers do need to be running DNS. Because the resolver behavior is to try the configured servers in order, until one responds, configuring very many servers can slow the user's networking. As long as a server answers, whether the query is successful or fails, the resolver will not move on to the next server. One should place the most local and reliable servers at the top of this list.

Setting the DNS Domain Suffix Order via Text File

The DNS domain suffix order can also be set during an unattended install. For Windows 2000, you should use the UNATTEND.TXT file rather than the method that follows. For Windows NT Workstation or Windows NT Server 4.0, you must use the Registry Editor because the unattended setup mode of Windows NT does not offer a way to specify the domain suffix order.

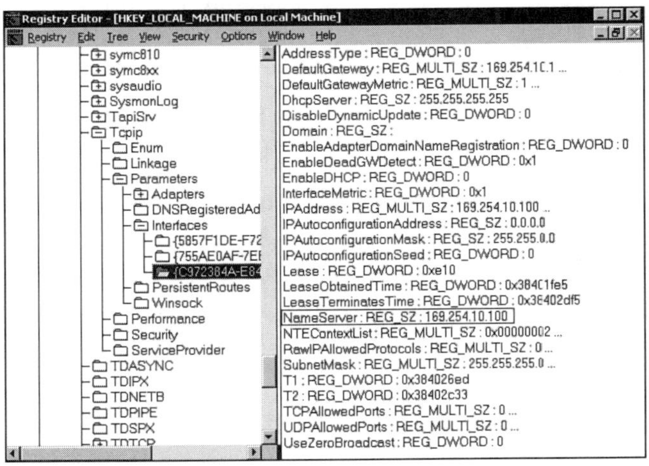

Figure 14.6 The Windows 2000 Registry opened to the per-interface TCP/IP settings.

Create a text file with the following two lines of text, and save it as SUFFIX.TXT. The spacing must appear exactly as shown below, where "xxxxxxxx.xxx" signifies a domain suffix. Up to six domain suffixes can be specified. The search order works left to right.

```
\\HKEY_LOCAL_MACHINE\System\CurrentControlSet\Services\TCPIP\Parameters
 "SearchList=textxxxx.com test2xxxx.net test 3xxxx.gov"
```

Copy REGINI.EXE and SUFFIX.TXT to the OEM subdirectory at the installation Sharepoint. REGINI.EXE is a Windows NT Resource Kit utility.

If one does not exist, create a CMDLINES.TXT file in the OEM subdirectory, and add the following line (including the quotation marks):

```
[Commands]
".\REGINI SUFFIX.TXT"
```

Only one instance of the [Commands] heading should exist in the CMDLINES.TXT file.

Make sure that the entry OEMPREINSTALL =Yes exists in the [UNATTEND] section of your UNATTENDED.TXT file

Setting the DNS Domain Suffix Order via Registry

Create a Registry file with the following two lines of text, and save it as SUFFIX.REG. The spacing must be exactly as shown in the example that follows, where xxxxxxxx.xxx signifies a domain suffix. Up to six domain suffixes can be specified. The search order works left to right.

```
\\HKEY_LOCAL_MACHINE\System\CurrentControlSet\Services\TCPIP\Parameters
"SearchList=textxxxx.com test2xxxx.net test 3xxxx.gov"
```

Copy REGEDIT.EXE and SUFFIX.REG to the OEM subdirectory at the installation Sharepoint.

If one does not exist, create a CMDLINES.TXT file in the OEM subdirectory, and add the following lines (including the quotation marks):

```
[Commands]
".\REGEDIT /s SUFFIX.REG"
```

Only one instance of the [Commands] heading should exist in the CMDLINES.TXT file.

Make sure that the entry OEMPREINSTALL =Yes exists in the [UNATTEND] section of your UNATTENDED.TXT file.

Code Styling

The preceding Registry key is one path; it has been wrapped for readability.

Use Registry Editor with Care

Once again, the importance of using the Registry Editor carefully cannot be stressed enough. Any incorrect use of the Registry can cause serious problems that may require you to reinstall your operating system!

Configuring Clients to Use WINS

A WINS-enabled client communicates with a WINS server to register the client names in the WINS database and to get IP addresses that have been mapped to NetBIOS names through WINS queries. WINS clients are configured with the IP address of one or more WINS servers: typically a primary and secondary should be entered. At startup, WINS clients communicate directly with a WINS server to register their computer name and corresponding IP address. The actual actions of WINS and WINS clients are covered in detail in Chapter 16, "WINS: Legacy Name Services and Resolution." The actual names registered with WINS may indicate more than just the machine name, such as the fact that domain control services may be obtained at the name. Chapter 17, "NetBIOS: Legacy Name Services and Resolution," covers the different uses of NetBIOS names.

Supported Clients

The following operating systems can currently act as WINS clients when using Windows as a WINS server:

- Windows 2000 all versions (Professional, Server, Advanced Server, Datacenter)
- Windows NT Workstation version 3.5x or version 4.0
- Windows NT Server version 3.5x or version 4.0
- Windows 95 and Windows 98
- Windows for Workgroups 3.11 (WFWG), with the Microsoft 32-bit TCP/IP stack installed
- Microsoft Network Client for MS-DOS, with real-mode TCP/IP-32
- LAN Manager for MS-DOS 2.2c (but not the OS/2 version)
- OS/2
- Linux and UNIX clients with SAMBA installed

Configuring the WINS Client

When Microsoft TCP/IP is installed under Windows 95 and Windows 98, the WINS client software is installed automatically. Windows NT and 2000 do not require any special effort other than having TCP/IP installed.

Windows 95, Windows 98, Windows 2000, and NT clients are configured with the IP address of one or more WINS servers by using the WINS Address tab of the TCP/IP Properties. Figures 14.7, 14.8, and 14.9 and the accompanying procedures show this configuration for Windows 95, Windows NT 4.0, and Windows 2000, respectively. Down-level clients are limited to specifying two WINS servers. IP addresses assigned to these Windows server computers running WINS should be provided by the network administrator. The most reliably available and local servers should be listed first, particularly in Windows 2000 where very many WINS servers may be listed.

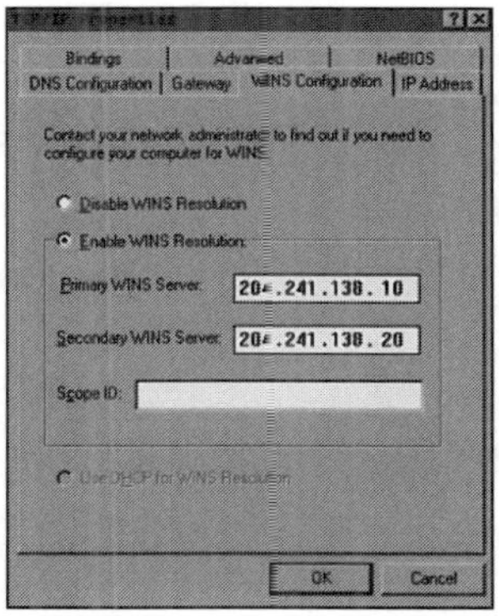

Figure 14.7 The process of enabling WINS in a Windows 95 client.

To configure a computer running Windows 95 and Windows 98 to use WINS for name resolution, follow these steps:

1. In the TCP/IP Properties, click the WINS Configuration tab.
2. If a DHCP server is available that is configured to provide information on available WINS servers, select Use DHCP for WINS Resolution. If a WINS server is available but a DHCP server isn't, select Enable WINS Resolution and type the IP addresses of the primary and secondary WINS servers.
3. If WINS is enabled, in the Scope ID box, type the computer's scope identifier, if used (usually this value is left blank).

To configure a computer running Windows NT 4.0 to use WINS for name resolution, follow these steps:

1. In the TCP/IP Properties, click the WINS Address tab.
2. Type the IP addresses of the primary and secondary WINS servers. If the client is obtaining TCP/IP configuration information from DHCP, entering this will override the WINS servers specified by DHCP.
3. In the Scope ID box, type the computer's scope identifier, if used (usually this value is left blank).
4. Check the boxes to Enable DNS for Windows Resolution and to Enable LMHOSTS for Lookup if needed. (discussed later).

To configure a computer running Windows 2000 to use WINS for name resolution, follow these steps:

1. In the TCP/IP Properties, click the Advanced button, and then select the tab labeled WINS.

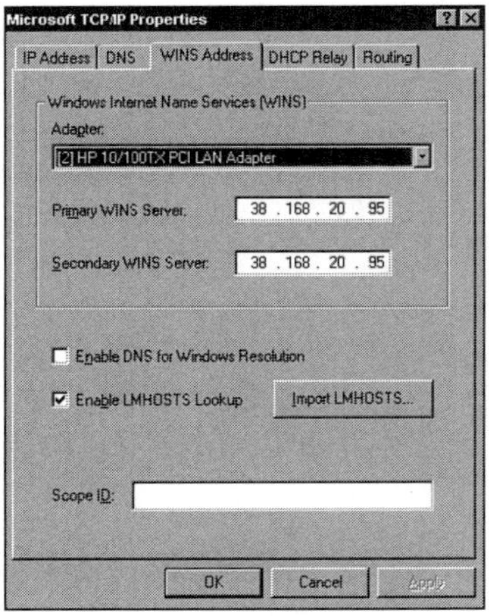

Figure 14.8 The process of enabling WINS in a Windows NT 4.0 client.

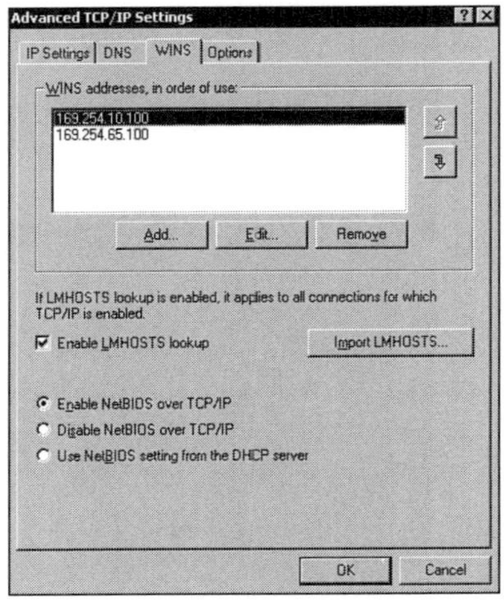

Figure 14.9 The process of enabling WINS in a Windows 2000 client.

2. Enter the WINS server IP addresses for this connection by using the Add button. You can add many WINS servers, and arrange them in the order they will be tried, but should make sure the most local and reliable are at the top.
3. Make sure that the Enable NetBIOS over TCP/IP selection is checked. Notice the option for using DHCP server-provided settings.

With Windows 2000, you will notice some extra options on the WINS tab. Disabling NetBT (by using Disable NetBIOS over TCP/IP) does not make sense in the context of this section where we are enabling WINS. When no interoperation with down-level Windows systems is needed, disabling NetBT effectively blocks calls by TCPIP.SYS to its helper NETBT.SYS, but in the first release of Windows 2000 you would be well-advised to test that all needed features are available before widely disabling NetBT. Also, it is worth noticing there is no option to Enable DNS for Windows Resolution in this Windows 2000 WINS configuration page as with the other systems (because it is always enabled, more on this a little later). Notice that there is no option to set the NetBIOS scope as there is in the other operating systems. For Windows 2000, this can only be set in the Registry key HKLM\SYSTEM\CurrentControlSet\Services\NetBT\Parameters\ScopeID or by the scope options from the DHCP server.

NetBIOS Scope

The NetBIOS scope can be, but is not often, used to segment the NetBIOS namespace. The NetBIOS scope enables interoperation with other NetBIOS implementations that use the same NetBIOS scope ID. Before any packets that contain a NetBIOS name are transmitted, the NetBIOS scope ID is appended to the name. On the receiving end, the NetBIOS scope in a packet must match the locally configured NetBIOS scope; otherwise, the packet is ignored. Therefore, only computers that have the same scope can communicate with each other using NetBIOS. Additionally, the scope ID is case sensitive; so computers configured with the scope ID "scope" that attempt to communicate with computers with scope ID "SCOPE" cannot communicate via NetBIOS over TCP/IP.

Windows 95 presents an unusual situation which sometimes requires manual intervention. In the Network option in the Windows 95 and Windows 98 Control Panel, you must first enable WINS name resolution so that you can manually configure the NetBIOS scope ID in the TCP/IP Properties. Therefore, you must also enter at least one IP address for a WINS server, even though a WINS server might not be present on the network. If you install Windows 95 or Windows 98 using a setup script and define the NetBIOS scope ID in the setup script, you do not also have to specify wins=1 plus a WINS server IP address. Remember that because NetBIOS scope IDs are used to segment network traffic, you must be very careful about assigning NetBIOS scope IDs. With a faulty scope ID configuration, users may not be able to connect to other computers. If WINS is not enabled, the NetBIOS scope ID can be changed only manually, by editing the Registry as follows:

1. Run Registry Editor (REGEDIT.EXE).
2. In the HKEY_LOCAL_MACHINE hive, go to the following key: System\CurrentControlSet\Services\VXD\MSTCP.
3. Add the new scope ID by clicking Edit, and then clicking New, and then selecting String Value. Type **ScopeID**, and press Enter. Double-click the value. A window appears for Edit String. Enter your scope ID under Value data.

Understanding Client Use of the Windows Resolver

To say "the" Windows resolver is really a misnomer. Windows computers have so many name-resolution options that it's hard sometimes to predict just how they'll behave. The way in which the resolver is configured, which is really what this chapter has covered so far by looking at the TCP/IP configuration settings, makes a huge difference in the resolver's behavior. Sometimes a computer just can't find others on the

> **Registry Editor Warning**
>
> Using Registry Editor incorrectly can cause serious systemwide problems that may require you to reinstall Windows 95 or Windows 98 to correct them.

network, even those showing in the browser list. If you know how resolvers work, the mysteries behind a success or failure are somewhat easier to solve. Helping you understand the Windows resolver is the purpose of this section. But this will only go so far, so take a look at Chapter 17 for further NetBIOS-specific browser information.

Introducing the Windows Resolver

A resolver is the collection of routines a client computer uses to take advantage of available name services. The Windows resolver is supplied within TCPIP.SYS and its helper NETBT.SYS. That is not to say that is all that these do. The former resolves IP host (DNS) names, and the latter handles NetBIOS name resolution for TCP/IP. For this section, resolution means the process of obtaining an answer about a name-to-IP mapping.

The UNIX resolver deals almost exclusively with IP host names. By contrast, the Windows resolver must support two name types: NetBIOS computer names and IP host names. What's more, the Windows resolver must decide which of several possible options to use to resolve the names. The resolver also must know what to do if the first approach doesn't succeed, if the second doesn't succeed, and so on. The resolver may first ask a WINS or a DNS name server for an address and then stay engaged until an answer comes back, even if it means that other servers must also be queried or other methods invoked. The resolver typically uses all options at its disposal until it has succeeded or exhausted its alternatives.

The general-purpose resolver facility inside a Windows operating system is available to any program that needs it, especially those with no name-resolving capabilities. Most applications needing name service use the general-purpose resolver by giving it computer names to resolve. The Windows name resolver submits queries to name servers and handles the various possible responses they can return. When names are resolved, applications can usually proceed with their tasks. If, for any reason, the resolver does not succeed in locating a name, it sends an appropriate failure message to the local application that requested service. Most Windows applications are designed to handle these conditions gracefully, messaging the user about the resolution failure.

Resolver Behavior Differences

Variations in resolver behavior among Windows 95, Windows 98, Windows NT, and Windows 2000 are not explored in detail here because the differences are too great. Having said that, the main differences are explored, and the characteristics of the settings available in the TCP/IP Properties as they impact the ordering of name lookup attempts are covered. The calling order and the method of deciding which are used or ignored are determined by configuration settings and the system version, making for very many different situations. The general rules here should be applied to understand specific configurations.

The Windows Resolution Methods

Chapter 17, discusses the six methods the resolver can have available to it. These methods are as follows:

- The local name cache
- NetBIOS broadcasts
- WINS servers
- LMHOSTS file
- DNS servers
- HOSTS files

Broadcast, WINS, and the LMHOSTS file deal with NetBIOS names, and are handled (mostly) by NetBT ("mostly" is used because of the DNS/WINS integration option). The last two in the list, DNS and the HOSTS file, deal with the DNS names. For simplicity, this discussion refers at times to these as the two name types, or the two routes the resolver may take, or distinguishes these as the NetBIOS methods and the DNS methods. If the client has the Enable DNS for WINS option and it is enabled, NetBIOS methods include the use of the two DNS methods.

Things are not as simple as sending a NetBIOS name down the NetBIOS track, however, and a DNS host name down the other route. First, there is the issue of which kind of name is a name likely to be. Then, there is the issue of what services the resolver does have available to it. Remember, it "can" have these six. Whether it does all depends on what is configured. Finally, there is the choice the resolver must make as to in what order to try the methods.

Windows Resolver Behaviors

One thing, thankfully, can be said simply: Of the resolution methods, the name cache is always checked first. This is much like a person recalling the definition of a word instead of going to the dictionary. Of course there are the two local caches, one for NetBIOS and one for DNS names. To view the local NetBIOS cache, use **nbtstat –n** in a command window. To view the local DNS name cache, use the **ipconfig /displaydns**, which is new in the updated ipconfig in Windows 2000, and not available in down-level NT at this time.

The first version difference to keep in mind is that Windows 2000 always attempts to resolve using both routes, at least if NetBT is enabled. Whichever resolution route answers first is used. This is not how any prior system version handled this; they all attempt to guess what kind of name they have been given. One consequence of this behavior in Windows 2000 is that if NetBIOS names are used, and DNS/WINS integration is enabled, frequently requested NetBIOS names are answered from the DNS server's cache very quickly and cheaply. It is therefore not surprising to see some Microsoft documents recommending this DNS/WINS configuration when using NetBIOS names.

Another difference between Windows 2000 compared to all other versions, is that Windows 2000 systems will always have DNS configured (or rather should to be functional in a network environment). DNS is strictly optional in all other systems. Because of this, in down-level systems the resolver must consider whether the DNS methods are available.

By looking back at the TCP/IP property configurations in the first part of this chapter, you will recall that the suffix list is also handled differently in Windows 2000. The two apparent differences are that one has more control, and that there is a primary and a connection-specific DNS suffix. This dual DNS identity, and per-adapter configuration is not available in any down-level system.

Because of the Windows 2000 dual use of both resolution routes, much of the remaining discussion needs to be taken with a grain of salt. Instead of repeatedly saying "for down-level systems," or "except for Windows 2000," this chapter just describes how all the other systems do things. Just keep in mind that for a Windows 2000 system these are fired off in parallel, when NetBT is not disabled. You were warned that this was an involved topic, after all.

When a name is obviously a DNS name—for example, because it is a FQDN or is too long to be a NetBIOS name—it is a candidate only for the DNS methods. Otherwise, the name is ambiguous and could be either kind, and is a candidate for both resolution routes. Resolution attempts via NetBIOS just query the provided name. Resolution attempts via DNS, however, may be repeated as the DNS suffix list is used, one at a time, to form the FQDNs that are successively tried. When a name is ambiguous, resolution as a NetBIOS name is, generally, first attempted; then, failing that, DNS resolution is attempted when it is enabled. Just what is an ambiguous name is difficult to precisely define, if only for version differences; for example, Windows NT allowed a period (.) character in a NetBIOS name.

If the client has the Enable DNS for WINS option and it is enabled, however, NetBIOS names are rerouted into the DNS methods, which means that they will also have the suffix list used. When this option is enabled on NT 4.0, DNS resolution is the first method that is tried for a NetBIOS name. A similar order for Windows 95 requires a Registry edit. In effect, this option is implied in Windows 2000, and you will notice that this is not surfaced in the TCP/IP Properties pages. Fully configuring DNS/WINS integration, as covered in Chapter 16, can be very important to guarantee that this route for NetBIOS resolution is successful. When used, it is quite important to make sure that a DNS suffix list appropriate for the DNS/WINS integration is configured in the client. Even without DNS/WINS integration, when static IP addresses are used, use of the same name in both namespaces and proper DNS registration of the name can make this option useful.

The order of the NetBIOS methods attempted depends on the NetBIOS node type of the client, which is fully covered in Chapter 17. Usually, we aim to prevent NetBIOS broadcasts, except in very small environments. When a client is configured to use WINS, it is configured to be a hybrid (h-node) type, meaning it will only use broadcast as a last resort after all direct communications with the configured WINS servers have failed. One may use the **ipconfig /all** command in Windows NT and 2000 or the corresponding **winipcfg** command in Windows 95 and Windows 98 (see Chapter 12, "Troubleshooting Tools and Utilities," for more information) to check a client node type. These are illustrated in Figure 14.10 for NT 4.0 and Figure 14.11 for Windows 95. Windows 2000 provides many more **ipconfig** options, but **ipconfig/all** has a very similar output. Most commonly one will see either hybrid or broadcast as the (NetBIOS) node type.

When a name is ambiguous, and failed to resolve as a NetBIOS name, it will be tried as a DNS name, but only if the client configuration is such that DNS methods have not yet been tried and the client is configured to use DNS. This is mostly the situation in the older clients configured for DNS.

One final thing that can be helpful, but which has fallen into disuse, is preloading the NetBIOS resolver cache by using a LMHOST file. You will find this covered in the appendixes. WINS mostly made these files obsolete, but many administrators still use them, to provide a guaranteed fallback in the event of worst-case WINS failure, especially on the servers forming the core of a deployment. The LMHOSTS file is also useful if forcing a client to use a specific domain controller for its secure channel.

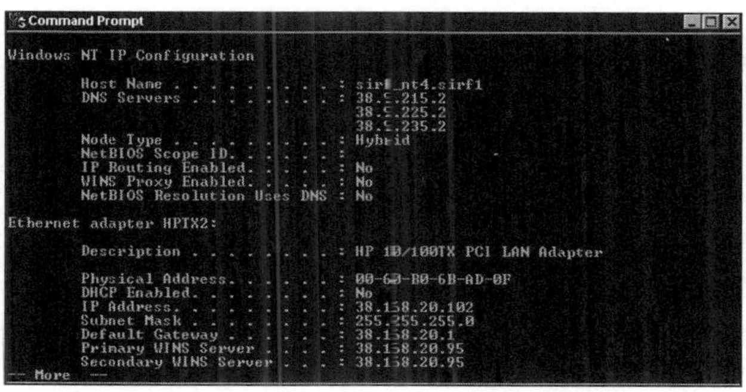

Figure 14.10 Viewing TCP/IP configuration with **ipconfig /all** in NT 4.0.

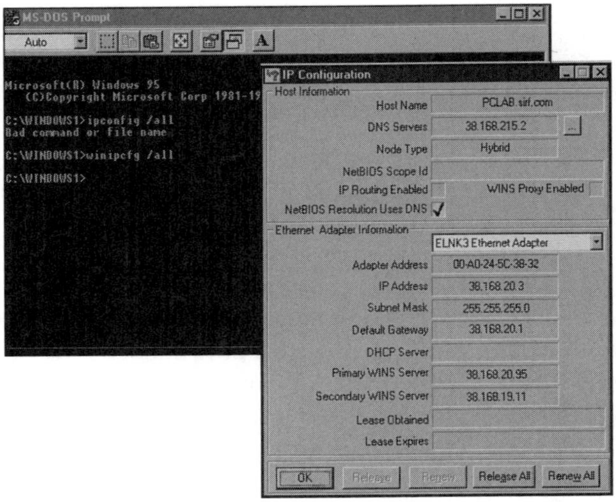

Figure 14.11 Viewing TCP/IP configuration with **winipcfg /all** in Windows 95.

Other Client-Support Information

This section addresses a few facts that may be of use in certain circumstances. The last of these are some of the Registry settings related to NetBT. The first, WINS proxies, is a little-used feature, but is needed when supporting the early era clients that cannot be directly WINS enabled, but that do use NetBIOS. The second provides information on the limitations of MS-DOS without and with the native mode TCP/IP 32-bit driver.

Wins Proxies

Windows-based networking clients can use WINS directly. Non-WINS computers that are b-node compatible (as described in RFCs 1001 and 1002) can access WINS through proxies. WINS proxies are WINS-enabled computers that listen to name registration and query broadcasts and then mediate these by forwarding them to the WINS server.

When a non-WINS enabled client broadcasts for a name resolution, it is actually asking all listening machines whether they know how to get to the machine named in the query. Any NetBIOS client might reply if it is the named machine or the name is in its cache. The proxy will step in and communicate with the WINS server to resolve names that are not answered. The proxy serves as an intermediary, by communicating with the WINS server and then supplying the WINS answer to the broadcast client. To handle name announcements, the proxy communicates with WINS, but the name is not registered. Rather, the broadcast client is only informed whether the name is available for use; the announced name is not reserved by registration in WINS.

With a Windows NT 3.5x platform, to designate a proxy you check the Enable WINS Proxy Agent option in the Advanced Microsoft TCP/IP Configuration dialog box.

With a Windows NT 4.0 or Windows 2000 platform, to designate a proxy you must use the Registry Editor (REGEDT32.EXE) and add an entry, which might correctly be taken as an indication of their being in current disfavor. To configure a WINS proxy anyway, edit the Registry on the machine becoming the proxy at HKLM\System\CurrentControlSet\Services\Netbt\Parameters. Set the key value EnableProxy to 1 to turn on the feature, and 0 to turn it off. If you are going to be using WINS proxies, make sure that there is one placed on each network segment having non-WINS clients and that they will be highly available. The better solution today is upgrading the older systems.

MS-DOS and the TCP/IP-32 Driver Upgrade

The MS-DOS TCP/IP implementation for Microsoft Network Client version 3.0 for MS-DOS supports the following:

- An MS-DOS–based interface
- Domain name resolver (DNR) to resolve host name–to–IP address mappings if your network has a DNS server
- The Dynamic Host Configuration Protocol (DHCP)
- Windows Internet Name Service (WINS) resolution
- Windows Sockets

MS-DOS–based clients do not support the following features, which are provided by TCP/IP-32 for Windows for Workgroups version 3.11, TCP/IP for Windows 95, and Windows NT Workstation and Windows NT Server versions 3.5, 3.51, and 4.0:

- Support for WINS resolution using DNS.
- Name registration with the WINS database. Note that MS-DOS computers are clients, not servers, so they generally do not need registration.
- Capability to act as a WINS proxy node.
- Support for multiple network adapters.
- Support for Internet Group Management Protocol (IGMP).

TCP/IP Registry Parameters

Very many TCP/IP parameters are located in the Registry under the HKEY_LOCAL_MACHINE\SYSTEM\CurrentControlSet\Services\Tcpip\Parameters key. Many of these are available for fine-tuning the behavior of TCP/IP and can have an impact on overall performance as well as resistance to network attack. Most of the needed settings are available through the Windows user interface, and are not mentioned here. Only a very few of this large number of parameters that might be of interest are listed.

DatabasePath Parameter

The DatabasePath parameter is used by Winsock services to locate the standard Internet data files (HOSTS, networks, protocols, services) and the LMHOSTS file. The attributes for this parameter are as follows:

- Key: Tcpip\Parameters
- Value type: REG_EXPAND_SZ
- Valid range: any valid directory path
- Default: %SystemRoot%\system32\drivers\etc

DisableDHCPMediaSense Parameter

The DisableDHCPMediaSense parameter is used to disable the behavior of the DHCP client where, on detecting a media sense event on an interface, it will obtain a lease (on a connect event) or invalidate the interface and related information (on a disconnect event). The attributes for this parameter are as follows:

- Key: Tcpip\Parameters
- Value type: REG_DWORD
- Valid range: 0,1 (0 false, 1 true)
- Default: 0

EnableDeadGWDetect Parameter

The EnableDeadGWDetect parameter when enabled (the default) allows TCP to have IP change the gateway being used when a number of connections are having problems and there are alternative gateways configured. The attributes for this parameter are as follows:

- Key: Tcpip\Parameters
- Value type: REG_DWORD
- Valid range: 0,1 (0 false, 1 true)
- Default: 1

IPAutoconfigurationEnabled Parameter

The IPAutoconfigurationEnabled parameter can be set globally or for specific interfaces and controls whether the client will fall back to IP auto-configuration when no DHCP server can be located. The attributes for this parameter are as follows:

- Key: Tcpip\Parameters
- Key: Tcpip\Parameters\Interfaces\<Interface>
- Value type: REG_DWORD
- Valid range: 0,1 (0 false, 1 true)
- Default: 1

IPAutoconfigurationSubnet Parameter

The IPAutoconfigurationSubnet parameter can be set globally or for specific interfaces and controls determines the IP subnet from which IP auto-configuration will pick an IP for the client when no DHCP server can be located. The attributes for this parameter are as follows:

- Key: Tcpip\Parameters
- Key: Tcpip\Parameters\Interfaces\<Interface>
- Value type: REG_SZ
- Valid range: Valid IP subnets
- Default: 169.254.0.0

IPEnableRouter Parameter

The IPEnableRouter parameter allows IP to route packets between its network connections. The attributes for this parameter are as follows:

- Key: Tcpip\Parameters
- Value type: REG_DWORD
- Valid range: 0,1 (0 false, 1 true)
- Default: 0

SynAttackProtect Parameter

The SynAttackProtect parameter allows TCP to adjust transmissions rates to cause connection attempts to time out more rapidly than they would otherwise. This will happen when the value of the TcpMaxPortsExhausted parameter makes it appear that a SYN-Attack is in progress. The attributes for this parameter are as follows:

- Key: Tcpip\Parameters
- Value type: REG_DWORD
- Valid range: 0,1 (0 false, 1 true)
- Default: 0

DNS Client Related Registry Parameters

The Registry contains under the HKEY_LOCAL_MACHINE\SYSTEM\CurrentControlSet\Services\Tcpip\Parameters key a number of parameters that relate to DNS resolution and to dynamic DNS client registration. These are listed in the following subsections. There are also a number of parameters that control the DNS caching resolver, including the capability to shut it off found under the HKEY_LOCAL_MACHINE\SYSTEM\CurrentControlSet\Services\Dnscache\Parameters Registry key. These are not listed here.

DefaultRegistrationTTL Parameter

The DefaultRegistrationTTL parameter specifies the time value sent with DDNS registration requests. The attributes for this parameter are as follows:

- Key: Tcpip\Parameters
- Value type: REG_DWORD (in seconds)
- Valid range: 0–oxFFFFFFFF
- Default: 0x4B0 (1,200 seconds, 20 minutes)

EnableAdapterDomainNameRegistration Parameter

The EnableAdapterDomainNameRegistration parameter is a per-interface setting that specifies that a adapter's configured domain name should be used in DDNS registrations. If DisableDynamicUpdate is false while this parameter is true, the interface will be registered under both domain names. The attributes for this parameter are as follows:

- Key: Tcpip\Parameters\Interfaces\<Interface>
- Value type: REG_DWORD
- Valid range: 0,1 (0 false, 1 true)
- Default: 0

DisableDynamicUpdate Parameter

The DisableDynamicUpdate parameter is available both as a global and as a per-interface setting that enables or disables DDNS registrations. The attributes for this parameter are as follows:

- Key: Tcpip\Parameters
- Key: Tcpip\Parameters\Interfaces\<Interface>
- Value type: REG_DWORD
- Valid range: 0,1 (0 false, 1 true)
- Default: 0

DisableReplaceAddressesInConflict Parameter

The DisableReplaceAddressesInConflict parameter is available as a global setting that controls how the DNS client behaves when encountering DNS registrations that conflict with its desired registrations for itself. The attributes for this parameter are as follows:

- Key: Tcpip\Parameters
- Value type: REG_DWORD
- Valid range: 0,1 (0 false, 1 true)
- Default: 0

DisableReverseAddressRegistrations Parameter

The DisableReverseAddressRegistrations parameter is available both as a global and as a per-interface setting that is used to disable registration of PTR resource records by the DDNS client. The attributes for this parameter are as follows:

- Key: Tcpip\Parameters
- Key: Tcpip\Parameters\Interfaces\<Interface>
- Value type: REG_DWORD
- Valid range: 0,1 (0 false, 1 true)
- Default: 0

UpdateSecurityLevel Parameter

The UpdateSecurityLevel parameter is a global setting used to set the security negotiation attempted with dynamic DNS updates. The default (0x0) is to attempt unsecured update, and then to attempt secured update if needed. The other values are do not use security, use security, and only use security for 0x00000010, 0x00000020, 0x00000100 respectively. The attributes for this parameter are as follows:

- Key: Tcpip\Parameters
- Value type: REG_DWORD
- Valid range: 0, 0x00000010, 0x00000020, 0x00000100
- Default: 0

AllowUnqualifiedQuery Parameter

The AllowUnqualifiedQuery parameter controls whether the resolver will send a query to DNS when it consists of only a host name. With this off, a resolution request for cowpoke on a computer where the domain is range.com results in a DNS query for cowpoke.range.com.. With this on, a DNS query for cowpoke. will be used. The attributes for this parameter are as follows:

- Key: Tcpip\Parameters
- Value type: REG_DWORD
- Valid range: 0,1 (0 false, 1 true)
- Default: 0

DisjointNamespace Parameter

The DisjointNamespace parameter controls whether the resolver will treat each interface as a separate DNS namespace. When this is on, the resolver will try all associated interfaces, as needed, before returning results. The attributes for this parameter are as follows:

- Key: Tcpip\Parameters
- Value type: REG_DWORD
- Valid range: 0,1 (0 false, 1 true)
- Default: 1

UseDomainNameDevolution Parameter

The UseDomainNameDevolution parameter controls whether the resolver will form DNS queries for ambiguous names by appending the clients domain, its parent, and so on provided that the appended domain is not a first-level domain. The attributes for this parameter are as follows:

- Key: Tcpip\Parameters
- Value type: REG_DWORD
- Valid range: 0,1 (0 false, 1 true)
- Default: 1

NetBT (NetBIOS over TCP/IP) Registry Parameters

All the NetBIOS over TCP/IP parameters are located in the Registry under subkeys of the HKEY_LOCAL_MACHINE\SYSTEM\CurrentControlSet\Services key at

- Netbt\Parameters
- Netbt\Adapters\<Adapter Name> on NT 4.0 (where <Adapter Name> refers to the subkey for a network adapter to which NetBT is bound, such as Lance01)
- Netbt\Parameters\Interfaces\<Interface Guid> on Windows 2000 (where <Interface Guid> is the unique system assigned name for the interface)

Values under the last two keys are specific to each adapter (interface). Windows NT 4.0 uses the Netbt\Adapters\<Adapter Name> and Windows 2000 uses parameters stored at Netbt\Parameters\Interfacs\<Interface Guid>. A reboot of the system is required for a change in any of these parameters to take effect, unless the client is using DHCP (in which case, the command **ipconfig /renew** can reconfigure the NetBT settings).

During the installation of the TCP/IP components, the TCP/IP Properties installs some of the parameters covered in the following sections with defaults or values provided in the install. Not all these key values are always present. You can also modify these parameters by using the Registry Editor.

> **Reboot May Be Required**
>
> To make sure there is a full registration, the server should be rebooted to regenerate WINS address entries if the **nbtstat -RR** option is not available.

The following listing is not exhaustive, but is a selection representative of the more common or interesting parameters. A set of DHCP-related parameters, to which the DHCP client stores values received from the DHCP server, are not included here. These DHCP-related parameters should not be set directly. Of the NetBIOS parameters, this list covers about half. Settings not included can be used to adjust timeout values for the different types of queries, to control NetBIOS connection creation, to adjust the caching of NetBIOS names, to adjust behaviors on multihomed systems, and to specify behaviors with proxying.

NetbiosOptions Parameter

This Registry parameter is a Windows 2000 parameter that is not present in Windows NT. The NetbiosOptions parameter specifies whether NetBIOS is enabled (a value of 1) or disabled (value of 2) on an interface. This parameter can be set via the TCP/IP Properties using the Disable NetBIOS over TCP/IP setting; you should not have to configure this parameter directly. When this key does not exist, the value of the DHCPNetbiosOptions parameter, which is only configurable through the use of DHCP, will be used if it exists; and if the NetbiosOptions parameter exists, the DHCPNetbiosOptions will be ignored. The attributes for this parameter are as follows:

- Key: Netbt\Parameters\Interfaces\<interface>
- Value type: REG_DWORD
- Valid range: 1 for enabled, 2 for disabled
- Default: 1

UseDnsOnlyForNameResolutions Parameter

This Registry parameter is a Windows 2000 parameter that is not present in Windows NT. This parameter can be used to disable all NetBIOS name queries. This does not disable NetBIOS, and name registrations and refreshes still take place. The attributes for this parameter are as follows:

- Key: Netbt\Parameters
- Value type: REG_DWORD
- Valid range: 0,1 (0, false; 1, true)
- Default: 0

SMBDeviceEnabled Parameter

This Registry parameter is a Windows 2000 parameter that is not present in Windows NT. The SMBDeviceEnabled parameter can be used to disable the new Server Message Block (SMB) device that is defined in Windows 2000 as a network transport protocol. The attributes for this parameter are as follows:

- Key: Netbt\Parameters
- Value type: REG_DWORD

- Valid range: 0,1 (0, false for disabled; 1, true for enabled)
- Default: 1

NodeType Parameter

The NodeType parameter controls what NetBIOS behaviors a client system follows for name registration and resolution. The attributes for this parameter are as follows:

- Key: Netbt\Parameters
- Value type: REG_DWORD
- Valid range: 1,2,4,8 (1 b-node, 2 p-node, 4 m-node, 8 h-node)
- Default: 1 or 8 depending on status as a WINS client

SessionKeepAlive Parameter

The SessionKeepAlive parameter determines the interval between NetBIOS session keep-alive communications, which are used to keep otherwise idle sessions open. The time interval is specified in milliseconds, and a value of 0xFFFFFFFF may be used to disable session keep-alives. The attributes of this parameter are as follows:

- Key: Netbt\Parameters
- Value type: REG_DWORD (milliseconds)
- Valid range: 60,000–0xFFFFFFFF
- Default: 3,600,000 (1 hour)

WinsDownTimeout Parameter

The WinsDownTimeout parameter determines how long the client will wait after all attempts to contact the configured WINS servers has failed. The time interval is specified in milliseconds, and after this interval the client will again attempt to WINS. This parameter is of use in speeding disconnected clients through their boot process. The attributes of this parameter are as follows:

- Key: Netbt\Parameters
- Value type: REG_DWORD (milliseconds)
- Valid range: 1,000–0xFFFFFFFF
- Default: 15,000 (15 seconds)

NameServerList Parameter

This Registry parameter is a Windows 2000 parameter that is not present in Windows NT. The NameServerList parameter specifies the IP addresses of WINS servers. If this parameter contains a valid value, it overrides the DHCP provided value(s). This parameter can be set via the TCP/IP Properties; you should not have to configure this parameter directly. The attributes for this parameter are as follows:

- Key: Netbt\Parameters\Interfaces\<interface>
- Value type: REG_MULTI_SZ (dotted-decimal IP address list, space delimited, such as 11.101.1.200 11.101.3.300)
- Valid range: Any valid IP address
- Default: Blank (no address)

NameServer Parameter

This Registry parameter is an NT 4.0 parameter that is no longer used in Windows 2000. The NameServer parameter specifies the IP address of the primary WINS server. If this parameter contains a valid value, it overrides the DHCP parameter of the same name. This parameter can be set via the TCP/IP Properties; you should not have to configure this parameter directly. The attributes for this parameter are as follows:

- Key: Netbt\Adapters\<Adapter Name>
- Value type: REG_SZ (dotted-decimal IP address, such as 11.101.1.200)
- Valid range: Any valid IP address
- Default: Blank (no address)

NameServerBackup Parameter

This Registry parameter is an NT 4.0 parameter that is no longer used in Windows 2000. The NameServerBackup parameter specifies the IP address of the backup WINS server. If this parameter contains a valid value, it overrides the DHCP parameter of the same name. This parameter can be set via the TCP/IP Properties; you should not have to configure this parameter directly. The attributes for this parameter are as follows:

- Key: Netbt\Adapters\<Adapter Name>
- Value type: REG_SZ (dotted-decimal IP address, such as 11.101.1.200)
- Valid Range: Any valid IP address
- Default: Blank (no address)

NameServerPort Parameter

The NameServerPort parameter determines the destination port number to which NetBT sends name service-related packets, such as name queries and name registrations, to WINS. The Microsoft WINS listens on port 0x89 (decimal 137). NetBIOS name servers from other vendors may listen on different ports. The attributes of this parameter are as follows:

- Key: Netbt\Parameters
- Value type: REG_DWORD (UDP port number)
- Valid range: 0–0xFFFF
- Default: 0x89

NameSrvQueryCount Parameter

The NameSrvQueryCount parameter determines the number of times NetBT sends a query to a WINS server for a given name when not receiving a response. The attributes of this parameter are as follows:

- Key: Netbt\Parameters
- Value type: REG_DWORD (count)
- Valid range: 0–0xFFFF
- Default: 3

NameSrvQueryTimeout Parameter

This parameter sets the wait period between query attempts to WINS for a given name. The attributes for this parameter are as follows:

- Key: Netbt\Parameters
- Value type: REG_DWORD (time in milliseconds)
- Valid range: 100–0xFFFFFFFF
- Default: 1,500 (1.5 seconds)

BroadcastAddress Parameter

The BroadcastAddress parameter can be used to force NetBT to use a specific address for all broadcast name-related packets. By default, NetBT uses the ones-broadcast address appropriate for each net. (That is, for a network of 11.101.0.0 with a subnet mask of 255.255.0.0, the subnet broadcast address would be 11.101.255.255.) This parameter would be set, for example, if the network uses the zeros-broadcast address (set using the UseZeroBroadcast TCP/IP parameter). The appropriate subnet broadcast address would then be 11.101.0.0 in the example given, and this parameter would be set to 0x0a650000. Note that this parameter is global and is used on all subnets to which NetBT is bound. This parameter normally does not exist in the Registry, but it may be created to modify the default behavior of the NetBT protocol driver. The attributes for this parameter are as follows:

- Key: Netbt\Parameters
- Value type: REG_DWORD (little-endian encoded IP address consisting of 4 bytes)
- Valid range: 0–0xFFFFFFFF
- Default: The ones-broadcast address for each network

EnableDns Parameter

If the EnableDns parameter is 1 (true), NetBT queries DNS for names that fail to resolve through WINS, broadcast, or the LMHOSTS file. For NT 4.0 this occurs first rather than last. This parameter can be set via the TCP/IP Properties; you should not have to configure this parameter directly. The attributes of this parameter are as follows:

- Key: Netbt\Parameters
- Value type: REG_DWORD (Boolean)
- Valid range: 0 or 1 (false or true)
- Default: 0 (False)

DNSServerPort Parameter

If the DNSServerPort parameter specifies what User Datagram Protocol (UDP) port will be used when NetBT sends queries to DNS. The attributes of this parameter are as follows:

- Key: Netbt\Parameters
- Value type: REG_DWORD
- Valid range: 0–0xFFFF
- Default: 0x35 (53 decimal value)

EnableLmhosts Parameter

If the EnableLmhosts parameter is 1 (true), NetBT will search the LMHOSTS file, if it exists, for names that cannot be otherwise resolved. By default, no LMHOSTS file database directory (specified by Tcpip\ Parameters\DatabasePath) exists, so no action is taken. This parameter can be set via the TCP/IP Properties; you should not have to configure this parameter directly. The attributes of this parameter are as follows:

- Key: Netbt\Parameters
- Value type: REG_DWORD (Boolean)
- Valid range: 0 or 1 (false or true)
- Default: 1 (True)

ScopeId Parameter

The ScopeId parameter defines the NetBIOS name scope for the machine. If valid, this value overrides the DHCP parameter of the same name. Setting this parameter to the value "*" indicates a null scope and overrides the DHCP parameter. The value of this parameter may not start with a period (.), and a blank value is ignored. This parameter can be set via the TCP/IP Properties; you should not have to configure this parameter directly. The attributes for this parameter are as follows:

- Key: Netbt\Parameters
- Value type: REG_SZ (character string)
- Valid range: Any valid DNS domain name consisting of two dot-separated parts, or an asterisk (*).
- Default: None

Summary

This chapter described in some detail how to configure Windows clients to use WINS and DNS name services. Following that, general rules of thumb that enable one to understand the variety of client resolution scenarios in use by the different Windows versions were discussed.

15

Windows DHCP Services

THIS CHAPTER REVIEWS THE *DYNAMIC HOST CONFIGURATION PROTOCOL* (DHCP) server installation and configuration, the use of DHCP services to simplify DNS namespace management through dynamic DNS (DDNS) updates, and issues of client configuration and scope options.

DHCP simplifies client machine management by handing out Internnet Protocol (IP) addresses and other client configuration information on request over the network. This also conserves IP address usage by distributing them to leasing clients for temporary use. DDNS updates allow a DHCP server to make entries into DNS zone files, reducing the amount of administration needed for DNS. Having DHCP update DNS works well in large-scale environments not just by reducing the amount of intervention needed by DNS administrators, but more importantly by reducing visits needed to client machines and accommodating their mobility. This is especially so for down-level clients that, unlike Windows 2000 clients, often cannot use DDNS for themselves.

This chapter reviews the following:

- **What Is DHCP?** Provides a brief history of DHCP and overview of its capabilities.
- **Installing a DHCP Server.** Covers the steps required to set up DHCP in Windows 2000.

- **Configuring a DHCP Server.** Looks at defining scopes and setting option values, at enabling the granting of leases, and at restrictions that can be used.
- **Configuring Clients to Use DHCP.** Briefly highlights client-side issues and references the complete client configuration information in Chapter 14, "Windows Client Configuration and Resolution."
- **DHCP Verses BOOTP.** Looks at BOOTP and at how DHCP server supports BOOTP clients.

So far, setting up DNS as a database of host name–to–IP address mappings has been fairly straightforward. Hosts on your network are assigned IP addresses and the associated resource records (RRs) are entered in the correct DNS domain. This is either done manually for down-level clients unless DDNS is not available, or with DDNS it is done automatically upon boot by Windows 2000 clients.

But what if there were a way to automatically hand out IP addresses? And what if at the same time DNS resource records could be automatically registered? This is what Dynamic Host Configuration Protocol (DHCP) can do in Windows 2000. When DHCP is used in conjunction with DDNS, virtually complete, automatic client networking configuration results.

What Is DHCP?

The DHCP is used to automatically assign Transmission Control Protocol/Internet Protocol (TCP/IP) settings to clients. Upon startup, a DHCP-enabled client requests an IP address and other information from a DHCP server. IP addresses come from a pool defined in the DHCP server's database called a *scope*. The server offers the IP address for a specified period of time called a *lease*.

This means users no longer have to obtain IP information from an administrator, or have to manually configure computers for these settings. Common problems stemming from manual TCP/IP configuration include duplicate IP addresses, mistyped information leading to no network connectivity, and administrative overhead from hosts moving to different subnets. DHCP was designed to alleviate these problems, and provides as benefits automation and centralized management of client TCP/IP configuration. Because IP addresses are returned to the scope pool when no longer needed, the number of IP addresses can be conserved. To complete the introduction to DHCP, you should understand where it fits in with DNS, and its relation to BOOTP—another rotocol designed to assign IP addresses.

DHCP is defined in RFCs 2131 and 2132, which build upon earlier RFCs 1533, 1534, 1541, and 1542. The Windows 2000 DHCP service supports the standards specified in 2131 and 2132. It should be pointed out that, at this writing, the interaction of DHCP in updating DNS dynamically is in the Internet Engineering Task Force (IETF) draft stage (refer to Appendix B, "RFCs Related to DNS"), which is the normal course preliminary to RFC standards track. Windows 2000 DHCP Server also supports the not-yet-standard user class option whereby the client provides information to the DHCP server which is used by the server to determine what class of special handling to provide.

The IP leasing occurs though a four-step exchange between the client and the DHCP server. After the client has received an IP lease and associated option information, it is bound to the terms of the lease. Prior to expiration, the client contacts the DHCP server to request lease renewal. When a client is refused an IP renewal it must stop all use of that IP and obtain another. It is possible to configure IP reservations in the DHCP server so that a client will always receive the same IP, a capability that has advantages in certain situations but which also reduces the administrative simplification provided by DHCP use.

What Can DHCP Provide for a Client?

DHCP is used for much more than just providing IP address to clients. When a client receives an IP address, it likely will also receive a number of configuration parameters, called options. Additionally, not all IP addresses are equal. Besides normal (Class A, B, or C) IP addresses, Windows 2000 DHCP can be used to provide multicast IP addresses (Class D) to clients through the same scope definition method that is covered later.

With Windows 2000, DDNS is fully integrated and standards based and the DHCP service can be configured to use Request for Comment (RFC)-compliant DNS update messages. The earlier Microsoft solution using Windows Internet Naming Service (WINS) integration with DNS provided some of this functionality but in a proprietary implementation, and remains the one alternative when dynamic DNS is not available. Older versions of BIND offered a series of API setups that administrators could use for controlling zone manipulation, but the newer versions of BIND provide standards-based implementations of DNS dynamic update messages that can articulate with Windows 2000 DHCP.

The Windows DHCP server can be configured to register any combination of the Address (A) and Pointer (PTR) resource records for the client, or neither record. The normal setting lets the client register the A record; DHCP will register the PTR record. By this means, the client has full TCP/IP networking support and is resolvable within the DNS namespace—a capability previously unavailable except through the nonstandard WINS and DNS integration. The DHCP server can detect when a request is not from a Windows 2000 client and use this information to determine what to register with DNS. For down-level and alien clients, DHCP server can be configured to register both the A and PTR records.

To provide for complete client configuration, DHCP scopes are configured to provide options during the leasing process. The complete standard options reference is RFC 2132. Table 15.1 lists some options commonly used in a Windows environment, as well as some, such as Option 47, which are of use only in a Windows environment although not often used.

Table 15.1 **Options Used for DHCP Clients in Windows 2000**

Option	Purpose
1	Subnet mask
3	Router
6	DNS server
15	Domain name
44	WINS server
45	NetBIOS Datagram Distribution Server
46	NetBIOS node type
47	NetBIOS Scope ID
51	Lease period
55	Client request for other options
58	Renewal time value (seconds)
59	Rebinding time value (seconds)

How DHCP Configures a Client

DHCP uses a four-phase process to configure a DHCP client. If a client is multi-homed, the process takes place separately for each adapter, with each adapter getting a unique IP address. This process, illustrated in Figure 15.1, is sometimes called the DORA process after the names of the messages used.

Discovery

In the first phase, the client initializes a limited version of TCP/IP and broadcasts a (DHCPDiscover) request for an IP address. This phase is called *discovery*, or the IP lease request phase. Because broadcast is used, routers between the client and the DHCP server must be configured to forward BOOTP/DHCP packets, or a DHCP relay agent needs to exist on the network segment of the client. Alternatively, a DHCP server needs to be deployed on each segment that has DHCP clients. This broadcast message includes the hardware *Media Access Control* (MAC) address of the requesting client, and even a field for an origin IP address. When a packet is proxied, this source IP is changed from 0.0.0.0 to the IP of the interface on which the broadcast was received by the BOOTP or DHCP relay agent.

Offer

In the second phase, DHCP servers (one or more) that receive the request broadcast an answer. This broadcast (DHCPOffer) message contains the requestor's hardware address, an offered IP address, subnet mask, length of lease, and the IP address of the

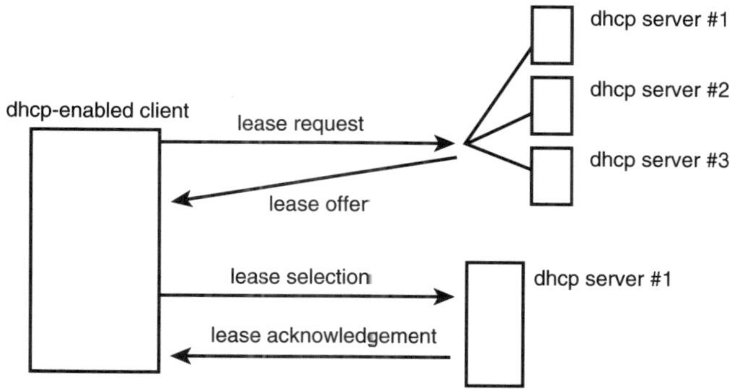

Figure 15.1 The four phases of the DHCP client-configuration process.

offering server. This phase is known as the IP lease offer phase. To reduce the number of offers while yet providing redundancy, intervening routers can be configured to forward discovery broadcasts to at most two IP addresses. It is possible that no DHCP server offers a lease. Windows 2000 clients can be configured to failover, after sufficient unsuccessful lease retries, into IP auto-configure.

Request

In the third phase, the client accepts an offer that reaches it, and broadcasts (DHCPRequest) that it has accepted the offer. This lets the offering server know to "close the deal" and lets the other DHCP servers know to retract their offers. This last part, informing the possible other DHCP servers, is why the client broadcasts this reply. This phase is called the *request*, or the IP lease selection phase.

Acknowledgement

In the fourth phase, the DHCP server with the accepted offer broadcasts an acknowledgement (DHCPAck) to the client. This message contains the valid IP address, lease duration, and other configuration information (DHCP options) if the server is set up to provide it. This phase is the IP lease acknowledgment phase.

Because DHCP clients can make specific requests, such as for a particular IP address, it is possible for the DHCP server to respond with a denial (DHCPNak) message. When this occurs, it is up to the client to determine its course of action. Usually the client, as is the case with Windows 2000 clients, begins the process from the start, possibly seeking any, rather than a particular, IP address.

Lease Renewal

After a Windows 2000 DHCP client has a leased IP address, it attempts to renew its lease after half of the lease duration has expired. The default lease is eight days; so in this case, after four days the client sends out a message to the DHCP server. If the client's IP address is still valid, the server responds with an acknowledgement and any updated information. The messages are similar to phases three and four in the initial configuration process, but are directed rather than broadcast. When attempting to refresh a lease, a client is said to be in the *renewal state*. If a client is unable to refresh a lease, when one eighth of the lease remains the client will start attempting to obtain a renewal of the current IP from any responding DHCP server. At this point the client is said to be in the *rebind state*. If the lease period has expired without successful renewal, the client stops using the IP and restarts the four-phase process to obtain a new IP lease.

The lease duration might be changed from the eight-day default used in Windows 2000 for a number of reasons. Factors include a highly volatile or an extremely rarely changing base of clients, or the ratio of machines to number of IPs. The eight-day default is sometimes said to have been selected because it accommodates weeklong absences. When adjusting the lease duration, one also needs to consider the impacts on dynamic DNS registrations, especially the time-to-live (TTL) default on the Start of Authority (SOA) record and the scavenging settings of the DNS server, and impacts on Active Directory churn if the DNS domain has been integrated.

Installing the Windows DHCP Server

Before installing a DHCP server, you need to consider your network configuration so that you can properly match your DHCP services configuration to it in the most efficient manner. In small- to medium-sized networks, the DHCP Server service can be run on the same computer where other services, such as WINS or DNS, are running. For small deployments, running these three (DNS, DHCP, and WINS) together when they are configured to interoperate presents efficiencies from reduced network communications. In networks with thousands of DHCP clients, you must take into account the network bandwidth, disk subsystem performance, and processor power required by the DHCP server. Also in larger enterprises with multiple authorities, coordination between all parties running DHCP services is essential.

If there are multiple subnets with DHCP clients, a simple solution is to have DHCP servers on each subnet. If you don't have a DHCP server on each subnet, you must install a relay agent, discussed later in this section, or configure the routers to act as one. It is usually a good idea to provide redundancy, which can be more easily accomplished with relay to a small number of DHCP servers.

Requirements and Enterprise Authority

Although there are third-party DHCP server software packages available, this book assumes that you will be using the Microsoft DHCP Server included with Windows 2000 Server version. The prerequisites are similar to those for installing WINS or DNS. You need the Windows 2000 Server installed with the TCP/IP protocol configured using a statically assigned IP address.

To install and configure DHCP, however, you need to be logged on with Enterprise Administrator privileges. Except on a network without an Active Directory, a plain administrator account will prove insufficient to set up DHCP, unless the account has been specifically delegated the ability by an Enterprise Administrator. The later section titled "Authorizing the Windows DHCP Server" discusses some of the specifics behind this requirement.

Installation

The installation process for DHCP server is very similar to that used for DNS server or WINS server. And as with these other servers, the effort is actually in the post-install configuration. One can use the Configure Your Server Wizard, or follow these few required steps:

1. Open the Control Panel.
2. Start the Add/Remove Programs applet.
3. Use the Add/Remove Windows Components icon on the left to start the Windows Component Wizard.
4. Scroll to and select Networking Services.
5. Use the Details button to get to the list of Networking Services.
6. Scroll down and check the box beside Dynamic Host Configuration Protocol (DHCP).
7. At this point, just finish the execution of the Windows Component Wizard using the Next and/or Finish buttons as needed based on whatever other options may have been selected while in the wizard.

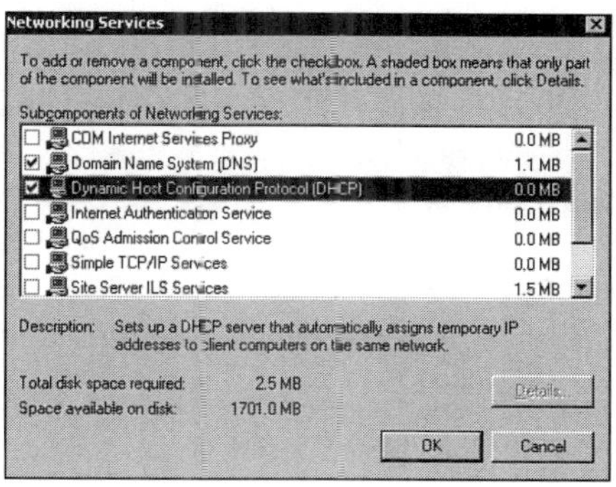

Figure 15.2 Selecting DHCP in Networking Components.

A Must Have

Any computer running a DHCP Server service *must* have a statically assigned IP address. In other words, the computer cannot be a DHCP client itself.

A number of steps remain, however, and at this point a newly installed DHCP server is not operational. We still need to look at enabling the server to hand out leases, defining pools of addresses, configuring options, and a few other factors.

The Management Interface to Windows DHCP Server

If you have not found it yet, this is a good time to open the DHCP server management console. You can find this now on the Start menu in the Administrative Tool folder, called DHCP. This may also be started from the Run box or at the command line by using **"dhcpmgmt.msc"**. You will probably want to select the Local Server the first time.

When this opens, you will find that the context menu (right-click) of the topmost node labeled DHCP is similar to the Action pull-down menu. We are interested in the Add Server option for the moment. First you will want to add whatever servers you will be managing. Not only does the management console enable you to easily manage multiple servers, you can also do this on your desktop version of Windows 2000 after installing the Administrative Tools (ADMINPAK.MSI).

Authorizing the Windows DHCP Server

Before a Windows 2000 DHCP server can grant leases, it must not only have a scope but must also be authorized. If you recall, the DORA leasing process is quite open, with no directed communication and no mutual authentication. Just ask and receive. This presents an environment in which interference by rogue DHCP servers can cause some major disruptions.

Because of the higher risk of interference with existing deployments, DHCP services in Windows 2000 can require high-level authority to start. If DHCP is installed on a standalone server, and there are no Windows 2000 domains visible on the network, the administrators of the server are allowed to configure and start the Windows 2000 DHCP server. If the server is part of a domain, or even if not but there are domains visible on the network, however, the machine must be authorized in the Active Directory for it to start. If the server is in a domain, this is done by an Enterprise Administrator for the Active Directory that includes the server's domain. If the DHCP server is not in a domain, the Enterprise Administrators of all Active Directory forests visible to the DHCP server need to authorize the server, each in his Active Directory.

To authorize a DHCP server as an Enterprise Administrator or by using a properly delegated account, follow these steps:

1. Open the DHCP server management interface.
2. Select Manage Authorized Servers in the Action menu or in the context menu of the DHCP node.
3. Click on the Authorize button.
4. In the Authorize DHCP Server pop-up window, enter the name or IP address of the server to be authorized.

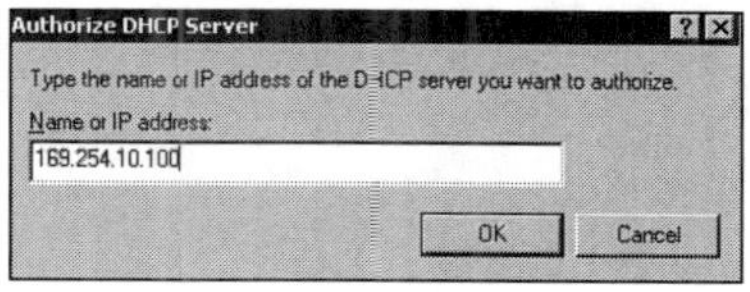

Figure 15.3 Authorizing a Windows 2000 DHCP Server.

5. Click OK, and then click Yes to confirm.
6. Close up returning from the authorization sequence.

Windows 2000 has features to control and detect what Windows 2000 DHCP Servers are operating on the network. Until a Windows 2000 DHCP Server is authorized, it will not start into operation. The details are many and not fully covered here. In essence, each Active Directory maintains a list of authorized DHCP servers in its enterprise context, listing them by IP. When a machine attempts to start Windows 2000 DHCP Server, inquiries are made to the enterprise context of a server's own domain, or if it is not joined to a domain, of all discoverable Active Directory enterprise contexts. DHCP server will not run unless it finds its IP address listed in all enterprise contexts that it checks (one if in a domain, else all).

For the purposes of this book on DNS, we will leave this subject. But you are encouraged to explore the rogue-detection features. One final reminder, this DHCP authorization mechanism applies to Windows 2000 DHCP Servers only.

DHCP Relay Agents

Now you have one DHCP server installed and ready to be configured. If you have more than one subnet, you need to find a way to handle clients that are on a different network segment than your server. Because DHCP is broadcast based, and broadcasts normally don't pass through routers, you must use a relay agent or have the routers configured for DHCP/BOOTP relay.

DHCP servers can provide IP addresses to clients across multiple subnets if the router that separates them can act as an RFC 1542 (BOOTP) relay agent. If the router cannot function as a relay agent, each subnet that has DHCP clients must have a DHCP server, or a service called DHCP Relay Agent can be installed on a Windows 2000 computer. When so configured, the DHCP Relay Agent intercepts DHCP (and BOOTP) broadcast messages, and sends packets directly to the DHCP server(s). These directed messages can cross routers, and contain information on the network interface that picked up the broadcast message. Thus the DHCP Relay Agent acts as a local proxy for the remote DHCP Servers, which use the interface information to determine where to send the response and what scope should be used.

The DHCP Relay Agent is installed through the Routing and Remote Access console found in the Administrative Tools folder of the Start menu. If this is your first time in the Routing and Remote Access console, you will probably need to set up and start the services (look in the Action menu).

1. Open the Routing and Remote Access management interface.
2. Expand the node representing your server.
3. Expand the IP Routing node.
4. If DHCP Relay Agent is not listed under IP Routing, use the context menu of the General node to select New Routing Protocol, and then select and add the agent.
5. Set the focus on the DHCP Relay Agent and then right-click and select its Properties, which appear as shown in Figure 15.4.
6. Enter and add the target DHCP servers' addresses.
7. When finished, use OK to close up.

At this point the agent knows where to forward the broadcasts, but you need to take control of where it listens for them. From the context menu of the DHCP Relay Agent node, use New Interface to select the interface(s) on which it is to listen. You are presented with the interface properties shown in Figure 15.5. At any later time, you can access this by double-clicking on the interface in the right pane when the DHCP Relay Agent node is selected in the left. In the interface properties, the Relay DHCP Packets option is used to enable and disable relay for that interface.

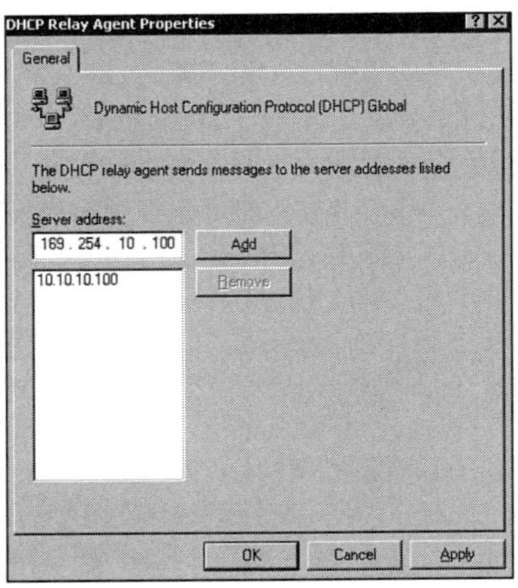

Figure 15.4 Setting DHCP servers addresses in Relay Agent.

Not Always Required

A DHCP server does not need to have, in fact in Windows 2000 it cannot have, the DHCP Relay Agent installed on it. The relay agent is installed on computers that are on subnets with no DHCP servers.

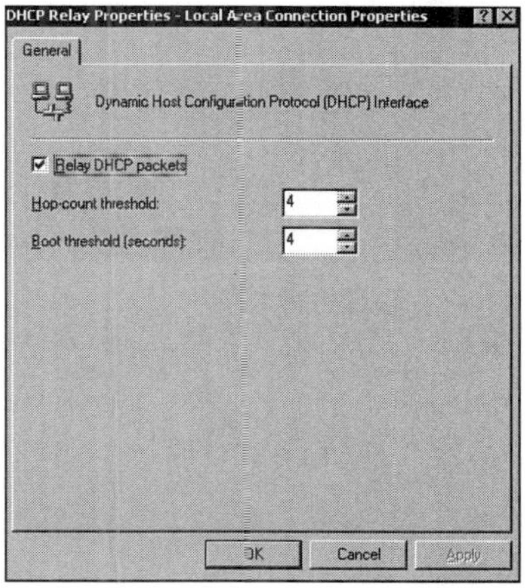

Figure 15.5 Enabling an interface for DHCP Relay Agent.

Configuring the Windows DHCP Server

Each DHCP server must have at least one pool of IP addresses for leasing to clients called a scope. A DHCP server can have scopes for more than one subnet, assuming client broadcasts can reach the server from each of those subnets. In this case, the DHCP server would have to be multihomed or have relay agents serving it, to service multiple subnets.

On each particular DHCP server, only one scope can be assigned to a specific subnet, but a subnet can be split between two or more DHCP servers for redundancy. Just make sure that the same IP address isn't available from each server unless it has been identically reserved (reservations are covered later). DHCP servers don't share information with each other so be very careful that there is no (unreserved) overlap in address pools. Figure 15.6 shows two DHCP servers with scopes providing redundancy in this way.

Consider DHCP server A on subnet 1, and DHCP server B on subnet 2. Server A and server B would have 75% of the IP address pool for subnet 1 and subnet 2, respectively, configured in their scope. Then another scope would be defined for the other 25% of the IP address pool in the remote subnet. Server A would in theory handle all client requests on its own subnet because it would respond faster than server B, which is farther away; if server A is down, however, server B would take over. In this configuration, the exact split—75/25, 80/20, and so forth—should be adjusted based on observed leasing rates and will depend on factors such as comparative network latency between client and the two servers.

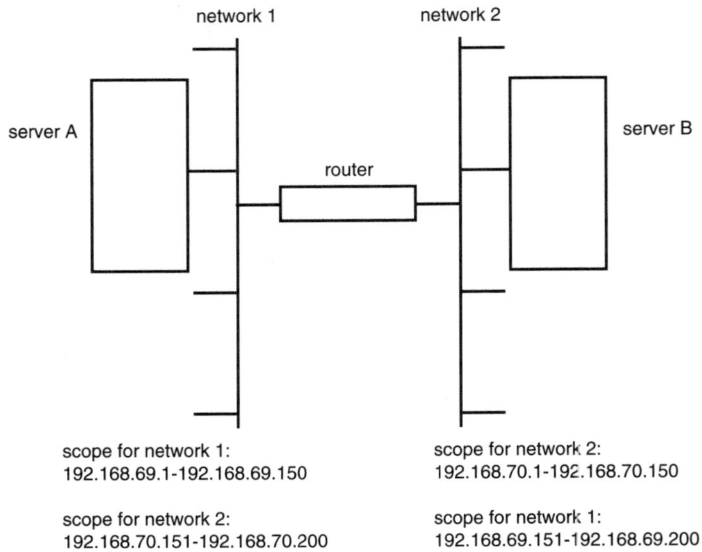

Figure 15.6 Distributed scopes among multiple DHCP servers.

Setting the interfaces on which a DHCP server will listen is global to the server. This setting as well as conflict detection is configured in the DHCP server's Properties page.

1. Open the DHCP server management interface.
2. Set the focus on your server's node and right-click and select the Properties of the server.
3. Select the Advanced tab.
4. Use the Bindings button to access the Bindings dialog box.
5. Check/uncheck interfaces in the Bindings dialog box to configure the interfaces on which DHCP will be made available, and then click OK.
6. On the Advanced tab of the server properties, enable conflict detection if desired, by entering the number of attempts.
7. Close the properties, saving changes, by clicking OK.

On the Advanced tab, did you notice that you can configure storage locations for the log and the DHCP database. Conflict detection is a feature the DHCP server can use to make sure that IP addresses it is about to lease are not in use by attempting to communicate with them on the network. Conflict detection obviously has its overheads, and slows the response DHCP gives to the clients. If you are in exclusive control of your environment, this would be an unneeded overhead as a production setting, but you should remain aware that this is available for problem resolution.

Defining Scopes

To create a new scope, in the DHCP management console, select the server to host the scope and bring up its context menu as is illustrated in Figure 15.7. You have the option of creating a new scope, superscope, or multicast scope. For our purposes, we will deal with a regular scope.

Multicast scopes implement MADCAP to provide multicast (Class D) IP addresses to clients. Superscopes in effect bundle scopes appropriate to a network segment into a larger logical entity, and can be very useful in transitioning between address pools. Both are created and managed similarly to regular scopes.

1. Open the DHCP Server management interface.
2. Set the focus on your server's node, and then right-click on it to open the server's context menu.
3. Select New Scope to start the wizard. Selecting either New Superscope or New Multicast Scope starts a wizard tailored to collect the needed information in each case.
4. Enter a name and description for the scope. These will be available later for modification in the scope's properties. Click Next.
5. Define the IP address pool, entering a beginning and ending IP address. Then specify the subnet mask to be used either in terms of its network part bit length or by entering its dotted-decimal form. Figure 15.8 shows this, where a portion of a Class B network has been allocated to the pool with a subnetting at the last octet. After defining these, click Next.

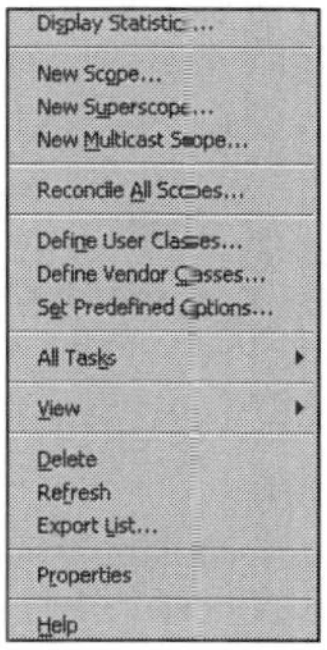

Figure 15.7 The main context menu of a DHCP server.

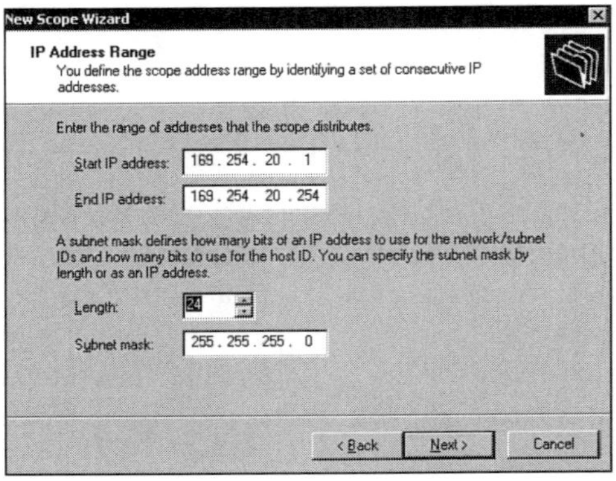

Figure 15.8 Allocating addresses to a new scope.

6. The New Scope Wizard provides a window where IP addresses in the range just provided may be excluded from use by the scope. It is not necessary to exclude any, and this can be modified later. Click Next.
7. The default lease duration of eight days can be changed. When doing so, understand the interactions this will have, especially with any dynamic DNS scavenging that might be enabled. Accept the default or set a value and click Next.
8. The New Scope Wizard now provides a choice to launch into setting scope options for this new scope. These may all be set manually, and when using predefined options, more conveniently if one has many scopes. Make your choice and click Next.
9. If you chose to configure options later, you are done. Otherwise, you are now guided, screen by screen, to provide values for the router (gateway), the DNS domain in which clients will have host names, the DNS servers to be used by the clients, and the WINS servers to be used by the clients. After this, you are asked to choose whether to activate the scope immediately or later.

When you click finish, the new scope is added to the left pane under your server, as you can see in Figure 15.9. It is not necessary to exclude any addresses from a scope. These exclusions can be modified at any time by expanding the scope node in the management window and then using the New Exclusion Range selection on an Address Pool node. The lease duration similarly may be set by days, hours, and minutes with a 999-day maximum at any time using the properties of the scope. Remember to coordinate with dynamic DNS configuration when adjusting the lease duration.

The newly created scope is shown listed in the management console, with a little red down-arrow in a white circle over the folder (in this case, the lower one named hq. example). This down-arrow icon indicates that the scope is not enabled. This isevident from the context menu of the scope, which has the Activate rather than the Deactive option available. It is best to set the scope options before making it available for leases.

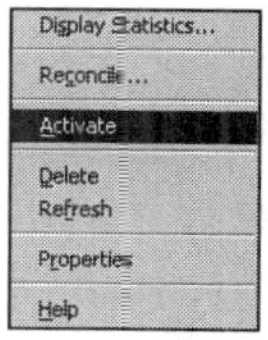

Figure 15.9 Allocating addresses to a new scope.

Notice that this ability to just deactivate a scope for maintenance or troubleshooting, instead of deleting it and having to re-create it, can be handy. This is usually only done within a *superscope*, which very briefly might be described as a collection of scopes made available as if it were a single scope, to make sure that existing clients are not left high and dry.

Setting DDNS Update on a Scope

Dynamically updating DNS entries for leased IP addresses is one of the advantages of using DHCP, particularly with down-level clients unable to register with DNS directly for themselves. Figure 15.10 shows the DNS tab of the properties of a scope, with the default settings. A very similar DNS tab is available in the DHCP properties as compared to the per-scope properties shown here. The server-level properties provide the defaults used on new scopes, and the scope-level properties are controlling of the scope behavior.

When enabled the DHCP server sends update messages to the DNS server configured in the server's TCP/IP Properties page. It may be prudent to configure the server to use a primary DNS server so that DNS updates do not need referral by a secondary to the primary, as would otherwise happen. Notice that one has the option of disabling this feature entirely, or of having DHCP issue updates either always or only when the client requests. Because the Microsoft DHCP clients send Vendor class information (covered later), the DHCP server can determine when a client is alien.

You have the option to have DHCP update DNS for all clients that are not identified as being able to do so for themselves. These are clients that do not provide a FQDN to the DHCP server by use of the proposed Option 81. Windows 2000 clients that do use this option are registered in the DNS domain specified by the provided *fully qualified domain name* (FQDN).

When DHCP registers with DNS for the client, it may be set as the owner of the DNS records if DNS security is exercised through Active Directory integration. If the machine account for the server running DHCP is a member of the Active Directory built-in group DnsUpdateProxy, the DHCP server does not automatically become the owner of records that it creates; if it is not a member of this group, however, it does become owner. Chapter 7, "Dynamic DNS and the Active Directory," discusses these issues; they should be considered when enabling updates in these circumstances.

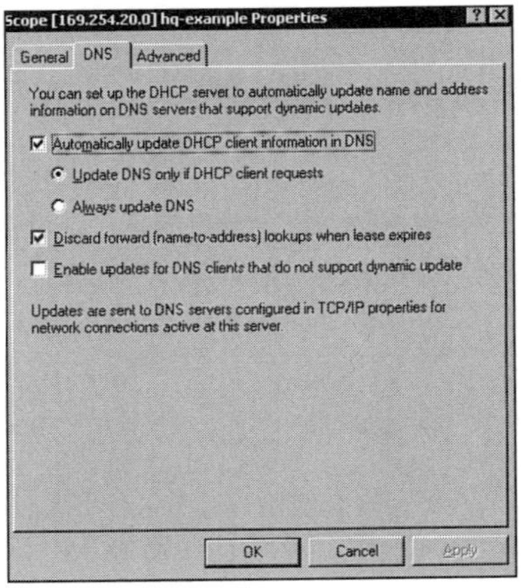

Figure 15.10 DDNS update settings of a scope.

Client Reservations

You can configure DHCP so that a DHCP server will always give the same IP address to a particular client. This is called a *client reservation.*

To configure a client reservation, follow these steps:

1. Open the DHCP server management interface.
2. Expand the server and then the scope node for the scope where reservations are to be created.
3. Right-click the Reservations folder for the scope, and then select New Reservations.
4. Fill in the reservation name, IP address, Ethernet address (or MAC address), description, and select the supported type (DHCP, BOOTP, or either). The MAC will have the form 23-a7-5f-77-d8-45 providing the 6-byte MAC in hex.
5. Click Add, and then close when finished.

The MAC address is used as a unique identifier for the machine. If you will recall, the MAC is sent by the client in the initial discovery message. When a lease DHCPDiscover request is received, the server checks to see whether there are any reservations in the appropriate scope before offering an IP. The MAC address can be found by issuing **ipconfig /all** on a Windows 2000 machine for which the reservation is being created or if it is possible to establish a network connection with the machine, by examining the local Address Recognition Protocol (ARP) table.

A client reservation also enables you to configure options at the individual client machine level. This allows DHCP to provide settings uniquely on a per-machine basis. Although this negates much of the administrative simplicity gained by using DHCP, using this degree of control through Client Options does still retain the centralized management benefit.

It is possible to use the same IP in scopes on separate DHCP servers that are used to share support for a subnet. When this is done, any IP address in both scopes should be reserved for the same client by MAC address. Do not forget, or free the reservation at some point making the IP address available for leasing, because this will lead to duplicate IPs in the serviced subnet.

DHCP Options

We have seen how the DHCP server delivers an IP address to the client, but what of other configuration information that is needed to use TCP/IP? The DHCP server does provide the subnet mask that was entered in defining the scope. It can also provide a list of further option values to the DHCP client. Table 15.1, "Options Used for DHCP Clients in Windows 2000," listed some of the most common options used with Windows clients. The entire list of options is controlled through the RFC standards process and continues to grow. A quick way to get a feel for the available options is by examining them as they are listed and briefly explained in the DHCP server interface.

Option Configuration Levels and Classes

Options can be configured at three levels: global, scope, and client. Options are identified by assigned numbers. Global, scope, and client options are DHCP server configuration differences, not differences in the options themselves. In other words, a specific option can be configured for use at any or all of these levels. Microsoft has chosen to term global options as *server options* in the Windows 2000 DHCP Server interface.

The options provided to a client can also be determined by information provided to the DHCP server by the client in what are called *classes*. There are user and also vendor classes supported in Windows 2000 DHCP server. It is worth noting that definition of standards for DHCP is a rather "hot" area of change at the moment. Some of what is implemented in Windows 2000 is in anticipation of emerging standards. The only vendor class predefined in the initial release of Windows 2000 is the Microsoft vendor class, but others can be installed for use. The emerging user class option is supported in both the Windows 2000 clients and the DNCP server, although the RFC for this is still in progress.

Global options are available to all DHCP clients on the server. Scope options are available to all clients in a particular scope and override any global options. Client options are created for a specific client that uses a reservation and override the global and scope options. By override, we mean that if a certain option is in conflict because it is specified at multiple levels, the option at the most specific level will be used. Otherwise, options accumulate. If user or vendor classes are used, these can be configured at any of these levels. When there is a conflict, if a class applies in determining the options sent to the client, the options specified for the class overrides options specified at the same or higher levels. That is, for example, user-class defined options at the scope level override the same option specified at the scope or global level.

Specifying Options

Predefined options are set on the DHCP Server node, and should not be confused with global, or server options. In Figure 15.7, the context menu for the server has selections to define classes or to set the predefined option defaults by selecting Set Predefined Options. As will be seen as we examine setting options, the predefined options function as default values when setting options at the global, scope, or client levels.

Defining either user or vendor classes, as shown in Figure 15.11, is done by the corresponding selections in the server's Properties dialog box. This first consists of entering a name, description, and the class ID (which clients must provided exactly as entered). This class ID may be entered in either the ASCII or the Binary area and will simultaneously appear in the other as it is entered.

After the class is defined, what options the class specifies need to be configured by choosing the Configure Options selection, such as in the Server Options node context menu. You should then, in the Advanced tab select the vendor or user class drop box and highlight your new class name, at which point you may begin setting the options by checking them and providing the information as required for each. Setting these options is very similar to how this is done outside of a class definition, which we will look at next. They will, however, only be applied at the selected level to clients that provide the class ID string.

Global options can be a little confusing at first. You can use the context menu on the server node and select Set Predefined Options to access a dialog box that enables you to set values for options that will then be available as default values when the options are used in the other configuration windows. This dialog box differs in not having check boxes beside the options, because the actual use or non-use of the options are set in the other dialog boxes. In this dialog box, just highlight the option to access and set the default values.

To configure global options, you need to use the Server Options node under a server; to configure scope options, use the Scope Options node within a scope; and to configure Client Options, use the reservation in the Reservations folder in a scope.

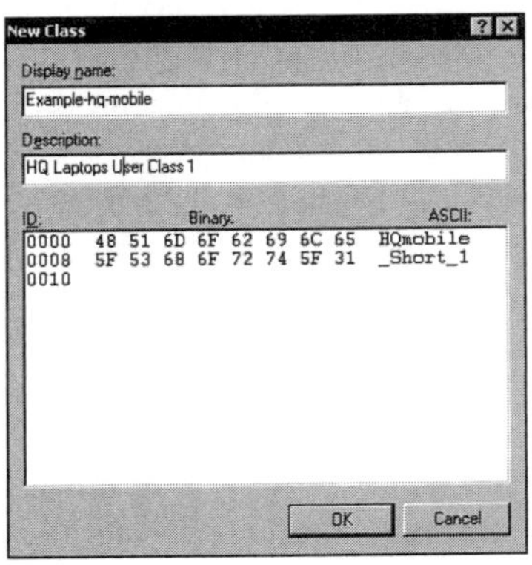

Figure 15.11 Defining a new user class.

Figure 15.12 shows the options dialog box used, with a differing focus, to specify options in all cases. You must first click and then highlight the appropriate node. With your choice highlighted, use the context menu and select Configure Options to bring up the options dialog box.

In Figure 15.12, the Advanced tab has been selected. The default user class is in use and the available options list box has been positioned to Option 5 for DNS server configuration, showing a server that was configured as a predefined default. The drop box for user classes has been expanded to show that the custom user class Example-hq-mobile is available for configuration.

To configure DHCP options, follow these steps:

1. Open the options dialog box at the desired level, either server, scope, or on a reservation as was just described.
2. On the General tab, check an option that is to be used.
3. As each option is checked, entry boxes appear for specifying the values to be used. To make this more convenient, you may want to use the predefined options discussed earlier, to set defaults so that you will not have to reenter information when configuring options in multiple places or multiple scopes.
4. Repeat steps 2 and 3 for all desired options.
5. If needed, switch to the Advanced tab of the dialog box.
6. Select the appropriate vendor or user class and proceed similarly to steps 2 through 4. The selection having Vendor Class of DHCP Standard Options and User Class of Default User Class corresponds to the options presented on the General tab.
7. Apply your changes and close by clicking on OK.

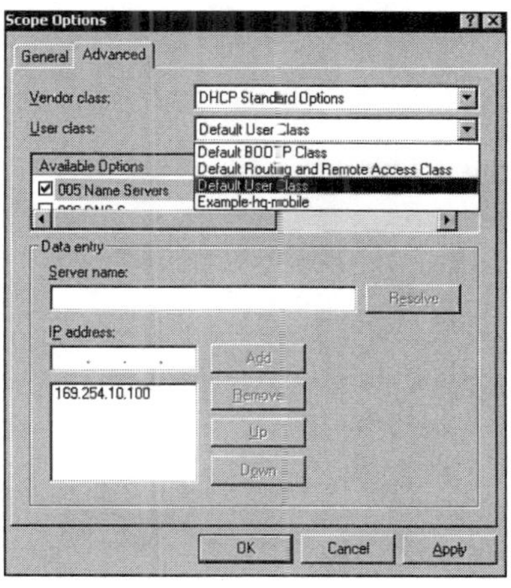

Figure 15.12 The advanced dialog box for setting options.

You may want to skip straight to the Advanced tab, because all settings are available there, including the Default User Class of the DHCP Standard Options shown on the General tab. You may find that you need to exit and reenter the options configuration dialog box for the General and Advanced lists to synchronize. When a specific vendor or user class is to cause specific option values to be used, these must be defined for that class at the appropriate global, scope, or client level. A class does not have to provide the same value for some option everywhere it is used, but instead provides the capability to specify values unique to each point of use.

You will want to remember the order of application of these settings in determining what options are returned to the client. Global, class at global, scope, class at scope, client (reservation), class at client is the order with the latter overwriting any conflicting values from the earlier. Remember that a client can provide only one user class. For the least amount of administrative effort, define options at the highest level and then override where needed. The downside of this approach is that it can become a task to understand exactly what options will be provided to a DHCP client because the settings at multiple levels must be examined.

Configuring Clients to Use DHCP

The main steps needed to configure a Windows client system to use DHCP were covered in Chapter 14. There it was pointed out that there is a check box in the TCP/IP Properties dialog box to obtain IP settings from a DHCP server. When the client has explicitly set TCP/IP property values, such as for DNS servers search order, these override the values provided as DHCP options. Clients differ, of course, and Windows 2000 has some extra places, quite clearly described in the screens, in the TCP/IP Properties dialog box that must be visited to enable some of these overrides.

A number of other client configuration factors were outside of the purpose of the discussion in Chapter 14, but are now covered.

Although the RFC defines many options, the older Microsoft DHCP clients were limited to accept only six of them:

- Default gateway (router) addresses (code 3)
- DNS server addresses (code 6)
- DNS domain name (code 15)
- WINS server addresses (code 44)
- NetBIOS node (name resolution) type (code 44)
- NetBIOS Scope ID (code 47)

You should make sure that the choices used for dynamic registration with DNS as set at the client and at the DHCP server are not in conflict.

Windows 2000 and Windows 98 clients support vendor classes, and at present Windows 2000 clients can be configured to use user classes. This is done with the updated **ipconfig** command-line tool.

ipconfig enables you to view and modify the user class. The **<interface>** parameter must be provided, and can be found by using **ipconfig /all**. The Local Area Connection is a common interface, and must be quoted because of the included space characters.

ipconfig /showclassid <interface> displays the DHCP class IDs allowed for this particular adapter (which can be specified if you have multiple adapters).

ipconfig /setclassid <interface> [<classID_string>] enables you to modify the class ID. The **<classID_string>** is case sensitive, and must match that on the DNCP server. If **<classID_string>** is omitted, any exiting value is removed.

Before leaving this topic, remember that the **ipconfig /renew** command is used to force any existing DHCP lease through release and renewal, and the **/release** option may be used to merely free a leased IP address, leaving the client without one on that interface.

DHCP Versus BOOTP

DHCP is an extension of *Bootstrap Protocol* (BOOTP). BOOTP (defined in RFCs 951 and 1532) was designed for two purposes: so that clients could request an IP address and other TCP/IP settings, and for diskless workstations to request the location of a boot file from which it boots after obtaining the image by the *Trivial File Transfer Protocol* (TFTP). The original BOOTP does not support the concept of leases, however, and each client's hardware address must be associated with a particular IP address.

Because Windows computers support DHCP but do not use BOOTP, there really is little reason to use BOOTP in a purely Windows environment. Because Windows provides DHCP services, and DHCP is derived from BOOTP, however, support for BOOTP clients was offered in Windows beginning with NT 4.0 Service Pack 2. This means that a DHCP server can respond to DHCP requests as well as BOOTP requests from UNIX clients and/or diskless workstations. This can be especially valuable in heterogeneous environments where DHCP/BOOTP server conflicts could otherwise be a problem. As with DHCP, Windows provides for BOOTP from subnets remote from the server through configuring relay agents. However, Windows 2000 does not provide a configurable TFTP service for delivering the boot image files.

This partial support may seem a strange situation, but when one considers the use of boot proms in network devices the limitation seems less major, and it certainly has no impact on Windows clients. DHCP options (or here call them BOOTP options) are used to inform BOOTP clients of the boot image filename and server. The Windows 2000 DHCP Server ignores BOOTP requests unless the BOOTP table has been configured with information on at least one boot image file. Also, a peculiarity with Windows 2000 is that BOOTP clients that do not specifically request options are not provided with any.

The dynamic BOOTP extension in Windows 2000 allows for simplified administration by the pooling of IP addresses into BOOTP scopes. With a BOOTP scope, linking hardware and IP addresses together one for one with reservations is unnecessary unless either the BOOTP clients do not support dynamic BOOTP or specific options are needed. BOOTP scopes are created just as is done for normal scopes, but they are then marked to be used for BOOTP requests by selecting either BOOTP Only or Both in the Advanced tab of the scope's Properties dialog box, as shown in Figure 15.13. While in the scope's Properties dialog box, it is worth noticing in the DNS tab that all options for having dynamic DNS updates performed are available for BOOTP clients.

To configure boot files, first change the defaults in the General tab of the DHCP server properties, shown in Figure 15.14, so that the box Show the BOOTP Table Folder is selected.

1. Open the DHCP server management interface.
2. Click the server node to give it focus, and then use the context menu (right-click) to select the server's Properties dialog box.
3. On the General tab, check the box labeled Show the BOOTP Table Folder.
4. Click OK to close the Properties dialog box.

Again, this is a necessary step, because the server ignores BOOTP requests if this table is empty. With the BOOTP Table node showing in the DHCP server console, it is then possible, by selecting New Boot Image from this node's context menu to provide boot image information. When responding to a BOOTP request, the information in this table is returned by the DHCP server.

1. Open the DHCP server management interface.
2. Expand the server node.

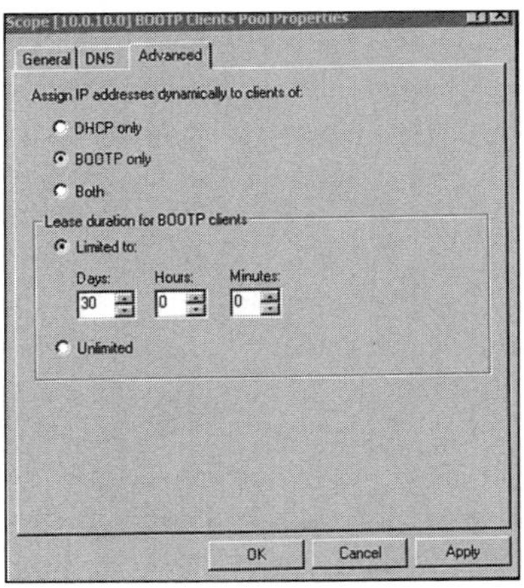

Figure 15.13 Setting a DHCP scope to service BOOTP clients.

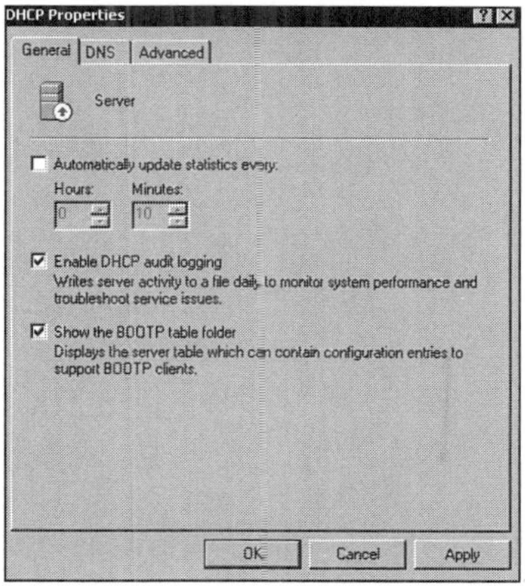

Figure 15.14 Setting DHCP server to access the BOOTP table.

3. Click on the BOOTP Table node. If this node is not visible, use the preceding procedure to enable the BOOTP table in the server's Properties dialog box.
4. BOOTP image files already defined are enumerated in the details pane on the right. To add a new image, use the context menu (right-click) of the BOOTP Table node and select New Boot Image.
5. Enter the TFTP server, image filename, and the image path on the TFTP server, and then click Add.

BOOTP and DHCP packets are formatted almost identically, and by default both use UDP ports 67 and 68 on the server and client, respectively. A BOOTP server response has a fixed, smaller size than is possible with DHCP, however, which means that care must be used in configuring the options returned for a scope used to support BOOTP. BOOTP clients have no concept of an IP lease. This is not an issue with traditional BOOTP usage where reservations are created for all BOOTP clients. The Windows 2000 DHCP Server, as you have seen, allows defining a scope to service BOOTP, dynamically allocating IP addresses in the process. If this dynamic BOOTP extension is used, the DHCP server recovers IP addresses leased to BOOTP clients based on expiration times followed by testing that the addresses are no longer in use. It is also worth noting that BOOTP uses a two-step rather than a four-step exchange between the client and server; and as just mentioned, there is no periodic renewal.

If per-BOOTP client options information is to be provided, reservations must be made for the BOOTP clients using their MAC address. This is done in the same way as for DHCP clients. Table 15.2 lists some of the options supported for BOOTP clients. The BOOTP client must request options or none will be returned.

Table 15.2 **Some Options Used for BOOTP Clients**

Option	Purpose
1	Subnet mask
3	Router
4	Time server
5	Name server
6	DNS servers
9	LPR server
12	Host name
13	Boot file size
15	DNS domain name
16	Swap server
17	Root path
28	Broadcast address
42	NTP servers
43	Vendor-specific information
48	X Window system font server
49	X Window system display manager
66	Boot server host name
67	Boot filename
69	SMTP server
70	POP3 server

Summary

Many people have been unable or hesitant to use DHCP because throughout its early history it could not normally integrate with DNS. Although the earlier Microsoft solution using WINS permitted this, the instability of the early generation of WINS and the proprietary character of this led many people to view this as not being a normal solution.

This chapter illustrates that by using a combination of Microsoft DHCP and DNS with dynamic updates enabled, network computers can have dynamically assigned IP addresses and yet still can participate in DNS. Further, this is done without a lot of administration. To use DHCP, thought must be given to the number and placement of DHCP servers, and impacts on DNS such as scavenging. Then the DHCP Server service is set up and authorized, scopes and options are defined and enabled, and clients are configured to become DHCP clients. When a base of DHCP clients exists, reconfiguring their networking configuration is centrally managed through the delivered DHCP options.

16

WINS: Legacy Name Services and Resolution

THIS CHAPTER COVERS THE *WINDOWS INTERNET NAMING SERVICE* (WINS). It is quite likely that an administrator will be dealing with this service. WINS is included in this book about DNS just because providing comprehensive name services for Windows computers, particularly down-level versions, requires familiarity with this Windows name service. Also, Microsoft is recommending that integrating Windows 2000 DNS services with WINS, when there are NetBIOS clients, is very effective in providing WINS name resolution to Windows 2000 clients. It's a mistake to view DNS and WINS as duplicates because they have different, although overlapping, capabilities. The benefits and methods of adding WINS lookups to a DNS server are described.

This chapter reviews the following:

- **WINS Services.** WINS performs an invaluable service in helping clients resolve NetBIOS names in segmented networks, but its legacy and implementation impose some limitations. This section describes the most important WINS advantages and offers suggestions for dealing with its limitations. The role that WINS, especially its integration with DNS, plays is an important consideration to a Windows 2000 deployment.
- **Installing WINS Servers.** WINS is fairly easily set up, as shown in this section.
- **Configuring DNS with WINS Integration.** The few required entries in DNS domains permitting DNS to use WINS are Microsoft specific. The considerations for correct use of this feature are clarified.

WINS Services

Every Windows computer has some applications that use NetBIOS names, and this remains true with Window 2000. Windows inherited NetBIOS name use from the early days when Microsoft and IBM were working together on communications products such as LAN Manager. Beginning with NT 3.5 versions, Microsoft introduced WINS as a service operating over Transmission Control Protocol/Internt Protocol (TCP/IP) able to translate between NetBIOS names and Internet Protocol (IP) addresses. WINS has gained a reputation as being something less than an administrator's favorite; with the NT 4 service packs from 3 through 5, however, WINS received major improvements and increased stability. WINS at Service Pack 5 in NT 4 is functionally equal to and interoperates with the WINS server provided in Windows 2000.

WINS provides *NetBIOS name service* (NBNS) in a TCP/IP network in compliance with RFC 1001 and RFC 1002. Before WINS, NetBIOS name servicing had very real problems in segmented networks. Broadcast operations either did not cross routers, or networks were subject to broadcast storms. Figure 16.1 shows the situation where clients Bob and Terri, not enabled to use WINS, are restricted from accessing anything on Broadcast Domain B by the router that joins the two segments.

When NetBIOS was first encapsulated in TCP/IP to overcome the segmentation problem, the LMHOSTS file was used to list names with IP pairs that could not be known by broadcast. This solution, similar to the early HOSTS file used before DNS

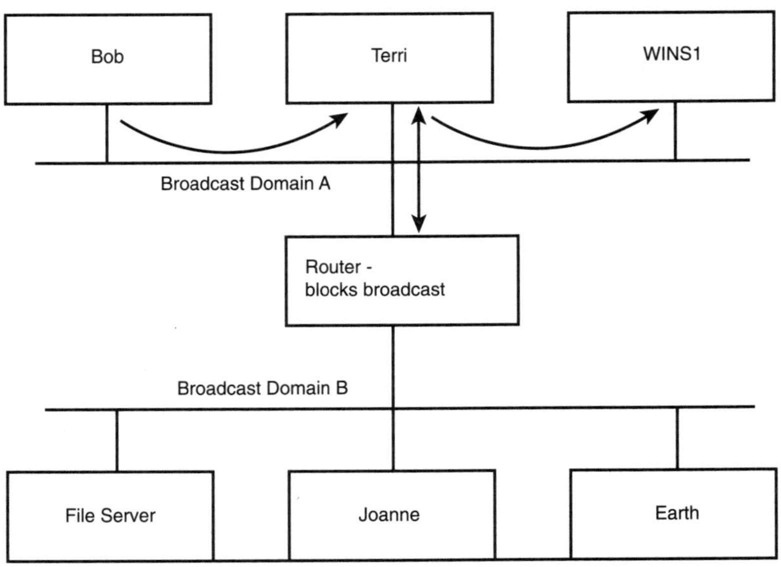

Figure 16.1 Segmentation in a routed network.

services, had the major problem of manual administrative maintenance. In the preceding example, all machines would need an LMHOSTS file listing IP addresses for each of the other machines' NetBIOS names. Obviously this could turn into much work as machines and networks changed. WINS provided a solution to these issues. In the example, it is only necessary that all machines be configured to point as WINS clients at the same WINS server, or a WINS server in the same replication cycle.

At about the time when WINS appeared, Dynamic Host Configuration Protocol (DHCP) was coming into use for dynamic IP assignment. The capability of a DHCP client to advertise itself in WINS on an IP network created a complete solution for Windows clients, provided that no machines needed to locate these clients using standard DNS name services. The growth in use of industry-standard TCP/IP as the protocol of choice, and the security practice of restricting NetBIOS resolution to the intranet, soon made the WINS and DHCP solution less than complete for all needs.

When DNS services were made part of Windows NT 4, the proprietary WINS and Windows Internet Naming Service-Reverse (WINS-R) records were also introduced to allow the DNS server to look up names in the WINS database. The integration of DNS and WINS at the time was the only way to provide this important service, the features and advantages of which are described later. Windows 2000 can now provide much of this functionality, for down-level NetBIOS registered clients, through use of the Windows 2000 DHCP Server. However, Microsoft has said that continuing to use WINS integration with DNS can provide a most efficient means for Windows 2000 clients to locate NetBIOS resources.

What the Future Holds for WINS and NetBIOS

Administrators should plan to support NetBIOS until all DOS LAN Manager, Windows 95/98, Windows NT 3.x, and Windows NT 4 computers are gone from their network. All these clients need NetBIOS, and they'll continue to need it. Although dynamic DNS (DDNS) and the use of DHCP in Windows 2000 together provide a newer, more standards-based means of accomplishing what the older, proprietary WINS integration with DNS provided, there are cases where immediately using these for older clients is not practical. Only when Windows 2000 and its successors have completely replaced the earlier operating systems will you be positioned to become free of NetBIOS. It's possible that Microsoft will build an alternative client for legacy systems, but so far this is only available for Windows 95 and Windows 98. Even with such an update, keep in mind that NetBIOS is a programming API and naming convention, not a networking protocol as such. (For more information on this, see Chapter 17, "NetBIOS: Legacy Name Services and Resolution."). Therefore, the use of NetBIOS is embedded within applications. It is very easy to confuse becoming free from *NetBIOS over TCP/IP* (NetBT) with becoming free from NetBIOS. Consequently, even if all client operating systems were fully functional without NetBIOS names, it is possible a legacy application could require them. And for this situation, WINS is the choice.

Purpose and Limitations of WINS

Without WINS, clients can locate other NetBIOS-named resources only by broadcasting on the local subnet or by finding them listed in the LMHOSTS file. This worked for extremely small networks. Originally in NetBEUI networks, the broadcast model was used; and then with increased use of TCP/IP, the LMHOSTS file was used. The limitations of these "networking in the small" approaches became obvious as Windows began to penetrate into larger-scale deployments.

WINS servers have one simple query-handling behavior: They reply positively with the address and name sought, or they reply negatively with a Requested Name Does Not Exist message. WINS servers search through the names in their database file of computers that have registered with them or with any of their replication-partner WINS servers.

WINS provides a central, but replicated, database of NetBIOS names. More importantly, WINS by design operates over the TCP/IP protocol and is dynamic. This solves the segmentation problem of broadcast protocols, and enables the use of dynamic IP assignment by DHCP while yet having user-friendly names for the machines. WINS clients request registration of names in the WINS database, and when they need to locate a resource by NetBIOS name they query this database to translate the name to an IP. NetBIOS names, as detailed in Chapter 17, can advertise different types of names. This feature allows the location of services in a way that could not be accomplished with the DNS name services before the introduction of the SRV resource record.

The mixture of the TCP/IP protocol and NetBIOS name use is implemented in NetBT in Windows systems. Microsoft has known for a long time that NetBIOS over TCP/IP is less than ideal and that, in fact, it creates problems because NetBIOS just wasn't designed for an expansive network such as the Internet. NetBIOS was designed for a small network and now operates on networks many thousands of times the size of those for which it was built. Although overcoming the routing problem, the WINS solution has had its own problems. One area of difficulty, particularly before NT 4 Service Pack 3, has been the replication architecture. A continuing problem is performance due to database size and the lack of hierarchical structure, which itself relates directly back to the NetBIOS namespace being flat. With the introduction of WINS, NetBT became easily able to provide a great deal of information about a Windows deployment, potentially to anyone in the world. One of the characteristics of the intranet phenomena was the blocking of the NetBIOS ports (137, 138, and 139) at the firewall to protect from public knowledge the advertised machines and services. Security concerns to protect some of the advertised services, such as the Server service, from public probing have been a driving factor. To be fair, with the introduction of Service (SRV) records, these concerns are now transferred to DNS services.

How WINS Works

All WINS communications is User Datagram Protocol (UDP) on port 137. The other ports often associated with NetBT are TCP 139, which is used for NetBIOS *Server Message Block* (SMB) sessions, and UDP 138, which is used for NetBIOS broadcast and unidirectional traffic. But it is port 137 that is used for NetBIOS name registration and resolution.

WINS servers maintain a database of NetBIOS name–to–IP mappings. Unlike DNS, this database is flat rather than hierarchically divided. This database can be replicated between multiple WINS servers for higher availability and fault tolerance. The originating WINS server that granted the name registration owns each registration in the database. Ownership becomes important when multiple WINS servers replicate. The replication architecture suiting a deployment depends on many factors and is beyond the scope of this chapter. Considerations include the number of servers needed for reasons of capacity and fault tolerance, and their distribution in the network topology. Microsoft has released a series of papers on the considerations, and which also recommend replication architectures, that have changed as WINS has evolved and that should be consulted for more information. In general, the recommendations have emphasized simplicity, with a minimum number of servers configured as Push/Pull replication partners to support all WINS clients in one database.

WINS is a service that might be considered as passive, or client driven. This overlooks the WINS database replication architecture, but is valid as a client view of WINS because WINS does not initiate any network communications with the client. Even in WINS integration with DNS, the relationship is that the DNS server is a client querying WINS.

WINS provides services in response to clients. WINS clients are responsible for four main actions: NetBIOS name registration, renewal, release, and query.

NetBIOS Name Registration

When a WINS client starts, or has its IP changed (in the case of a DHCP client), the client sends a registration request containing its name and IP to the WINS server. If the name is not in use, the WINS server replies with an acknowledgement granting the name and providing a renewal interval or *time-to-live* (TTL) value. The WINS server itself makes use of this value in its periodic cleanup activities, because it knows clients must renew within this time or the name may be freed. In the event of a name collision, the WINS server tries to verify that the registered name is still in use. A name collision happens when the requested name matches but the associated IP does not match for a pair already listed in the database. The WINS server verifies the registration by sending a NetBIOS adapter status request to the IP associated with the name in the WINS database, or to each IP if the name is a multihomed registration.

If the machine is alive and replies, within the three trials the WINS server uses, and the name returned matches the database for that IP, the requesting machine receives a denial. If no response is received to the three adapter status requests, the name is made available and the registration request is granted.

When a client attempts to register, it can happen that the primary WINS server is unavailable. The client retries and then switches over to the next configured WINS server, after three unsuccessful attempts. If all attempts to contact a WINS server fail, the client may failover to broadcast announcement of its name if the client's NetBIOS node type permits this.

When a client is multihomed, it registers for each interface bound to NetBT. But only the first IP is registered on each interface bound to NetBIOS. Multihomed is used in different ways; but for NetBIOS, multihomed strictly means multiple network cards. Again, NetBIOS uses only one IP per card. The use of multihomed to mean multiple IP addresses on a card does not apply in this case.

NetBIOS Name Renewal

After being granted a name registration by WINS, the client is responsible for retaining that grant by periodically renewing it. This is a little complex, and in practice has been less than reliable in earlier NT 4 implementations. The renewal algorithm in Windows 2000 for the very first renewal differs from that used at all other renewals. This accommodates the new burst-handling feature of the WINS server (described later). After the first renewal, the client attempts name renewal at half the TTL, and retries renewal if needed, before then switching over to a secondary WINS server(s). If the client has encountered problems with its primary and switched to the secondary, supposedly it will periodically attempt to switch back to the primary. In practice, this has been one of the weak points during earlier NT 4, and whether this is entirely fixed will need some time to see. It is not germane to provide exact timings for the retry intervals, because this seems to differ by platform and version.

The administrator should be aware that the switch newly added to the Nbtstat command-line utility in NT 4 Service Pack 4, **"nbtstat –rr"**, is also available in Windows 2000. This can be used to force a WINS client to refresh the registration of its NetBIOS name(s). Previously we were forced to reboot the machine to achieve this, which was all too frequent for important registrations such as on domain controllers (DCs).

NetBIOS Name Query

Name query is, of course, the main purpose of WINS. Registrations, and static entries, create the database that is queried but queries are typically more frequent. When a NetBIOS application needs to connect to a machine or service known by its NetBIOS name, a WINS client sends a query to the WINS server. NetBIOS name resolution can follow different paths depending on the client configuration and operating system; for a WINS client, however, the resolver in NetBT contacts WINS. In general, this query is sent to the primary WINS server. If the server replies with a positive or negative reply, the resolver accepts this response. Only when the

WINS server does not respond will the resolver continue with its other alternatives, the first of which will be any secondary WINS server(s), if configured. A successful WINS query delivers an IP to the requesting client.

NetBIOS Name Release

When a client shuts down gracefully, it sends a release message to its WINS server. To this, the WINS server does reply, either positively or negatively. The purpose of name release is to keep the database current and to reduce the amount of name testing the WINS server needs to do when an attempt is made to recycle a name, such as when one merely reboots a WINS client. The usefulness of a name release denial is uncertain, with clients likely ignoring such a response.

Name and Database Characteristics in WINS Systems

As just discussed, in a WINS system all names are registered with a WINS server. The names are stored in a database on the WINS server that answers requests for name-to-IP address resolution based on the entries in this database. NetBIOS names are used for many purposes, as is discussed in Chapter 17, which are distinguished by the last character in their names. WINS entries are also of different types. Figure 16.2 shows these as the choices one has when creating a static WINS entry.

Normally, one does not need to be concerned with these different WINS entry types, because this is managed automatically during registration. The different types of entries are as follows:

- **Unique.** Used to associate a NetBIOS name with a single IP, usually for [00h], [03h], and [20h] names
- **Group.** Used to associate multiple IP addresses with a NetBIOS name used for multicast communications.

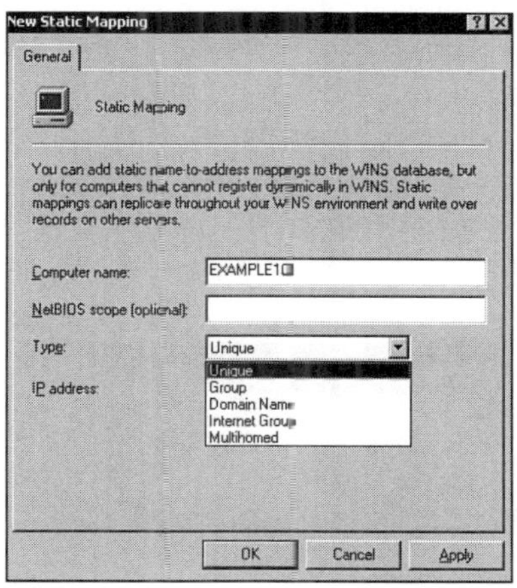

Figure 16.2 WINS entry type selections.

- **Domain name.** Used to associate a [1Ch] NetBIOS name with the IP addresses of the domain controllers
- **Internet group.** Used for custom associations of a [20h] NetBIOS name with up to 25 IP addresses
- **Multihomed.** Associates a NetBIOS name with one IP for each adapter in a machine that has multiple adapters

Redundancy and load balancing are maintained by allowing more than one WINS server in the WINS system. These servers replicate their database entries among one another to maintain a consistent view of the namespace. The latency of this replication, often called the convergence of the database, determines how rapidly a new registration or release is made visible to all WINS clients. Most Windows installations use one WINS database for all clients of all domains, thus providing an installationwide location capability.

Each registered name has an entry in the database. The name is owned by the WINS server it registered with and is a replica on all other WINS servers. Within the WINS management console, the view of the database can be filtered based on this owner. This gives the illusion of an internal structure to the database. But the database is one undivided collection of these NetBIOS names in a Jet database. This has some management implications that are discussed when we set up a WINS server.

Each entry has a state associated with it. Entries are also assigned a version ID used in guiding the replication process. The entry may be in the active, released, or extinct (also known as tombstone) state. The way that entries marked for extinction are handled has been improved for Windows 2000, and what can be manually marked for extinction has also been changed. Because this is such a significant an improvement, Figure 16.3 shows the choice presented when deleting a record.

Previously, only the owning WINS server could extinguish a name, and manual deletion could only be done on static entries. Now, one can delete any record and choose to use the new tombstone method that will replicate the deletion to all partners. These new algorithms have much improved the overall stability of a replicated database and its management.

The WINS system also allows the registration of static names. This enables the administrator to register names for servers running operating systems that are not capable of dynamic WINS registration, to reserve names from being preempted. If you register non-WINS computers as static entries, WINS clients will not be allowed to

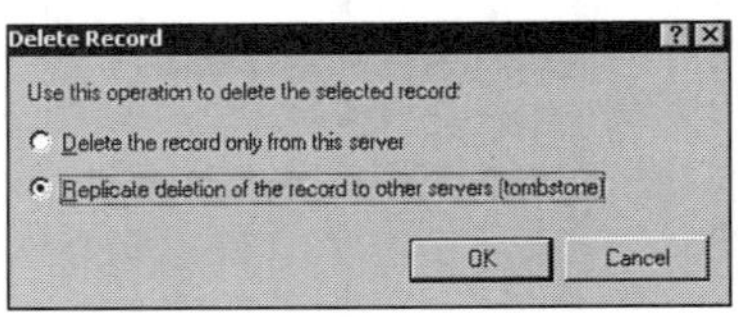

Figure 16.3 Choices when deleting a WINS entry.

register that name. Static names have lead to many headaches, and their use is to be discouraged. WINS distinguishes between dynamic and static entries and treats static names somewhat differently than dynamic names. Whether static entries can be overwritten by replication is now a configurable feature. Static entries have in the past been a major problem in a replicated WINS database. The Windows 2000 WINS improvements, also in the associated upgrade to NT 4, promise to prevent this problem, and also the problem of deleted records becoming resurrected through replication.

Benefits and Issues of Combining WINS and DNS

The Microsoft DNS Server works hand in hand with the Microsoft WINS Server and provides a great deal of interoperability. To provide this interoperability, a new record was defined as part of the zone file. The WINS record is specific to Windows DNS and may be attached only to the zone root domain. The presence of a WINS record instructs the name server to use WINS to look up any requests for hosts in the zone that do not have resource records in the DNS database. This functionality is particularly useful for UNIX-based clients that need to contact clients enabled for both DHCP and WINS.

You can configure a Microsoft DNS Server to use WINS for host name resolution because the host name part of a DNS fully qualified domain name is like a NetBIOS computer name. During the resolution process, the DNS client queries a Microsoft DNS Server that refers the query to an associated WINS server. Microsoft proprietary WINS and WINS-R records are used to enable the DNS server to refer to a WINS server, which it will do if it is otherwise unable to satisfy a query against one of its authoritative domains.

By using WINS and a Microsoft DNS Server on an IP network, your clients can use NetBIOS or DNS names to locate and connect with other computers. If DNS cannot find a name, it forwards this to the WINS server. After the WINS server finds the correct host, it returns the address of that host to the DNS server, which then forwards a reply to its client. All the interactions between the WINS server and DNS server are transparent to clients. To the clients, the WINS/DNS transaction appears as though the DNS server handled the request by itself.

In NT 4 this DNS/WINS integration solved what is possibly the number one problem of the busy DNS administrator: not needing to update the name registration. By removing most Address (A) records from the DNS server and pointing it to the local WINS server, you can make the DNS server work as if it were dynamically updated. This same approach also solved the problem associated with DHCP-assigned IP addresses. In this case, the WINS client updates the WINS database and DNS can return an IP under circumstances the DNS administrator could not possibly have solved.

Prior to DDNS, the only way to reduce the number of static resource records you would normally have to maintain in a DNS server's zone file was by integrating WINS and Microsoft DNS, enabling the use of the dynamic name services of WINS. This is a particularly powerful option for Windows computers configured to use both DHCP and WINS because in such a case you don't even need to configure the Windows clients manually, leaving the whole setup to be handled dynamically by DHCP and the client. Now that DHCP has been enhanced in Windows 2000 to use dynamic DNS (DHCP is covered in Chapter 15, "Windows DHCP Services"), and can register even down-level clients, this role of WINS in namespace maintenance is of lower value. Windows 2000 has introduced new alternatives, with either the client or the DHCP server able to register these records with DNS through dynamic updates. One needs to look at the needs and abilities of all clients, at whether DHCP and DDNS are used, and then determine the role that DNS/WINS integration holds for an environment.

The Client-Level WINS via DNS Setting

Related to, but independent from WINS and DNS integration, in down-level systems there is a setting in the TCP/IP properties to Enable DNS for Windows Resolution (as it is phrased in NT 4). This setting is used by the client resolver to control forwarding of WINS resolution queries to the DNS server (and also enables use of the HOSTS file if needed). A client so configured will first try DNS, and will then use other means when needed. Most down-level client resolvers will otherwise first use NetBIOS resolution methods (NetBIOS cache, WINS, LMHOSTS) before reaching and attempting to use DNS to resolve a NetBIOS name. It is important to notice that WINS integration into DNS by use of the WINS and WINS-R proprietary records complements the use of this client setting. It does not, however, require it. The DNS server refers to WINS when needed if it is enabled, without regard to this client setting. This client setting just provides the client resolver with a direct route to this extended DNS service capability. For these same reasons, it is important that this client configuration option be used only if DNS servicing of WINS queries will be successful. This success can be provided either through DNS/WINS integration or by a careful strategy both of host naming and of the DNS domains that the client resolver will append when forming DNS queries.

Considerations and Strategies for DNS/WINS Integration

Even though a computer name in WINS is a NetBIOS name, it can also be the host name of the Windows computer in an IP domain name sense. This assumes, however, that the naming schemes are complementary, such as when you are using one name for both namespaces. For this DNS and WINS integration to work most simply, computers should be using one name in both namespaces.

In Windows NT, one recommended practice when using WINS and DNS integration is to set aside a delegated DNS domain for use by all WINS clients. The reason for this recommendation is simple: There is usually one WINS database. If WINS is enabled in multiple DNS zones, a WINS-registered machine is reachable under equally multiple DNS zones, and hence fully qualified names. That is, the WINS name would be visible to the DNS server in multiple zones. As this would lead to confusion, and in some situations configuration problems, the practice of using WINS and WINS-R records in only one subdomain came about. This way, the client machines' DNS domain as set in its TCP/IP properties could always accurately reflect the answers obtained from DNS resolution using WINS integration.

This strategy now seems in conflict with Windows 2000, where synchronizing the Windows domain and the DNS domain is recommended by Microsoft. (In fact, with the first release of Windows 2000, doing otherwise involves handling a number of further issues.) It is true that Windows 2000 DNS Server provides a way to specify what DNS domain is used to form the Fully Qualified Domain Name (FQDN) when reverse lookups are satisfied using WINS. It is also true, however, that a single WINS database is recommended to hold all NetBIOS clients. But these may be from many Windows domains, each of which most often has a different DNS domain. One possible solution lies in the little-documented capability of Windows 2000 network interfaces to have secondary DNS domains configured. The more straightforward path, however, involves recognizing that this legacy name resolution issue is one of legacy clients. Providing the legacy clients with a separate DNS domain while yet having them as members within differently named Windows 2000 domains raises fewer issues than does doing so with up-level clients. These can be segregated in such a specifically delegated DNS domain as
second-class clients of a Windows 2000 directory services architecture. After all, is not the objective to upgrade these over time to Windows 2000 clients?

WINS and DNS services can be run on the same computer or on different computers. Where these are placed depends on a number of factors, however, such as whether Active Directory integration of DNS is used. In this case, it might be advised to place WINS servers on systems with lighter load than the DCs have. Remember that a heavily used WINS server drives the disk subsystem intensively, which is surely not what one wants to add to a Windows 2000 DC's load.

WINS Versions

As mentioned earlier, the WINS server in NT 4 was upgraded by Service Pack 5 to where it has equivalent function to the WINS server in Windows 2000. Many of the problems encountered with the earlier versions of the WINS server have received new algorithms, and improvements have been made to the underlying processes.

Among the main improvements in Windows 2000 WINS are the following:

- Persistent connections can be configured for replication partners that are well connected, reducing the overhead from repeatedly establishing connections. This improves replication speed while reducing the load on the servers.
- Enhancements to the database storage engine improve reliability and performance of the WINS database.
- Manual tombstoning of records with the tombstone replicating to guarantee extinction of deleted records.
- Improved management interface with significant new enhancements, making the administration of WINS a more productive experience.

If you are considering on which release to place WINS, you may find that the administrative interface in Windows 2000 is more convenient. Certainly, there is probably no reason to continue running a prior version of WINS (considering the improved performance and reliability features). The last bullet in the preceding list does not do justice to the many new features added for managing WINS servers and for navigating within the WINS database. Besides the ease-of-use enhancements, Windows 2000 WINS also provides for database verification, database export, and command-line administration.

Installing WINS Servers

Installing WINS is extremely easy. In fact, it is so easy that when worse comes to worst, more than one administrator has resorted to uninstall/reinstall as a cure. The few required steps are as follows:

1. Open the Control Panel.
2. Start the Add/Remove Programs applet.
3. Use the Add/Remove Windows Components icon on the left to start the Windows Component Wizard.
4. Scroll to and select Networking Services, as shown in Figure 16.4.
5. Use the Details button to get to the list of networking services.
6. Scroll to the bottom and check the box beside Windows Internet Name Service (WINS).
7. At this point, just finish the execution of the Windows Component Wizard using the Next and/or Finish buttons as needed based on whatever other options may have been selected while in the wizard.

Believe it or not, at this point you are ready to start using WINS. It is now as simple as setting the clients to use your new WINS server. Of course, that is not all there is to it,

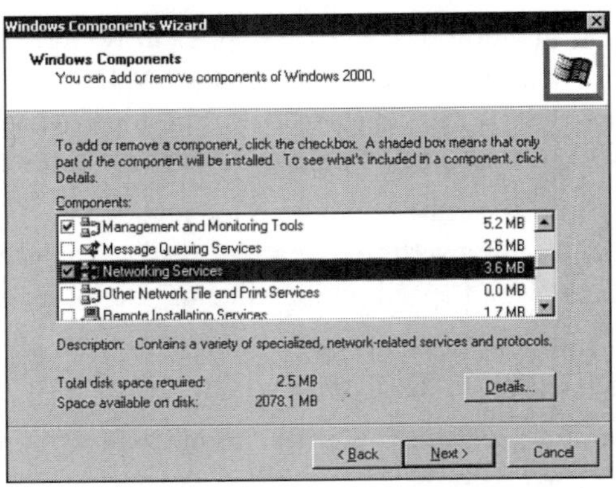

Figure 16.4 Selecting networking components to install.

but you do have a functional WINS server at this point. If your network is at all large, you will want to install more WINS servers and configure replication between them. The other thing you should do, besides becoming familiar with the WINS service, and its management needs, and its interface, which you will find named WINS in the Start menu Administrative Tools under Programs, is to set a few properties.

Figure 16.5 shows the entry WINS server Properties page accessed by right-clicking on the WINS server and selecting Properties.

In this figure a location for backups of the WINS database has been set, and the check box enabling backup of the database on server shutdown (a default behavior in NT 4) has been enabled. If you do not enable this option, you should have a practice of periodic backup, which can be done through the management console.

Other options found in these property pages enable one to configure the different time intervals such as the TTL sent to the WINS client as the renewal interval, the location of the WINS database storage, and the behavior of the WINS server when under bursts of service requests. Before jumping in and changing the interval time values, you should do yourself a favor by reading up on their interactions in the online documentation and considering the implications in your WINS system.

By spending some time in the management console, you will notice commands for scavenging, for backup and restore, for verifying the database, and other actions. Many are in the context menu accessed by right-clicking on the server node. Verifying the database is a high-overhead operation, and not frequently needed. When used, do this when the network impact will not be noticed if at all possible.

The Windows 2000 WINS Server provides background database compacting and also permits manual, offline compacting. Because WINS performance is so directly tied to database size and background compacting does not recover space as well as can be done with offline compacting, large WINS databases are sometimes taken offline for

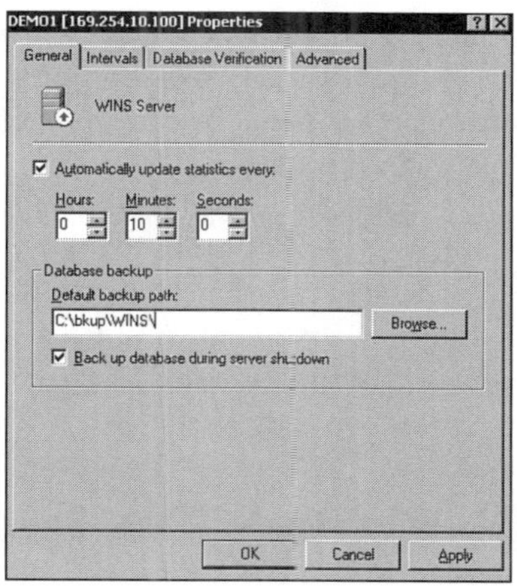

Figure 16.5 Windows 2000 WINS server Properties page.

this servicing. Because WINS is actually a database application, hardware selection should emphasize disk performance. So, has the message become clear yet? To run WINS you must be aware of and provide for "backup, scavenge, and compact" to keep your WINS database healthy and performing at its peak.

The new burst-handling feature in the Windows 2000 WINS server allows the deferring of work when the server is under heavy load. When needed the server issues immediate name registration grants with short TTL values when they are requested without first verifying their availability. This gets a response back to the client, relieving the WINS system of retries or switches to secondaries, and effectively queues the work for later. Because the Windows 2000 client performs its first renewal at one-eighth of this extra short TTL used in a burst response, the unchecked grant does not have a long lifetime.

As mentioned earlier, WINS replication will not be discussed in detail. But, there are a few observations we would like to make. First, the default configuration is to replicate only with explicitly configured partners. This is likely the way you will want to leave this. This setting is a security consideration as much as anything, enabling you to control who may get a dump of your WINS database. Turning on the automatic discovery and replication configuration is of use only in very small environments, where there are only two or three WINS servers. The other observation is that you are faced with the choice of configuring partners as Push, as Pull, or as Push/Pull partners. These methods of replication have some different properties. Push replication is not scheduled, whereas Pull replication is. This difference helps in configuring replication when there are slow links involved. But this also has an impact on the time it takes for the database to converge to the same content at all WINS servers. When replication is not over a slow link, use of the new option of having replication partners remain connected should be considered for use. This is not appropriate for a Pull-only replication, but where usable it will greatly reduce overhead and improve convergence. On Pull-only replications, you may want to adjust the threshold on the number of changes collected before replication is triggered. You will want to balance these against your deployment needs. When there are no overriding factors, replications partners should be configured for both Push and Pull.

Before moving on, the WINS statistics available in the management console should be mentioned because these can give you an overall feel of the health of your WINS system and even more so of its load. Two other tools for WINS monitoring and management deserve mention. You can probably guess. The WINS object in System Monitor and the WINS context in netsh. (netsh was reviewed in Chapter 12, "Troubleshooting Tools and Utilities.") Learning to use these will ease your life if WINS is a key, and heavily used part of your environment.

Configuring DNS with WINS Integration

For ideal integration, NetBIOS and DNS hosts should support both name resolution and reverse address lookups. Name resolution is a process in which a NetBIOS or DNS host name is resolved to an IP address. This just means that a name such as

Host.example.net (the DNS name) or Host (the NetBIOS name) should uniquely resolve to an IP address such as 198.25.40.31. A reverse address lookup resolves an IP address to a unique NetBIOS or DNS host name. This just means that an IP address, such as 198.25.40.31, should uniquely resolve to such a name as Host.example.net or Host.

This section discusses how to integrate DNS and WINS name resolution methods and identifies issues you may face when implementing this support. When dealing with name resolution, the part that involves more effort is the process to ensure that DNS hosts can resolve dynamic NetBIOS names. The opposite is trivial because NetBIOS hosts can use a DNS resolver to resolve any static DNS host names.

Before showing the actual steps to enable this support, the next section looks in a scenario-based manner at the types of client combinations to make clear the options between which one can, or may be forced to, choose. This will be a review if you have followed everything that has been said in this chapter so far, but it is presented to illustrate more plainly the variety of situations one might encounter.

How Integration Works

DNS is configured to use WINS by adding special, Microsoft-specific resource records (RRs) to the DNS database. This is always done at the root of a DNS zone. When DNS attempts to resolve a name query in a WINS-enabled domain, if it does not find the A record that is needed it can then send the host part of the FQDN to WINS. If WINS returns an IP, DNS caches this and returns it to the client. For this to work, the DNS domain in the FQDN must be WINS enabled. For this to work without confusion, the WINS clients should also understand that this is their DNS domain.

Understanding Different Name Resolution Situations

Depending on the amount of interaction between the DNS hosts and NetBIOS hosts, the whole name resolution issue brings some interesting scenarios.

One scenario is where the clients connect to the servers and no interaction is necessary between clients. If the connectivity involves NetBIOS hosts (such as Microsoft hosts) and DNS hosts (such as UNIX hosts), the integration can often be done without many problems just because of the following:

- The NetBIOS hosts can query a DNS server for DNS host name resolution. This ensures that the UNIX servers can be accessed from the NetBIOS clients.
- The NetBIOS hosts (such as a Windows server used to run FTP, IIS, or other TCP/IP-based Server services) can be assigned static IP addresses that can be mapped in the DNS database. UNIX clients will be able to use DNS to resolve these NetBIOS hosts. It is also possible to use either static or DHCP-assigned IP addresses in conjunction with dynamic DNS registration, although for major servers static IP assignment is favored.
- The WINS clients continue to use WINS servers to resolve NetBIOS host names to IP addresses.

This scenario did not really need to have DNS enabled to look for resolutions in WINS. If Dynamic Host Configuration Protocol (DHCP) is used to assign IP addresses and DDNS is not enabled, however, the preceding scenario will not permit the UNIX clients to find NetBIOS hosts serviced by DHCP. If these clients register with WINS and DNS uses WINS, however, any client can find these hosts through DNS queries.

A second scenario is where every host may need to connect to every other host, such as in a workgroup setting, especially where DHCP is used or when static IP assignments to NetBIOS hosts are not recorded in DNS with static A resource records. The integration becomes more challenging because of the peer-to-peer connectivity between NetBIOS hosts and UNIX hosts and the absence of dynamic (or manual) DNS updates. This is the situation Windows DNS Server can service through integration with WINS.

In addition to being a regular DNS server, the Windows DNS Server helps in checking the WINS database for a given host name that can't be found in the DNS database. If a UNIX client that knows nothing of WINS is querying for a NetBIOS host, for example, the DNS resolver software on the UNIX box can be configured to point to the Windows DNS service. The Windows DNS Server will go through the DNS part of the resolution and then use the WINS database (located either on the same machine or on a remote machine) to resolve the name. In effect, this enables non-WINS clients to resolve NetBIOS names by querying a DNS server. Previous to the WINS integration, there was no way to reliably resolve the names of DHCP clients, because of the dynamic IP addressing and absence of DNS A records.

Windows 2000 has now added to the available alternatives through its implementation of DDNS. This provides the ability to have these DNS updates performed either by the clients themselves, or by DHCP on their behalf. In fact, the Windows 2000 DHCP Server can even do this for non-Windows DHCP clients. This extends the ability to dynamically assign IP addresses and yet have DNS resolution even of non-Microsoft clients systems. But here we are covering WINS, which is integrated in the same way whether we are looking at NT 4 or Windows 2000. This integration will continue to be available, and used mostly for non-DHCP or non-Microsoft DHCP clients that do register with WINS.

Examining WINS/DNS Integration Situations

The first example considered here shows problems, not with DNS/WINS integration, but rather arising from the inablility to understanding client needs and where to use it appropriately. The example involves clients trying to reach a server in a network where the DNS administrator is far behind schedule on updating the DNS because dynamic DNS is not enabled. Consider the network shown in Figure 16.6.

Suppose Terri tries to ping a new host recently installed (frenchy.example.net) on the corporate side of the network.

If a NetBIOS broadcast query is performed by Terri's computer (terri.example.net) it would not reach over the router. If it checked its LMHOSTS file for a frenchy and

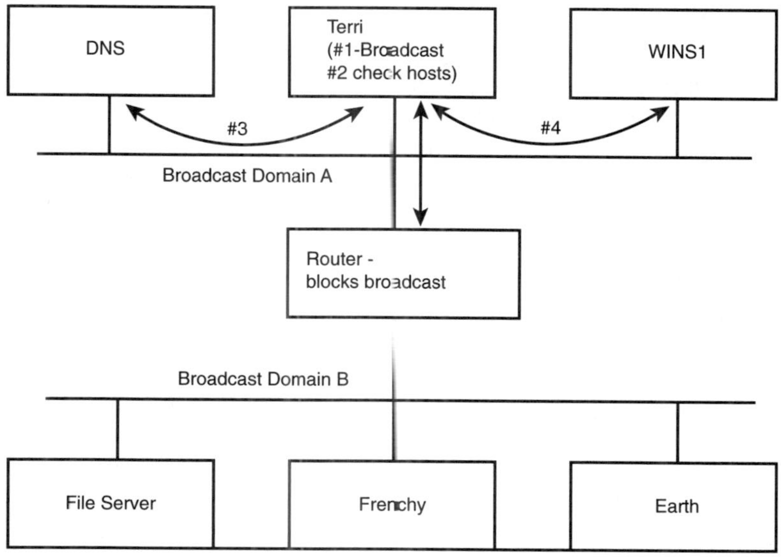

Figure 16.6 Windows NetBIOS client resolution alternatives.

its HOSTS file for a frenchy.example.net entry, it is likely this new machine would not be found. The other two alternatives are to check with DNS whether terri.example.net is a DNS client and to check with WINS whether terri.example.net is a WINS client. Perhaps one does not remember that Windows machines are not always DNS clients, at least before Windows 2000, and that being a WINS client is also optional.

If the DNS administrator hasn't yet manually updated the configuration files for example.net, Terri's DNS request fails. If Terri is a WINS client, a query is sent to the WINS server on wins1.example.net. If this WINS server has a mapping for \\FRENCHY, Terri receives the IP and can ping the machine. Of course, with DNS/WINS integration Terri's DNS request would have resolved successfully if \\FRENCHY is WINS registered.

There are some observations and issues to point out in this example. If the new machine is a WINS client, it will register \\FRENCHY with a WINS server, which should either be wins1.example.net itself or should be a replication partner with it. Next, if terri.example.net is a down-level DNS client and the name being resolved is frenchy.example.net rather than \\FRENCHY, the query will first be sent to DNS. If terri.example.net is a Windows 2000 client, queries to DNS and to WINS are undertaken simultaneously. In either of these cases, using DNS/WINS integration allows the most rapid resolution. In the first case, because WINS will not be tried until DNS has failed, and in the Windows 2000 case because of the better performance of DNS (assuming frenchy.example.net is in the DNS cache from an earlier query)compared to

WINS with its flat database. Also, notice that where the DNS and WINS servers are located on the network is immaterial provided that there is TCP/IP connectivity with them. Finally, it should be observed that if frenchy.example.net is a Windows 2000 client or a client of Windows 2000 DHCP services, either of these cases can provide for direct registration with DNS using dynamic updates.

One problem you can face when integrating WINS and DNS involves networks that manage IP addresses with DHCP servers other than the one provided with Windows 2000. If frenchy.example.net has a static IP address of 192.168.10.41 and the DNS administrator manually creates an A record in the configuration file to reflect that address, Terri can ping frenchy.example.net. If \\FRENCHY uses a DHCP server that does not update DNS, however, the IP address is dynamic and can therefore change and the administrator has no chance of maintaining the DNS A record. In this situation, making \\FRENCHY a WINS client and using WINS/DNS integration is a solution. However, this also means that \\FRENCHY is a Windows system or perhaps a UNIX Samba system. Other, NetBIOS-unaware clients cannot be provided for with this older DNS/WINS integration as is possible using Windows 2000 DHCP with dynamic DNS updates.

WINS/DNS Integration Requirements

To query DNS, a FQDN must be used. Therefore, to query a WINS database by DNS hosts (using the Windows DNS Server), you must decide the zone of the DNS namespace in an organization that will have dynamic (WINS-enabled) hosts. If an organization has an Internet domain called example.net assigned to it, for example, it could delegate a zone (say, interactive.example.net), where the zone interactive will contain all the dynamic DHCP (WINS-enabled) clients.

A Windows DNS server can be designated as the primary DNS server for the interactive zone. The primary Windows DNS machine for this zone can also be a WINS server or can point to a WINS server on the network. The UNIX hosts (and the Windows hosts for that matter) can be configured to query the Windows DNS Server for all host names to be resolved in the interactive.example.net part of the DNS namespace. The Windows DNS Server will in turn use the WINS database (local or remote) to resolve the names in the NetBIOS zone.

This approach was the recommended practice during NT 4. Delegating such a zone for WINS clients provided a clear and simple way to integrate their DNS visibility into an existing DNS services architecture. Also, delegating one zone to Microsoft DNS was more palatable to existing DNS shops than migrating from BIND. This solution makes it easy for all parties—the DNS server, the NetBIOS clients, and host resolving them by name—to all be in agreement as to the FQDN.

Now consider another situation, with the same company, but with the dynamic NetBIOS hosts split among two zones (such as, interactive1.example.net and interactive2.example.net). In this situation, having a Windows DNS Server as the primary host for both the interactive1 and interactive2 zones allows resolving the NetBIOS host names by the process previously described. These two zones could also be placed on separate Windows DNS Servers to achieve the same result. However, the DNS Server, although using WINS to resolve names, won't know that a given dynamic NetBIOS host truly belongs to the interactive1 or interactive2 zone from a DNS perspective (because WINS is just a flat database of names). In fact DNS can find any of the NetBIOS hosts in either zone, which can be a problem. But, the forward lookup still does accomplish its purpose: returning the correct IP address.

In summary, the leading issues involved are as follows:

- Is DHCP used?
- Is dynamic DNS in use?
- If both of these first two are affirmative, can all DHCP clients have their DNS records dynamically updated? This is nearly equivalent to asking whether Microsoft DHCP and DNS are in use and enabled for dynamic updating.
- Is there a desire to reduce manual DNS RR entry overhead, but without using DDNS?

Then, if the answers to these questions show that there are IP assignments that will not normally have corresponding DNS entries, the issues involved are as follows:

- Do any non-WINS clients need to resolve names to these IP assignments?
- Is it more convenient or efficient to have WINS clients resolve these using DNS?
- If so, what DNS domain name(s) should be used? And, if multiple domains are to be used, or zone transfers are to be made to non-Microsoft DNS servers, will the resulting confusions be acceptable?

Configuring DNS to use WINS

By now it should be clear that WINS is easily set up. Because enabling DNS to use WINS is equally simple, the question naturally arises as to what then are the issues.

First, before using this capability, one should have a plan as to what clients will be resolvable in which DNS domain as was just discussed. This decision is not as simple in Windows 2000 as it was in NT due to the use of DNS domains as Windows 2000 names. You may also want to review the discussions of WINS-R reverse lookup later in this chapter before deciding on your plan. There does not seem to be a clear signal from Microsoft on this other than what was discussed earlier and the option to upgrade down-level clients to Windows 2000.

Second, and much more well defined, is that one needs to be aware that WINS records in DNS zones will not transfer to any non-Microsoft DNS servers without causing problems. This situation is accommodated by a setting discussed shortly. However, this implies that one will have secondaries that will not be able to resolve all the names resolvable by Microsoft DNS Servers for the zone. This can lead to erratic behavior as seen by the DNS clients.

Enabling WINS Forward Lookups

This section discusses the use of the DNS management console to configure DNS to use WINS. But first, you will see that this can also be done by the zone files.

In addition to the standard resource records that the DNS zone files support, Windows DNS allows a WINS and a WINS-R record. As the PLACE.DNS sample file that Microsoft provides in the %windir%\SYSTEM32\DNS\Samples directory states the following:

> The presence of a WINS record at the zone root instructs the name server to use WINS to look up any request for A (address) records for names that are DIRECT children of zone root, and which do NOT have A records in the zone file.

This file is seemingly unchanged between NT 4 and Windows 2000 and offers some limited advise on using this feature.

The following is the general syntax of a WINS record:

```
<domain> IN WINS [LOCAL] [L<Lookup timeout>] [C<Cache timeout>] (<WINS servers>)
```

The optional LOCAL flag indicates that this record should not be included in zone transfers. Between the optional LOCAL flag and the specification of WINS server(s) to be used, one can provide L<Lookup timeout> and C<Cache timeout> values in seconds.

To add the WINS record to the zone file, use code similar to that demonstrated in Listing 16.1.

Listing 16.1 **DNS file resource records for WINS**

```
@      IN WINS LOCAL L900 C2  (
                198.25.40.20
                198.25.40.30 )
earth.example.net.      IN A     198.25.40.20
mars.example.net.       IN A     198.25.40.30
```

In this example, the two WINS servers to be used are specified by IP in the order in which they will be tried. Omit the LOCAL flag if the WINS record should be included in zone transfers.

WINS lookup can be more easily enabled for a zone through the DNS management console instead of manual entry of the WINS record.

In NT 4 this is accomplished as follows:

1. Open the NT 4 DNS Manager.
2. Select the zone and then use its context menu (right-click) to access the zone Properties dialog box.
3. In the zone Properties dialog box, select the WINS tab.
4. Check the Use WINS Resolution check box and type in the IP address(es) of the WINS server(s) to be used, clicking Add.

5. Use the Do Not Replicate check box option if it is appropriate to prevent the WINS record from being propagated in zone transfers.

In Windows 2000, the setting for use of WINS integration is similar.

1. Open the Windows 2000 DNS Server management console.
2. Expand the server in the tree at left, and then highlight the root node of the zone to be enabled for WINS.
3. With the focus set on the zone, use its context menu (right-click) to access the zone Properties dialog box.
4. In the zone Properties dialog box, select the WINS tab, as is shown in Figure 16.7.
5. Check the box to Use WINS Forward Lookup, and then enter the IP address(es) of the WINS servers, using Add for each one.
6. Use the Do Not Replicate check box option if it is appropriate to prevent the WINS record from being propagated in zone transfers.
7. If appropriate, adjust the TTL value used on the answers returned by DNS.
8. Click the Advanced button of the WINS tab.
9. If appropriate, modify the default values for how long WINS responses are cached by the DNS server and for how long DNS server waits for WINS to reply.
10. Complete the changes by use of Apply and OK as needed.

Figure 16.7 shows the Windows 2000 DNS Server's WINS configuration sheet. If you did not have your DNS server listed when the DNS Server management console started, you need to highlight the DNS node at the top in the left pane and then use Connect to Computer from either the Action menu or the context menu.

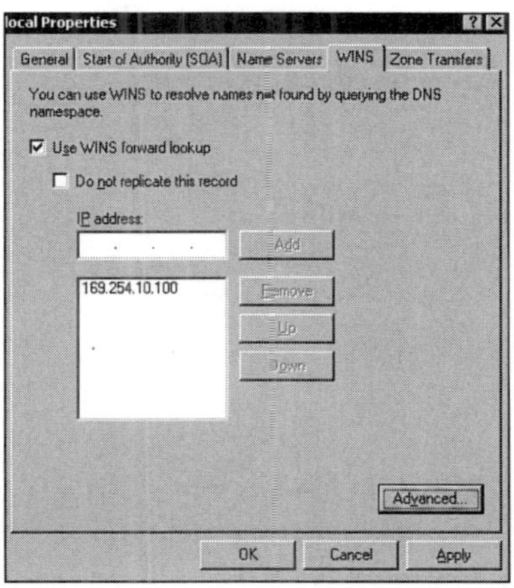

Figure 16.7 Configuring WINS forward lookup in DNS.

The check box labeled Do Not Replicate This Record controls whether the WINS record will be included in zone transfers and corresponds to the LOCAL flag on the WINS record. By clicking on Advanced, adjustment may be made to the cache time-out and the timeout applied to WINS queries. The cache timeout governs how stale data is allowed to become in the DNS server cache, and should not be confused with the TTL value WINS provides to WINS clients or the TTL value DNS will use in answers. It is sensible, however, to keep these relatively the same so that changes in registered WINS names will be reflected in DNS use of WINS. You should also be aware that many WINS servers can be added, but that they will be tried as needed, possibly delaying WINS lookups if the first and second listed are not highly available and reliable. Figure 16.8 shows the same but for a secondary zone that does not receive a WINS record from the primary.

Here you can override the absence of a WINS record in the transfer from the zone primary. Notice that the indented check box is grayed out because Use Local WINS Resource Record is implied when one provides a WINS record that overrides the zone primary. Also, this implies that the record is treated as LOCAL, and will not be transferred to any secondaries to which this secondary server is a master.

Reverse Lookups with WINS

Although WINS was not constructed to provide reverse lookup capabilities, this functionality can still be accomplished, effectively mimicking PTR records for WINS-enabled clients, when using Microsoft's DNS Server. The presence of a WINS-R record at the in-addr.arpa zone root instructs the name server to use a NetBIOS node adapter status lookup for any reverse lookup requests for IP addresses in the zone if they are not defined with Pointer (PTR) records. This means that both the DNS server and the machine using the IP are involved in answering the DNS query. This then means that

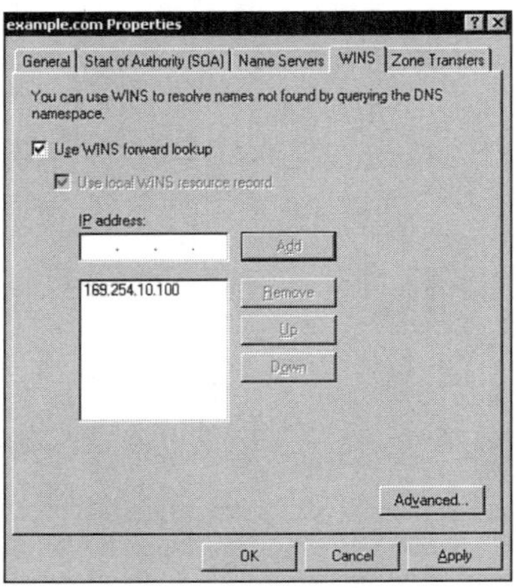

Figure 16.8 Configuring WINS for a secondary zone.

a fair amount of network latency is built in to the process. Reverse WINS lookup is not a high-performance act, but is a useful functionality, particularly when it cannot be done otherwise.

The following is the general syntax of a WINS-R record:

```
<domain> IN WINS-R [LOCAL] <domain to append to returned NetBIOS names>
```

Between the optional LOCAL flag and the specification of the domain to be appended, one can provide L<Lookup timeout> and C<Cache timeout> values in seconds. Using a real-world domain, a WINS-R record would appear as follows:

```
@     IN WINS-R LOCAL L900 C2  example.net.
```

Using the DNS management console to configure WINS reverse lookup is very similar to configuring WINS for forward lookup zones, except one first selects the in-addr.arpa reverse lookup zone in the DNS server's tree at the left in the DNS management console. Then, in the zone Properties dialog box, as shown in Figure 16.9, a WINS-R tab is used to enable this capability.

Remember to check the Do Not Replicate This Record box if this DNS server will transfer this zone to any non-Microsoft DNS servers. The Advanced button again gives access to the cache and the lookup timeout values.

The box labeled Domain to Append to Returned Name is where the DNS domain that should be used is provided. Remember that the NetBIOS name is not qualified by the DNS hierarchy, which is what this provides. WIN-R does not actually enable the use of WINS at all. Rather, when this is enabled and a PTR query is received that DNS cannot otherwise resolve in a zone for which it is authoritative, DNS sends a NetBIOS adapter status inquiry using the IP. If the machine is reachable

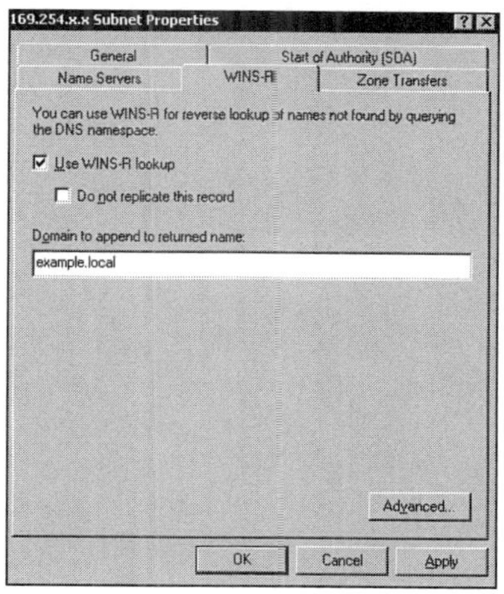

Figure 16.9 Configuring WINS-R lookup in DNS.

and running NetBT, it replies, providing its NetBIOS name in the response. DNS then appends the value entered in this box and returns the result as a FQDN in response to the original PTR query. You are clearly free to use different domain names for each zone that is WINS-enabled, but you should carefully consider the implications.

Reverse address lookups allowing one to obtain the DNS FQDN of a host given its IP address, are becoming increasingly used for logon, firewall, and other anti-spoofing and sensitive applications. The process tends to complicate WINS and DNS integration, but its use is recommended to provide full service for the down-level clients that rely on DNS/WINS integration.

Summary

This chapter described the purpose of WINS, how it works, and how it can be used with DNS to provide full networking support to down-level clients. A number of interacting factors were examined and the main considerations for successfully deploying WINS and its DNS integration were covered. The steps needed to install and configure WINS and to configure its integration with DNS were detailed with emphasis on key settings.

17

NetBIOS: Legacy Name Services and Resolution

THIS CHAPTER COVERS THE *Network Basic Input/Output System* (NetBIOS), which has highly visible uses in Windows Internet Naming Service (WINS) and browsing. This chapter shows what these do for you, and how, and gives recommendations for dealing with NetBIOS on a practical level. Although Windows 2000 has made large strides toward NetBIOS independence, it will be some time until we are running larger Windows deployments without NetBIOS. For these reasons, and because in general, legacy NetBIOS name resolution is not well understood, this chapter is included.

This chapter reviews the following:

- **NetBIOS History and Characteristics.** NetBIOS is a legacy application interface with services designed to make small peer-to-peer networking easy. NetBIOS works on more than one transport protocol. This section gives you an overview of NetBIOS so that you can understand precisely what it is and how, for example, it differs from NetBEUI. One goal of Windows 2000 is to begin removing dependence on NetBIOS. If you have down-level clients, you likely need to continue supporting NetBIOS and also need to keep your options open with WINS.
- **NetBIOS Name Registration.** NetBIOS names must be advertised, as is explained in this section.

- **NetBIOS Names and Resource Codes.** NetBIOS names contain a hidden character used to identify special resources, such as message services and domain controllers. This section provides a reference for these.
- **Resolving NetBIOS Names.** NetBIOS has many ways to resolve names. This section introduces the operation of the Windows resolver.
- **NetBIOS Node Types.** NetBIOS clients are classified into node types based on their registration and resolution behavior. This section defines their types and their behaviors.
- **Browsing: The NetBIOS Discovery Service.** The Browser service is a very much automated capability hiding behind Computers Near Me and Network Neighborhood.
- **NetBIOS on the Wire.** NetBIOS is used for naming and services over connections, but not as a network transport protocol. NetBIOS is available in both the old form and in new ways to provide Server Message Block support through Direct Hosting within Windows 2000, as covered in this section.

NetBIOS History and Characteristics

There is nothing quite like NetBIOS in the UNIX world. Windows administrators have struggled with NetBIOS namespace support because of its architectural limitations. Although the introduction of WINS and its stabilization with the later NT 4 service packs helped make the flat NetBIOS namespace reliably useful, Microsoft has aimed Windows 2000 squarely at bringing their operating system out of this troublesome networking model.

A number of things make learning NetBIOS essential for system administrators. NetBIOS isn't going away soon but rather will be around as long as legacy applications and operating systems need to be supported. NetBIOS needs a non-DNS name server (such as WINS to make all of its other services and dependent applications run properly. The NetBIOS resolver, over time, has gained so many alternatives that understanding its operation can be quite important for client performance. When misconfigured, NetBIOS clients can incur much unneeded network load.

The Windows 2000 network configuration settings enable you to disable the *NetBIOS over* Transmission Control Protocol/Internet Protocol *(TCP/IP)* (NetBT) implementation. This is provided for use if backward compatibility is not necessary in your environment (such as a Windows 2000–only network). However, some features in the first release of Windows 2000 appear to still require the use of NetBIOS names. The work of making Windows 2000 completely independent from its NetBIOS legacy will continue for a time, and because of this thorough testing of a planned NetBIOS-disabled deployment is recommended. Finally, it is important to recognize that removing NetBIOS over TCP/IP does not necessarily mean removing all use of NetBIOS naming.

A Nutshell History of NetBIOS

NetBIOS isn't a name service, although it does have some related capabilities as well as a formal name service called WINS. NetBIOS started out as a network *application programming interface* (API) for MS-DOS computers in small, single-segment networks, but was forced into larger network roles because of Microsoft's success with Windows 3.x and Windows for Workgroups. NetBIOS also isn't a network protocol in the sense that IP is a transport protocol, but rather has come to be used with a number of protocols. Figure 17.1 shows this situation, where it is clear that NetBIOS provides its service at the upper layers of the protocol stack.

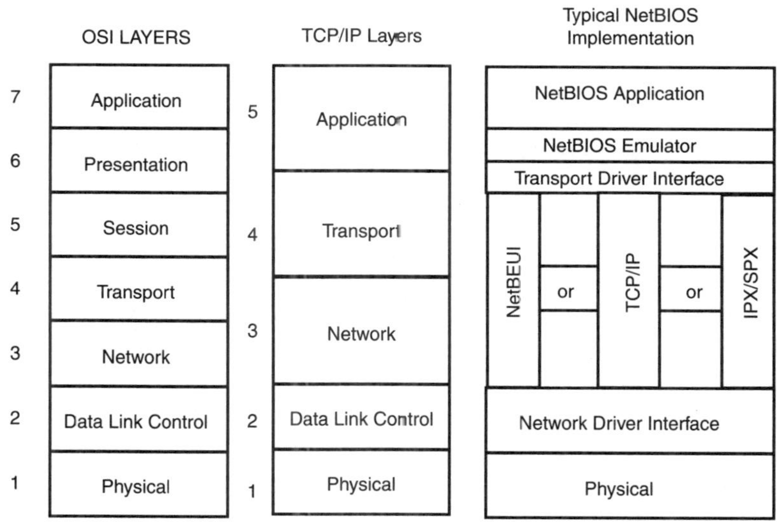

Figure 17.1 The Network Layers and NetBIOS.

The network layers and NetBIOS.NetBIOS was developed in the personal computer environment to enable programmers to develop client/server programs and was implemented in the *NetBIOS Extended User Interface* (NetBEUI) protocol by IBM in 1985. IBM packaged NetBIOS support with the NetBEUI network protocol to give MS-DOS PC applications easy-to-use network services in *local area networks* (LANs).

NetBEUI is only practical for a few hundred computers, and doesn't scale to *wide area networks* (WANs) because it can't be routed. A frustrating example of this legacy is sometimes evident when the list of computer names showing up in one browser list differs from another because the users are on opposite sides of a router. This limitation of being nonroutable has been addressed with NetBT first by LMHOSTS files, and then by WINS.

3Com and Microsoft jointly developed LAN Manager to run as a process on OS/2. IBM's version, LAN Server, differed slightly, but they both used NetBEUI. In

1993, Microsoft abstracted NetBIOS from NetBEUI for binding to TCP/IP, and in 1995 for binding to Novell's IPX/SPX. This made NetBIOS services more useful in WANs, but it didn't remedy all of its architectural limitations. NetBIOS can still use more broadcasts than other TCP/IP service protocols, and uses an altogether different convention to name computers and services. (These are discussed later in this chapter in the section titled "NetBIOS Names and Resource Codes.")

NetBIOS Services

The features NetBIOS provides are outlined in RFC 1001 and 1002. Some widely used and very convenient services depend on NetBIOS, such as the pre-Windows 2000 version of the Browser service (which provides a list of computers in the Computers Near Me and the Network Neighborhood windows), Server and Workstation services (which, for example, use *Server Messenger Block* [SMB] to share files in what is sometimes called Microsoft networking), and the Messenger service (which provides the capability to send messages to users with only their logon name for reference).

Some other services depend on NetBIOS, but let's leave the particulars for a moment to describe NetBIOS more generally. NetBIOS is best described as a suite of *interprocess communication* (IPC) services falling into three categories:

- **Name services get, release, and resolve resource names.** NetBIOS names must be unique. They are used for individual users, computers, services, and other resources. Names in the flat namespace are located through broadcasts, or in the case of WINS, through point-to-point communications with a persistent naming authority capable of addressing computers on any reachable IP network.
- **Session services include messaging commands that give a pair of NetBIOS applications full-duplex, sequenced, and reliable connections.** Multiple connections are supported, and names identify both participants.
- **Datagram services transmit and receive messages between participants by broadcasting to group names or unicasting to unique, individual names.** Unlike session services, datagram services are non- sequenced, unreliable, and connectionless.

NetBIOS supports name registrations and resolutions, a service that has a close relationship with DNS, the core subject of this book. NetBIOS can be caused to broadcast frequently, even on TCP/IP. Name service broadcasts have an architecturally imposed scope, limiting them to a single network segment. Because the broadcasts aren't always appreciated, and in routed networks are ineffective, NetBT emerged. With the advent of NetBT, and then WINS, different NetBIOS node types have been defined (more on this later) in order to set the default NetBIOS name services behavior. Even still, until the upgrades in NT 4 Service Packs 3 to 5, NetBIOS name services using WINS were to often less than fully reliable. Fortunately, NetBIOS session services usually work fine if name service issues are resolved.

Figure 17.2 shows the Windows 2000 Registry expanded to HKLM\System\CurrentControlSet\Services\NetBT to show the adjacent NetBIOS and NetBT keys.

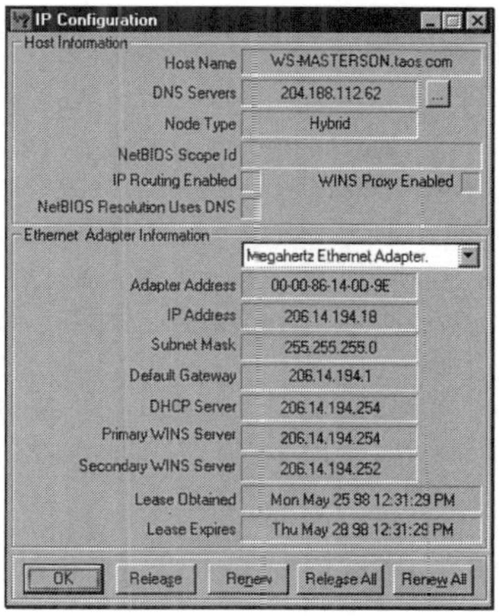

Figure 17.2 The Registry showing NetBIOS and NetBT keys.

As stated here and elsewhere in this book, Windows 2000 has a switch on the TCP/IP properties to disable NetBT. This should not be confused with disabling NetBIOS. Properly speaking, NetBT is a helper to TCP/IP and is only one means by which NetBIOS is made available. That said, it is easy to confuse these. We usually are using NetBT, so most of our experience with NetBIOS is when used with TCP/IP, and so is colored by the glasses of NetBT. This chapter tries to use NetBIOS and NetBT appropriately, even though it deals with NetBIOS when used in the TCP/IP protocol.

NetBIOS Name Registration

Obviously NetBIOS session and datagram services are useless without name services. Machines must locate one another to communicate. As part of the name services, a client must announce, or advertise, itself so that it may be located.

This autonomous origin of names is both a strong and a weak point. This has the advantage of being dynamic, or self-configuring, in a way unavailable with DNS until dynamic updates were defined. The downside of this is shown by the long history of finding a satisfactory implementation.

Originally, a NetBIOS client would periodically broadcast on the network to let others know of its presence. Other NetBIOS clients, by listening for these, could then build lists in their NetBIOS name cache of what was on the network, or rather, on their network segment.

Two approaches used before WINS to overcome the limitations of this broadcast architecture are still in use. One is the Browser service that, sort of like carpooling, frees a number of machines from the name list formation duties by having a few machines elected to assume the responsibility. This is covered in the later section titled "Browsing: the NetBIOS Discovery Service." The other early approach was the LMHOSTS file. With NetBT and the ability to cross routers, the LMHOST file was used to provide a simple table of name-to-IP mappings. (Appendix A, "LMHOSTS and HOSTS Files," cover this in more detail.)

Finally, WINS was introduced to provide for NetBIOS name services in a larger TCP/IP environment. A machine that is a WINS client registers itself directly with WINS and periodically renews the registration. (For details, see Chapter 16, "WINS: Legacy Name Services and Resolution.") Without WINS, a client can only broadcast. Either way, a NetBIOS client is driven, compelled if you will, to make its presence known.

NetBIOS Names and Resource Codes

NetBIOS names and DNS names each have their own rules. With Windows 2000 it has become increasingly important that machines, whenever possible, have the same name in both namespaces. This limits both DNS, where otherwise the same name could be used within different domains, and also NetBIOS names that then need to use the more restricted DNS character set. Although Windows 2000 accommodates independent DNS and down-level names, the immediate benefits, especially during migration, may well not be worth the long-term confusion. If one has a "situation" because of a preexisting name convention, one can "Rob Peter to pay Paul" but eventually there will be a tax collected.

A Flat Namespace and NetBIOS Scopes

The NetBIOS namespace isn't hierarchical; it's flat, which creates some challenges for administrators. Limited capacity for names is one such challenge because in a flat namespace no two computers can have the same name. Can you imagine what would happen if two companies couldn't both name their Web servers WWW? In the larger enterprise environment, this translates into the need to use naming standards to avoid conflicts. This is especially true now that Windows 2000 imposes a uniqueness restriction on down-level names in the local Windows 2000 forest.

NetBIOS does provide one attempt at overcoming the limitations of its flat namespace. This is the introduction of NetBIOS ScopeIDs. NetBIOS can use a ScopeID, but most of the time it is not configured and left to default. When two machines are configured with the same ScopeID, they can interoperate as NetBIOS peers. When the machines have different ScopeIDs, they will not acknowledge each other or interoperate. The ScopeID is transparently appended in NetBIOS name registrations, renewals, queries, and releases. It is that simple, and limited. Using

NetBIOS ScopeIDs allows multiple NetBIOS namespaces on a network, possibly reducing the size of each, but does nothing to introduce any hierarchy among the multiple flat namespaces. In practice, NetBIOS ScopeIDs have not been a popular feature.

NetBIOS Name Characteristics

NetBIOS names are always 16-byte strings. When a name has fewer than 15 characters, it's automatically padded out with space characters to 15 bytes in length, with one byte reserved for a suffix that's really a resource or service code. These are automatically appended after the 15th byte. The suffix is usually hidden unless you're looking at a WINS database, a trace, or the output of a command such as **nbtstat**.

Whenever you see a NetBIOS name shorter than 15 characters, it has been truncated for display purposes by removing all white space after the last printable character.

NetBIOS names can consist of alphanumeric characters including the blank space and special characters such as the following: ! @ # $ % ^ & ( ) - ' { }_ . ~. In fact, the NT 4 administrative interfaces increasingly limited one's machine name choices, but any character is valid in a NetBIOS name except for certain characters with special uses—namely ?*:;|/\<>[],'+=, which are disallowed. In the Windows 2000 administrative interfaces, the period (.) character is now not allowed in NetBIOS names.

NetBIOS names can't start with an asterisk (*), which is reserved for broadcast addressing. Even though the period (.) is legal in NetBIOS names and allowed by NT 4, it's not valid for host names in the DNS domain namespace because it is used to delimit portions of *fully qualified domain names* (FQDNs). Take a look at the "Host Name Characteristics" section of Chapter 1, "Introducing the Domain Name System," where there's more information about naming, particularly for compatibility with DNS.

Just because one can do something does not constitute a good reason to do so. This is especially true if you want a NetBIOS name to be compatible with DNS. Use only the special hyphen, or minus, character ([ms]), anything else will be rejected by many modern DNS machines running in default configuration. Some printer applications have problems with the hyphen (-) character; so for maximum compatibility, use strictly alphanumeric characters with the first character being an alphabetic character only. On the other hand, if your objective is protecting your internal namespace, the ability of the Microsoft DNS implementation to use an extended character set presents some alternatives for your consideration.

NetBIOS Name Resource Codes

Resource codes give NetBIOS the capability to register not just names but computers, standard services, and other resources. Because NetBIOS already knows where services reside—that is, what IP address to use to reach them—clients can query to reach those services by name without first having to know where they are. With the addition of SRV records to DNS, this previously unique capability of the NetBIOS namespace can be provided in part by DNS, and in fact is heavily used by a Windows 2000 domain environment now and will likely become increasingly used for service advertisement throughout the DNS system over time.

Table 17.1 lists the more commonly seen NetBIOS service resource codes. Most of the codes are used only to identify computers and resources. Some codes might only infrequently appear in a WINS database, such as those used by custom applications, and are not listed.

Table 17.1 **NetBIOS (16th Byte) Service Resource Codes**

Resource Code	Type of Entry	What's Registered; Service Performing the Registration
<00>	A computer or domain name	NetBIOS computer name or domain of membership; Workstation service
<01>	Literally: "_MSBROWSE_"	IP of local master browser for announcement to other browsers; Browser service
<03>	A user or computer name	Message target: a NetBIOS username or NetBIOS computer name; Messenger service
<06>	A computer name	NetBIOS computer name running RAS; RAS service
<1B>	A domain name	Domain master browser; the PDC's special Domain Master Browser service
<1C>	A domain name	Domain group name; PDC or BDC (up to 25 DCs can register per domain)
<1D>	A domain name	Local master browser publishing browse lists for retrieval by backup local browsers; Browser service
<1E>	A domain name	Normal group name targeted by broadcasts to elect local master browsers; Browser service
<1F>	A computer name	NetBIOS computer name capable of Network Dynamic Data Exchange; NetDDE service
<20>	A computer or group name	NetBIOS computer or special administrative group name; Server service

Resource Code	Type of Entry	What's Registered; Service Performing the Registration
<21>	A computer name	NetBIOS computer name; RAS client
<BE>	A computer name	NetBIOS computer name; Network Monitor agent
<BF>	A computer name	NetBIOS computer name, by Network Monitor utility

Following are some examples of NetBIOS names commonly used by Microsoft components:

- **computer_name[00h]** Registered by the Workstation service on the WINS client.
- **computer_name[03h]** Registered by the Messenger service on the WINS client.
- **computer_name[06h]** Registered by the *Remote Access Service* (RAS), when started on a RAS Server.
- **computer_name[1Fh]** Registered by the *Network Dynamic Data Exchange* (NetDDE) services, and only appears if the NetDDE services are started on the computer. By default, the NetDDE services are not automatically started.
- **computer_name[20h]** Registered by the Server service on the WINS client.
- **computer_name[21h]** Registered by the RAS Client service, when started on a RAS client.
- **computer_name[BEh]** Registered by the Network Monitoring Agent service, and only appears if the service is started on the computer. If the computer name is not a full 15 characters, the name is padded with plus (+) symbols.
- **computer_name[BFh]** Registered by the Network Monitoring utility (included with Microsoft Systems Management Server). If the computer name is not a full 15 characters, the name is padded with plus (+) symbols.
- **username[03h]** Usernames for the users currently logged on are registered in the WINS database. The username is registered by the Server component so that the user can receive any **net send** commands sent to his username. If more than one user is logged on with the same username, only the first computer at which a user logged on with that username registers the name.
- **domain_name[1Bh]** Registered by the Windows NT Server *primary domain controller* (PDC) running as the domain master browser and that is enabling the remote browsing of domains. When a WINS server is queried for this name, a WINS server returns the IP address of the computer that registered this name.

- **domain_name[1Dh]** Registered only by the local master browser, of which only one can exist for each subnet. This name is used by the backup browsers to communicate with the master browser to retrieve the list of available servers.

  WINS servers always return a positive registration response for domain_name[1D], even though the WINS server does not "register" this name in its database. Therefore, when a WINS server is queried for the domain_name[1D], the WINS server returns a negative response, which causes the client to broadcast to resolve the name.
- **domain_name[00h]** Registered by the Workstation service so that it can receive browser broadcasts from LAN Manager–based computers.
- **domain_name[1Ch]** Registered for use by the domain controllers within the domain; can contain up to 25 IP addresses. One IP address will be that of the PDC, and the other 24 will be the IP addresses of *backup domain controllers* (BDCs).
- **domain_name[1Eh]** Registered for browsing purposes and used by the browsers to elect a master browser When a WINS server receives a name query for a name ending with [1E], the WINS server always returns the network broadcast address for the requesting client's local network.
- **__MSBROWSE__[01h]** Registered by the master browser for each subnet. When a WINS server receives a name query for this name, the WINS server always returns the network broadcast address for the requesting client's local network.

Resolving NetBIOS Names

NetBIOS name services provide a way to register names via broadcast in small networks and via directed communications when a WINS server is available. These names are then available to answer queries in a process called *resolution*. With NetBT, resolution returns an IP address that corresponds to a registered name. NetBIOS doesn't require a name server like DNS or WINS does. Name servers are useful, and necessary under some circumstances, but they are only one of several name resolution mechanisms that NetBIOS can use.

Name Resolution Methods

Windows computers can resolve network names from six possible sources, not counting any LDAP methods. Chapter 14, "Windows Client Configuration and Resolution," describes some other aspects of the query order clients use depending on their Windows version, how they're configured, and what methods they have at their disposal. Figure 17.3 shows what happens when three of the more commonly seen methods are used. Notice that broadcast resolutions don't typically return the addresses of hosts outside the local network, a limitation that's best overcome by deploying a WINS server.

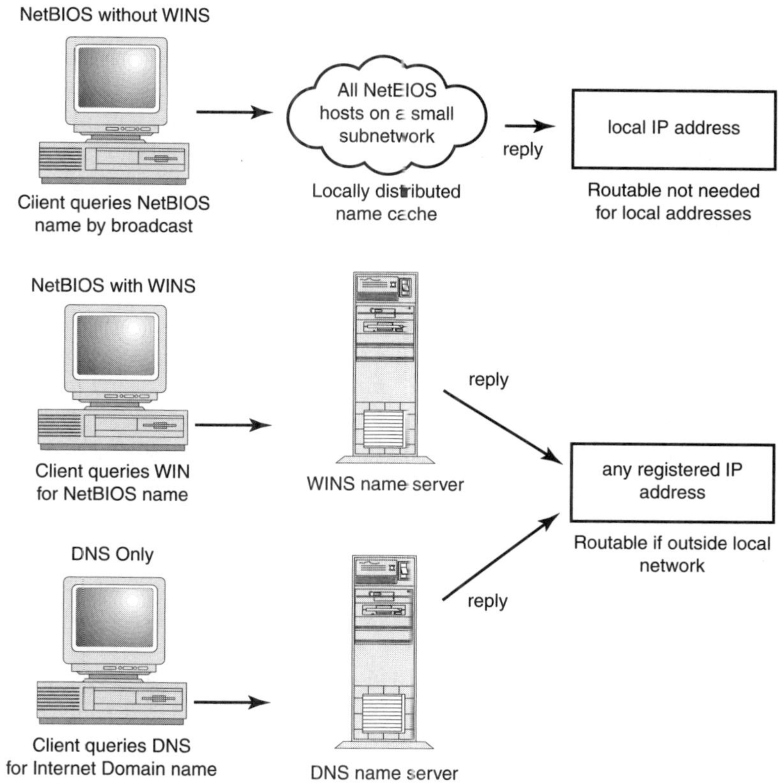

Figure 17.3 NetBIOS and DNS name query methods and results.

The rest of this chapter presumes that TCP/IP is the NetBIOS transport protocol being used. For various reasons, this is increasingly the most commonly used transport protocol. The following are short descriptions of the name resolution sources Windows computers can employ. NetBIOS name resolution sources are primarily the first four listed, especially in NT 4. Under conditions of name normalization between DNS and NetBIOS, however, all are applicable. The last two, namely DNS and HOSTS file, are also used for NetBIOS resolution by some Windows versions when the client is configured to "Enable DNS for Windows Resolution" (or by a similar check box selected on the WINS tab of the TCP/IP Properties dialog box). Window 2000 clients are a little different in always using both DNS and NetBIOS resolution routes if both are available. For Windows 2000 clients, being able to successfully resolve NetBIOS names through DNS/WINS integration can have a performance advantage.

- **NetBIOS name cache.** The locally stored cache of names gathered into each client's memory by preloading (see LMHOSTS in this list) or by successfully resolving an address. Subsequent queries from cache are quick, but cache life for an entry is only 10 minutes, after which it will have to be refreshed.

- **Broadcast queries.** Use the NetBIOS *Datagram Distribution Service* (NDDS) on UDP ports 137 and 138 if names can't be found in cache and a WINS server acting as a *NetBIOS Name Service* (NBNS) is not configured. Broadcasts ask computers on the local network to search their name tables. The target host, if on the same network, responds. Routers normally block NDDS broadcasts, limiting this method to single network segments. If a segment is large, broadcast methods can congest network traffic, in which case further network segmentation or nonbroadcast methods should be used.
- **WINS: Microsoft's *NetBIOS Name Server*.** Clients register and release their own names at the WINS server address they have been configured to use. For resolutions, they query the same address. WINS/client communications are directed messages at UDP ports 137 and 138, enabling them to pass through routers. If WINS fails, some clients can then resort to broadcast queries.
- **LMHOSTS.** A locally stored LAN Manager–style hosts (text) file a client can query if broadcasts fail. LMHOSTS names can be preloaded into local NetBIOS name cache using the #PRE tag to prevent broadcasting for frequently queried hosts. #PRE is also useful for hosts outside the local network so that sure-to-fail broadcasts won't be attempted. Prior to Windows 2000, if a domain controller was not on the client's immediate network, preloading a domain controller's address was required (using the #PRE and #DOM tags) when not using WINS to log on to a Windows domain. Appendix A discusses LMHOSTS file.
- **DNS.** Clients will query a DNS Server for a NetBIOS name. In NT 4 this required checking the Enable DNS for Windows Resolution box in the client's TCP/IP Properties dialog box. With Windows 2000, you get this functionality by default, out of the box. Also, the order for NT and 2000 differs from the default client behavior for other Windows platforms. NT (if DNS is enabled) checks DNS first. Windows 2000, of course, must have DNS configured, and always checks with DNS simultaneously with any NetBIOS resolution efforts. In other platforms, DNS Servers are always queried last, which means that DNS is their least-practical method for resolving NetBIOS names. For this to be of use, DNS integration of WINS (as covered in Chapter 16) should be used, although careful use of the same NetBIOS and DNS host names and planning of domains and the resolver search list is needed.
- **HOST.** A locally stored UNIX-style hosts (text) file, which a client can also query if other methods fail. It is available for use whenever DNS is configured, which for some clients (see DNS entry) is only if all other query methods fail. Appendix A discusses the HOST file.

For both LMHOST and HOST files, the main disadvantage is that maintaining the file on a number of client machines can be a headache. The LMHOSTS, however, can be maintained on a server and included into the clients' LMHOSTS files. In either case, when used, try to use only hosts that are unlikely to change often in these files.

There is much more to the resolver's behavior, such as when it uses which of these methods. For that, however, we need to discuss the next topic, NetBIOS node types.

NetBIOS Node Types

Every NetBIOS computer has a node type. Node type has nothing to do with DNS domains and IP hosts name resolution; it is a configuration parameter for NetBIOS computers only.

Four possible node types exist, specifying which method is used to register and resolve NetBIOS computer names:

- b-node clients use broadcasts only.
- p-node clients use point-to-point with the name server only.
- m-node clients, sometimes called a mixed node, use broadcasts first and then point-to-point.
- h-node clients, sometimes called a hybrid node, use point-to-point first and then broadcasts.

Some Microsoft documents actually mention a fifth, which is an h-node client, that uses DNS first when resolving a NetBIOS name (the Enable DNS for Windows Resolution option again).

A machine configured as a WINS client is an h-node; one with the WINS address empty is a b-node, by default. DHCP options may be conveniently used to set the node type. The m-node and p-node types are rare and, in fact, don't even occur unless configured manually via the Registry or with a DHCP server. The following section briefly discusses p-nodes and m-nodes before moving on to a fuller explanation of the more common h-node and b-node types. During resolution, all node types first check their NetBIOS name cache before then following the resolution behaviors described.

The Rarest Node Types: p-node and m-node

The p-nodes don't ever broadcast to register themselves or to find addresses. They only communicate point-to-point using directed *User Datagram Protocol* (UDP) datagrams and TCP sessions to register with a NetBIOS name server (WINS) and resolve names using the same server.

These p-nodes are a practical configuration to have for clients on the remote side of a WAN link from the main office, for example, where broadcasts would surely fail often because the computers being resolved live on the other side of a router.

The m-nodes broadcast and then go directly to a WINS server if this fails. This is by far the least-used configuration because it's so impractical. The m-nodes might be useful where a remote WAN site has no WINS server and the client mostly needs servers located in the same subnet. If a local broadcast name resolution attempt fails, the client connects with a WINS server over the router, in the main office. The delays could be as long as several seconds, but if there's a slow WAN link anyway, the delay may not bother users.

b-node Resolution

The b-nodes resolve names by broadcast only, which usually means that their effective scope is limited to the single subnet they're on. Because routers typically block broadcasts, they prevent b-nodes from resolving any computers on the other side. These b-nodes never use a name server. Figure 17.4 illustrates the resolution methods available to b-nodes.

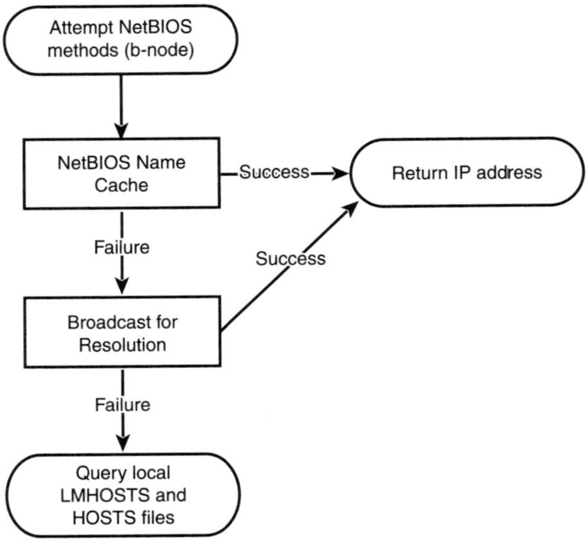

Figure 17.4 Resolution by a NetBIOS b-node.

A downside to b-nodes is that they put unnecessary traffic on the network that can be removed just by employing a WINS server. If you don't want to use WINS and plan to rely mostly on broadcasts, you can still get the benefit of some direct addressing across routers by preloading addresses into the local NetBIOS name cache. To do this, just employ an LMHOST file and the #PRE directive. This technique also reduces broadcasts from b-nodes because every preloaded address that would otherwise require a broadcast will be first found in cache.

h-node resolution

The h-nodes, or hybrid nodes, resolve names by asking the WINS server. If that fails, they broadcast. The h-nodes overcome the limitations of b-node address resolution because the queries pass directly through routers to get to the name server. Because an h-node's resolver already knows the address of one or more WINS servers, it's easy to resolve a target computer's address. Then the client can pass through routers again to connect with the target computer. This is where h-nodes really shine. Figure 17.5

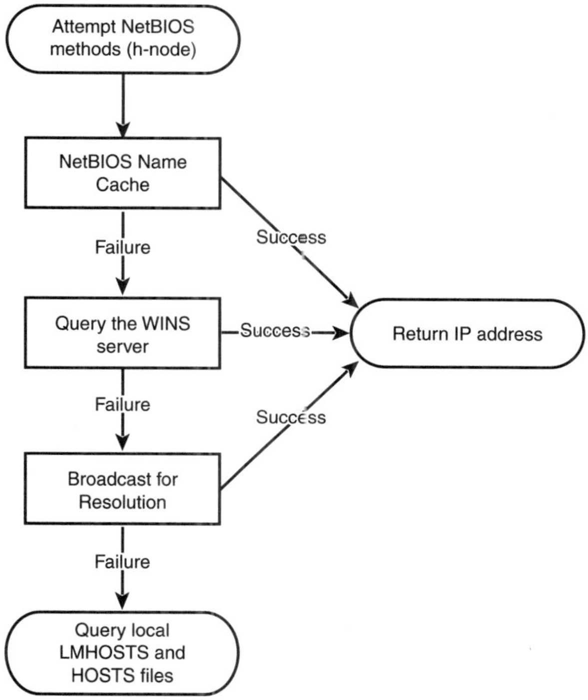

Figure 17.5 Resolution by a NetBIOS h-node.

illustrates how h-nodes work. These nodes can locate any computer that's registered in their same WINS server, in contrast to b-nodes, which typically can't locate any addresses outside their own subnet without resorting to LMHOSTS files.

There's little to dislike about hybrid nodes: Just install a WINS server and use them! The following sequence illustrates the operation of a typical h-node, from startup to shutdown:

1. **Registration.** At startup, the h-node registers its own name and address with the WINS server using point-to-point communications with the server via the address configured in its TCP/IP properties or received from DHCP.
2. **Registration renewal.** The h-node is required to refresh its name registration with the WINS server periodically, with the frequency based on a time provided by the WINS server at registration.
3. **Resolution.** Until shutdown, the h-node resolves names as often as necessary by asking the WINS server directly. The h-node uses addresses the WINS server sends back to directly contact other computers.
4. **Release.** At shutdown, the h-node releases its own registration from the WINS server to indicate that it is no longer available.

The h-nodes always use the WINS server after checking the local NetBIOS name cache. They resort to b-node behavior only if that fails, which is to say, if all configured WINS servers don't respond or if, for some other reason, the client can't register itself upon startup. Even in such cases, the client continues to attempt to contact the WINS server to try to return to a direct addressing method.

Browsing: The NetBIOS Discovery Service

The Browser service creates a list of NetBIOS computer names, sorted by a group name, that is viewable in the Computers Near Me and the Network Neighborhood windows or with the **net view** command. The Browser service monitors announcements made by all the computers on the network and gathers them into lists organized by workgroup or domain. This service itself has no address information, however, and instead relies on the available NetBIOS name services. The Computers Near Me browse list does still work in Windows 2000 when NetBT has been disabled, but it will not show down-level machines. This section deals with NetBT operation of the Browser service.

When you double-click on a name in the browser list, you are requesting a connection directly with the selected computer using the addressing information in the browser list and asking it to enumerate all its shares for you. If this operation is successful, you'll quickly see what printers and files are available. If it is not, something has changed in how to correctly address the listed computer. It might have gone offline more recently than the last refresh of the list, have had its IP changed, and so forth. In this case, the NetBIOS calls initiate attempts to resolve the name afresh, at which point WINS may be queried. If these work, one again sees the available shares and printers, just not as quickly; but if this fails, one receives a message that the name or network path was not found.

Browsing works fine when there are no routers because it discovers computer names primarily by listening to announcement broadcasts. As soon as you introduce routers, browsing can become unreliable and certainly becomes more complex. Think of the browser server as listing everything it can touch. In a routed network, however, it may only touch resources on its segment. So one gets many lists, each isolated in a segment, and somehow these lists must be consolidated to become useful.

The way to establish reliable browsing is to first realize how it works, and second to design the support it needs to function properly.

At least one *local master browser* (LMB) exists for every protocol (such as NetBEUI, TCP/IP, and IPX, if you have a computer using these protocols) on every subnet. Microsoft's documents refer to the master browser and distinguish these from the *domain master browser* (DMB) in several ways. Further, Microsoft's documents refer to LMBs as being either master browsers, backup master browsers, or potential master browsers.

The DMB for a domain has the responsibilities of collecting the lists from the LMBs, consolidating them, and redistributing them to the LMBs. Figure 17.6 illustrates this process. The DMB is also responsible for maintaining and validating the

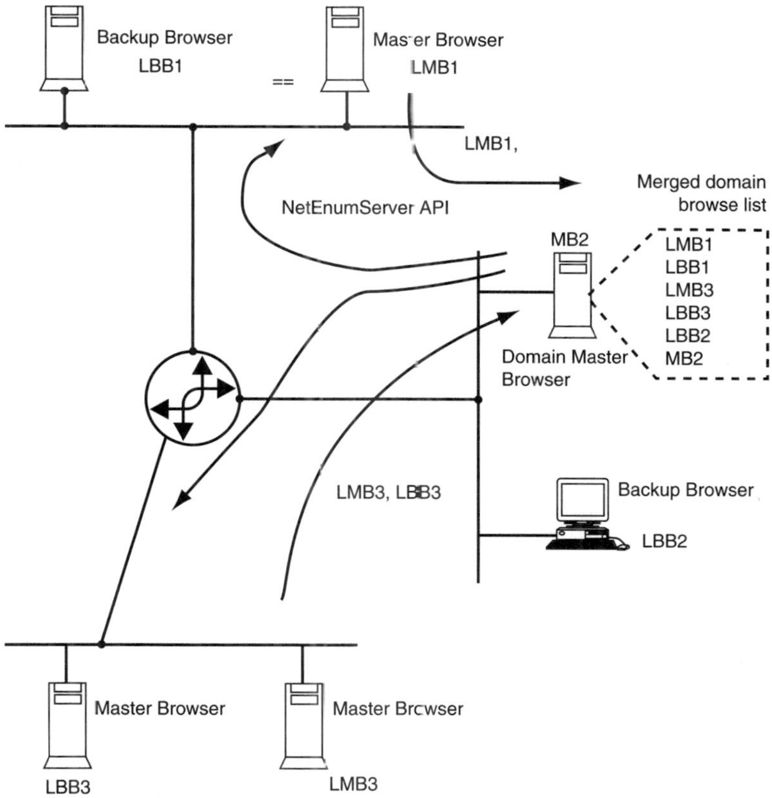

Figure 17.6 The Domain Master Browser controls the browse list.

Entire Network listing distributed to the LMBs. For the Microsoft Windows Network list, in NT 4, the DMB would periodically list all domain name registrations from its WINS server and would then verify their existence.

The different LMB roles are that the master assembles the local list, communicates with the DMB, and controls the backup master browsers. The backup master browsers receive the list from the master and provide the browse list to machines on the local segment when requested. The potential master browsers are there ready to assume one of the other LMB roles if needed.

Note

Here browsers are called either a local master browser or a domain master browser to emphasize the role they play as important to this discussion. LMBs are responsible only for the names on one network segment, or subnet. The DMB is always the primary domain controller and it has domainwide responsibilities over the browser list.

The LMB that NetBIOS contacts and uses for name service is the one for the protocol bound first to the network adapter. It's a good idea to use only one protocol, or as few as absolutely necessary. If you must have more than one, make sure that all the computers have the same binding order to ensure that NetBIOS name services work reliably and efficiently. If you're using TCP/IP, you will also discover an LMB for each workgroup or domain name on the subnet. The rule of thumb here is to reduce the workgroup and domain names, if possible, as this will impact Browser service load on the network.

To make browsing reliable, you need a domain environment with a member on each subnet where you want reliable browsing. In a workgroup model, the browser list is dominated by the highest priority machine booted at the time that identifies itself as being in the workgroup. Priority runs from domain controllers, member servers, professional or workstation versions, down to Windows 9x machines, with higher release levels within each having priority. When a machine attempts to contact an LMB and fails, unless prohibited in its Registry, the machine announces itself on the network as an LMB. On hearing this announcement, higher priority machines counter by announcing their intention to be the LBM. When a machine has made such and announcement and is not challenged, it begins filling the role of LMB for that network subnet. When the LMB is part of a domain environment, the LMB role includes interfacing with the DMB, and it is this that has proved very important in stabilizing the browsing environment.

A PDC is the only server that can act as a DMB. DMBs are critical because they merge the browse lists received from LMBs and then pass them back, sorted. As mentioned previously, DMBs also maintain the list of all domains and workgroups. What might not be apparent is that there is a fairly large amount of network communication involved in all of this list assemblage, checking, and distribution happening at scheduled intervals four or five times per hour. Also, the LMBs are using volunteered machine cycles. On average roughly 3% of the machines on the network will be active as LMBs, not counting potential master browsers. For each protocol on each subnet, there is always at least one LMB. Then, as the number of clients using a protocol on a subnet increases, one LMB is added in a backup role for every 32 clients. In the limit, this works out at a minimum to 1 out of every 32 (or at least approximately 3%) of the machines are volunteering cycles to support browsing.

Use of a WINS server is recommended, because a way is needed for the DMB and the LMBs on various subnets to find one another by querying WINS (for the 1Bh, 1Dh, or 1Eh names). It is possible to use special entries in the LMHOSTS files rather than WINS, which is exactly the solution to Browser service consolidation that was used before WINS. On nomadic networks, such as those where users dial in but no permanent users exist, one can install a Windows NT Server to act as the master browser, and make all dial-in users' workgroup or domain names the same as that used for the server.

In the past one had to take measures to make sure that the DMB didn't lose an election, and it is still a good practice to keep a close watch on this in highly interpenetrating environments. This was previously a problem but seems to have been mostly, if not totally, solved by Service Pack 3 for NT 4. Earlier, multiple domains did not always seem to keep their elections separate at all times. Also earlier, a partial solution was to not put a PDC on the same network segment on which a newer version of Windows Server was running because the newer Windows Server would win the election. This newer version would then become an LMB, sometimes apparently putting the DMB out of business. Browse lists for distinct domains are now more tolerant about sharing network segments without disrupting one another. However, it is worth keeping watch on election results and investigating when it seems needed. Using Network Monitor to sniff election traffic sometimes reveals needlessly repetitive or frequent elections.

To hide a Windows Server service from the browse list, in the usual services location HKEY_LOCAL_MACHINE\System\CurrentControlSet\Services change the following Registry key LanmanServer\Parameters\Hidden value from 0 to 1. The Server service will still be active, and users will be able to connect, but the server won't announce its Server service and won't appear in any browse lists.

NetBIOS on the Wire

This section identifies other factors that relate to NetBIOS and its use. The first is actually a recap of the issues about which administrators have been concerned, but drawn together from their mentions earlier in the chapter. The other headings presented here focus on a few points that may have received too little visibility so far in this chapter.

Issues Faced When Using NetBIOS

Possibly the biggest issue with NetBIOS is the control, for security purposes, of access to the NetBIOS ports. Also very high on the list of concerns is the control of broadcasts. Behind these in importance is the reliability of the Browser service, or more correctly, of WINS services and browser elections. A further issue is network load caused by the Browser service, in elections and in list maintenance.

NetBIOS broadcasts can be controlled by using WINS and having reliable connectivity. A Windows client configured as a WINS client is automatically a hybrid (h-node), whereas one that is not a WINS client defaults to being a broadcast (b-node) client. This preceding fact should not be forgotten if you are configuring Windows 2000 machines and think that you have no need to make them WINS clients.

The reliability of Windows name and browser services has seemingly been corrected by service releases in NT 4. Service pack 3 solved much of the browser election problems, and Service Packs 4 and 5 introduced major changes to WINS to improve manageability and stability of a large WINS database. Also, and importantly, the addition of

nbtstat –rr switch to force client re-registration with WINS has solved the issue of unwanted reboots.

Previously, many wrestled with multihomed machines. With the addition of the multihomed WINS registration type, however, one can steer clear of these old problems, if one just remembers that only the first protocol bound to an adapter, and/or the first IP per adapter can be bound with NetBIOS.

Given that these services are fairly self-maintaining and hopefully now trouble-free, the remaining reasons to be concerned about using them are then the security issues and the network load. The chapter earlier detailed the type of load the Browser service creates, and avoiding broadcast clients has been mentioned. So, there does not appear to be anything else that may be usefully said here, except that one needs to be aware of these.

The simplest way to find out what node type your local machine is configured as is to open a command windows and issue the command **ipconfig /all**. The tool for NetBT that is similar to the **netstat** tool for TCP/IP is **nbtstat**. Both of these were mentioned in Chapter 12, "Troubleshooting Tools and Utilities." Listing 17.1 shows output from the **nbtstat -r** command on a Windows 95/98 computer. The use of **nbtstat -r** reveals resolution statistics since boot up, illustrating in this case that a WINS server resolved all 18 of the name queries the client performed.

Listing 17.1 **nbtstat -r Showing Name Resolution History**

```
C:\WINDOWS>nbtstat -r

NetBIOS Names Resolution and Registration Statistics
----------------------------------------------------
Resolved By Broadcast          = 0
Resolved By Name Server        = 18

Registered By Broadcast        = 0
Registered By Name Server      = 4
```

Listing 17.2 shows output from the **nbtstat -n** command on the same Windows 95/98 computer, revealing what names it successfully registered on the name server.

Listing 17.2 **nbtstat -n Showing Registered Names**

```
C:\WINDOWS>nbtstat -n

Node IpAddress: [10.14.194.8] Scope Id: []
            NetBIOS Local Name Table
   Name                 Type         Status
---------------------------------------------
WS-EXAMPLE     <00>     UNIQUE           Registered
COMPANY                 <00>     GROUP            Registered
WS-EXAMPLE     <03>     UNIQUE           Registered
MEXAMPLE       <03>     UNIQUE   Registered
```

As to the NetBIOS security concerns, these traditionally are that the less information made available to possible villains the better. When WINS is used, this becomes a broader concern, because NetBT enables the distribution of the NetBIOS name information much more broadly than in the network-segment-limited non-WINS forms of NetBIOS. The general recommendation has been to filter out or disable the routing of NetBIOS traffic between your installation and the open network.

NetBIOS on TCP/IP and Other Transport Protocols

NetBIOS over TCP/IP, documented in RFCs 1001 and 1002, is named NetBT, or NBT. NetBIOS provides the same suite of services on NetBEUI , IPX/SPX, or TCP/IP. It's important to note, however, that NetBIOS services operating on one transport protocol can't communicate with NetBIOS services operating on another transport protocol. You can use NetBEUI (which always includes NetBIOS) on one computer, for example, and NetBIOS over TCP/IP on another, but they won't communicate. The earlier Figure 17.1 depicted the relationship of NetBIOS to the familiar seven-layer OSI networking model. What this means is that using NetBIOS at the upper networking layers on two machines to establish a NetBIOS session will only work when the two machines have a common protocol at the lower layers and NetBIOS has been enabled to use that protocol on both machines. For this to work most efficiently, if NetBIOS is enabled on multiple protocols, that common protocol should be the first one tried by NetBIOS.

Server Message Blocks (SMBs) and the Common Internet File System

In an historical overview of NetBIOS, we can't overlook the networking functions of *Server Message Blocks* (SMBs), which give Windows computers a native file redirection facility for accessing remote file systems. Some developers refer to SMB as the LanMan protocol because it was first made popular by 3Com's now defunct LAN Manager products. It is more correct to think of the session and datagram services of NetBIOS when talking of SMB than to even mention the name services.

Although SMB and NetBIOS have a closely related history, SMB is more enduring. It was subsumed into the open *Common Internet File System* (CIFS) standard proposed by Microsoft, Network Appliance, and others. The CIFS proposal was much like the *Network File System* (NFS) common on UNIX computers, but with some significant feature differences.

> **Note**
>
> NetBIOS uses the well-known TCP/IP ports:
>
> - NetBT name services use UDP port 137.
> - NetBT session services use TCP port 139.
> - NetBT datagram services use UDP port 138.

With the release of Windows 2000, SMB needed a new way to operate because of the ability to disable NetBT on Windows 2000 computers. To provide for SMB, a NetBT-disabled Windows 2000 machine will use DNS resolution to obtain the IP of the target machine. At that point, it will use port 445 to establish a session with the machine for SMB use. Microsoft has dubbed this *direct hosting*. If both machines can support direct hosting, SMB sessions are possible without the use of NetBT—which is to say, when the TCP/IP properties switch to disable, NetBIOS over TCP/IP is used.

There is increasing use of SMB in the popular open-licensed application for UNIX named SAMBA. SAMBA enables UNIX hosts to share files and printers with Windows computers, and in most ways behaves as a down-level client that may be WINS enabled. Now through direct hosting in Windows 2000, SMB support does not require NetBT. It is fair to say that the NetBIOS legacy will remain part of the computing scene for at least the near term.

Summary

This chapter introduced the main features of NetBIOS, focusing on NetBT. It presented concepts to help administrators make design decisions affecting WINS, browsing, and other services in a Windows networking environment.

IV

Appendices

A

The LMHOSTS and HOSTS Files

THIS APPENDIX OFFERS INFORMATION ABOUT the LMHOSTS file used for NetBIOS name resolution and the HOSTS file used for DNS name resolution in Windows systems. At one time, these files were all important, but they have fallen to disuse in recent years. They are quite useful still for certain purposes. Many administrators, perhaps from thoroughness or from force of habit, still like to configure their key servers with LMHOSTS files both to preload the NetBIOS cache and to ensure a fallback resolution in the event the other methods are disrupted. These files are also very useful for a user who likes pet private names, or the developer who needs shortcuts to test Web sites or temporary machines that will not be formally registered with the name services.

When these files are used, it is not unwise to place individual host entries into both in parallel, unless one is absolutely sure of his resolver's search order. One thing, also, to keep in mind is that each is parsed on demand when needed from the top down. For this reason, it is best to list the most frequent entries highest, to place all entries above any comments, and actually, to trim the files to contain nothing but the needed entries.

LMHOSTS File

The LMHOSTS file plays two roles. First, it is parsed to preload the NetBIOS resolver cache (that can be examined with **nbtstat –n**). Second, it is the NetBT resolver's method of last resort. The LMHOSTS file is really easier to use than it may appear from the following. Just remember to make sure the Enable LMHOSTS Lookup check box is checked in the WINS area of your TCP/IP Properties dialog box.

LMHOSTS is kept in the %windir%\drivers\etc directory, where you'll find a sample named LMHOSTS.SAM that Microsoft provides to get you started. If you decide to use the sample, remove the .SAM extension. LMHOSTS is much like a hosts file on UNIX, but, as mentioned earlier, it works with NetBIOS names and uses the same syntax as Microsoft LAN Manager 2.x. LMHOSTS functions like a HOSTS file for simple name-to-address mappings, but it also supports directives that aren't allowed in a HOSTS file.

The # character appearing as the first character on a line is the comment symbol, indicating that the line contains only comments for users to read. If the characters immediately following the # are reserved words, as shown in Table A.1, however, they are interpreted as directives, not comments. These directives are mostly used to preload the cache. The LMHOST file management can be centralized off of a server by using the INCLUDE capability.

Table A.1 **Reserved Words in the LMHOSTS.SAM File**

Reserved Word	**Description**
#PRE	Preloads an entry into the NetBIOS name cache, where it remains as long as the computer is running. It's required and must precede computer names that will be # INCLUDED. Up to 100 entries may be preloaded.
#DOM: <domain_name>	Identifies the name of a computer acting as a domain controller. It's important, especially in the absence of WINS, that DCs be identified on any domain member. The entry will have the form <IP address><machine_name>#PRE #DOM: <domain_name>.
#BEGIN_ALTERNATE	Indicates the beginning of a section where #INCLUDE <filename> statements exist. The first <filename> successfully included (loaded) in any group during processing causes the others to be skipped.
#INCLUDE <filename>	Used to specify one or more LMHOST files on other computers to be read and included in the list of names and addresses. Uses UNC syntax for <filename>.
#END_ALTERNATE	Indicates the end of a section where #INCLUDE statements exists, delimiting the group.

Reserved Word	Description
\0xnn	Specifies the hex value of a nonprinting character to be appended to the NetBIOS name at the 16th byte. This enables you to manually identify service codes with computers in a manner similar to the registrations in WINS. If you use this feature with a name with fewer than 15 characters, enclose the name in quotation marks, pad it with spaces, and insert the \xnn within the quotation marks beginning at the 16th character position. See Table 17.1 for the resource codes these represent. Other special application codes may also be used as documented in product literature. Note that this feature is not backward compatible with LAN Manager.

There is probably no more direct explanation of the use of the LMHOSTS file than Microsoft's own in its distributed sample file. Listing A.1 is the sample (found in %windir%\system32\drivers\etc as LMHOSTS.SAM) automatically installed on Windows 2000/NT computers.

Listing A.1 **The Sample LMHOSTS.SAM* File**

```
#
# This is a sample LMHOSTS file used by the Microsoft TCP/IP for Windows.
#
# This file contains the mappings of IP addresses to NT computernames
# (NetBIOS) names.  Each entry should be kept on an individual line.
# The IP address should be placed in the first column followed by the
# corresponding computername. The address and the comptername
# should be separated by at least one space or tab. The ?#? character
# is generally used to denote the start of a comment (see the exceptions
# below).
#
# This file is compatible with Microsoft LAN Manager 2.x TCP/IP lmhosts
# files and offers the following extensions:
#
#      #PRE
#      #DOM:<domain>
#      #INCLUDE <filename>
#      #BEGIN_ALTERNATE
#      #END_ALTERNATE
#      \0xnn (non-printing character support)
#
# Following any entry in the file with the characters "#PRE" will cause
# the entry to be preloaded into the name cache. By default, entries are
# not preloaded, but are parsed only after dynamic name resolution fails.
#
```

continues

```
# Following an entry with the "#DOM:<domain>" tag will associate the
# entry with the domain specified by <domain>. This affects how the
# browser and logon services behave in TCP/IP environments. To preload
# the host name associated with #DOM entry, it is necessary to also add a
# #PRE to the line. The <domain> is always preloaded although it will not
# be shown when the name cache is viewed.
#
# Specifying "#INCLUDE <filename>" will force the RFC NetBIOS (NBT)
# software to seek the specified <filename> and parse it as if it were
# local. <filename> is generally a UNC-based name, allowing a
# centralized lmhosts file to be maintained on a server.
# It is ALWAYS necessary to provide a mapping for the IP address of the
# server prior to the #INCLUDE. This mapping must use the #PRE directive.
# In addition the share "public" in the example below must be in the
# LanManServer list of  "NullSessionShares" in order for client machines to
# be able to read the lmhosts file successfully. This key is under
# \machine\system\currentcontrolset\services\lanmanserver\parameters\
nullsessionshares
# in the registry.  Simply add "public" to the list found there.
#
# The #BEGIN_ and #END_ALTERNATE keywords allow multiple #INCLUDE
# statements to be grouped together. Any single successful include
# will cause the group to succeed.
#
# Finally, non-printing characters can be embedded in mappings by
# first surrounding the NetBIOS name in quotations, then using the
# \0xnn notation to specify a hex value for a non-printing character.
#
# The following example illustrates all of these extensions:
#
# 102.54.94.97     rhino         #PRE #DOM:networking  #net group's DC
# 102.54.94.102    "appname  \0x14"                    #special app server
# 102.54.94.123    popular            #PRE             #source server
# 102.54.94.117    localsrv           #PRE             #needed for the include
#
# #BEGIN_ALTERNATE
# #INCLUDE \\localsrv\public\lmhosts
# #INCLUDE \\rhino\public\lmhosts
# #END_ALTERNATE
#
# In the above example, the "appname" server contains a special
# character in its name, the "popular" and "localsrv" server names are
# preloaded, and the "rhino" server name is specified so it can be used
# to later #INCLUDE a centrally maintained lmhosts file if the "localsrv"
# system is unavailable.
#
# Note that the whole file is parsed including comments on each lookup,
# so keeping the number of comments to a minimum will improve performance.
# Therefore it is not advisable to simply add lmhosts file entries onto the
# end of this file.
```

HOSTS File

The HOSTS file plays the exact same role in Windows systems as for UNIX systems. You might recall that at one time, before BIND, all network host name resolution on TCP/IP was done with HOSTS files. It provides a local IP address–to–DNS host name table. If the NetBT resolver is configured to use DNS for NetBIOS names, however, this file will also be checked by that resolver rather than just by the DNS resolver.

The HOSTS file is also stored in the %windir%\drivers\etc directory. The file syntax is pretty self-explanatory, except that no mention is made that one can list multiple names per IP address line. In other words, with a line like

```
charlie  paul  tom.here
```

one could ping tom.here and it would be the same as ping 102.54.94.97, which it in fact would be. The names given can of course also be the proper FQDNs for the listed IP addresses.

Listing A.2 is the Microsoft's sample HOSTS file that comes with Windows 2000/NT.

Listing A.2 **The Sample HOSTS* File**

```
#
# This is a sample HOSTS file used by Microsoft TCP/IP for Windows NT.
#
# This file contains the mappings of IP addresses to host names. Each
# entry should be kept on an individual line. The IP address should
# be placed in the first column followed by the corresponding host name.
# The IP address and the host name should be separated by at least one
# space.
#
# Additionally, comments (such as these) may be inserted on individual
# lines or following the machine name denoted by a `#' symbol.
#
# For example:
#
#      102.54.94.97     rhino.acme.com          # source server
#       38.25.63.10     x.acme.com              # x client host
127.0.0.1       localhost
```

B

RFCs Related to DNS

REQUEST FOR COMMENT (RFC)DOCUMENTS SERVE SEVERAL PURPOSES. Some RFCs describe how the Internet works, defining standards. Others are informational, and others, still, are for discussion, providing suggestions that can lead to future standards or observations that can promote better practices. At the top of every RFC is a statement of its status, indicating what kind of document it is.

The RFCs are maintained by the RFC editor at the Information Sciences Institute (ISI), who is responsible for publishing the documents in their final form. RFCs can be found by visiting a number of sites, with `http://www.rfc-editor.org/rfc.html` being the most direct. For an overview of what RFCs are and how the RFC process works, visit `http://www.rfc-editor.org`. If you know the RFC `NNNN` number, forming a link to the Internet Engineering Task Force (IETF) at `http://www.ietf.org/rfc/rfcNNNN.txt` is direct. The IETF home `http://www.ietf.org` is also the best route to the Internet drafts.

The rest of the appendix provides the RFC numbers for the RFCs concerning DNS, NetBIOS, and the technologies used in association with DNS (see Table B.1). For brevity in this list, X.500, Lightweight Directory Access Protocol (LDAP), public key infrastructure (PKI), and related RFCs have been excluded. Some of the current

IETF drafts that are particularly relevant to DNS, or rather Windows 2000 DNS, are noted at the end.

Table B.1 **RFCs Used with DNS, NetBIOS, and Associated Technologies**

RFC	Description
RFC 819:	*The Domain Naming Convention for Internet User Applications*
RFC 830:	*A Distributed System for Internet Name Service*
RFC 920:	*Domain Requirements*
RFC 974:	*Mail Routing and the Domain System*
RFC 986:	*Guidelines for the Use of Internet-IP Addresses in Connectionless-Mode Network Protocol*
RFC 1001:	*Protocol Standard for a NetBIOS Service on a TCP/UDP Transport: Concepts and Methods*
RFC 1002:	*Protocol Standard for a NetBIOS Service on a TCP/UDP Transport: Detailed Specifications*
RFC 1032:	*Domain Administrators Guide*
RFC 1033:	*Domain Administrators Operations Guide*
RFC 1034:	*Domain Names: Concepts and Facilities*
RFC 1035:	*Domain Names: Implementation and Specification*
RFC 1069:	*Guidelines for the Use of Internet-IP Addresses in ISO Connectionless-Mode Network Protocols*
RFC 1101:	*DNS Encoding of Network Names and Other Types*
RFC 1118:	*The Hitchhiker's Guide to the Internet*
RFC 1122:	*Requirements for Internet Hosts—Communication Layers*
RFC 1123:	*Requirements for Internet Hosts—Application and Support*
RFC 1183:	*New DNS RR Definitions* (Updates RFC 1034 and 1035)
RFC 1348:	*DNS NSAP RRs* (Made obsolete by RFC 1637)
RFC 1464:	*Using the Domain Name System to Store Arbitrary String Attributes*
RFC 1508:	*Generic Security Service Application Program Interface* (Made obsolete by RFC 2078)
RFC 1510:	*The Kerberos Network Authentication Service (V5)*
RFC 1519:	*Classless Inter-Domain Routing (CIDR): An Address Assignment and Aggregation Strategy*
RFC 1531:	*Dynamic Host Configuration Protocol*
RFC 1535:	*A Security Problem and Proposed Correction with Widely Deployed DNS Software*
RFC 1536:	*Common DNS Implementation Errors and Suggested Fixes*
RFC 1537:	*Common DNS Data File Configuration Errors*
RFC 1591:	*Domain Name System Structure and Delegation*
RFC 1597:	*Address Allocation for Private Internets*
RFC 1611:	*DNS Server MIB Extension*
RFC 1612:	*DNS Resolver MIB Extension*

continues

RFC	Description
RFC 1627:	*Network 10 Considered Harmful (Some Practices Shouldn't be Codified)*
RFC 1631:	*The IP Network Address Translator*
RFC 1632:	*A Revised Catalog of Available X.500 Implementations*
RFC 1637:	*DNS NSAP Resource Records* (Obsoletes RFC 1348)
RFC 1664:	*Using the Internet DNS to Distribute RFC 1327 Mail Address Mapping Tables*
RFC 1700:	*Assigned Numbers*
RFC 1706:	*DNS NSAP Resource Records* (Obsoletes RFC 1637)
RFC 1712:	*DNS Encoding of Geographical Location*
RFC 1713:	*Tools for DNS Debugging*
RFC 1794:	*DNS Support for Load Balancing*
RFC 1876:	*A Means for Expressing Location Information in the Domain Name System*
RFC 1884:	*IP version 6 Addressing Architecture*
RFC 1886:	*DNS Extensions to Support IP version 6*
RFC 1912:	*Common DNS Operational and Configuration Errors*
RFC 1964:	*The Kerberos Version 5 GSS-API Mechanism*
RFC 1982:	*Serial Number Arithmetic* (Updates RFC 1034 and 1035)
RFC 1995:	*Incremental Zone Transfer in DNS*
RFC 1996:	*A Mechanism for Prompt Notification of Zone Changes (DNS NOTIFY)*
RFC 2010:	*Operational Criteria for Root Name Servers*
RFC 2025:	*The Simple Public-Key GSS-API Mechanism (SPKM)*
RFC 2044:	*UTF-8, a Transformation Format of Unicode and ISO 10646*
RFC 2052:	*A DNS RR for Specifying the Location of Services (DNS SRV)*
RFC 2065:	*Domain Name System Security Extensions* (Made obsolete by RFC 2535)
RFC 2078:	*Generic Security Service Application Program Interface, Version 2* (Obsoletes RFC 1508)
RFC 2097:	*The PPP NetBIOS Frames Control Protocol (NBFCP)*
RFC 2100:	*The Naming of Hosts*
RFC 2131:	*Dynamic Host Configuration Protocol*
RFC 2132:	*DHCP Options and BOOTP Vendor Extensions*
RFC 2136:	*Dynamic Updates in the Domain Name System (DNS UPDATE)* (Updates RFC 1035)
RFC 2137:	*Secure Domain Name System Dynamic Update* (Updates RFC 1035)
RFC 2148:	*Deployment of the Internet White Pages Service*
RFC 2151:	*A Primer on Internet and TCP/IP Tools and Utilities*
RFC 2163:	*Using the Internet DNS to Distribute MIXER Conformant Global Address Mapping (MCGAM)*
RFC 2168:	*Resolution of Uniform Resource Identifiers using the Domain Name System*
RFC 2181:	*Clarifications to the DNS Specification*
RFC 2182:	*Selection and Operation of Secondary DNS Servers*
RFC 2196:	*Site Security Handbook*
RFC 2200:	*Internet Official Protocol Standards*

continues

Table B.1 **Continued**

RFC	Description
RFC 2203:	*RPCSEC_GSS Protocol Specification*
RFC 2219:	*Use of DNS Aliases for Network Services*
RFC 2279:	*UTF-8, a Transformation Format of ISO 10646*
RFC 2308:	*Negative Caching of DNS Queries (DNS NCACHE)* (Updates RFC 1034 and 1035)
RFC 2317:	*Classless IN-ADDR.ARPA Delegation*
RFC 2345:	*Domain Names and Company Name Retrieval*
RFC 2352:	*A Convention for Using Legal Names as Domain Names*
RFC 2478:	*The Simple and Protected GSS-API Negotiation Mechanism*
RFC 2535:	*Domain Name System Security Extensions* (Updates RFC 2181, 1035, 1034)
RFC 2536:	*DSA KEYs and SIGs in the Domain Name System*
RFC 2537:	*RSA/MD5 KEYs and SIGs in the Domain Name System*
RFC 2538:	*Storing Certificates in the Domain Name System*
RFC 2539:	*Storage of Diffie-Hellman Keys in the Domain Name System*
RFC 2540:	*Detached Domain Name System (DNS) Information*
RFC 2541:	*DNS Security Operational Considerations*
RFC 2671:	*Extension Mechanisms for DNS (EDNS0)*
RFC 2672:	*Non-Terminal DNS Name Redirection (DNAME RR)*
RFC 2279:	*UTF-8, a Transformation Format of ISO 10646* (Obsoletes RFC 2044)
RFC 2308:	*Negative Caching of DNS Queries (DNS NCACHE)*
RFC 2317:	*Classless IN-ADDR.ARPA Delegation*
RFC 2345:	*Domain Names and Company Name Retrieval*
RFC 2517:	*Building Directories from DNS*
RFC 2535:	*Domain Name System Security Extensions* (Obsoletes RFC 2065)
RFC 2541:	*DNS Security Operational Considerations*
RFC 2606:	*Reserved Top-Level DNS Names*
RFC 2694:	*DNS Extensions to Network Address Translators (DNS_ALG)*

There are several current changes to the RFC standards that are tied up in the draft stage of the process. You might find that some things in Windows 2000 do not have a consistent list of RFC documents to back up what is being done. Microsoft has a number of white papers available on their Web site that can help you decipher what the thoughts were on each subject and how it relates to IETF drafts. You can also research the previously listed sites, `http://www.rfceditor.org/rfc.html` and `http://www.ietf.org/ID.html`, to see these drafts as they progress through revisions to either become RFC standards or fail to do so.

IETF drafts of particular note to the initial release of Windows 2000 are (you will likely need to search for higher numbered versions):

RFC 2052, *A DNS RR for specifying the location of services (DNS SRV),* has been under a revision that is sometimes referred to as RFC 2052bis, which, among other things, introduced the "_" underscores into the service and protocol specification seen in the SRV RRs. The current draft, dated November 1999, has the same title as RFC 2052 (see `http://www.ietf.org/internet-drafts/draft-ietf-dnsind-rfc2052bis-05.txt`).

The IETF draft *Interaction between DHCP and DNS* relates to the update of DNS by Dynamic Host Configuration Protocol (DHCP), dated October 1999 (see `http://www.ietf.org/internet-drafts/draft-ietf-dhc-dhcp-dns-11.txt`).

Included in Windows 2000, but not fully documented, is *The User Class Option for DHCP*, dated October 1999 (see `http://www.ietf.org/internet-drafts/draft-ietf-dhc-userclass-04.txt`).

Discovering LDAP Services with DNS, dated September 1999, makes a brief motion toward stating how DNS is being used at such uppermost levels as the directory services within the Windows 2000 LDAP architecture (see `http://www.ietf.org/internet-drafts/draft-ietf-ldapext-locate-00.txt`).

Relating to the securing of DNS, especially the dynamic update process, are: *Secret Key Transaction Authentication for DNS (TSIG)*, dated December 1999 (see `http://www.ietf.org/internet-drafts/draft-ietf-dnsind-tsig-12.txt`), *Secret Key Establishment for DNS (TKEY RR)*, dated December 1999 (see `http://www.ietf.org/internet-drafts/draft-ietf-dnsind-tkey-02.txt`), and *GSS Algorithm for TSIG (GSS-TSIG)*, dated June 1999 (see `http://www.ietf.org/internet-drafts/draft-skwan-gss-tsig-04.txt`).

On the use of UTF-8 labels in DNS is *Using the UTF-8 Character Set in the Domain Name System*, dated June 1999 (see `http://www.ietf.org/internet-drafts/draft-skwan-utf8-dns-02.txt`).

C

Top-Level Internet Domains

THIS APPENDIX PROVIDES A LIST of top-level domains (TLDs). In the domain name system (DNS), all DNS servers and computer hosts belong to one country or one type of organization. You've probably seen some of these TLDs. They also frequently appear at the end of Web server names: `com` is for commercial organizations, `edu` is for educational organizations, `net` is for network support centers, and so on. These and others appear in Table C.2. Table C.1 contains examples of TLDs for countries.

TLDs can contain many computer host names, but the DNS servers that service TLDs don't usually store the names of all those hosts. This is important. There are simply too many names for one server to manage. Instead, top-level DNS servers have delegation entries that refer to lower-level DNS servers.

Low-level domain names in the DNS name hierarchy can change frequently and without many consequences, just as the leaves and branches of a real tree can change by season or by trimming. However, TLD names are like large tree branches. Although not necessarily permanent, TLDs can't change easily or frequently because they support all the lower domains. Other proposed TLDs are listed in Table C.3.

Some TLDs have their own DNS servers. Others are managed by root DNS servers, such as the us and edu domains illustrated in Figure 2.6 in Chapter 2, "How DNS Works".

Table C.1 **Country Code Top-Level Internet Domains**

Domain Name	Country or Region
AC	Ascension Island
AD	Andorra
AE	United Arab Emirates
AF	Afghanistan
AG	Antigua and Barbuda
AI	Anguilla
AL	Albania
AM	Armenia
AN	Netherlands Antilles
AO	Angola
AQ	Antarctica
AR	Argentina
AS	American Samoa
AT	Austria
AU	Australia
AW	Aruba
AZ	Azerbaijan
BA	Bosnia and Herzegovina
BB	Barbados
BD	Bangladesh
BE	Belgium
BF	Burkina Faso
BG	Bulgaria
BH	Bahrain
BI	Burundi
BJ	Benin
BM	Bermuda
BN	Brunei Darussalam
BO	Bolivia
BR	Brazil
BS	Bahamas
BT	Bhutan
BV	Bouvet Island
BW	Botswana
BY	Belarus
BZ	Belize

continues

Domain Name	Country or Region
CA	Canada
CC	Cocos (Keeling) Islands
CD	Congo, Democratic Republic of the
CF	Central African Republic
CG	Congo, Republic of the
CH	Switzerland
CI	Cote d'Ivoire (Ivory Coast)
CK	Cook Islands
CL	Chile
CM	Cameroon
CN	China
CO	Colombia
CR	Costa Rica
CU	Cuba
CV	Cape Verde
CX	Christmas Island
CY	Cyprus
CZ	Czech Republic
DE	Germany
DJ	Djibouti
DK	Denmark
DM	Dominica
DO	Dominican Republic
DZ	Algeria
EC	Ecuador
EE	Estonia
EG	Egypt
EH	Western Sahara
ER	Eritrea
ES	Spain
ET	Ethiopia
FI	Finland
FJ	Fiji
FK	Falkland Islands (Malvinas)
FM	Micronesia, Federated States of
FO	Faroe Islands
FR	France
GA	Gabon
GD	Grenada
GE	Georgia
GF	French Guiana

Table C.1 **Continued**

Domain Name	Country or Region
GG	Guernsey
GH	Ghana
GI	Gibraltar
GL	Greenland
GM	Gambia
GN	Guinea
GP	Guadeloupe
GQ	Equatorial Guinea
GR	Greece
GS	South Georgia and the South Sandwich Islands
GT	Guatemala
GU	Guam
GW	Guinea Bissau
GY	Guyana
HK	Hong Kong
HM	Heard and McDonald Islands
HN	Honduras
HR	Croatia/Hrvatska
HT	Haiti
HU	Hungary
ID	Indonesia
IE	Ireland
IL	Israel
IM	Isle of Man
IN	India
IO	British Indian Ocean Territory (Diego Garcia Islands)
IQ	Iraq
IR	Iran (Islamic Republic of)
IS	Iceland
IT	Italy
JE	Jersey
JM	Jamaica
JO	Jordan
JP	Japan
KE	Kenya
KG	Kyrgyzstan
KH	Cambodia
KI	Kiribati
KM	Comoros

continues

Domain Name	Country or Region
KN	Saint Kitts, Nevis, and Anguilla
KP	Korea, Democratic People's Republic (North Korea)
KR	Korea, Republic of (South Korea)
KW	Kuwait
KY	Cayman Islands
KZ	Kazakhstan
LA	Laos, People's Democratic Republic
LB	Lebanon
LC	Saint Lucia
LI	Liechtenstein
LK	Sri Lanka
LR	Liberia
LS	Lesotho
LT	Lithuania
LU	Luxembourg
LV	Latvia
LY	Libyan Arab Jamahiriya
MA	Morocco
MC	Monaco
MD	Moldova, Republic of
MG	Madagascar
MH	Marshall Islands
MK	Macedonia
ML	Mali
MM	Myanmar
MN	Mongolia
MO	Macau
MP	Northern Mariana Islands
MQ	Martinique
MR	Mauritania
MS	Montserrat
MT	Malta
MU	Mauritius
MV	Maldives
MW	Malawi
MX	Mexico
MY	Malaysia
MZ	Mozambique
NA	Namibia
NC	New Caledonia

continues

Table C.1 **Continued**

Domain Name	Country or Region
NE	Niger
NF	Norfolk Island
NG	Nigeria
NI	Nicaragua
NL	Netherlands
NO	Norway
NP	Nepal
NR	Nauru
NT	Neutral Zone
NU	Niue
NZ	New Zealand
OM	Oman
PA	Panama
PE	Peru
PF	French Polynesia
PG	Papua New Guinea
PH	Philippines
PK	Pakistan
PL	Poland
PM	Saint Pierre and Miquelon
PN	Pitcairn
PR	Puerto Rico
PT	Portugal
PW	Palau
PY	Paraguay
QA	Qatar
RE	Reunion Island
RO	Romania
RU	Russian Federation
RW	Rwanda
SA	Saudi Arabia
SB	Solomon Islands
SC	Seychelles
SD	Sudan
SE	Sweden
SG	Singapore
SH	Saint Helena
SI	Slovenia
SJ	Svalbard and Jan Mayen Islands
SK	Slovak Republic

continues

Domain Name	Country or Region
SL	Sierra Leone
SM	San Marino
SN	Senegal
SO	Somalia
SR	Suriname
ST	Saint Tome and Principe
SV	El Salvador
SY	Syrian Arab Republic
SZ	Swaziland
TC	Turks and Caicos Islands
TD	Chad
TF	French Southern Territory
TG	Togo
TH	Thailand
TJ	Tajikistan
TK	Tokelau
TM	Turkmenistan
TN	Tunisia
TO	Tonga
TP	East Timor
TR	Turkey
TT	Trinidad and Tobago
TV	Tuvalu
TW	Taiwan
TZ	Tanzania
UA	Ukraine
UG	Uganda
UK	United Kingdom (Great Britain)
UM	US Minor Outlying Islands
US	United States of America
UY	Uruguay
UZ	Uzbekistan
VA	Vatican City State (Holy See)
VC	Saint Vincent and Grenadines
VE	Venezuela
VG	Virgin Islands (British)
VI	Virgin Islands (US)
VN	Vietnam
VU	Vanuatu
WF	Wallis and Futuna Islands
WS	Samoa

continues

Table C.1 **Continued**

Domain Name	Country or Region
YE	Yemen
YT	Mayotte
YU	Yugoslavia
ZA	South Africa
ZM	Zambia
ZR	Zaire
ZW	Zimbabwe

Table C.2 **Standard TLDs**

Organization	Scope
COM	Commercial Sites
EDU	Educational Sites
GOV	US Government Sites
INT	International Organizations
MIL	US Military Sites
NET	Network Related Sites
ORG	Organizations

Table C.3 **Other Proposed TLDs**

Organization	Scope
FIRM	For businesses, or firms
SHOP	For businesses offering goods to purchase (initially introduced as .STORE)
WEB	For entities emphasizing activities related to the WWW
ARTS	For entities emphasizing cultural and entertainment activities
REC	For entities emphasizing recreation/ entertainment activities
INFO	For entities providing information services
NOM	For those wishing individual or personal nomenclature

D

Registering Addresses on the Internet

INTERNET DNS DELEGATIONS ARE HANDLED BY THE *InterNIC* (Internet Network Information Center). (Name registrations were previously managed exclusively by Network Solutions, Inc.) InterNIC is a registered name of the U.S. Department of Commerce and was previously used exclusively by Network Solutions, Inc. The *Internet Corporation for Assigned Names and Numbers* (ICANN) is the new nonprofit organization taking responsibility from the U.S. government over a number of Internet functions, including the domain name system (www.icann.org). A group of Accredited Registrars are authorized by ICANN to register names in the .com, .org, and .net top-level domains. Any network entity that an individual or organization wants to use on the Internet must have a registered name, delegated by InterNIC, to be seen by others. Network Solutions is no longer the only provider of registration; you may want to contact a number of others. ICANN maintains a complete list of registrars at www.icann.org/registrars/accredited-list.html, and InterNIC maintains a list of active registrars at www.internic.net/regist.html.

The process is relatively painless and the cost is minimal. Organizations on the Net will perform the service of registering domains, but they often charge an additional fee. The standard charge for registering a .com, .org, or .net domain is $35 per year, but the amount you'll be charged to register a domain is $70 to cover the first two years. After two years, a new invoice will be issued to you for $35 each year for renewal. Many registrars are also offering renewals for multiple years, up to ten in some cases. Registrars are free to set their charges, however, and may offer bundled packages that increase or reduce the name registration costs. Country code domains can be considerably more expensive, with each country code being independently administered. The .us TLD is handled at www.nic.us, for example, and the *Internet Assigned Numbers Authority* (IANA) maintains an index at www.iana.org/cctld.html that lists the authorities for each country code.

Organization new to the Internet must deal with a couple of issues before registering. You must have a valid IP network address. That is, the numbers used for the IP addresses of your hosts must be assigned (numbers cannot be randomly chosen), and the network portion of the IP address must be routable. The Internet service provider you'll use to provide your connection to the Internet usually deals with both issues.

The next thing to do is decide on a domain name. In reality, having several names in mind is wise because someone else might have already registered your first and second choices. You can check whether the name you want is already registered with the **whois <domain name>** command, or by using a Web interface that many sites, including Network Solutions provides at **Error! Hyperlink reference not valid.** www.networksolutions.com/cgi-bin/whois/whois. After you have selected a good domain name, complete the registration forms and submit them.

You can register a domain name in a few different ways. The easiest is to follow the step-by-step Web instructions found on your chosen registrar's Web page. The preceding version of this book presented Network Solution's agreement (version 4.0) and template, because it was the only alternative at the time. You can also download the text version of the Network Solution's form directly from ftp://rs.internic.net/templates/domain-template.txt. For one running DNS, this template has been the quickest, simplest way to occasionally register names. Internet addresses will either be managed by your ISP, delegated to you from your ISP, or assigned by the *American Registry for Internet Numbers* (ARIN), http://www.arin.net. Many service providers will not delegate authority for blocks of addresses smaller than a /24 (Class C network). Your ability to manage your own reverse zone will depend highly on the size of your organization and your justification/need for address space. The template form received is available at the ftp site listed just below, along with the legal agreement to which it refers. Take these as examples, and verify the current information at the source when applying for a name registration; the information that you are required to provide is outlined below. The NIC handle will be assigned after you complete your first registration, and can be referenced on any future submissions you may make. Questions 9 and 10 are only for new registrations.

[Templates are available at ftp://www.networksolutions.com/templates]

Authorization

0a. (N)ew (M)odify (D)elete......:

0b. Auth Scheme..................:

0c. Auth Info....................:

1. Comments.....................:

2. Complete Domain Name.........:

Organization Using Domain Name
3a. Organization Name............:
3b. Street Address...............:
3c. City.........................:
3d. State........................:
3e. Postal Code..................:
3f. Country......................:

Administrative Contact
4a. NIC Handle (if known)........:
4b. (I)ndividual (R)ole..........:
4c. Name (Last, First)...........:
4d. Organization Name............:
4e. Street Address...............:
4f. City.........................:
4g. State........................:
4h. Postal Code..................:
4i. Country......................:
4j. Phone Number.................:
4k. Fax Number...................:
4l. E-Mailbox....................:

Technical Contact
5a. NIC Handle (if known)........:
5b. (I)ndividual (R)ole..........:
5c. Name (Last, First)...........:
5d. Organization Name............:
5e. Street Address...............:
5f. City.........................:
5g. State........................:
5h. Postal Code..................:
5i. Country......................:
5j. Phone Number.................:
5k. Fax Number...................:
5l. E-Mailbox....................:

Billing Contact
6a. NIC Handle (if known)........:
6b. (I)ndividual (R)ole..........:

6c. Name (Last, First)...........:
6d. Organization Name............:
6e. Street Address...............:
6f. City.........................:
6g. State........................:
6h. Postal Code..................:
6i. Country......................:
6j. Phone Number.................:
6k. Fax Number...................:
6l. E-Mailbox....................:

Primary Name Server
7a. Primary Server Hostname......:
7b. Primary Server Netaddress....:

Secondary Name Server(s)
8a. Secondary Server Hostname....:
8b. Secondary Server Netaddress..:

Product/Service Options (For New Registrations Only)
9a. Registration Period (1-10yrs):
9b. Bulk Whois Optout (Y/N)......:

Channel Payment/Identifier Options
10a. Channel Identifier...........:

E

Sample Network Traces for DNS Resolutions

THIS APPENDIX DISPLAYS SOME BASIC CAPTURES from the Microsoft Network Monitor (NetMon) utility. A fully capable version is included with Systems Management Server (SMS), enabling you to capture the traffic to and from any machine on the network. A less-capable version, which comes with Windows 2000 Server, is able to trace traffic to and from the machine on which it is running.

NetMon provides basic packet capture and decode capability. The figures presented in this appendix have the header sections of the packets that were captured on the name server for several DNS queries submitted through `nslookup`.

DNS Query Trace: The Question

Figure E.1 shows the DNS question being sent for `reston.va.us`. Working down the header information, the listing starts with frame properties, Ethernet, Internet Protocol (IP), User Datagram Protocol (UDP) packet headers, and finally the DNS information. The highlighted line is the question in the DNS packet.

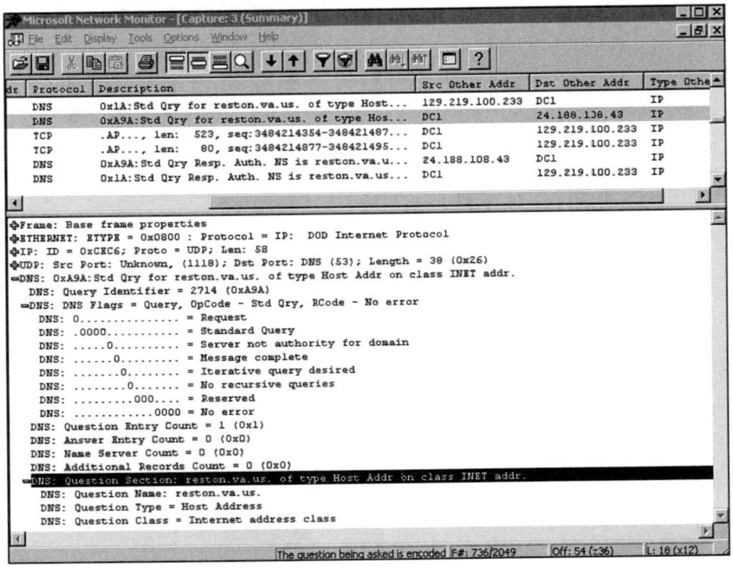

Figure E.1 A DNS query packet viewed in NetMon.

From the information displayed, the packet can be identified as a DNS query for the Internet class host address of `reston.va.us`. The upper frame shows the packets, in time order, within the capture. The highlighted packet in the upper frame is detailed in the lower frame. A further, hex-level view of the packet is not shown here. If you look at the upper window, the part of the packet list shown begins with two packets in which the protocol is DNS. The first of these is the DNS query sent by `nslookup` to the server named DC1, and the next, which is expanded in detail, is the resulting query that was sent by the DNS server on DC1 working recursively to resolve the `nslookup` query. The details of these two packets are almost identical.

Figure E.2 displays the returned packet with the answer to the query. Examining the lines for the DNS answer, the first thing that should be noticed is that `reston.va.us` is actually resolved as a host Address (A) record with the IP address provided.

In the upper frame of the figure, it can be seen that the detailed packet was received by DC1 from the same host to which the DNS query was sent. Then, the next DNS packet is outbound from DC1 returning the answer to the originating `nslookup` system. However, examining the details of the answer packet shows that there is something more to `reston.va.us` than just an A record. At the same level as the Answer Section can be seen an Authority Section and an Additional Records Section. Figure E.3 shows the same packet with these added sections partially expanded.

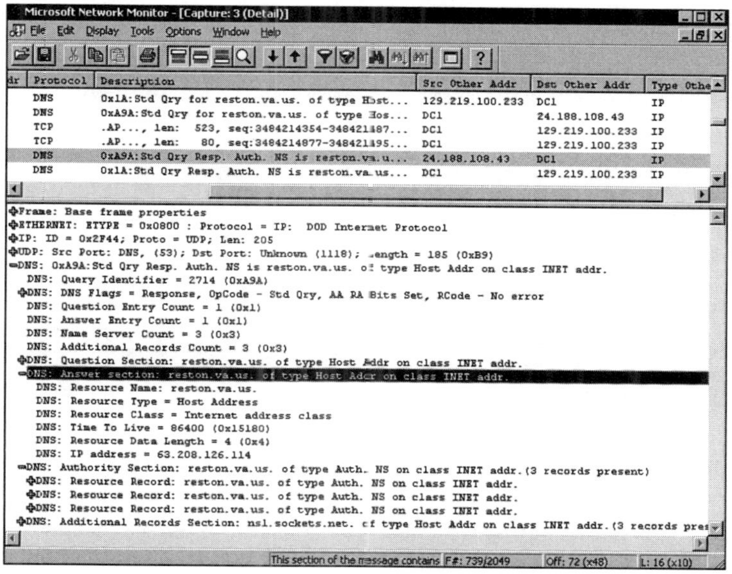

Figure E.2 A NetMon trace showing an answer to a DNS query.

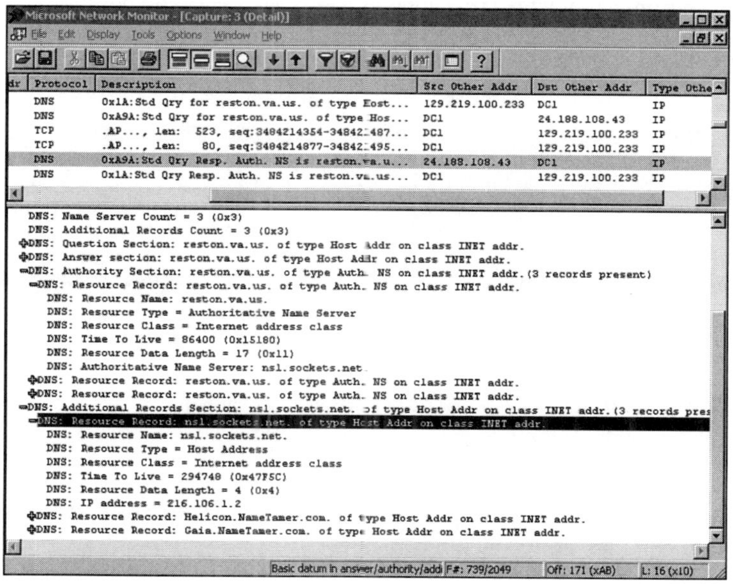

Figure E.3 The DNS answer packet showing DNS RR information.

The Authority Section shows that the name `reston.va.us` was also found on three NS records. The first of these has been expanded to show the name of the DNS server that the record delegates for the `reston.va.us` domain. Then, in the Additional Records Section, the corresponding A RR is expanded to show that the IP for use in further queries has been included in the answer.

In this example, the `nslookup` setting was to query for records of type=any, and so, both A and Name Server (NS) records with the name `reston.va.us` were returned.

Windows NT 4 DNS Query Trace: DNS with Windows Internet Naming Service (WINS) Integration

With the WINS lookup enabled, the DNS server can query for WINS-registered hosts, and if they exist, the server can report them as members of the Internet domain served by the name server. Recall that any NetBIOS name in the WINS database is resolved by DNS as if it was represented by an A RR in domains that are enabled to use WINS resolution. Because of this, the same NetBIOS name can potentially resolve to many fully-qualified domain names (FQDNs) if the WINS record is used in a zone having multiple DNS domains.

Certain changes have been made between NetMon version 1.1, provided in Windows NT 4, and version 2.1, provided in Windows 2000. Because of the possible confusion resulting from how NetMon represents these packets in Windows NT 4, we first look in Figures E.4

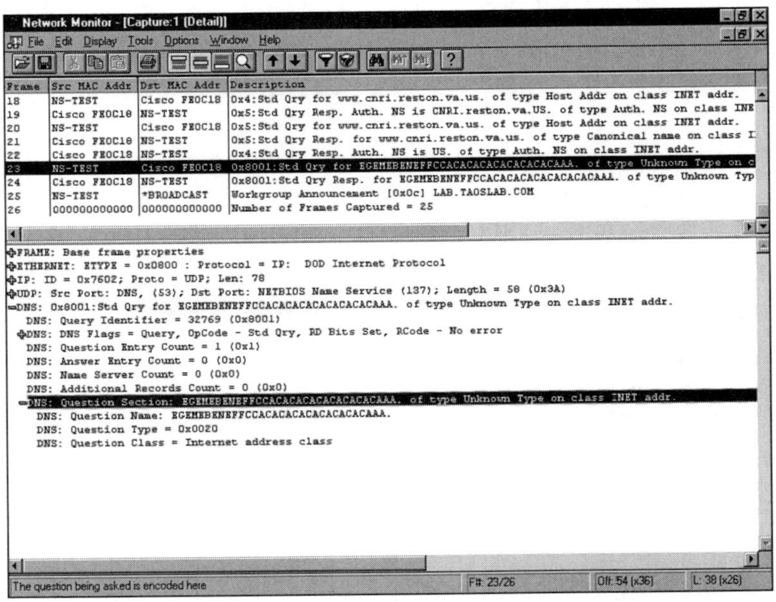

Figure E.4 A NetMon 1.1 trace showing how DNS queries WINS in Windows NT 4.

and E.5 at a NetMon version 1.1 trace. Figure E.4 shows the query for a host address being passed from the DNS server to the WINS server.

There are a couple of points of interest in this query. The first is the UDP header line in which the source port is 53 (standard DNS), but the destination port is 137 (the NetBIOS name service).

The second point of interest is that the name being used in the query is some encoded, alphanumeric string and that the type is "Unknown." Obviously, this is a problem. Microsoft has acknowledged it in Knowledge Base (KB) article Q160828, *Network Monitor Parses DNS WINS Lookup Queries as DNS Packets*. The article says ". . . the Protocol column will say DNS even when the packet being sent to the WINS server is a NetBT (NetBIOS over Transmission Control Protocol [TCP]) packet destined for port 137."

In Figure E.5, the answer for the query, as resolved through WINS, is displayed. Here again, some nonstandard information is being passed in the DNS packet. The same name is returned with a resource type equal to 20 (hex), which is an unknown resource type code in standard DNS, and the RDATA field that would normally contain an IP address isn't present. Instead, a series of numbers that look somewhat like a MAC address appears under the "Additional Resource Data" heading.

This answer is not very useful, and it's clear that hidden, undocumented information of some kind is passing between the DNS and WINS server. The problem with this trace is that there really aren't any references to tell what is happening. The request

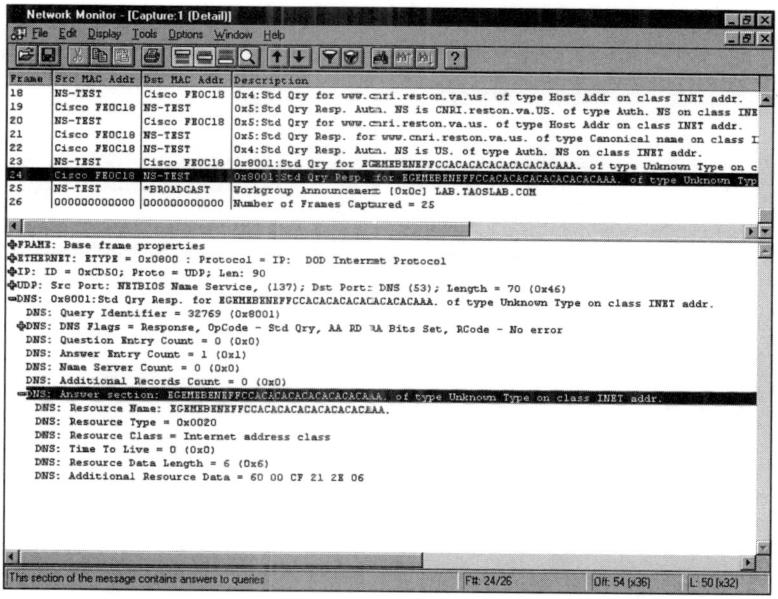

Figure E.5 A NetMon 1.1 trace showing how WINS answers DNS in Windows NT 4.

goes to the WINS server and comes back with an answer, but how can anyone really be sure that the information is correct? Incidentally, the numeric string that came back from the WINS server is not a MAC address; this is evidenced by requesting the MAC address from a workstation:

```
> arp -d machine.example.NET

Net to Media Table
Device  IP Address              Mask            Flags   Phys Addr
---     -----------             ---------         ---       -----
le0     machine.example.NET     255.255.255.255         00:20:af:f0:77:0e
```

Windows 2000 DNS Query Trace: DNS with WINS Integration

The packet parser in NetMon 2.1 that shipped with Windows 2000 has resolved these packets, which are typically difficult to decipher with any other tool. Figure E.6 shows an initial query for a machine, `3of5.pc.example.local`, which was sent to the DNS server by `nslookup`.

In this case, there is no A record in the zone for this host name, but the zone does have a WINS record. As a result, the DNS server sends a name query to the WINS server for the unqualified host name. In the upper frame in Figure E.6, a pair of NBT

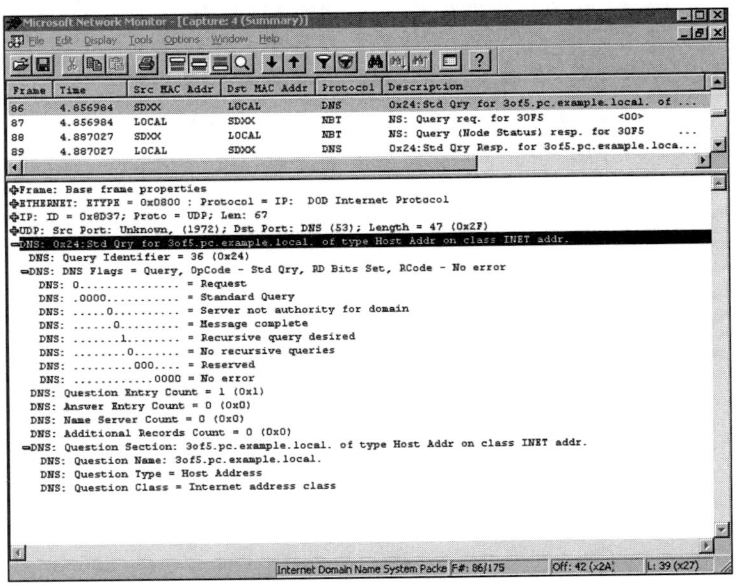

Figure E.6 A NetMon 2.1 trace showing a recursive DNS query.

NetBT) packets can be seen followed by the DNS answer to this query. Figures E.7 and E.8 show these two NBT packets.

Looking at Figure E.7, you can see that this is a normal NetBIOS name query, (directed at UDP port 137. Toward the bottom, it can be seen in the Query Name line that the first label has been stripped from the original DNS query and padded to a length of 15 characters before appending a hex 0, resulting in the NetBIOS name being queried.

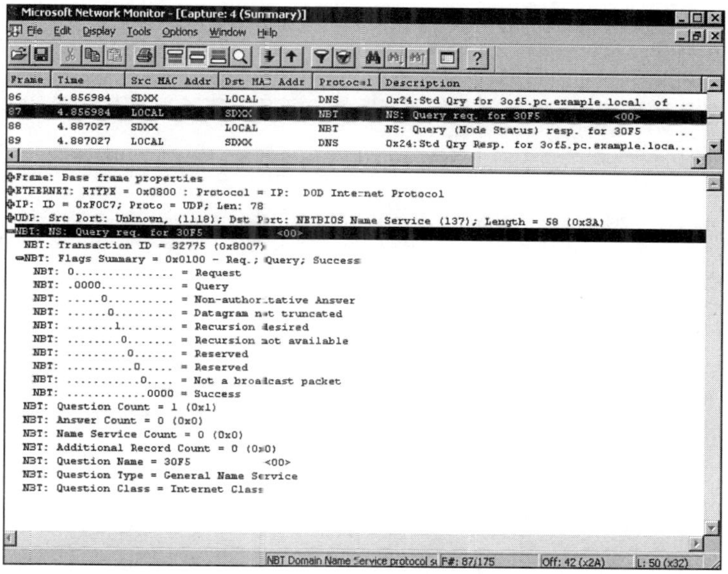

Figure E.7 A NetMon 2.1 trace showing DNS sending WINS a name query.

Figure E.8 shows a normal successful WINS name resolution answer for a unique name. If we were to then look at the next packet in the sequence of four, labeled "DNS 0x24 Std Qry Resp.," we would see a completely normal looking DNS answer being sent to the originating `nslookup` resolver.

Despite some shortcomings, NetMon is an excellent tool for administrators because it decodes and parses Server Message Block (SMB) and NBT messages, and it parses Lightweight Directory Access Protocol (LDAP) messages. As long as you are using legacy applications on your network, the parsing on NetBIOS-related packets (which a number of third-party tools treat as unknown) in itself makes NetMon a quite useful tool.

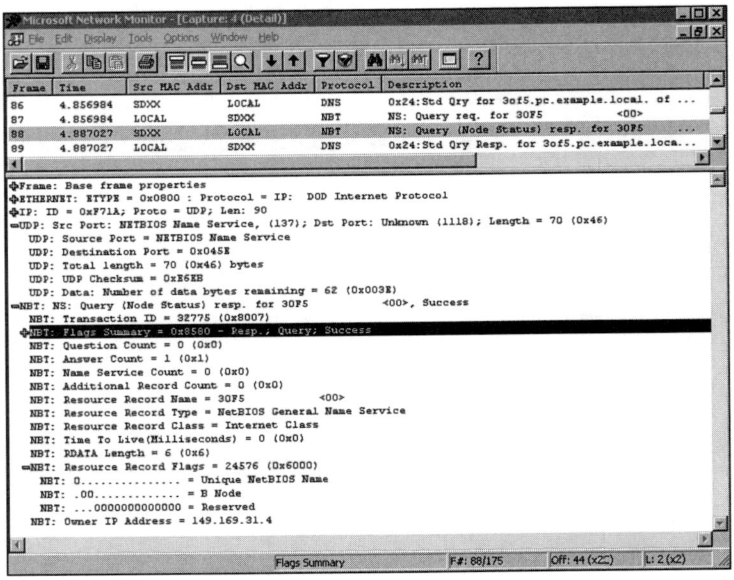

Figure E.8 A NetMon 2.1 trace showing DNS receiving the WINS answer.

F

Resource Records and the InterNIC Cache File

THIS APPENDIX FURNISHES TWO KINDS of information, a list of resource records (RRs) and a sample of InterNIC's root server cache file for your reference (both current as of this writing).

RRs

The following is a complete list of RR types, unlike the list of RRs in Chapter 4, "Domain Information Details." Refer to Chapter 4 for the most commonly used RR types. In addition to an explanation of each RR type, I've included its syntax for the zone file and an example showing how it's used. Note that the `<class>` and `<ttl>` fields for the RRs are reversible. All cited Requests for Comments (RFCs) are Standards track unless otherwise indicated.

Address (A) Records (RFC 1035)

A records are used to map host names to Internet Protocol (IP) addresses (see Chapter 4 for more detail). The syntax for the A record looks like:

```
<owner>     <ttl>     <class>     A     <address>
```

A sample A record might look like:

```
socrates             IN     A     10.1.1.1
```

Quad A (AAAA) Records (RFC 1886)

AAAA records are the address records for a host using IP version 6 (IPv6). The AAAA records is also the address record type for IPv6 Internet addresses. The syntax is basically the same as the standard A record:

```
<owner>     <ttl>     <class>     AAAA     <IPv6 address>
```

A sample AAAA RR would look something like:

```
v6gtwy.taos.com.          IN     AAAA     1234:5678:abc:0:0:0:356:70
```

Andrew File System Database (AFSDB) Records (RFC 1183)—Experimental

AFSDB records (experimental at this stage) are pointers for either Andrews File System (AFS) cell database servers or DCE-authenticated name servers. AFS is a distributed network file system, for which the locations of all the filesets are stored in the cell database. Information about the location of Open Software Foundation distributed computing environment (DCE) services is obtained from the authenticated name server in a DCE cell. A cell is a group of hosts that share services. The syntax for the AFSDB record looks like:

```
<owner>     <ttl>     <class>     AFSDB     <subtype>     <host>
```

In this syntax, the `<subtype>` is a `1` for an AFS cell database, and `2` for a DCE-authenticated name server. A sample AFSDB record might look like:

```
taos.com.     IN     AFSDB     1     afssrv.taos.com.
```

Canonical Name (CNAME) Records (RFC 1035)

CNAME records are used to provide "aliases" for hosts (see Chapter 4 for more detail). The syntax of the CNAME record looks like:

```
<owner>     <ttl>     <class>     CNAME     <host.domain-name.>
```

A sample CNAME record might look like:

```
ftp          IN     CNAME     www.domain.com.
```

Domain Redirection (DNAME) Records (RFC 2672)

DNAME records are used to provide redirection for domain sub trees. This can be quite useful if merging domains because of acquisitions or renumbering a network becomes a necessity. The syntax of the DNAME record looks like:

```
<owner> <ttl> <class> DNAME <target>
```

A sample DNAME record might look like:

```
hq.example.com          IN DNAME corp.example.net.
```

DNS Encoding of Geographical Location - Global Positioning (GPOS) Records (RFC 1712)—Obsolete

Host Information (HINFO) Records (RFC 1035)

The HINFO record was designed to provide some basic information about a host's architecture or hardware type and operating system. Originally designed to aid clients connecting to hosts with services like File Transfer Protocol (FTP), the HINFO record is now used primarily by local administrators to help keep track of the machines on their network. The syntax is as follows:

```
<owner>     <ttl>     <class>     HINFO     <cpu>     <os>
```

A sample HINFO record might look like:

```
flamer.taoslab.com.     IN     HINFO     PC     Win95

flamer.taoslab.com.     IN     HINFO     "Intel PC"     "Solaris x86"
```

Notice that the `<cpu>` and the `<os>` types need to be enclosed in quotes if a white space is going to be used.

Integrated Services Digital Network (ISDN) Records (RFC 1183—Experimental)

The ISDN record (experimental at this stage) is designed to provide addresses for ISDN resources. The unique thing about ISDN is that the ISDN address is really a phone number. The ISDN record contains the telephone number (with country and area code); it can also include a `<subaddr>` field, following the primary address (telephone number), to contain the telephone extension, if there is one. The syntax for the ISDN record is as follows:

```
<owner>     <ttl>     <class>     ISDN     <ISDN-address>     <subaddr>
```

A sample ISDN RR could be represented as:

```
pbx.taos.com.     IN     ISDN     14083302562     100
```

KEY Records (RFC 2535, obsoletes 2065)

The KEY record is used to identify the public key associated with a DNS name. The public key is required by a security-aware DNS, and it specifies the key algorithm and MD5/RSA algorithm. A security-aware DNS server must include the KEY record as additional information if retrieving Name Server (NS), A, or AAAA RRs. The KEY record is authenticated by the Digital Signature (SIG) record (described later). The syntax for a KEY record looks like:

```
<owner>     <ttl>     <class>     KEY     <1024 bit zone key>
```

An example of the KEY record might look like:

```
domain.com          IN     KEY     <1024 bit key>
```

Key Exchange (KX) Records (RFC 2230)—Informational

The KX record provides a mechanism for delegating the authority to a node to act as a key exchanger for other hosts via Secure DNS. Syntax for the KX record looks like:

```
<domain-a>     <ttl>     <class>     KX     <preference>     <domain-b>
```

A sample KX record might look like:

```
eng.domain.com.          IN     KX     10     corp.domain.com.
```

Location Information (LOC) Records (RFC 1876)

The LOC record can be used to provide information, such as latitude and longitude, which identifies the location of a network or host. The syntax for the LOC record looks like:

```
<owner>     <ttl>     <class>     LOC     <lat & long>     <size>
```

A sample LOC record might look like:

```
host.mydomain.com          IN     LOC     21 21 N 157 56 W     500m
```

Mailbox (MB) Records (RFC 1035) Experimental

The MB record (experimental at this stage) was initially designed as a pointer to the mail accounts in a DNS domain. The record never caught on for implementation, although the `<mailbox>` field in the Start Of Authority (SOA) record uses the MB format specification. The syntax for the MB record looks like:

```
<owner>     <ttl>     <class>     MB     <mailbox domain name>
```

An example of the MB record might look like:

```
hknief.taos.com.     IN     MB     mailhost.taos.com.
```

Mail Destination (MD) Records (RFC 1035)—Obsolete

Mail Forwarder (MF) Records (RFC 1035)—Obsolete

Mail Group (MG) Records (RFC 1035) Experimental

The MG record (experimental in DNS at this stage, per the RFC) is another mail handling record that is similar to the MB record. The purpose of the MG record is to provide a record for mail groups (also known as mail-lists). The syntax for the MG record is essentially the same as the MB record, with multiple mailboxes listed under the mail group owner:

```
<owner>     <ttl>     <class>     MG     <mail group domain name>
```

A mail group (list) would look like:

```
sysadmin.taos.com.     IN     MG     hknief.taos.com.
                                 IN     MG     gtal.taos.com.
                                 IN     MG     mmasterson.taos.com.
```

Mailbox Information (MINFO) Records (RFC 1035) Experimental

The MINFO record (experimental at this stage) is similar in function to the `Owner-<maillist>` and `<maillist>-response` aliases for many list manager software packages. The `<resp-mbox>` is the person responsible for list maintenance, and the `<error-mbox>` is the mail address to which messages concerning errors should be routed. The formal syntax looks like:

```
<owner>     <ttl>     <class>     MINFO  <resp-mbox>  <error-mbox>
```

In an actual zone file, the MINFO record format could be represented as:

```
sysadmin.taos.com.  IN  MINFO  hknief.taos.com. hknief.taos.com.
```

Mailbox Rename (MR) Records (RFC 1035) Experimental

The functionality of the MR record (experimental at this stage) is the equivalent of the redirected mail capability of the mail alias. It represents an alternative mail address to which mail should be forwarded or, for the mailer, which mail address to rewrite in the "To:" field. The basic syntax is represented as:

```
<owner>     <ttl>     <class>     MR     <new mbox>
```

In practical application, the entry in the zone file might look like:

```
hknief.isi.edu.     IN     MR     hknief.taos.com.
```

Mail Exchanger (MX) Records (RFC 1035)

The MX record is used by mail transport agents (MTA) to determine where mail should be routed for a given domain (see Chapter 4 for more details). The syntax of the MX record looks like:

```
<owner>     <ttl>      <class>     MX     <preference>     <mail-exchange.domain.>
```

A sample MX record might look like:

```
domain.com           IN     MX     10     mailhost.domain.com
```

(NS) Records Name Server(RFC 1035)

The NS record is used for delegating name servers for a given domain (see Chapter 4 for more details). The syntax for the NS record looks like:

```
domina.com     <ttl>     <class>     NS     hostname.domain.com.
```

A sample NS record might look like:

```
root-servers.net            IN      NS      ns.ripte.net.
```

Network Service Access Point (NSAP) Records (RFCs 1348, 1637 and 1706)

The NSAP record provides a DNS name to NSAP mapping for Open Systems Interconnect (OSI) Connectionless Network Protocol (CLNP) . This record is only used to support the existing CLNP deployment in the Internet. The syntax for the NSAP record looks like:

```
<owner>     <ttl>     <class>     NSAP     <length>     <NSAP Address>
```

A sample NSAP record might look like:

```
host.domain.com.            IN      NSAP      21
47102589283400000002344FFFF29342847AB23CD
```

NSAP-PTR Records (RFC 1348—Obsolete)

The NSAP-PTR records are handled by standard Pointer (PTR) records.

NULL Records (RFC 1035) Experimental

NULL records are experimental and not enabled in "master" zone files. They're only used as placeholders in some extensions for DNS. The record can contain any data the does not exceed 65535 octets.

Non-Existence (NXT) Records (RFC 2535, obsoletes 2065)

The NXT record provides a mechanism that enables a name server to deny the existence of a queried name or a RR in an authenticated manner. Instead of returning a simple non-existent error, it instead returns any known information about the known security domain along with any specified RRs (NS, SIG, KEY) that should be queried next. The syntax for the NXT records looks like:

```
<owner>     <ttl>     <class>     NXT     <domain> RR RR RR
```

A sample NXT record might look like:

```
yourdomain.com            IN      NXT      mydomain.com. NS SIG KEY
```

Pointer (PTR) Records (RFC 1035)

The PTR record is used to map IP addresses back to host names (see Chapter 4 for more detail). The syntax for the PTR record looks like:

```
<owner>     <ttl>     <class>     PTR     <host.name.domain.>
```

A sample PTR record might look like this:

```
1.1.27.10.in-addr.arpa.     IN     PTR     myhost.domain.com.
```

Pointer to X.400 (PX) Records (RFC 1664)

The PX record is similar in function to the MX record, except that it uses mapping from Internet domain-style addresses (RFC 822) to X.400 (RFC 1327) addresses. The syntax for the PX record looks like:

```
<owner>     <ttl>     <class>     PX     <preference>     <RFC 822 map>     <RFC
1327 map>
```

A sample PX record might look like:

```
*.domain.com.          IN     PX     10     domain.com.     PRMD-domain.ADMD-
p400.C-com.
```

Responsible Person (RP) Records (RFC 1183—Experimental)

The RP record (experimental at this stage) enables the administrator to designate, through the DNS, who is responsible for the individual machines on a network. This can be a good thing or a bad thing depending on your job title and how the machine in question is performing. The syntax for a RP record looks like:

```
<owner>     <ttl>     <class>     RP     <mbox name>  <txt RR domain>
```

If this was implemented on an actual server, it could look like:

```
www.taos.com.     IN     RP     hknief.taos.com.     txt.taos.com.
txt.taos.com.     IN     TXT     "Help Desk - (408) 588-1296"
```

This record says that `hknief` is the responsible person, and further digging by querying the Text (TXT) record reports the phone number of the help desk.

Route Through (RT) Records (RFC 1183—Experimental)

The RT record (experimental at this stage) looks like the MX record type; its purpose is to provide multiple addresses through which packets can be routed. If a host was not directly connected to the Internet but needed to have Telnet access, the idea that intermediate hosts could act as gateways for the session could be established with these RT records. Priorities can be specified to provide alternative routes, should one host fail. The syntax looks like:

```
<owner>     <ttl>  <class>  RT  <preference>  <intermediate-host>
```

In application, the record might look like:

```
internal.taos.com.     IN     RT     5     gateway.taos.com.
                       IN     RT     10     bkupgtwy.taos.com.
```

Digital Signature (SIG) Records (RFC 2535, obsoletes 2065)

The SIG record is used to "sign," and thereby authenticate, other RRs for a specified time interval using encryption techniques and the signer's "private" key (see also the KEY RR section). The syntax for a SIG record looks like:

```
<owner>    <ttl>    <class>    SIG    <RR signed>    <signer's name>
```

A sample SIG record might look like:

```
my.domain.com         IN    SIG    SOA    <Signature>
```

Start of Authority (SOA) Records (RFC 1035)

The SOA record is used to identify the authoritative source for the records contained within a domain's zone file (see Chapter 4 for more detail). The syntax of a SOA record looks like:

```
<owner>    <ttl>    <class>    SOA    <zone source>    <mailbox>
( <serial #> <refresh> <retry> <expire> <m-ttl>
```

A sample SOA record might look like:

```
domain.com          IN    SOA    ns.domain.com    root.domain.com
( 1 3600 300 21600 1800)
```

Service (SRV) Records (RFC 2052—Experimental)

The SRV record (experimental at this stage) was designed to enable clients to find the servers that offer a type of service without tying a "brand name" to the machine. If a group of servers are going to provide Web services, there is no need to call all them www or some sort of modifier. The hosts can be identified as Web servers by listing their machines with the SRV record. The syntax of the SRV record looks like:

```
<service>.<protocol>    <ttl>    <class>    <priority>    <weight>    <port>
<target>
```

A sample SRV record might look like:

```
_ldap._tcp   IN  SRV  0 0 389  adserver.example.net.
```

TXT Records (RFC 1035)

The TXT record enables the administrator to associate some text string with a particular record (as in the case of the RP RR). The basic syntax for this RR is:

```
<owner>    <ttl>    <class>    TXT    <text string>
```

Another example of the TXT record could give information about the location of a particular host:

```
www.taos.com.    IN    TXT    "Santa Clara Office"
```

Well Known Services (WKS) Records (RFC 1035)

The WKS record was designed to let outside agents learn that certain hosts were providing specific services. The services are associated with the protocol, Transmission Control Protocol (TCP) or User Datagram Protocol (UDP), and the service type. The protocols might be any of those listed in the `PROTOCOLS` file (`\%systemroot%\system32\drivers\etc\protocol`). The services can be any services below port 256 from the `SERVICES` file (`\%systemroot%\system32\drivers\etc\services`). The syntax for the WKS record looks like:

```
<owner>      <ttl>      <class>      WKS      <address> <protocol> <service>
```

An example of a WKS record might look like:

```
taos.com.          IN      WKS      207.33.46.130      tcp      telnet
                   IN      WKS      207.33.46.135      upd      domain
                   IN      WKS      207.33.46.140      tcp      smtp
```

Windows Internet Name Service (WINS) Records

The WINS record was designed to let outside agents learn the IP addresses of systems that might not have entries configured in DNS zones, but rather registered with NetBIOS name servers. The WINS record allows the Microsoft DNS server to query a WINS server to resolve the Netbios name to an IP address, which is then used to satisfy a DNS query. This is provided in a very limited number of name servers and is designed to operate only in a Windows network environment. This was a widely used part of the NT 4.0 configuration, but is being obsoleted as Microsoft as Windows 2000 fully embraces the standard TCP/IP suite of protocols.

```
owner class WINS [LOCAL] [L<lookup_timeout>] [C<cache_timeout>]
<wins_ip_addresses>

@      IN       WINS      LOCAL L10 C10 172.16.77.100
```

Windows Internet Name Service-Reverse (WINS-R) Records

The WINS-R record is similar in function to the PTR record, but uses a call to the Netbios NBTSTAT function to resolve an IP address to a Netbios name. As with the WINS RR, this functionality is designed to operate only within a Microsoft environment and is being phased out with the move to Windows 2000.

```
<owner domain>  IN  WINS-R [local]  <lookup timout> <cache timeout> <domain name
to append>
```

For most installations of DNS on Windows 2000, the WINS and WINS-R records will likely not be used.

X.25 Addressing (X25) Records (RFC 1183—Experimental)

The X.25 record (experimental at this stage), like the ISDN record, is designed to provide addressing for X.25 circuits. The address itself is actually an X.121 address for use in X.25 networks. The syntax is:

```
<owner>     <ttl>     <class>     X.25     <psdn address>
```

An example of an X.25 record could look like:

```
remote.taos.com.          IN     X.25     31547622562
```

The InterNIC Cache File

InterNIC's root cache file is automatically loaded into the DNS server during installation using the latest copy that Microsoft received before distributing the server. The file's name is `cache.dns`.

Changes to the root cache records rarely occur, and changes that do occur usually have little or no affect on the functioning of other DNS servers. You can download the root cache file directly from the InterNIC via FTP at `ftp://rs.internic.net/domain/named.root`.

The cache file contains the names and IP addresses of the root-level servers. There's a NS record for each root name server and, because the DNS architecture requires it, an A record as well. When the DNS was first implemented, several name servers around the network were made root name servers. To simplify things and to make it easier to recognize these important name servers, they were moved to the `root-servers.net` domain. For informational purposes, you see, in its record, each server's old name—the one used before it was moved to the `root-servers.net` domain. The old name provides a clue to each server's actual location.

The `cache.dns` file contains entries like these:

```
; formerly NS.INTERNIC.NET
.                          3600000  IN  NS    A.ROOT-SERVERS.NET.
A.ROOT-SERVERS.NET.        3600000      A     198.41.0.4
;
; formerly NS1.ISI.EDU
.                          3600000      NS    B.ROOT-SERVERS.NET.
B.ROOT-SERVERS.NET.        3600000      A     128.9.0.107
;
; formerly C.PSI.NET
.                          3600000      NS    C.ROOT-SERVERS.NET.
C.ROOT-SERVERS.NET.        3600000      A     192.33.4.12
;
; formerly TERP.UMD.EDU
.                          3600000      NS    D.ROOT-SERVERS.NET.
```

```
D.ROOT-SERVERS.NET.      3600000      A    128.8.10.90
;
; formerly NS.NASA.GOV
.                        3600000      NS   E.ROOT-SERVERS.NET.
E.ROOT-SERVERS.NET.      3600000      A    192.203.230.10
;
; formerly NS.ISC.ORG
.                        3600000      NS   F.ROOT-SERVERS.NET.
F.ROOT-SERVERS.NET.      3600000      A    192.5.5.241
;
; formerly NS.NIC.DDN.MIL
.                        3600000      NS   G.ROOT-SERVERS.NET.
G.ROOT-SERVERS.NET.      3600000      A    192.112.36.4
;
; formerly AOS.ARL.ARMY.MIL
.                        3600000      NS   H.ROOT-SERVERS.NET.
H.ROOT-SERVERS.NET.      3600000      A    128.63.2.53
;
; formerly NIC.NORDU.NET
.                        3600000      NS   I.ROOT-SERVERS.NET.
I.ROOT-SERVERS.NET.      3600000      A    192.36.148.17
;
.                        3600000      NS   J.ROOT-SERVERS.NET.
J.ROOT-SERVERS.NET.      3600000      A    198.41.0.10
;
; housed in LINX, operated by RIPE NCC
;
.                        3600000      NS   K.ROOT-SERVERS.NET.
K.ROOT-SERVERS.NET.      3600000      A    193.0.14.129
;
; temporarily housed at ISI (IANA)
;
.                        3600000      NS   L.ROOT-SERVERS.NET.
L.ROOT-SERVERS.NET.      3600000      A    198.32.64.12
;
; housed in Japan, operated by WIDE
;
.                        3600000      NS   M.ROOT-SERVERS.NET.
M.ROOT-SERVERS.NET.      3600000      A    202.12.27.33
; End of File
```

G

Using IPv6

THIS APPENDIX BRIEFLY DESCRIBES THE NEXT generation suite of protocols for the Internet and provides some insight into using DNS with these protocols. As this appendix is read, the importance of DNS in the near future becomes obvious, especially for those who aren't great at recalling long series of numbers. It is key to note that Windows 2000 has full support for the IPv6 suite and provides an easy mechanism for transferring to the newer technologies.

What is IPv6?

To start off, let's be sure that everyone understands what IPv6 is. Most people know of (or have at least heard of) Transmission Control Protocol/Internet Protocol (TCP/IP)—the suite of protocols used by the Internet for communications. In reality, these are two separate entities and are only part the big picture. TCP is a transmission protocol that provides a connection-oriented mechanism for reliably transferring data between source and destination applications on the Internet. TCP rides on top of IP, which provides the functionality of a connectionless environment and accounts for unique addresses among hosts that want to communicate. Along with TCP and IP, other protocols are necessary to provide added functionality. Some of these additional protocols are User Datagram Protocol (UDP), Internet Control Message Protocol (ICMP), and Address Resolution Protocol (ARP).

The version of TCP/IP currently used on the Internet is based on IP version 4, or IPv4. This appendix talks about the version that will be implemented next, IP version 6 (IPv6). IPv6 provides a number of improvements over IPv4, the most obvious difference being the addresses used by the two. IPv4 uses a 32-bit address, usually represented by four octets in the form `aaa.bbb.ccc.ddd`. IPv6 on the other hand uses 128-bit addresses that are represented by eight hextets, such as `1111:aaaa:3333:bbbb:5555:eeee:7777:ffff`.

How is IPv6 Different?

Now that the general concept behind IPv6 has been presented, let's examine some of the reasons for changing from IPv4 to IPv6 and the effects of that change. IPv4, with its 32-bit address, has a potential four billion addresses (2 raised to the 32nd power = 4294967296), which must be shared among all the world's computers. That might seem like a lot, but with the tremendous growth of the Internet, it has been predicted that the current pool of addresses will be depleted by 2005. The advent of Network Address Translation (NAT) and the use of private Internet address space (RFC 1918) have eased the burden of keeping network entities unique; however, it has not eliminated the need for an expanded address space. Other shortcomings in IPv4 are the lack of: security, Quality of Service (QoS), and mobility.

The capabilities of IPv6, as defined by RFC 1752, provide: expanded addressing and routing, source routing, support for dynamic addressing in the form of Dynamic Host Configuration Protocol (DHCP), header extensions, authentication, QoS, and a simplified header format. On top of this, IPv6 was designed to enable an easy transition, or migration, to the new suite. In addition to IPv6, a new version of the ICMP (ICMPv6) has been developed under RFC 1885. ICMPv6 handles the basic functionality of reporting packet processing errors and path diagnosis, as does ICMPv4; in addition, ICMPv6 also handles the Internet Group Membership Protocol (IGMP) functions as specified in RFC 1112. The Address Resolution Protocol (ARP) is being replaced with a new Neighbor Discovery Protocol (NDP), which also handles ICMP router discovery and ICMP redirects.

IPv6 Addresses Structure

As previously stated, IPv6 addresses use 128-bits in a colon separated hex notation. Just as with IPv4, IPv6 prefixes have special meaning and provide insight as to the use and format of the IPv6 address.

For example, IPv6 addresses that begin with the first eight bits equal to zero are generally reserved. Addresses beginning with the prefix 0000 001 binary are reserved for Network Subnet Access Protocol (NSAP), and addresses beginning with the prefix 0000 010 binary are reserved for Internet Packet eXchange (IPX). Addresses beginning with the prefix 1111 1111 binary are reserved for multicast traffic, much as the 224.0.0.0 network for IPv4 is. Two special IPv6 addresses are 0::0 (or just ::) and 0::1 (or just ::1) addresses, in which :: is an unspecified address. The unspecified address can be used for nodes that are newly attached to a network and might not have been assigned a value yet. The other special case of ::1 is used for the loopback address (the equivalent of 127.0.0.1 for IPv4).

To assist with the migration to IPv6, some special categories of addresses for IPv4-mapped addresses and IPv4-compatible addresses. IPv4-mapped addresses are quit literally IPv4 addresses that are mapped into the IPv6 address structure. For IPv6 nodes that need to speak to IPv4-only nodes, the IPv4 address can be mapped via an IPv6 gateway using the following:

> IPv4 address `207.33.46.71` (literally `207.033.046.071`) will be represented as `0000:0000:0000:0000:FFFF:2070:3304:6071`, or `::FFFF:2070:3304:6071`.

IPv4-compatible addresses are used by IPv6 nodes that need to communicate with each other but through an IPv4 network. The address notation is similar to the address in the previous example, the notable difference being that the value of `FFFF` is replaced by `0000`. In this way, two IPv6 nodes can "tunnel" through an IPv4 network. The IPv6-compatible address for the previous IPv4 address would simply be represented as `::2070:3304:6071`.

Using IPv6 with DNS

So, you might ask, how does all this affect the DNS server? Well, with a new addressing scheme, there of course needs to be new Resource Records (RR) to handle the new format. Enter the Quad A record (`AAAA`) (see Appendix F), which handles the 128-bit address for IPv6. Additionally, a special domain, called IP6.INT, handles reverse lookups of pointer records. Reverse lookups are the real difficulty, in that IPv6 prefixes do not need to fall on even byte boundaries. Without this restriction, the reverse map must view each digit of the IPv6 address as a separate and significant entity while performing lookups at each point. Using the IP6.INT domain, the pointer records for the previous addresses would look like:

```
7.5.0.0.0.9.6.2.1.0.0.0.4.6.0.0.0.0.0.0.0.0.0.0.0.0.0.0.0.0.0.0.IP6.INT.
```

and

```
6.0.0.0.0.0.0.0.0.0.0.0.0.0.0.0.0.0.0.0.0.0.0.0.0.0.0.0.0.0.0.0.IP6.INT.
```

This could be simplified slightly by identifying the prefix for the addresses and defining the zone for the address range to which the pointer records pertain. The prefix is essentially the equivalent of a subnet mask, for a range of assigned addresses. The `/xx` notation of the prefix is the style taken from classless inter-domain routing (CIDR). Hence, if a network using a prefix of /68 was used, the result would look like the following:

Network address = 2345:7003:F167:0A41:A000:0000:0000:0000/68

IP6.INT domain = A.1.4.A.0.7.6.1.F.3.0.0.7.5.4.3.2.IP6.INT.

The entries in the zone file are now represented by 60-bit numbers that append the domain tag of the IP6.INT domain. Example:

IPv6 Address: 2345:7003:F167:A41:A000::268

PTR Record: .6.2.0.0.0.0.0.0.0.0.0.0.0.0.0.A.1.4.A.0.7.6.1.F.3.0.0.7.5.
4.3.2.IP6.INT.

The zone file entry for the A.1.4.A.0.7.6.1.F.3.0.0.7.5.4.3.2.IP6.INT. zone would just be:

```
8.6.2.0.0.0.0.0.0.0.0.0.0.0.0       IN       PTR      <Host>
```

With each digit being significant in its value and location, DNS functioning becomes of the utmost importance. Windows 2000 has general IPv6 support for both, configuring a host to operate on an IPv6 network and handling the expanded requirements of DNS in an IPv6 environment.

The American Registry of Internet Numbers (ARIN) has begun assigning some IPv6 address blocks, although most of these blocks are going to research organizations and large carriers (tier-one service providers). These folks are the "early adopters," and, hopefully, they will get most of the wrinkles ironed out for the rest of us before it comes time for us to make the jump. The main reasons for deploying IPv6 now are the quality of service features and the added security. However, as mentioned earlier, the use of "private" IP space and the use of NAT have dramatically slowed the rate of consumption of publicly routable addresses. This coupled with the CIDR push has enabled a number of public addresses to be reclaimed or reallocated. In general, I suspect that IPv6 will not be in general use for probably two more years. For more information on IPv6, please refer to the Requests for Comments (RFCs) or visit the Web sites for the 6Bone, http://www.6bone.net, and 6REN, http://www.6ren.net. 6Bone is the IPv6 backbone test bed that was set up in 1995 to assist in the evolution and deployment of IPv6. 6REN is a voluntary coordination initiative that was set up to provide a production IPv6 transit service. The idea is to encourage the use of IPv6 networks and to provide a high-quality, robust service for the interconnection of the deployed IPv6 infrastructures on research and educational networks. More information about IPv6 and its status can be obtained from the IPv6 home page at http://www.ipv6.org.

H

Multihomed Windows Servers

MULTIHOMING ENTAILS A NUMBER OF ISSUES, most of which are not important for Windows 2000 DNS services. Especially in early NT 4 systems, however, multihoming always carried with it a share of pain. Because not all readers will be immediately moving all their DNS servers out of NT 4 systems, and to be clear about the state of things in Windows 2000, this appendix is included.

Windows 2000 has much improved support for multihomed machines. The Routing and Remote Access services provide a suite of services for machines having multiple interfaces, whether real or virtual and whether using open Transmission Control Protocol/Internet Protocol (TCP/IP) or an encryption technology for private networking. The routing component enables one to configure a machine's first-hop choice by management of the routing table. One definitely needs to become familiar with the networking services provided in Windows 2000 when running machines with multiple interfaces. Other than the few name service considerations discussed here, using DNS on multihomed servers should be trouble-free.

Multihoming DNS Servers

Modern BIND 8 can configure its DNS service delivery to a very fine grain tuned by interfaces and ports. This capability is missing in the Windows 2000 DNS Server. The Windows 2000 version can be configured to, or not to, provide DNS services to specific interfaces using the Interfaces tab of the DNS server's Properties dialog box.

When doing so, one is setting a serverwide configuration. In other words, the server provides resolution from all zones on all enabled interfaces. Other serverwide settings, such as refusing recursive queries or using a list of forwarders, are also equally used for all enabled interfaces. In contrast, BIND 8 can present different resolution services, making selected zones available to specific interfaces or ports.

Partly because of this behavior, configuring multiple IP addresses on a single adapter usually brings no benefit. Clients may think that their DNS services are more directly available, but otherwise one has only increased in small measure the overhead of supporting the TCP/IP stack. When large numbers of Internet Protocol (IP) are used in this way, the total extra overhead may indeed become significant.

By default, when DNS server is on a machine with multiple interfaces, it services all of them unless otherwise explicitly configured. The Windows 2000 DNS Server also includes the option to prioritize the IP addresses in its answers. When a query is received about a multihomed machine, DNS server might find multiple A records for the queried name. In this situation, if it recognizes an IP and the set forming the answer corresponds to an interface on which the query was received, DNS server can place this IP first in the answer it sends. If your DNS server is not itself multihomed, all queries are received on the same interface, and no benefit can be obtained from this feature, even if many queries are asking to resolve multihome machines. If this feature is not of benefit to your multihomed deployment sufficient for the overhead, it should be disabled.

Multihoming with NetBIOS

Although only marginally related to providing DNS, one does need to be clear of the limitation of NetBIOS names relative to multihomed machines. Because Windows Internet Naming Service (WINS) was covered in some depth because of its use with Windows DNS Servers, some of the following may be relevant to your DNS server deployment. What is said here applies equally to up-to-date NT 4 systems and Windows 2000 systems.

The early history of NT 4 included the evolution of the system's capability to handle real-world TCP/IP networking. As NT was pushed into more complex network configurations, the evolution of some aspects of the NetBIOS name service for NetBT, called WINS, was inescapable. Along the way to the present WINS, the war stories were collected by more than one system manager.

WINS today does include a multihomed registration type that provides for multiple IP addresses (maximum is 25) to be associated with a NetBIOS name registration. However, one needs to understand that the NetBIOS implementation in the operating system binds only to the first IP address on a network card. Similarly, it registers only this IP address with WINS. However, each network card to which the "WINS client" is bound has its first IP registered. Although it had a shaky start, by Service Pack 3 the use of multihomed machines, when these limitations were understood, became quite manageable. And, with NT 4 Service Pack 5 the WINS implementation in NT 4 became the functional equivalent to that shipped with Windows 2000.

That said, Microsoft in Windows 2000 is still recommending that a WINS server not be multihomed. And, this is probably a good practice for any machine used for NetBT-based services, such as file and print sharing in down-level fashion. Although each card bound to NetBT registers one IP address, there is apparently no guarantee on the order in which these bind. Because most multihomed machines have multiple interfaces in order to have a presence in otherwise separate networks, rather than to aggregate bandwidth within one switched network, this randomness can apparently lead to problems. Previously in NT 4 this led to erratic Browser service election processes, for example, and so it has been recommended in NT 4 not to multihome PDC machines in order to guarantee that they do retain the domain master browser (DMB) role. The best advice has been just not to bind NetBIOS to multiple adapters in machines providing critical NetBIOS-based services.

Index

A

D

F

K-L

M

N

O

P

Q

S

U

V-W

X-Z

Windows 2000 Answers

Selected Windows 2000 Titles from New Riders Publishing

This is the updated edition of New Riders' best-selling *Inside Windows NT Server 4.* Taking the author-driven, no-nonsense approach that we pioneered with our *Landmark* books, New Riders proudly offers something unique for Windows 2000 administrators—an interesting and discriminating book on Windows 2000 Server, written by someone in the trenches who can anticipate your situation and provide answers you can trust.

ISBN: 1-56205-929-7

Architected to be the most navigable, useful, and value-packed reference for Windows 2000, this book uses a creative "telescoping" design that you can adapt to your style of learning. It's a concise, focused, and quick reference for Windows 2000, providing the kind of practical advice, tips, procedures, and additional resources that every administrator will need.

ISBN: 0-7357-0869-X

Windows 2000 Active Directory is just one of several new Windows 2000 titles from New Riders' acclaimed *Landmark* series. Perfect for network architects and administrators, this book describes the intricacies of Active Directory while keeping real-world systems and constraints in mind. It's a detailed, solution-oriented book which addresses the need for a single work to planning, deploying, and managing Active Directory in an enterprise setting.

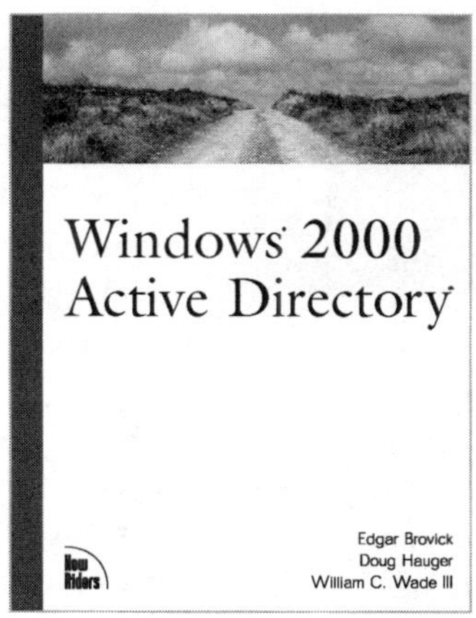

ISBN: 0-7357-0870-3

Windows NT Performance: Monitoring, Benchmarking, and Tuning

By Mark T. Edmead and Paul Hinsberg
1st Edition
288 pages, $29.99
ISBN: 1-56205-942-4

Performance monitoring is a little like preventive medicine for the administrator: No one enjoys a checkup, but it's a good thing to do on a regular basis. This book helps you focus on the critical aspects of improving the performance of your NT system by showing you how to monitor the system, implement benchmarking, and tune your network. The book is organized by resource components, which makes it easy to use as a reference tool.

Windows NT Terminal Server and Citrix MetaFrame

By Ted Harwood
1st Edition
400 pages, $29.99
ISBN: 1-56205-944-0

It's no surprise that most administration headaches revolve around integration with other networks and clients. This book addresses these types of real-world issues on a case-by-case basis, giving tools and advice for solving each problem. The author also offers the real nuts and bolts of thin client administration on multiple systems, covering relevant issues, such as installation, configuration, network connection, management, and application distribution.

Windows NT Power Toolkit

By Stu Sjouwerman and Ed Tittel
1st Edition
800 pages, $49.99
ISBN: 0-7357-0922-X

This book covers the analysis, tuning, optimization, automation, enhancement, maintenance, and troubleshooting of Windows NT Server 4.0 and Windows NT Workstation 4.0. In most cases, the two operating systems overlap completely and are discussed together. Where the two systems diverge, each platform is covered separately. This advanced title comprises a task-oriented treatment of the Windows NT 4 environment. By concentrating on the use of operating system tools and utilities, Resource Kit elements, and selected third-party tuning, analysis, optimization, and productivity tools, this book will show its readers how to carry out everyday and advanced tasks.

Windows NT Network Management: Reducing Total Cost of Ownership

By Anil Desai
1st Edition
450 pages, $34.99
ISBN: 1-56205-946-7

Administering a Windows NT network is kind of like trying to herd cats—an impossible task characterized by constant motion, exhausting labor, and lots of hairballs. Author Anil Desai knows all about it; he's a consulting engineer for Sprint Paranet, which specializes in Windows NT implementation, integration, and management. So, we asked him to put together a concise manual of the best practices—a book of tools and ideas that other administrators can turn to again and again in managing their own NT networks.

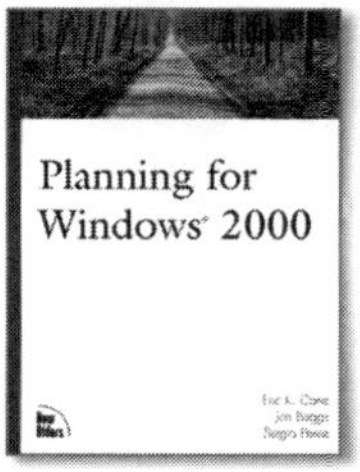

Planning for Windows 2000

By Eric K. Cone, Jon Boggs, and Sergio Perez
1st Edition
400 pages, $29.99
ISBN: 0-7357-0048-6

Windows 2000 is poised to be one of the largest and most important software releases of the next decade, and you are charged with planning, testing, and deploying it in your enterprise. Are you ready? With this book, you will be. *Planning for Windows 2000* lets you know what the upgrade hurdles will be, informs you how to clear them, guides you through effective Active Directory design, and presents you with detailed rollout procedures. Eric K. Cone, Jon Boggs, and Sergio Perez give you the benefit of their extensive experiences as Windows 2000 Rapid Deployment Program members by sharing problems and solutions they've encountered on the job.

Inside Windows 2000 Server

By William Boswell
1st Edition
1533 pages, $49.99
ISBN: 1-56205-929-7

Finally, a totally new edition of New Riders' best-selling *Inside Windows NT Server 4*. Taking the author-driven, no-nonsense approach we pioneered with our *Landmark* books, New Riders proudly offers something unique for Windows 2000 administrators—an interesting, discriminating book on Windows 2000 Server written by someone who can anticipate your situation and give you workarounds that won't leave a system unstable or sluggish.

BackOffice Titles

Implementing Exchange Server

By Doug Hauger, Marywynne Leon, and William C. Wade III
1st Edition
400 pages, $29.99
ISBN: 1-56205-931-9

If you're interested in connectivity and maintenance issues for Exchange Server, this book is for you. Exchange's power lies in its capability to be connected to multiple email subsystems to create a "universal email backbone." It's not unusual to have several different and complex systems all connected via email gateways, including Lotus Notes or cc:Mail, Microsoft Mail, legacy mainframe systems, and Internet mail. This book covers all of the problems and issues associated with getting an integrated system running smoothly, and it addresses troubleshooting and diagnosis of email problems with an eye toward prevention and best practices.

Exchange System Administration

By Janice Rice Howd
1st Edition
300 pages, $34.99
ISBN: 0-7357-0081-8

Okay, you've got your Exchange Server installed and connected; now what? Email administration is one of the most critical networking jobs, and Exchange can be particularly troublesome in large, heterogeneous environments. Janice Howd, a noted consultant and teacher with over a decade of email administration experience, has put together this advanced, concise handbook for daily, periodic, and emergency administration. With in-depth coverage of topics like managing disk resources, replication, and disaster recovery, this is the one reference every Exchange administrator needs.

SQL Server System Administration

By Sean Baird, Chris Miller, et al.
1st Edition
352 pages, $29.99
ISBN: 1-56205-955-6

How often does your SQL Server go down during the day when everyone wants to access the data? Do you spend most of your time being a "report monkey" for your coworkers and bosses? *SQL Server System Administration* helps you keep data consistently available to your users. This book omits introductory information. The authors don't spend time explaining queries and how they work. Instead, they focus on the information you can't get anywhere else, like how to choose the correct replication topology and achieve high availability of information.

Internet Information Services Administration

By Kelli Adam
1st Edition,
200 pages, $29.99
ISBN: 0-7357-0022-2

Are the new Internet technologies in Internet Information Services giving you headaches? Does protecting security on the Web take up all of your time? Then this is the book for you. With hands-on configuration training, advanced study of the new protocols the most recent version of IIS, and detailed instructions on authenticating users with the new Certificate Server and implementing and managing the new e-commerce features, *Internet Information Services Administration* gives you the real-life solutions you need. This definitive resource prepares you for the release of Windows 2000 by giving you detailed advice on working with Microsoft Management Console, which was first used by IIS.

SMS 2 Administration

By Michael Lubanski and Darshan Doshi
1st Edition
350 pages, $39.99
ISBN: 0-7357-0082-6

Microsoft's new version of its Systems Management Server (SMS) is starting to turn heads. Although complex, it allows administrators to lower their total cost of ownership and more efficiently manage clients, applications, and support operations. So if your organization is using or implementing SMS, you'll need some expert advice. Darshan Doshi and Michael Lubanski can help you get the most bang for your buck with insight, expert tips, and real-world examples. Darshan and Michael are consultants specializing in SMS and have worked with Microsoft on one of the most complex SMS rollouts in the world, involving 32 countries, 15 languages, and thousands of clients.

UNIX/Linux Titles

Solaris Essential Reference

By John P. Mulligan
1st Edition,
300 pages, $24.95
ISBN: 0-7357-0023-0

Looking for the fastest, easiest way to find the Solaris command you need? Need a few pointers on shell scripting? How about advanced administration tips and sound, practical expertise on security issues? Are you looking for trustworthy information about available third-party software packages that will enhance your operating system? Author John Mulligan—creator of the popular "Unofficial Guide to The Solaris™ Operating Environment" Web site (`sun.icsnet.com`)—delivers all that and more in one attractive, easy-to-use reference book. With clear and concise instructions on how to perform important administration and management tasks and key information on powerful commands and advanced topics, *Solaris Essential Reference* is the book you need when you know what you want to do and only need to know how.

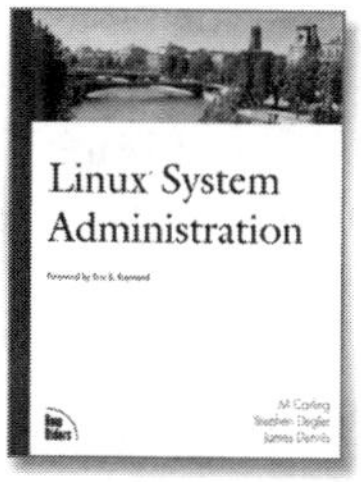

Linux System Administration

By M Carling, Stephen Degler, and James Dennis
1st Edition
450 pages, $29.99
ISBN: 1-56205-934-3

As an administrator, you probably feel that most of your time and energy is spent in endless firefighting. If your network has become a fragile quilt of temporary patches and work-arounds, this book is for you. Have you had trouble sending or receiving email lately? Are you looking for a way to keep your network running smoothly with enhanced performance? Are your users always hankering for more storage, services, and speed? *Linux System Administration* advises you on the many intricacies of maintaining a secure, stable system. In this definitive work, the authors address all the issues related to system administration, from adding users and managing file permissions, to Internet services and Web hosting, to recovery planning and security. This book fulfills the need for expert advice that will ensure a trouble-free Linux environment.

GTK+/Gnome Application Development

By Havoc Pennington
1st Edition
492 pages, $39.99
ISBN: 0-7357-0078-8

This title is for the reader who is conversant with the C programming language and UNIX/Linux development. It provides detailed and solution-oriented information designed to meet the needs of programmers and application developers using the GTK+/Gnome libraries. Coverage complements existing GTK+/Gnome documentation, going into more depth on pivotal issues, such as uncovering the GTK+ object system, working with the event loop, managing the Gdk substrate, writing custom widgets, and mastering GnomeCanvas.

Developing Linux Applications with GTK+ and GDK

By Eric Harlow
1st Edition
490 pages, $34.99
ISBN: 0-7357-0021-4

We all know that Linux is one of the most powerful and solid operating systems in existence. And as the success of Linux grows, there is an increasing interest in developing applications with graphical user interfaces that take advantage of the power of Linux. In this book, software developer Eric Harlow gives you an indispensable development handbook focusing on the GTK+ toolkit. More than an overview of the elements of application or GUI design, this is a hands-on book that delves deeply into the technology. With in-depth material on the various GUI programming tools and loads of examples, this book's unique focus will give you the information you need to design and launch professional-quality applications.

Linux Essential Reference

By Ed Petron
1st Edition
350 pages, $24.95
ISBN: 0-7357-0852-5

This book is all about getting things done as quickly and efficiently as possible by providing a structured organization for the plethora of available Linux information. We can sum it up in one word—value. This book has it all: concise instructions on how to perform key administration tasks, advanced information on configuration, shell scripting, hardware management, systems management, data tasks, automation, and tons of other useful information. All of this coupled with an unique navigational structure and a great price. This book truly provides groundbreaking information for the growing community of advanced Linux professionals.

Lotus Notes and Domino Titles

Domino System Administration

By Rob Kirkland, CLP, CLI
1st Edition
850 pages, $49.99
ISBN: 1-56205-948-3

Your boss has just announced that you will be upgrading to the newest version of Notes and Domino when it ships. How are you supposed to get this new system installed, configured, and rolled out to all your end users? You understand how Lotus Notes works—you've been administering it for years. What you need is a concise, practical explanation of the new features and how to make some of the advanced stuff work smoothly by someone like you, who has worked with the product for years and understands what you need to know. *Domino System Administration* is the answer—the first book on Domino that attacks the technology at the professional level with practical, hands-on assistance to get Domino running in your organization.

Lotus Notes & Domino Essential Reference

By Tim Bankes, CLP
and Dave Hatter, CLP, MCP
1st Edition
650 pages, $45.00
ISBN: 0-7357-0007-9

You're in a bind because you've been asked to design and program a new database in Notes for an important client who will keep track of and itemize a myriad of inventory and shipping data. The client wants a user-friendly interface that won't sacrifice speed or functionality. You are experienced (and could develop this application in your sleep) but feel you need something to facilitate your creative and technical abilities—something to perfect your programming skills. The answer is waiting for you: *Lotus Notes & Domino Essential Reference*. It's compact and simply designed. It's loaded with information. All of the objects, classes, functions, and methods are listed. It shows you the object hierarchy and the relationship between each one. It's perfect for you. Problem solved.

Networking Titles

Cisco Router Configuration & Troubleshooting

By Mark Tripod
1st Edition
300 pages, $34.99
ISBN: 0-7357-0024-9

Want the real story on making your Cisco routers run like a dream? Why not pick up a copy of *Cisco Router Configuration & Troubleshooting* and see what Mark Tripod of Exodus Communications has to say? They're the folks responsible for making some of the largest sites on the Net scream, like Amazon.com, Hotmail, USAToday, Geocities, and Sony. In this book, they provide advanced configuration issues, sprinkled with advice and preferred practices. You won't see a general overview on TCP/IP. This book addresses more meaty issues, like security, monitoring, traffic management, and more. In the troubleshooting section, the author provides a unique methodology and lots of sample problems to illustrate. By providing real-world insight and examples instead of rehashing Cisco's documentation, Mark gives network administrators information they can start using today.

Network Intrusion Detection: An Analyst's Handbook

By Stephen Northcutt
1st Edition
267 pages, $39.99
ISBN: 0-7357-0868-1

Get answers and solutions from someone who has been in the trenches. The author, Stephen Northcutt, original developer of the Shadow intrusion detection system and former Director of the United States Navy's Information System Security Office at the Naval Security Warfare Center, gives his expertise to intrusion detection specialists, security analysts, and consultants responsible for setting up and maintaining an effective defense against network security attacks.

Other Books By New Riders

Windows Technologies

Internet Information Services Administration
0-7357-0022-2
SMS 2 Administration
0-7357-0082-6
Planning for Windows 2000
0-7357-0048-6
Windows NT Network Management: Reducing Total Cost of Ownership
1-56205-946-7
Windows NT DNS
1-56205-943-2
Windows NT Performance Monitoring, Benchmarking, and Tuning
1-56205-942-4
Windows NT Power Toolkit
0-7357-0922-X
Windows NT Registry: A Settings Reference
1-56205-941-6
Windows NT TCP/IP
1-56205-887-8
Windows NT Terminal Server and Citrix MetaFrame
1-56205-944-0
Implementing Exchange Server
1-56205-931-9
Inside Window 2000 Server
1-56205-929-7
Exchange Server Administration
0-7357-0081-8
SQL Server System Administration
1-56205-955-6
Windows 2000 Active Directory
0-7357-0870-3

Networking

Understanding Directory Services
0-7357-0910-6
Understanding the Network
0-7357-0977-7
Domino System Administration
1-56205-948-3
Cisco Router Configuration and Troubleshooting
0-7357-0024-9
Understanding Data Communications, Sixth Edition
0-7357-0036-2
Network Intrusion Detection: An Analyst's Handbook
0-7357-0868-1

Certification

A+ Certification TestPrep
1-56205-892-4
A+ Certification Training Guide, 2E
0-7357-0907-6
A+ Fast Track
0-7357-0028-1
MCSD Fast Track: Visual Basic 6, Exam 70-176
0-7357-0019-2
MCSE Fast Track: Internet Information Server 4
1-56205-936-X
MCSE Fast Track: Networking Essentials
1-56205-939-4
MCSE Fast Track: TCP/IP
1-56205-937-8
MCSD Fast Track: VB 6, Exam 70-175
0-7357-0018-4
MCSE Fast Track: Windows 98
0-7357-0016-8
MCSE Fast Track: Windows NT Server 4
1-56205-935-1
MCSE Fast Track: Windows NT Server 4 Enterprise
1-56205-940-8
MCSE Fast Track: Windows NT Workstation 4
1-56205-938-6
MCSE Simulation Guide: Windows NT Server 4 Enterprise
1-56205-914-9
MCSE Simulation Guide: Windows NT Workstation 4
1-56205-925-4
MCSE TestPrep: Networking Essentials, Second Edition
0-7357-0010-9
MCSE TestPrep: TCP/IP, Second Edition
0-7357-0025-7
MCSE TestPrep: Windows 98
1-56205-922-X
MCSE TestPrep: Windows NT Server 4 Enterprise, Second Edition
0-7357-0009-5
MCSE TestPrep: Windows NT Server 4, Second Edition
0-7357-0012-5
MCSE TestPrep: Windows NT Workstation 4, Second Edition
0-7357-0008-7
MCSD TestPrep: VB 6 Exams
0-7357-0032-X
MCSE Training Guide: Networking Essentials, Second Edition
1-56205-919-X
MCSE Training Guide: TCP/IP, Second Edition
1-56205-920-3
MCSE Training Guide: Windows 98
1-56205-890-8
MCSE Training Guide: Windows NT Server 4, Second Edition
1-56205-916-5
MCSE Training Guide: Windows NT Server Enterprise, Second Edition
1-56205-917-3
MCSE Training Guide: Windows NT Workstation 4, Second Edition
1-56205-918-1
MCSD Training Guide: VB 6 Exams
0-7357-0002-8

Graphics

Inside 3D Studio MAX 2, Volume I
1-56205-857-6
Inside 3D Studio MAX 2, Volume II: Modeling and Materials
1-56205-864-9
Inside 3D Studio MAX 2, Volume III: Animation
1-56205-865-7
Inside 3D Studio MAX 2 Resource Kit
1-56205-953-X
Inside AutoCAD 14, Limited Edition
1-56205-898-3
Inside Softimage 3D
1-56205-885-1
HTML Web Magic, Second Edition
1-56830-475-7
Dynamic HTML Web Magic
1-56830-421-8
Designing Web Graphics.3
1-56205-949-1
Illustrator 8 Magic
1-56205-952-1
Inside trueSpace 4
1-56205-957-2
Inside Adobe Photoshop 5
1-56205-884-3
Inside Adobe Photoshop 5, Limited Edition
1-56205-951-3
Photoshop 5 Artistry
1-56205-895-9
Photoshop 5 Type Magic
1-56830-465-X
Photoshop 5 Web Magic
1-56205-913-0

We Want to Know What You Think

To better serve you, we would like your opinion on the content and quality of this book. Please complete this card, and mail it to us or fax it to 317-581-4663.

Name ______________________________

Address ______________________________

City______________ State______________ Zip ______________

Phone ______________________________

Email Address ______________________________

Occupation ______________________________

Operating system(s) that you use ______________________________

What influenced your purchase of this book?

- ❑ Recommendation
- ❑ Cover Design
- ❑ Table of Contents
- ❑ Index
- ❑ Magazine Review
- ❑ Advertisement
- ❑ New Riders' Reputation
- ❑ Author Name

How would you rate the contents of this book?

- ❑ Excellent
- ❑ Very Good
- ❑ Good
- ❑ Fair
- ❑ Below Average
- ❑ Poor

How do you plan to use this book?

- ❑ Quick Reference
- ❑ Self-Training
- ❑ Classroom
- ❑ Other

What do you like most about this book? Check all that apply.

- ❑ Content
- ❑ Writing Style
- ❑ Accuracy
- ❑ Examples
- ❑ Listings
- ❑ Design
- ❑ Index
- ❑ Page Count
- ❑ Price
- ❑ Illustrations

What do you like least about this book? Check all that apply.

- ❑ Content
- ❑ Writing Style
- ❑ Accuracy
- ❑ Examples
- ❑ Listings
- ❑ Design
- ❑ Index
- ❑ Page Count
- ❑ Price
- ❑ Illustrations

What would be a useful follow-up book for you? ______________________________

Where did you purchase this book? ______________________________

Can you name a similar book that you like better than this one, or one that is as good? Why?

____

How many New Riders books do you own? ______________________________

What are your favorite computer books? ______________________________

What other titles would you like to see us develop? ______________________________

Any comments for us? ______________________________

Windows 2000 DNS: 0-7357-0973-4

www.newriders.com • Fax 317-581-4663

Fold here and tape to mail

Place
Stamp
Here

New Riders Publishing
201 W. 103rd St.
Indianapolis, IN 46290

How to Contact Us

Visit Our Web Site

www.newriders.com

On our Web site you'll find information about our other books, authors, tables of contents, indexes, and book errata.

Email Us

Contact us at this address:

nrfeedback@newriders.com

- If you have comments or questions about this book
- To report errors that you have found in this book
- If you have a book proposal to submit or are interested in writing for New Riders
- If you would like to have an author kit sent to you
- If you are an expert in a computer topic or technology and are interested in being a technical editor who reviews manuscripts for technical accuracy

nrfeedback@newriders.com

- To find a distributor in your area, please contact our international department at this address.

nrmedia@newriders.com

- For instructors from educational institutions who want to preview New Riders books for classroom use. Email should include your name, title, school, department, address, phone number, office days/hours, text in use, and enrollment, along with your request for desk/examination copies and/or additional information.
- For members of the media who are interested in reviewing copies of New Riders books. Send your name, mailing address, and email address, along with the name of the publication or Web site you work for.

Write to Us

New Riders Publishing

201 W. 103rd St.

Indianapolis, IN 46290-1097

Call Us

Toll-free (800) 571-5840 + 9 + 4511

If outside U.S. (317) 581-3500. Ask for New Riders.

Fax Us

(317) 581-4663